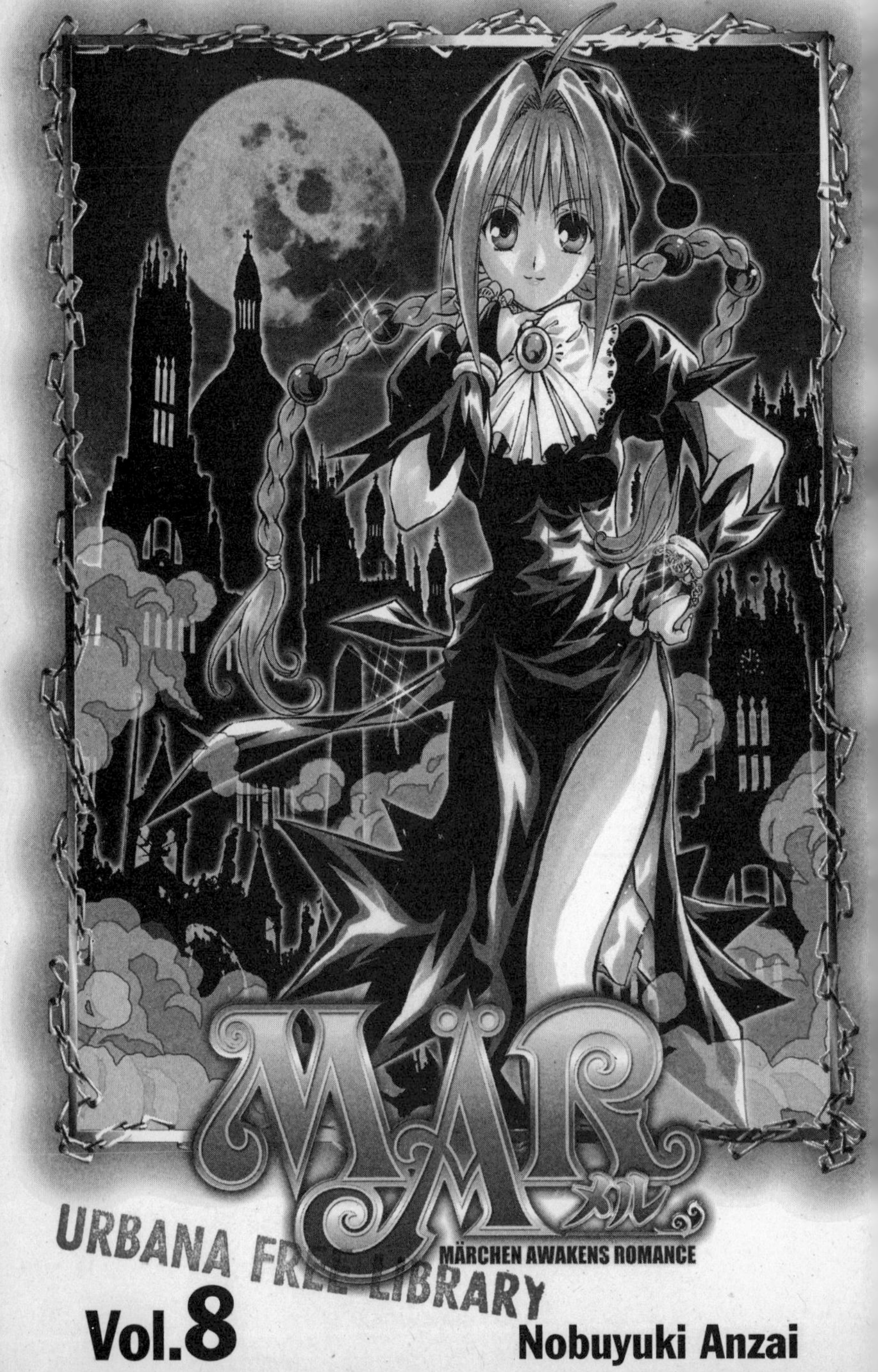

MÄR メル

MÄRCHEN AWAKENS ROMANCE

Vol.8

Nobuyuki Anzai

Characters

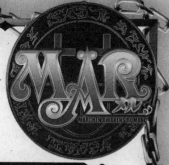

Alan

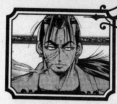

A warrior who played a major role in the war six years ago. For a while, a curse trapped him in the form of Edward.

Edward

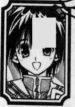

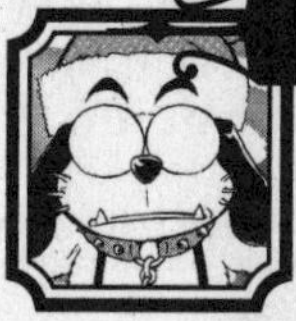

The dog who devotedly serves Princess Snow.

Snow

The Princess of the Great Kingdom of Lestava, freed from a pillar of ice by Ginta.

Nanashi

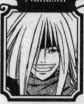

Leader of the Thieves Guild, Luberia. Detests the Chess Pieces.

Alviss

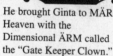

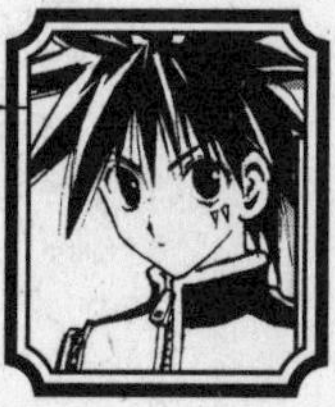

He brought Ginta to MÄR Heaven with the Dimensional ÄRM called the "Gate Keeper Clown."

Ginta Toramizu

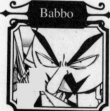

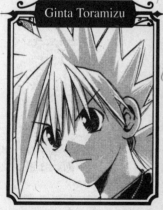

A second-year middle school student who dreams about the world of fairy tales—and suddenly finds himself there!

Babbo

A rare talking ÄRM, who by synchronizing with Ginta is able to change shape. He once belonged to Phantom.

Jack

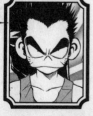

A farmboy who left his mother and his farm to go on adventures with Ginta.

Previous Volume

Ginta jumps through a "door" that suddenly appears in his classroom, and finds himself in Märchen, the magical world of his dreams. Now, at the "request" of the Chess Pieces, the War Games have begun—and Ginta and his friends, calling themselves MÄR, must battle the Chess warriors. The MÄR team won their first three battles, but now as Battle 4 begins on the Glacier Field, they are outraged by the cruel and vicious nature of their opponent Rapunzel, a Zodiac Knight of the Chess Army!

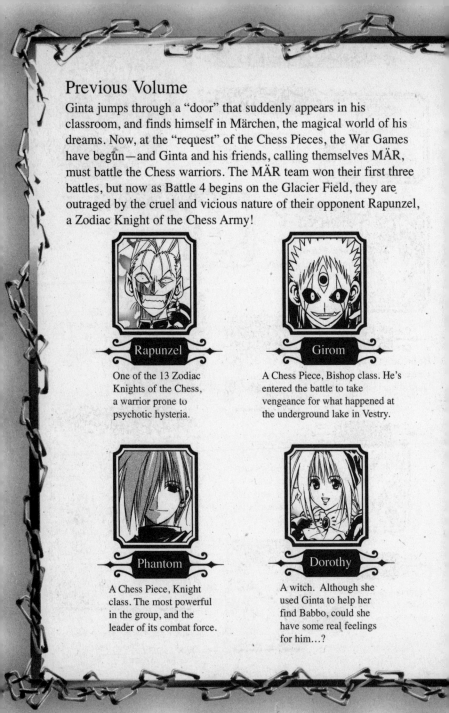

Rapunzel

One of the 13 Zodiac Knights of the Chess, a warrior prone to psychotic hysteria.

Girom

A Chess Piece, Bishop class. He's entered the battle to take vengeance for what happened at the underground lake in Vestry.

Phantom

A Chess Piece, Knight class. The most powerful in the group, and the leader of its combat force.

Dorothy

A witch. Although she used Ginta to help her find Babbo, could she have some real feelings for him…?

CONTENTS

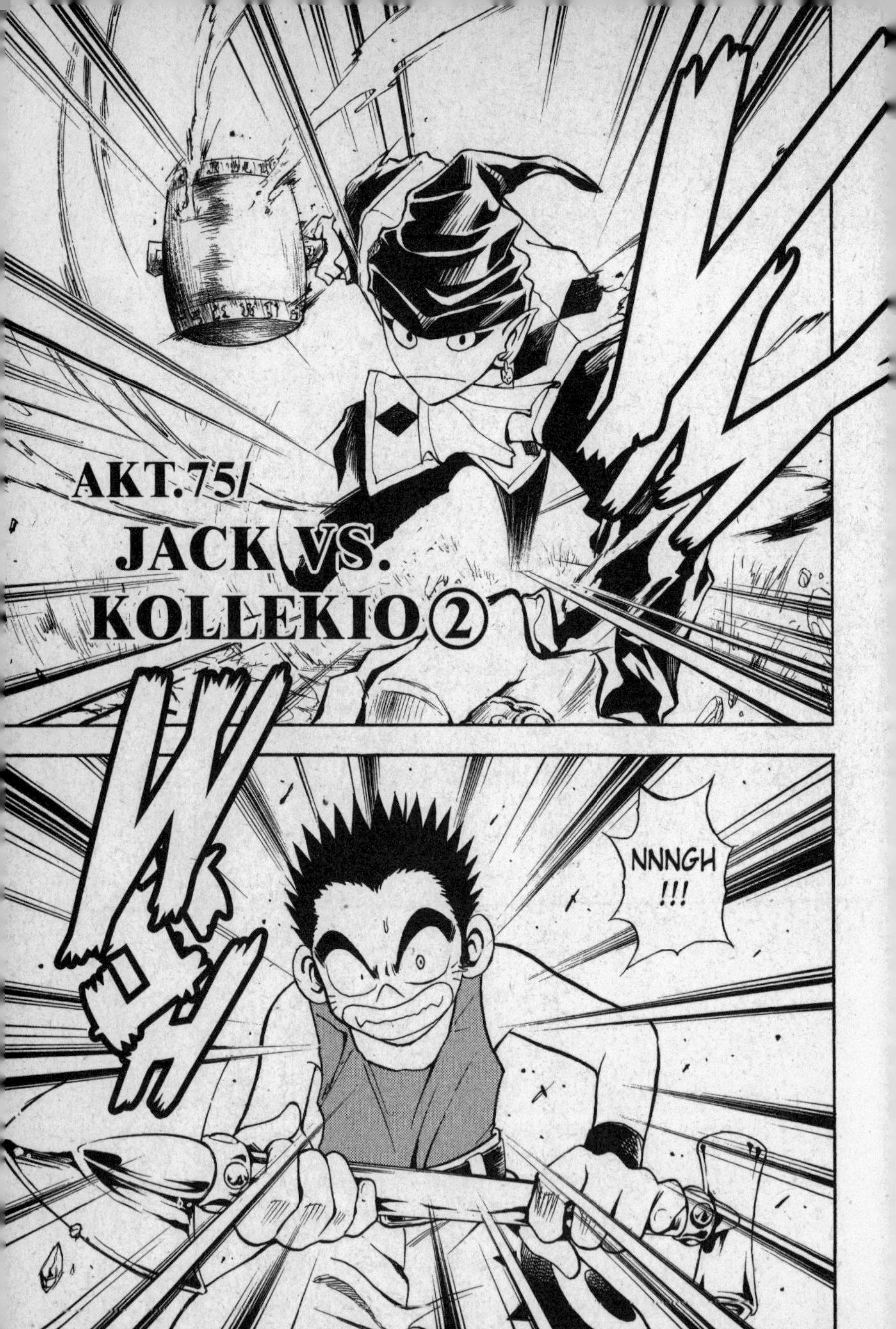
AKT.75/
JACK VS.
KOLLEKIO②
NNNGH
!!!

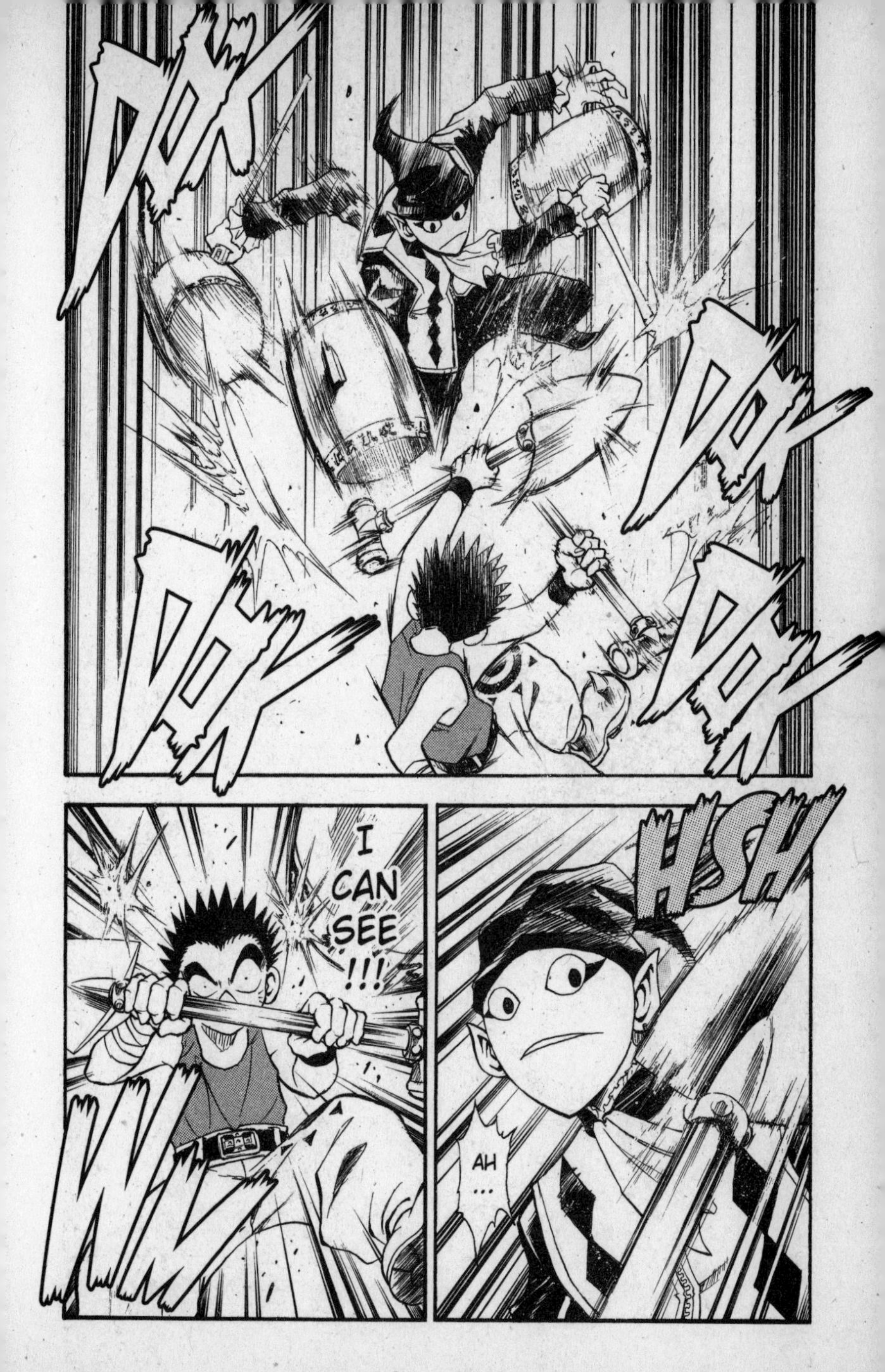
DAK
DAK
DAK
DAK
HSH
AH ...
I CAN SEE !!!

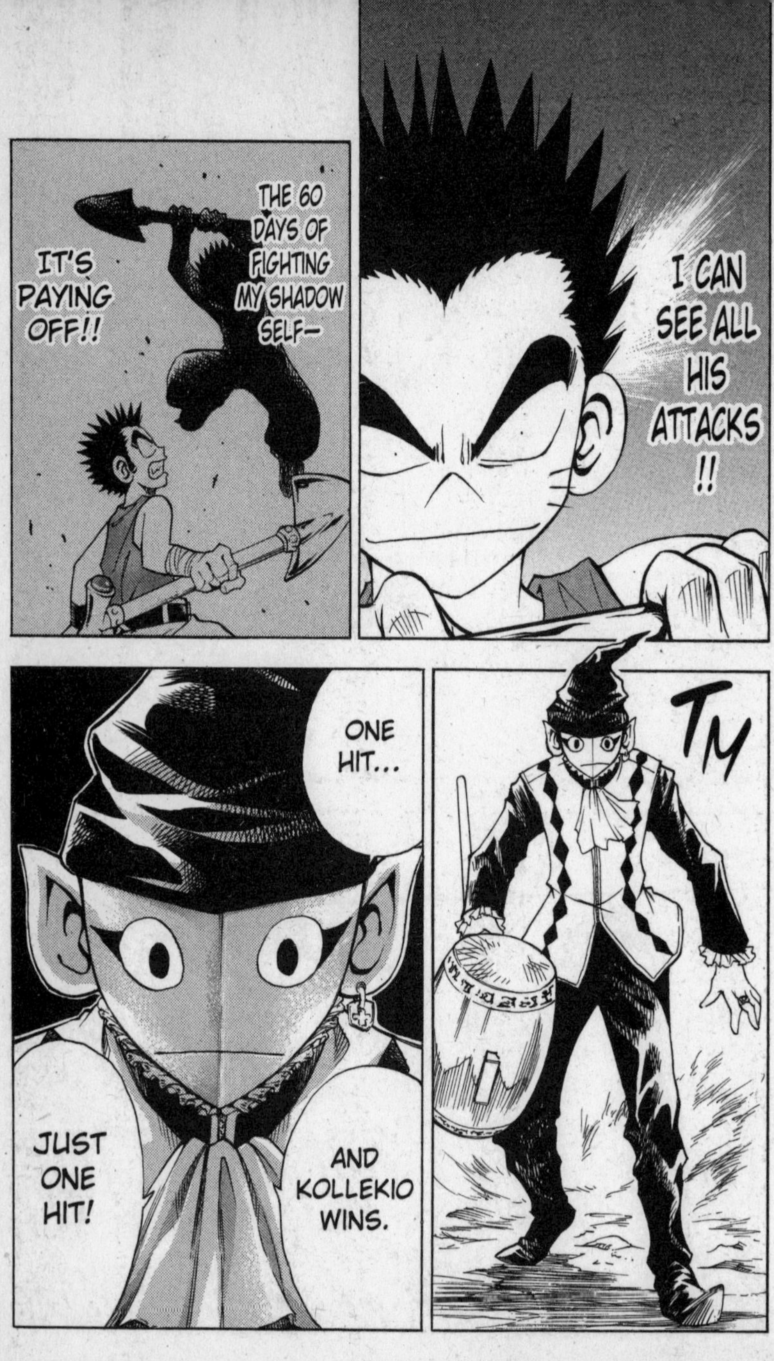
I CAN SEE ALL HIS ATTACKS !!
THE 60 DAYS OF FIGHTING MY SHADOW SELF—
IT'S PAYING OFF!!
TM
ONE HIT...
AND KOLLEKIO WINS.
JUST ONE HIT!

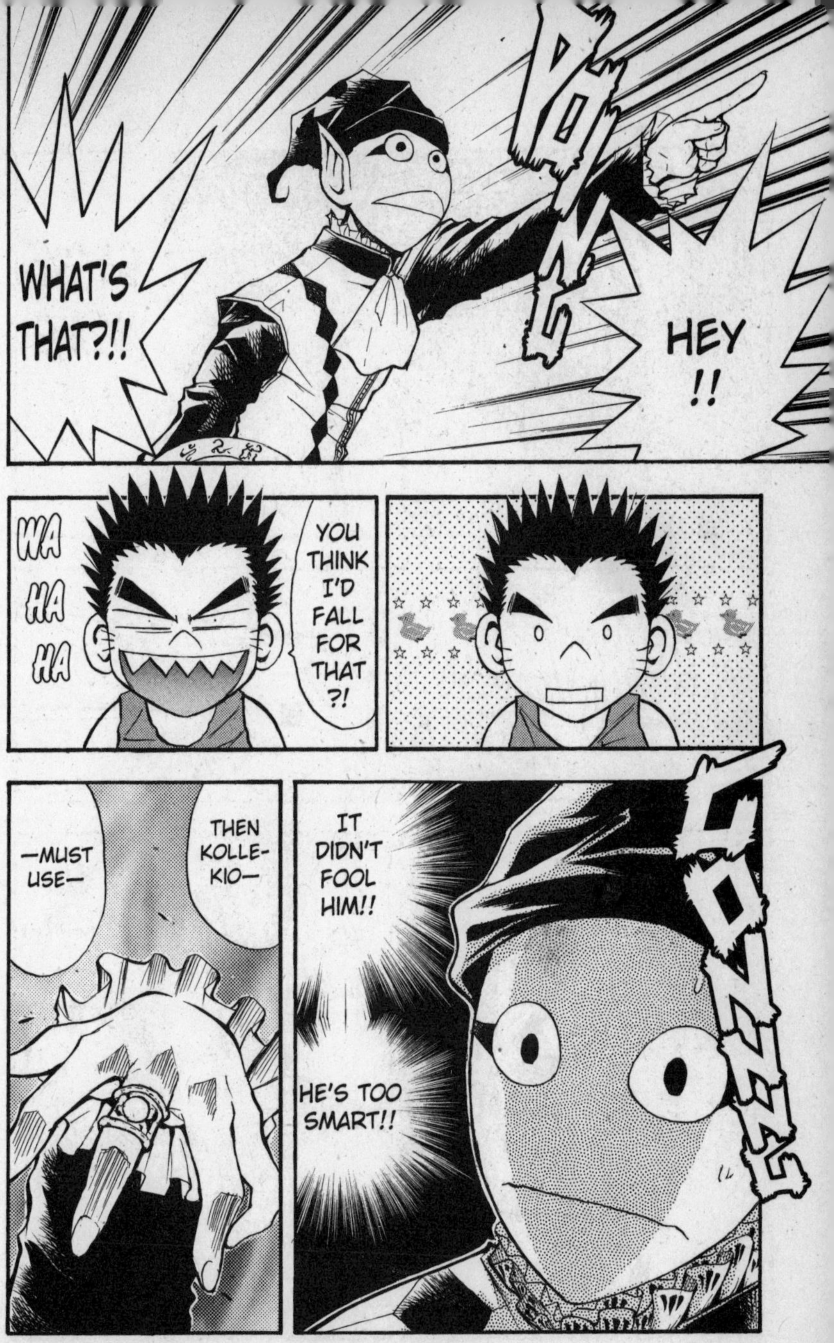
HEY !!
WHAT'S THAT?!!
YOU THINK I'D FALL FOR THAT?!
WA HA HA
IT DIDN'T FOOL HIM!!
HE'S TOO SMART!!
THEN KOLLE-KIO—
—MUST USE—

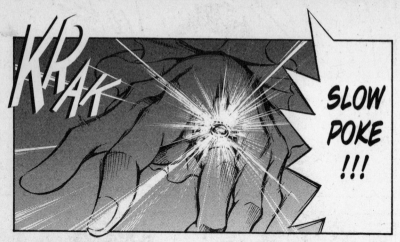

SLOW POKE !!!

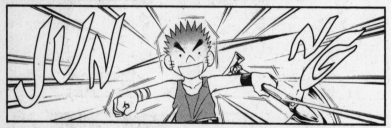

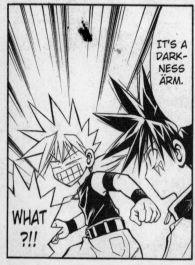

IT'S A DARK-NESS ÄRM.

WHAT ?!!

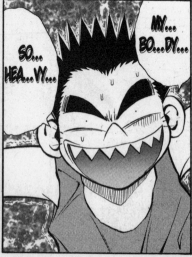

SO... HEA...VY...

MY... BO...DY...

11

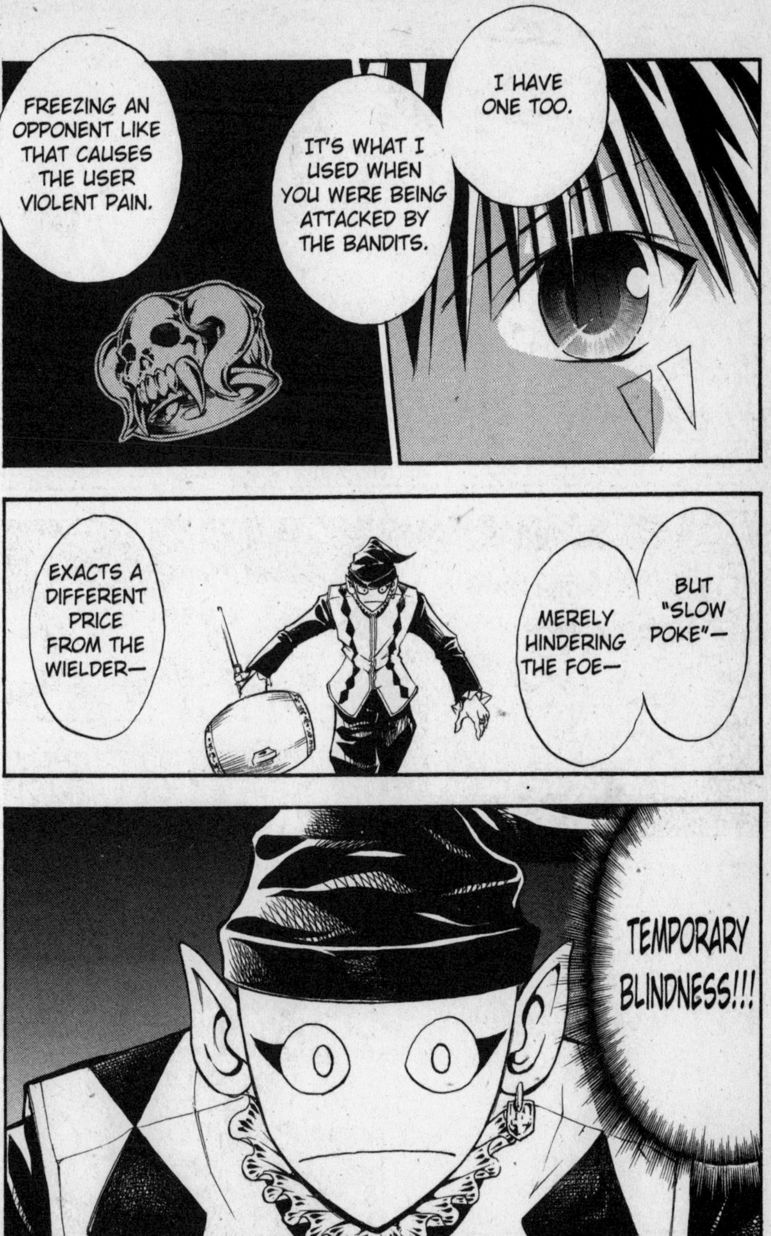
I HAVE ONE TOO.
IT'S WHAT I USED WHEN YOU WERE BEING ATTACKED BY THE BANDITS.
FREEZING AN OPPONENT LIKE THAT CAUSES THE USER VIOLENT PAIN.
BUT "SLOW POKE"—
MERELY HINDERING THE FOE—
EXACTS A DIFFERENT PRICE FROM THE WIELDER—
TEMPORARY BLINDNESS!!!

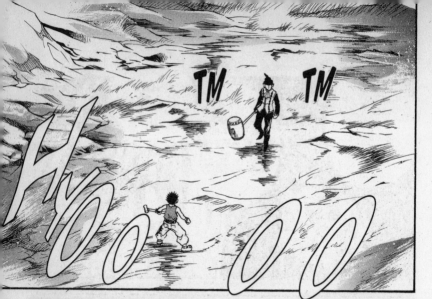

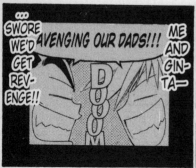

SWORE WE'D AVENGING OUR DADS!!! ME AND GET REV-ENGE!! GIN-TA—

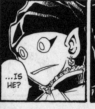

...IS HE?

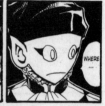

WHERE...

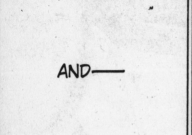

AND—

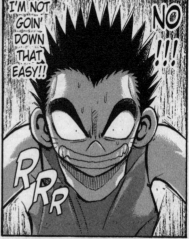

I'M NOT GOIN' DOWN THAT EASY!! NO!!!

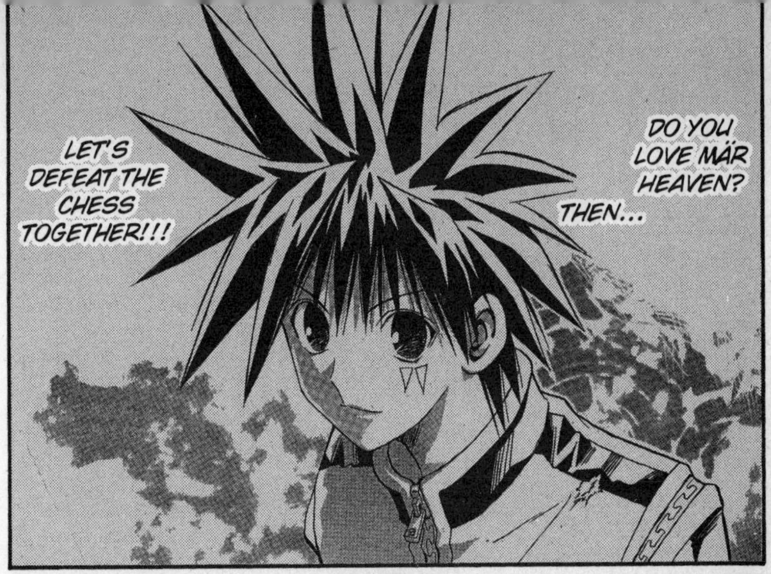
DO YOU LOVE MÄR HEAVEN?
THEN...
LET'S DEFEAT THE CHESS TOGETHER!!!

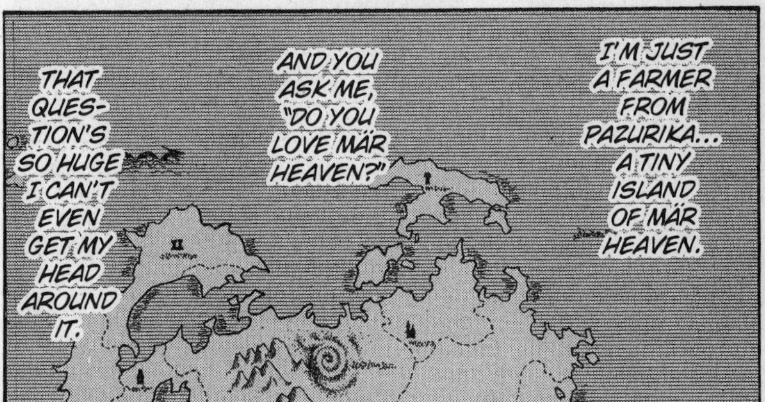
I'M JUST A FARMER FROM PAZURIKA... A TINY ISLAND OF MÄR HEAVEN.
AND YOU ASK ME, "DO YOU LOVE MÄR HEAVEN?"
THAT QUES-TION'S SO HUGE I CAN'T EVEN GET MY HEAD AROUND IT.

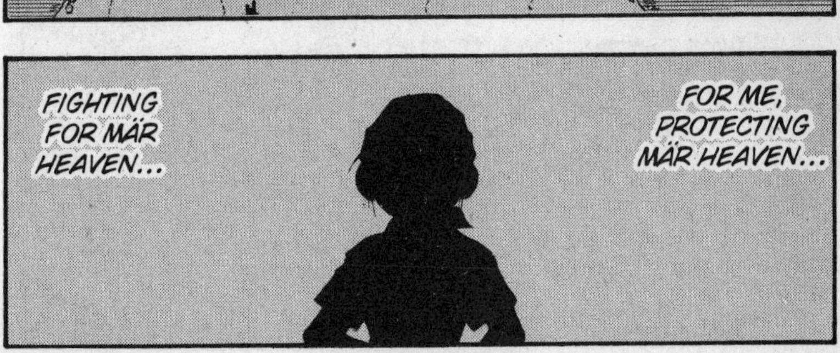
FOR ME, PROTECTING MÄR HEAVEN...
FIGHTING FOR MÄR HEAVEN...

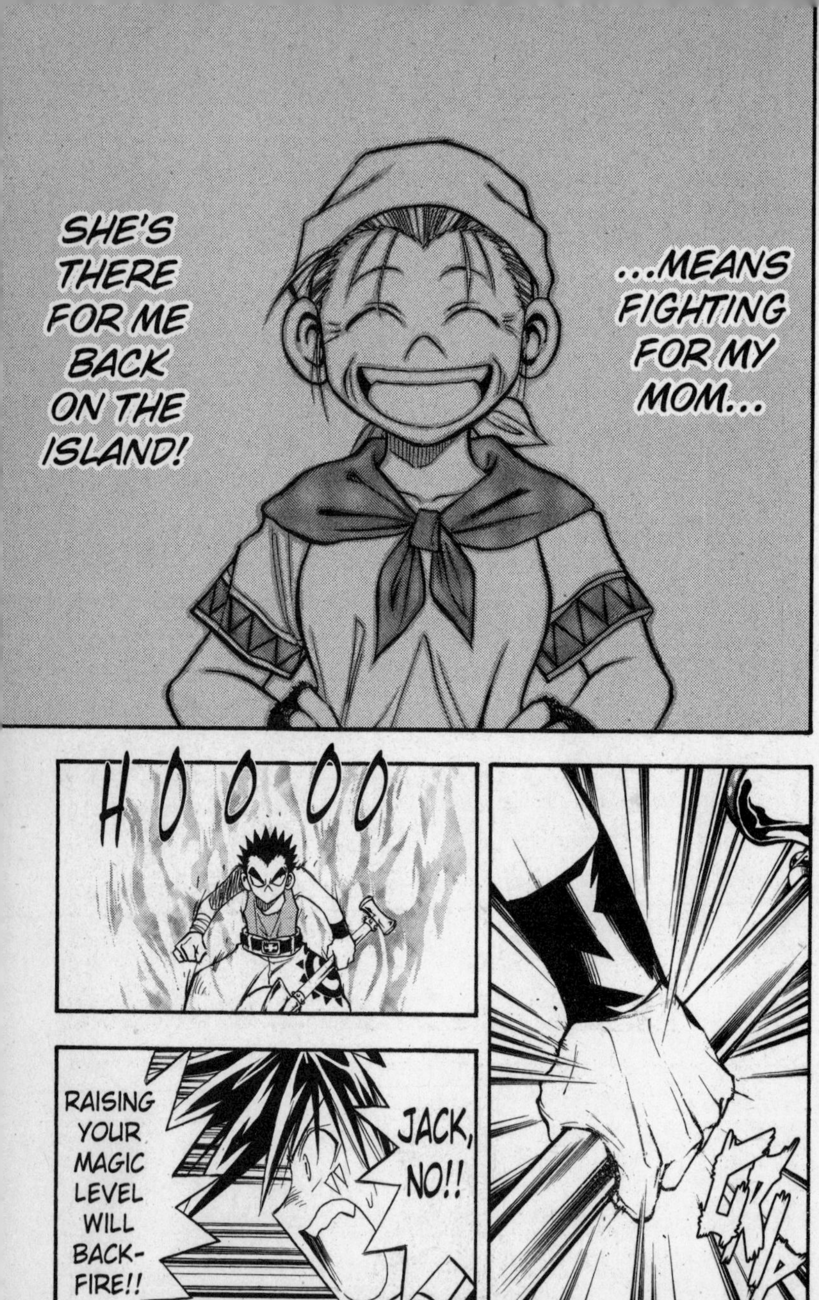
...MEANS FIGHTING FOR MY MOM...
SHE'S THERE FOR ME BACK ON THE ISLAND!
HOOOO
JACK, NO!!
RAISING YOUR MAGIC LEVEL WILL BACK-FIRE!!

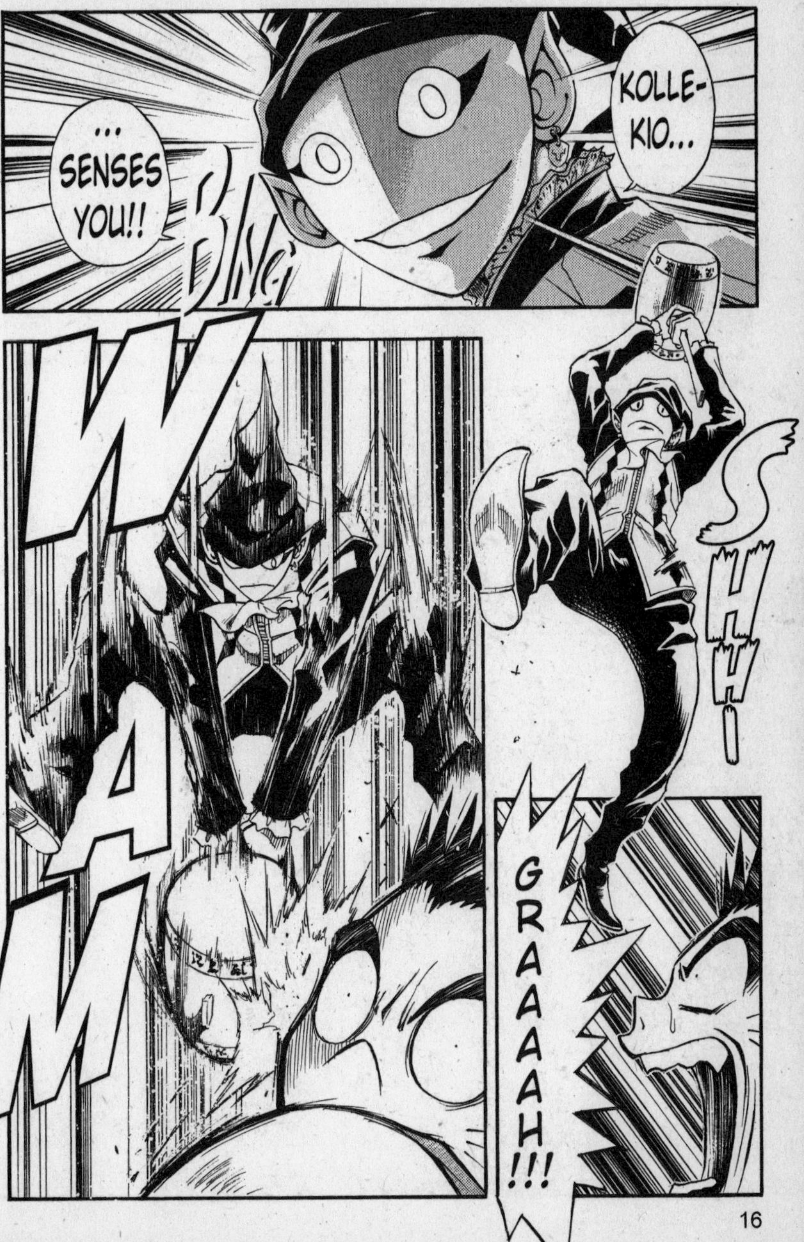
KOLLE-KIO...
... SENSES YOU!!
BING
SHHH
GRAAAAH!!!
WHAM

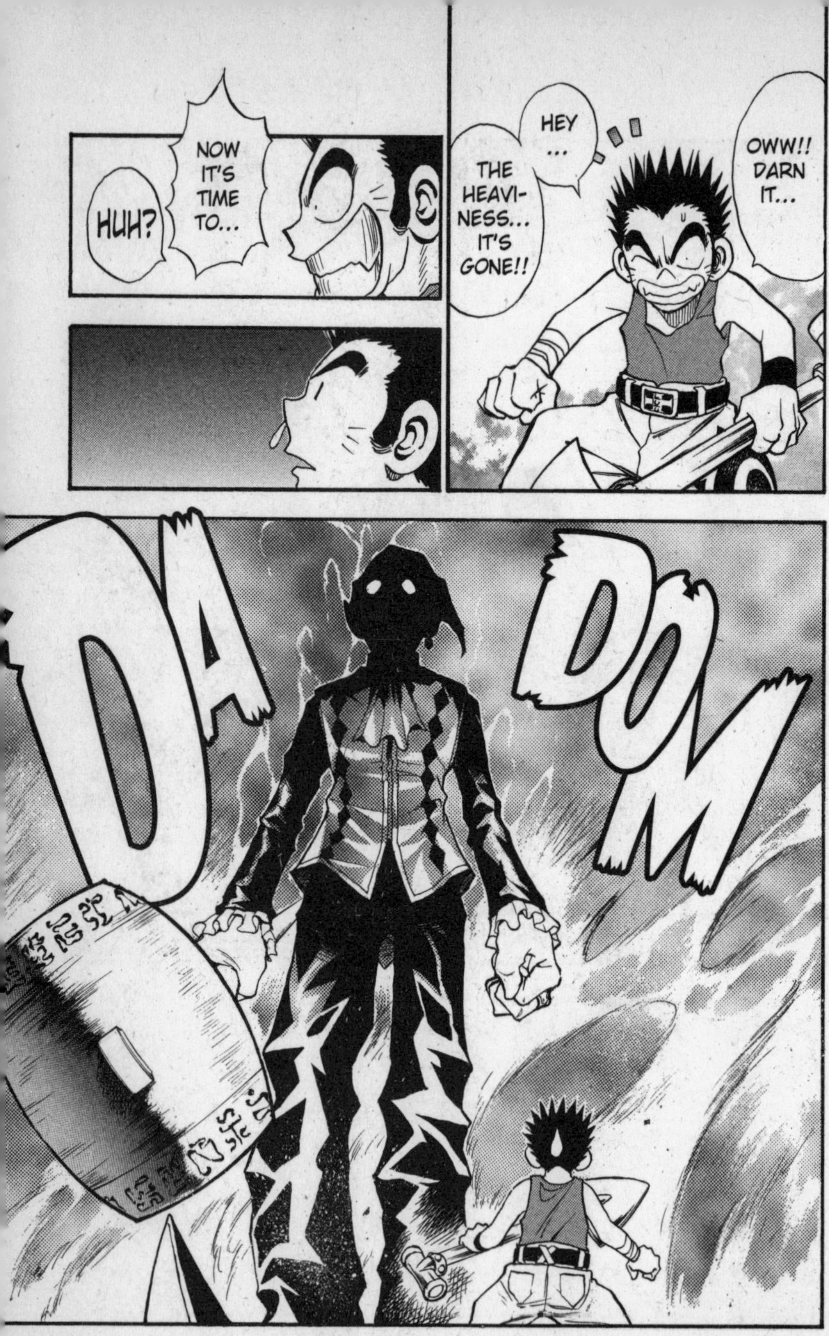
OWW!! DARN IT...
HEY ...
THE HEAVI-NESS... IT'S GONE!!
NOW IT'S TIME TO...
HUH?
DA DOM

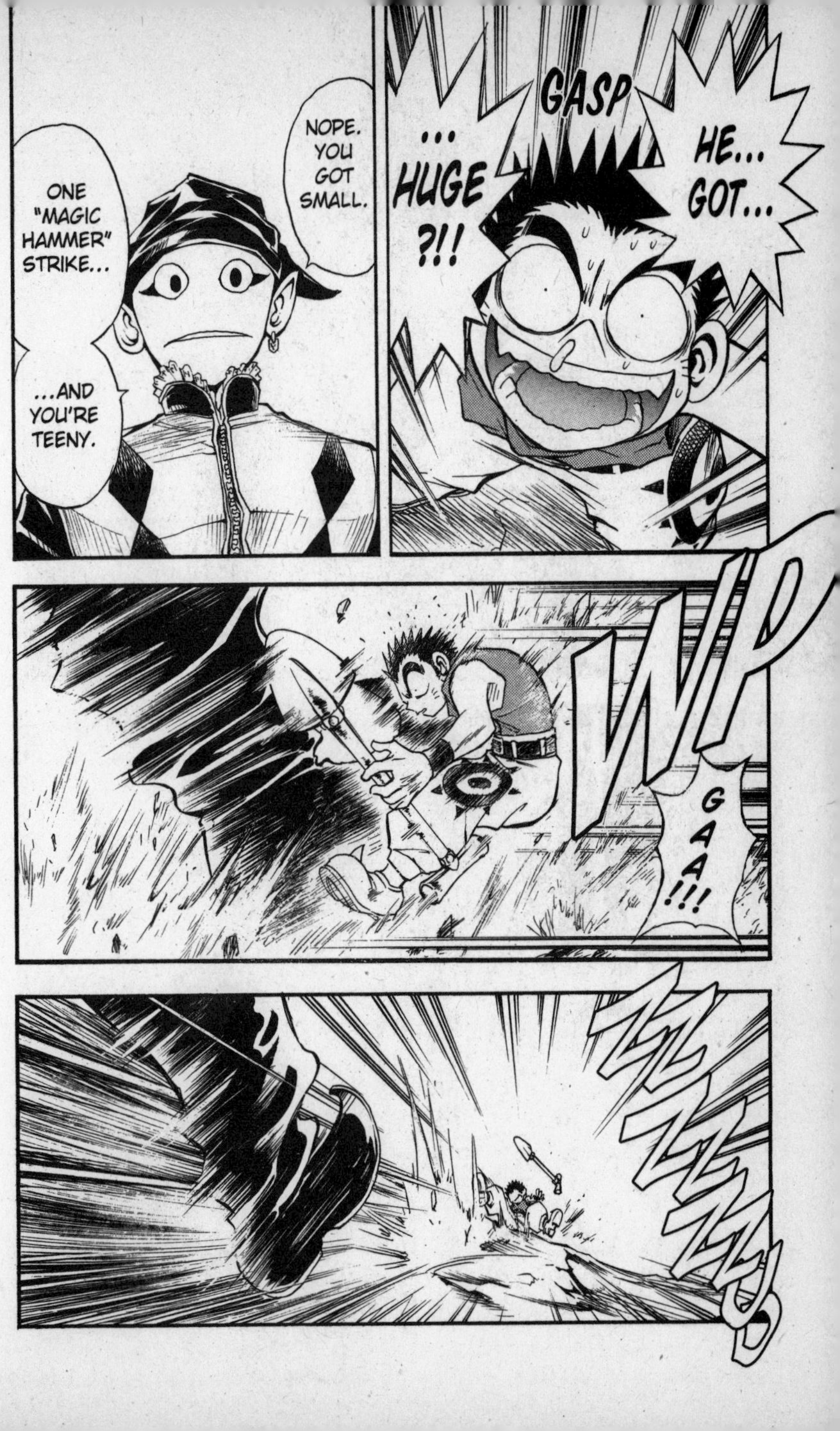
GASP
HE... GOT...
... HUGE ?!!
NOPE. YOU GOT SMALL.
ONE "MAGIC HAMMER" STRIKE...
...AND YOU'RE TEENY.
WIP
GAAA!!!

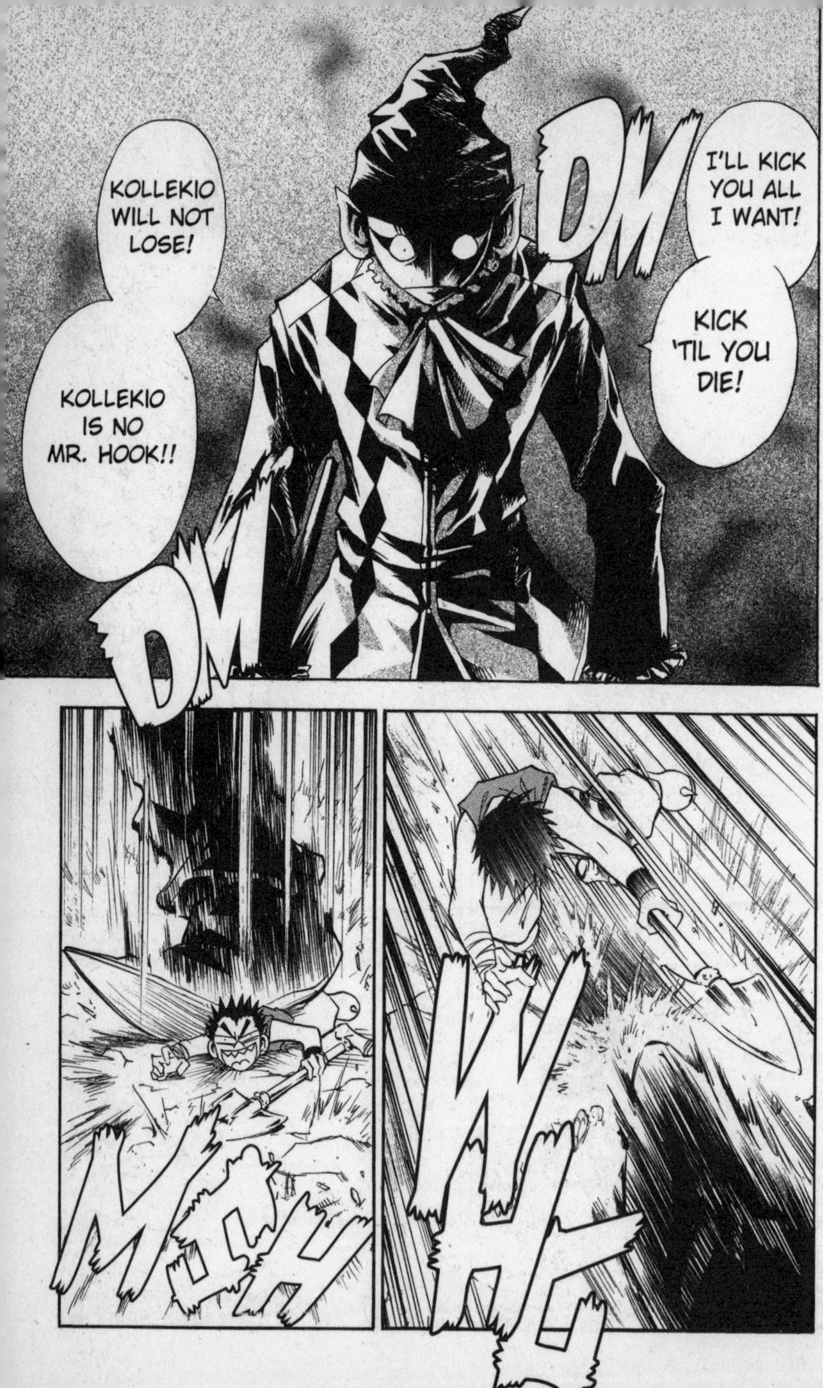
DM
I'LL KICK YOU ALL I WANT!
KICK 'TIL YOU DIE!
KOLLEKIO WILL NOT LOSE!
KOLLEKIO IS NO MR. HOOK!!
DM

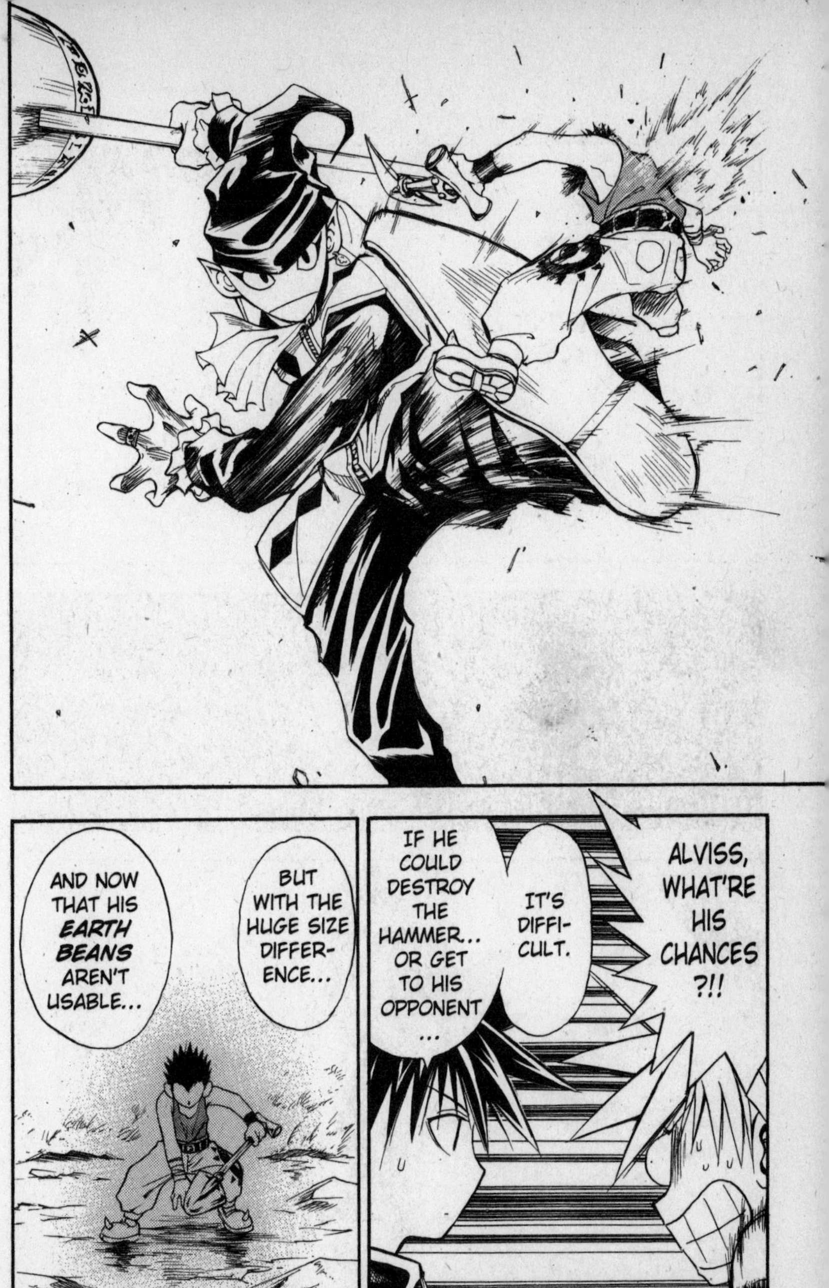
ALVISS, WHAT'RE HIS CHANCES?!!
IT'S DIFFICULT.
IF HE COULD DESTROY THE HAMMER... OR GET TO HIS OPPONENT...
BUT WITH THE HUGE SIZE DIFFERENCE...
AND NOW THAT HIS *EARTH BEANS* AREN'T USABLE...

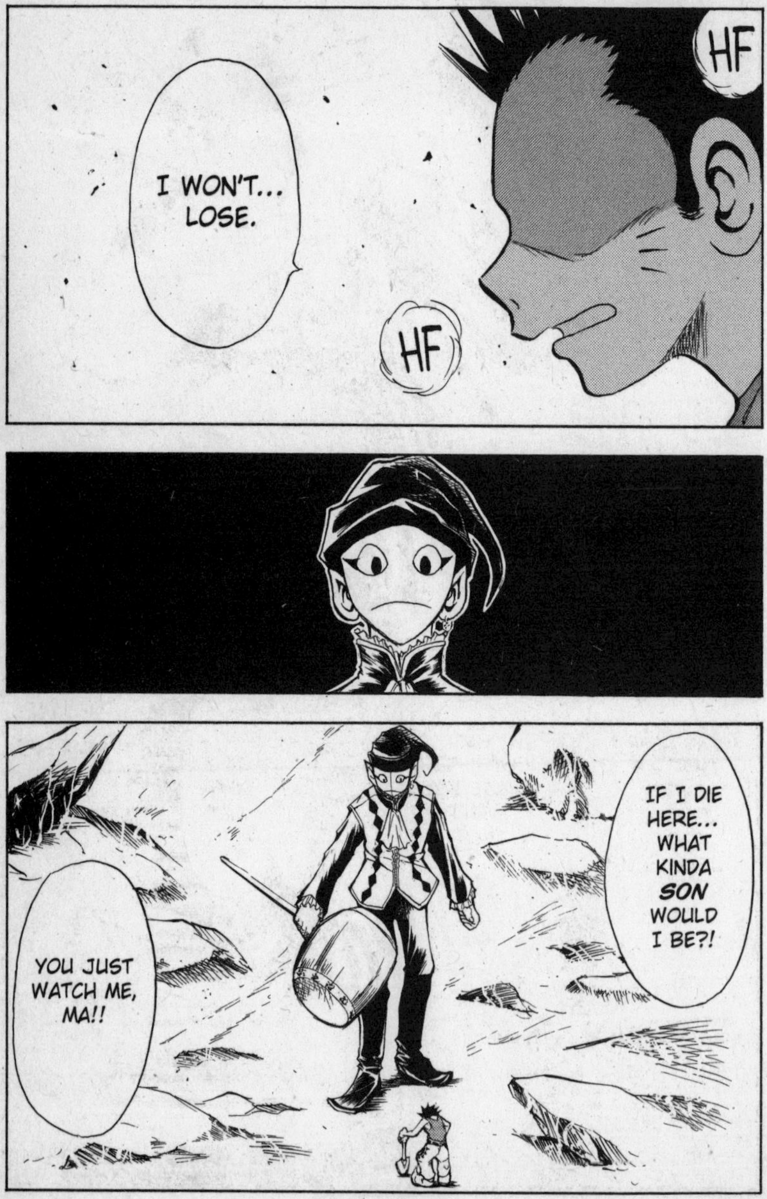
HF
I WON'T... LOSE.
HF
IF I DIE HERE... WHAT KINDA *SON* WOULD I BE?!
YOU JUST WATCH ME, MA!!

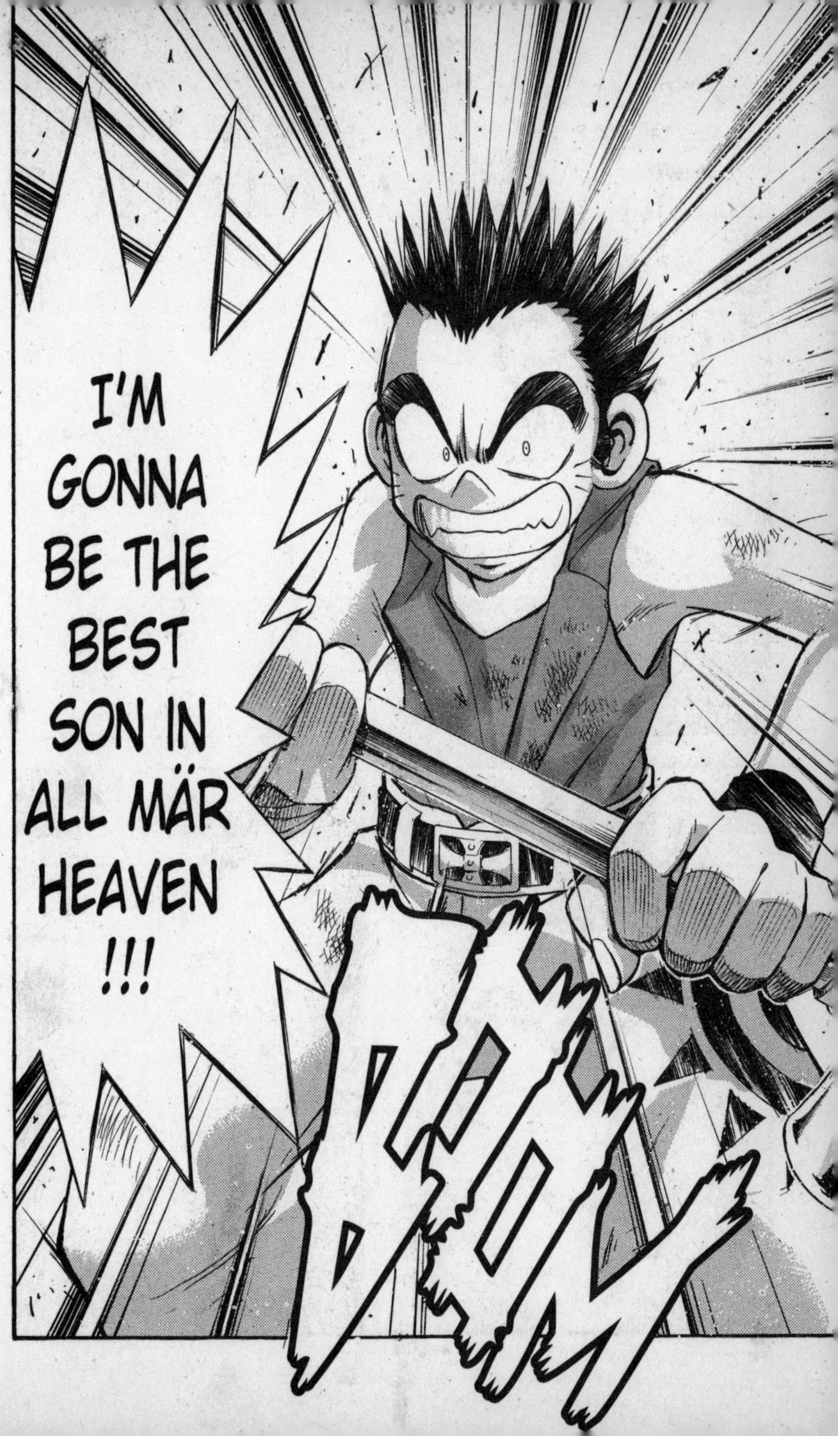
I'M GONNA BE THE BEST SON IN ALL MÄR HEAVEN !!!

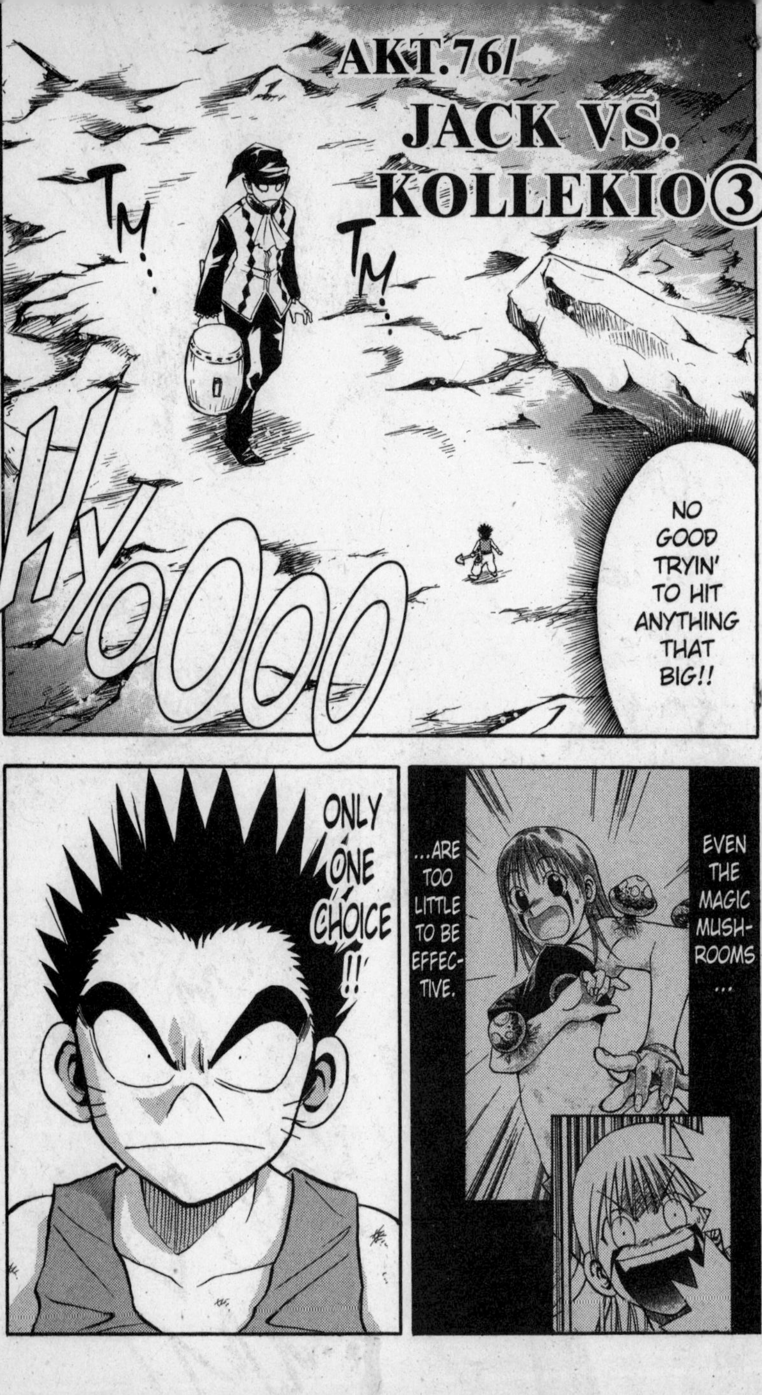
AKT.76/
JACK VS.
KOLLEKIO③
TM...
TM...
NO GOOD TRYIN' TO HIT ANYTHING THAT BIG!!
HYOOOOO
EVEN THE MAGIC MUSH-ROOMS...
...ARE TOO LITTLE TO BE EFFEC-TIVE.
ONLY ONE CHOICE!!

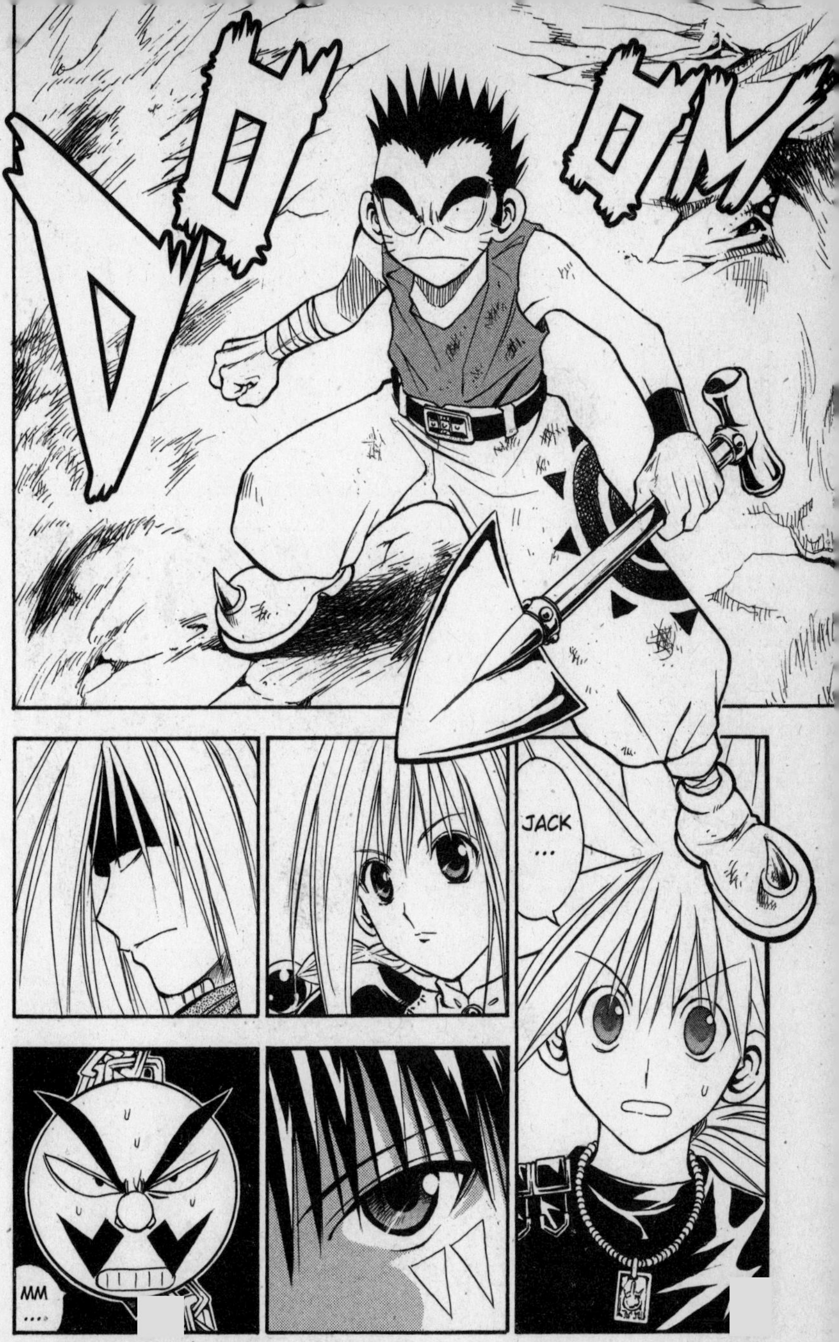
DOOM
JACK ...
MM ....

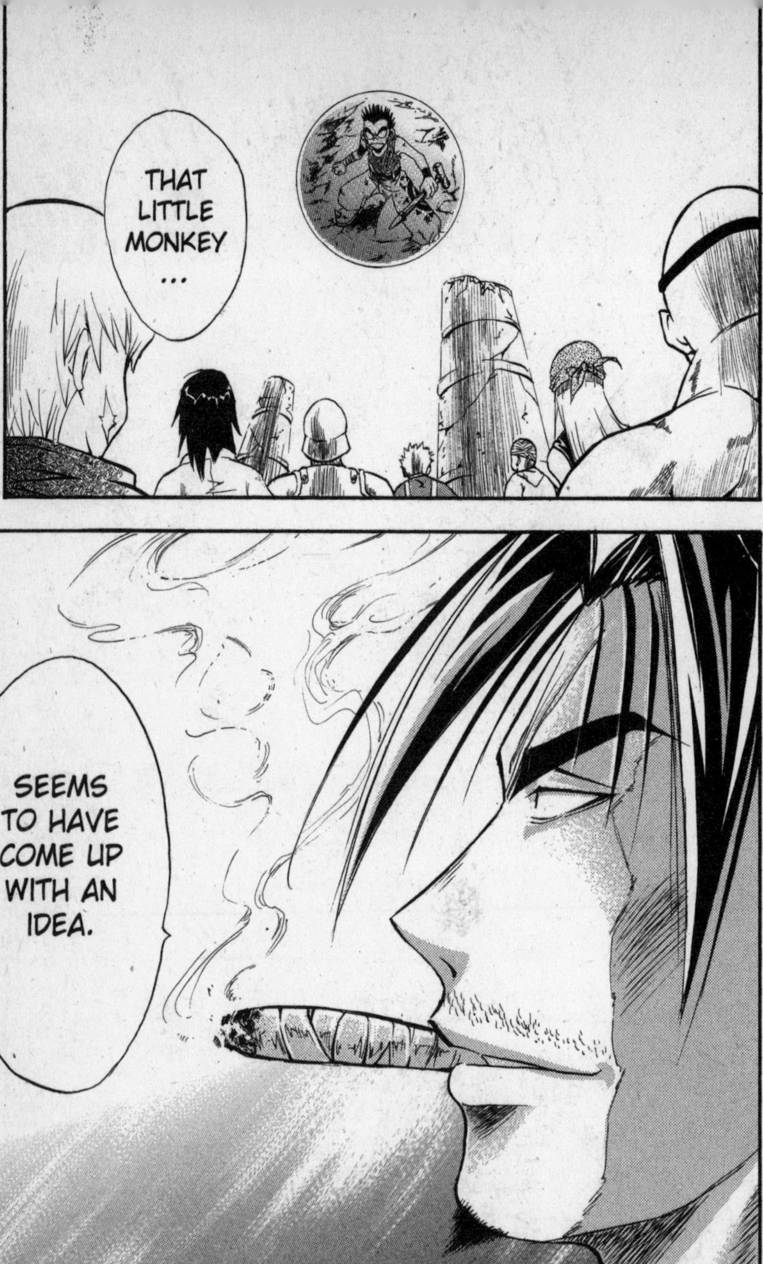
THAT LITTLE MONKEY ...
SEEMS TO HAVE COME UP WITH AN IDEA.

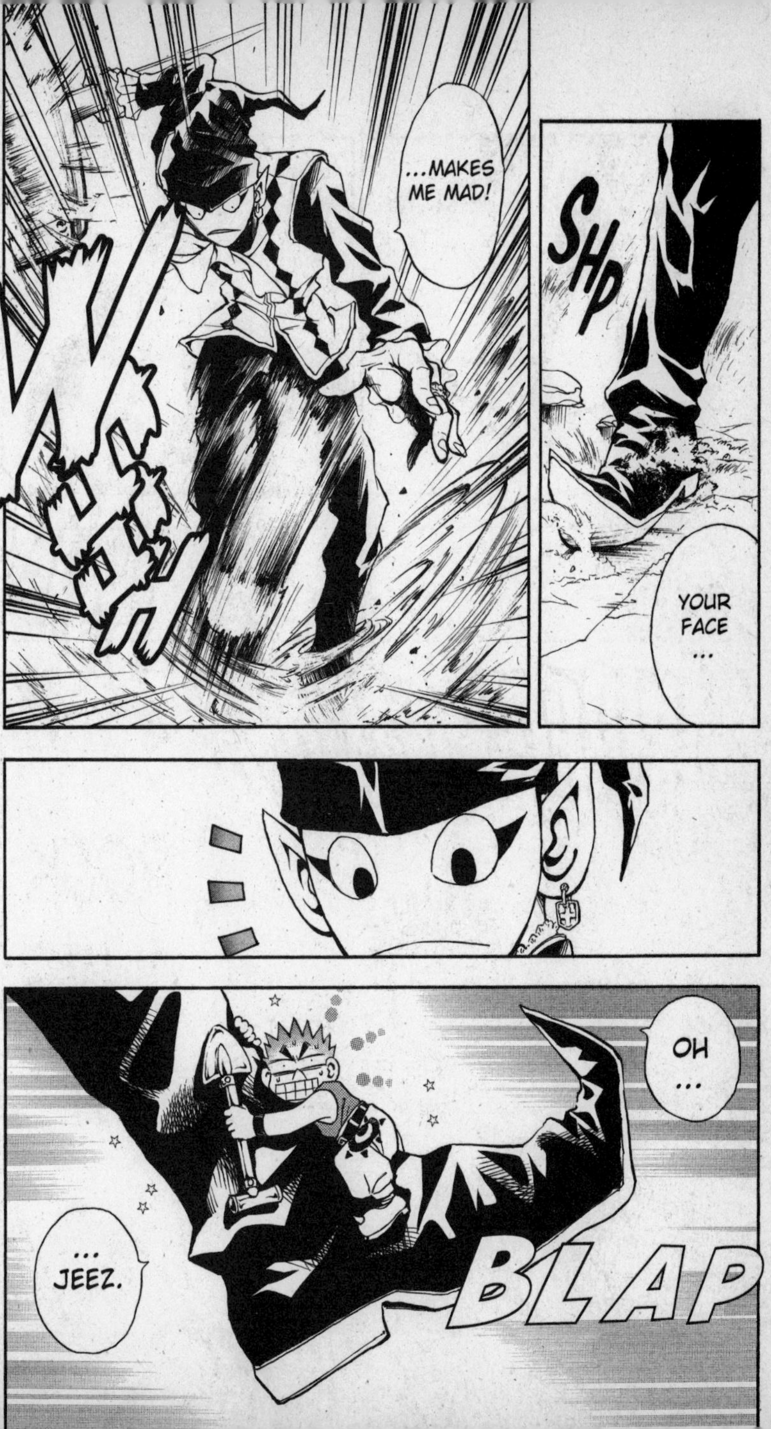
SHP
YOUR FACE ...
...MAKES ME MAD!
OH ...
BLAP
... JEEZ.

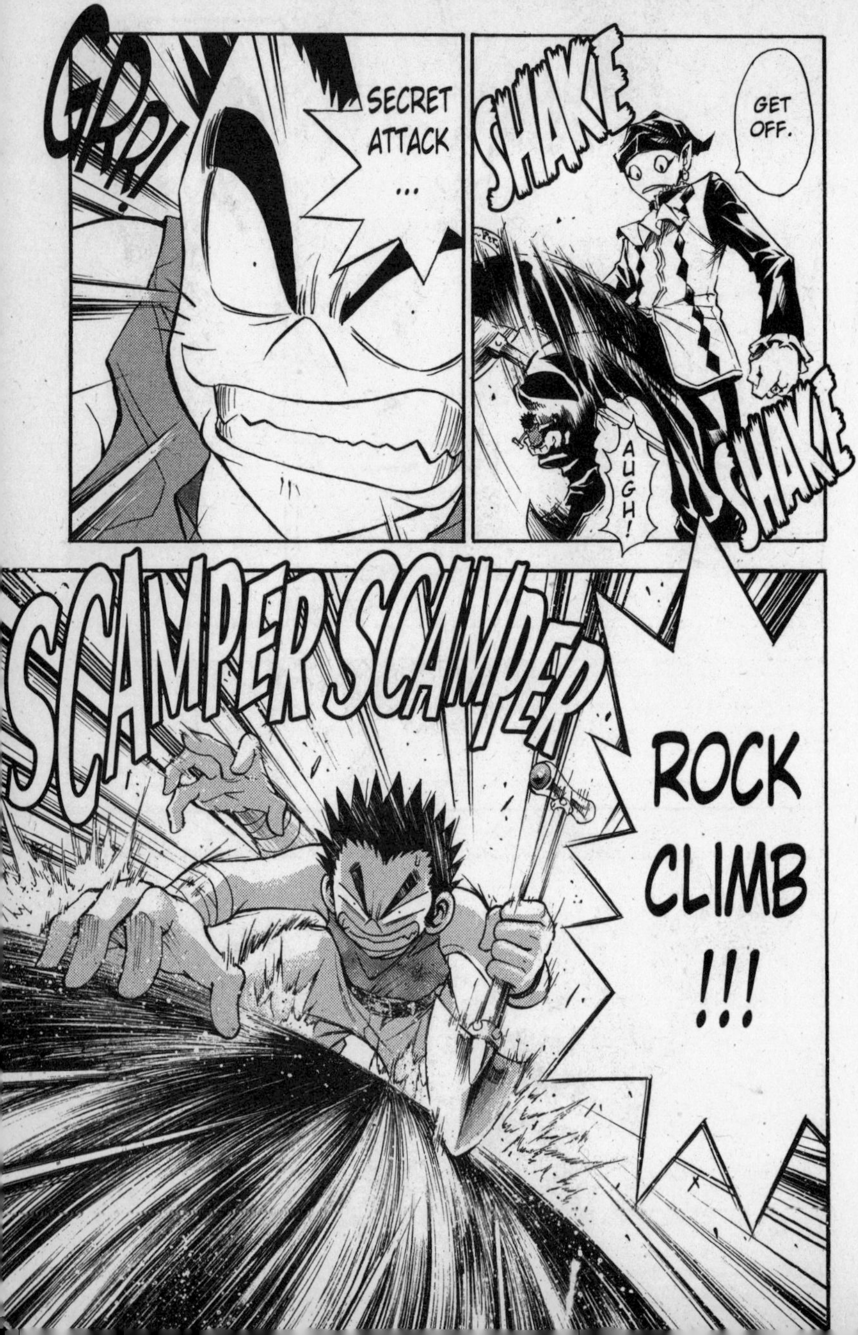
SHAKE
GET OFF.
AUGH!
SHAKE
GRR!
SECRET ATTACK ...
SCAMPER SCAMPER
ROCK CLIMB !!!

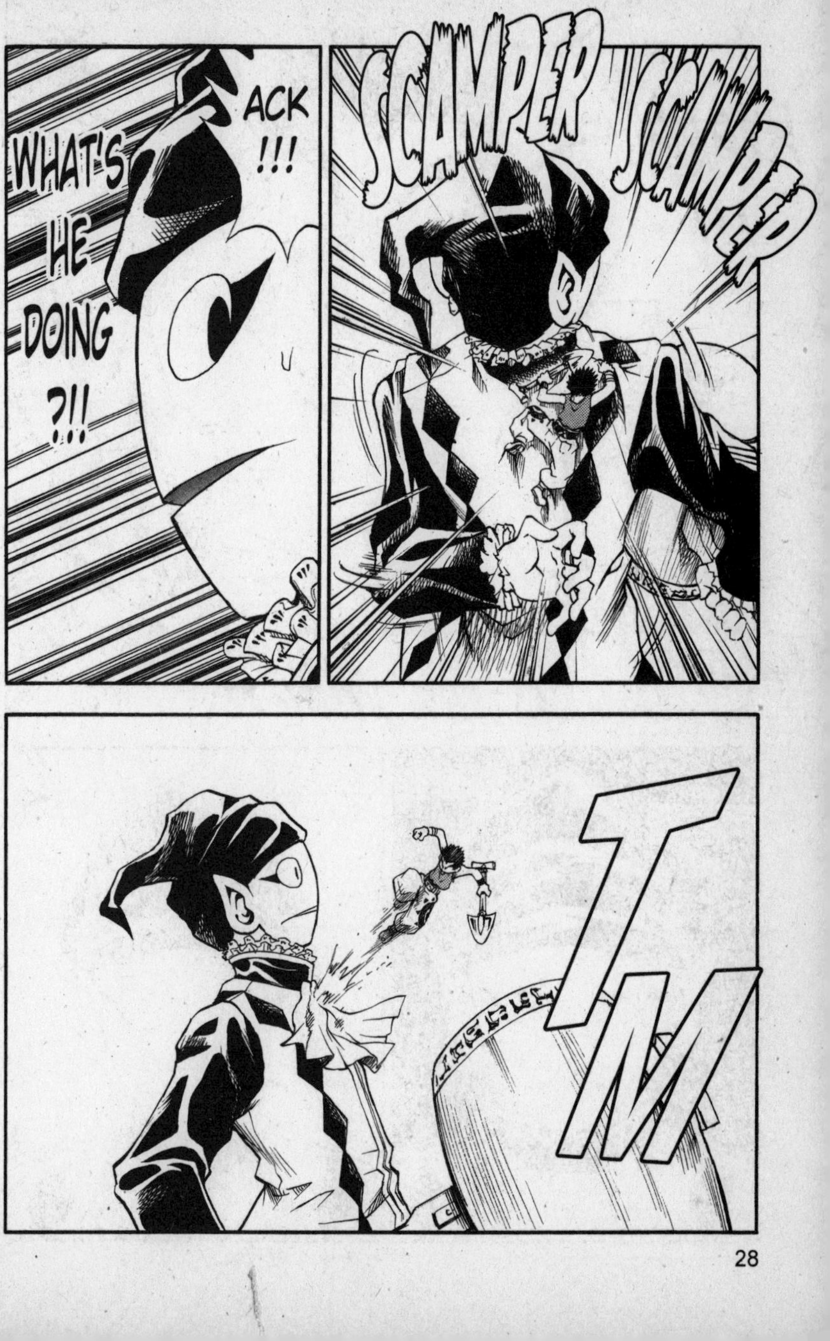
SCAMPER SCAMPER
ACK !!!
WHAT'S HE DOING ?!!
TM

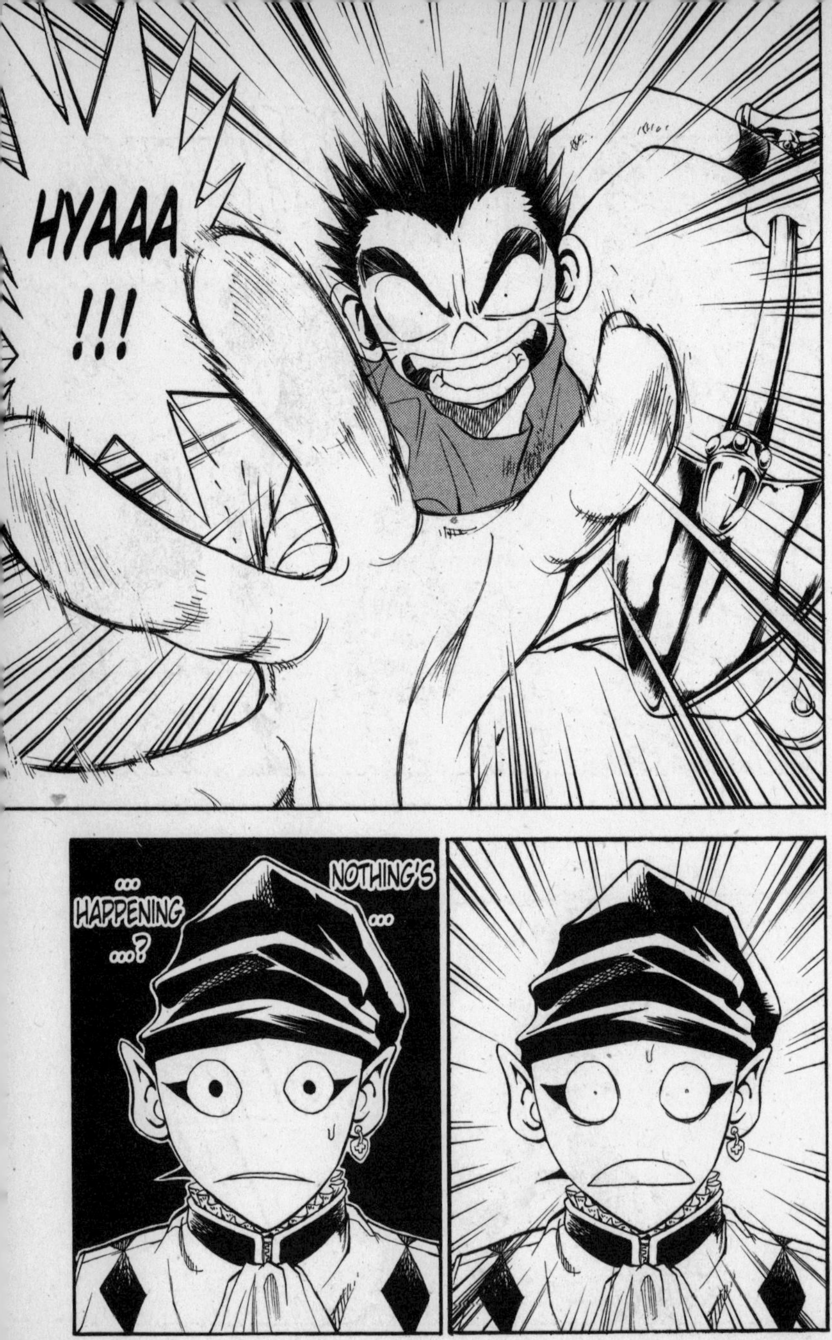
HYAAA !!!
NOTHING'S ...
... HAPPENING ...?

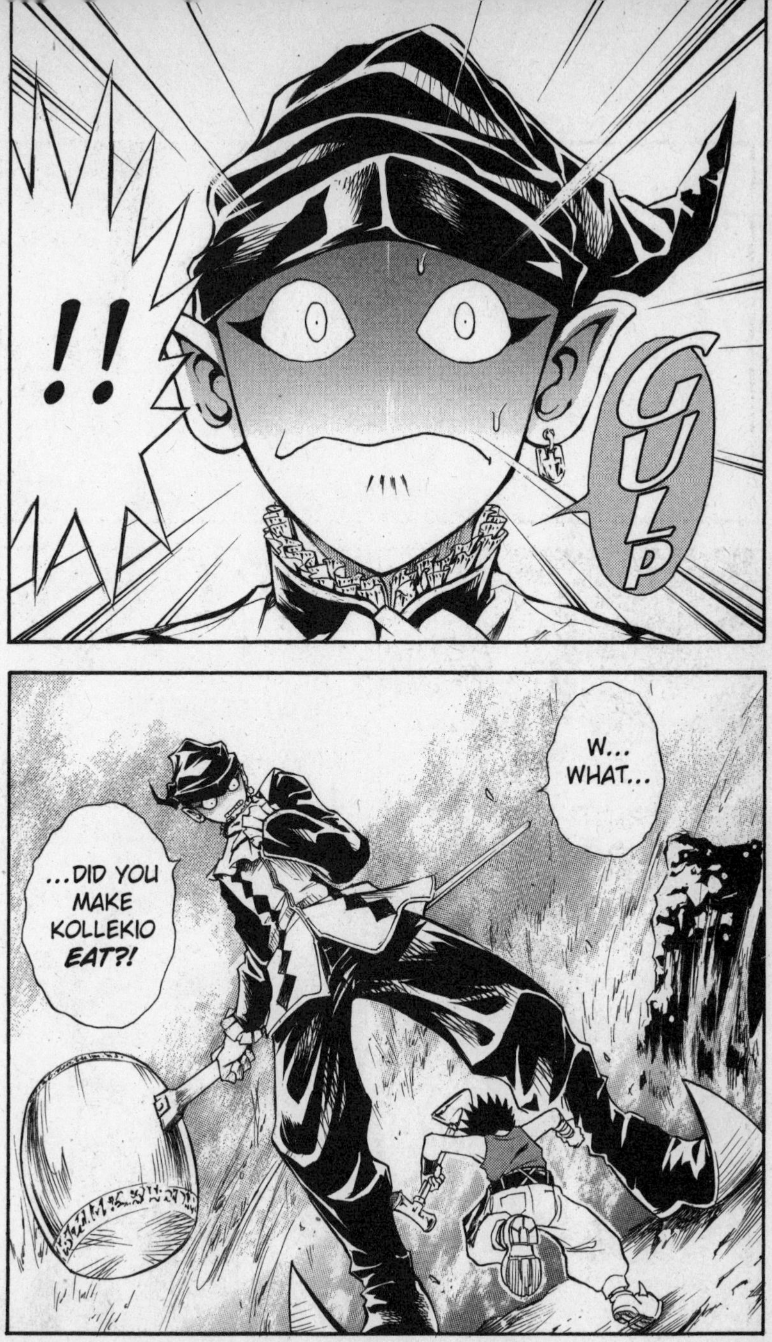
GULP
!!
W... WHAT...
...DID YOU MAKE KOLLEKIO *EAT?!*

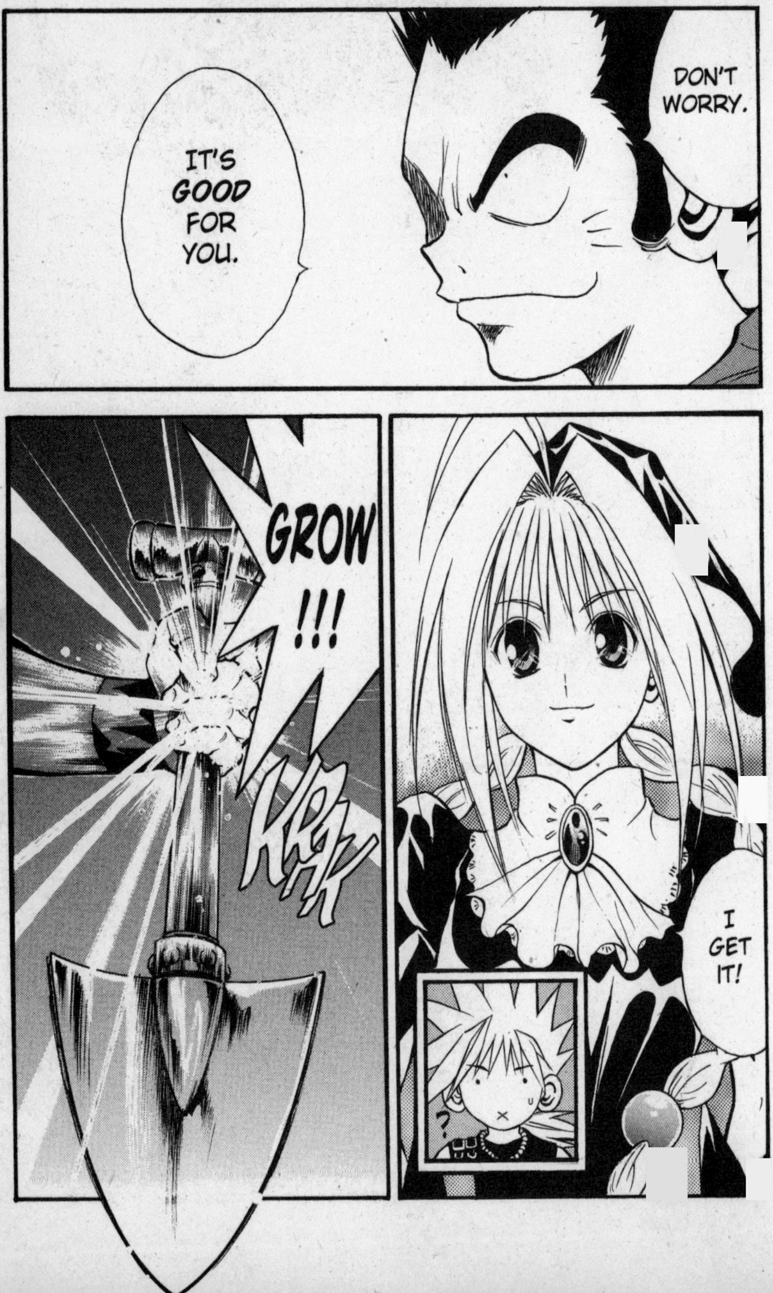
DON'T WORRY.
IT'S GOOD FOR YOU.
I GET IT!
GROW!!!
KRAK

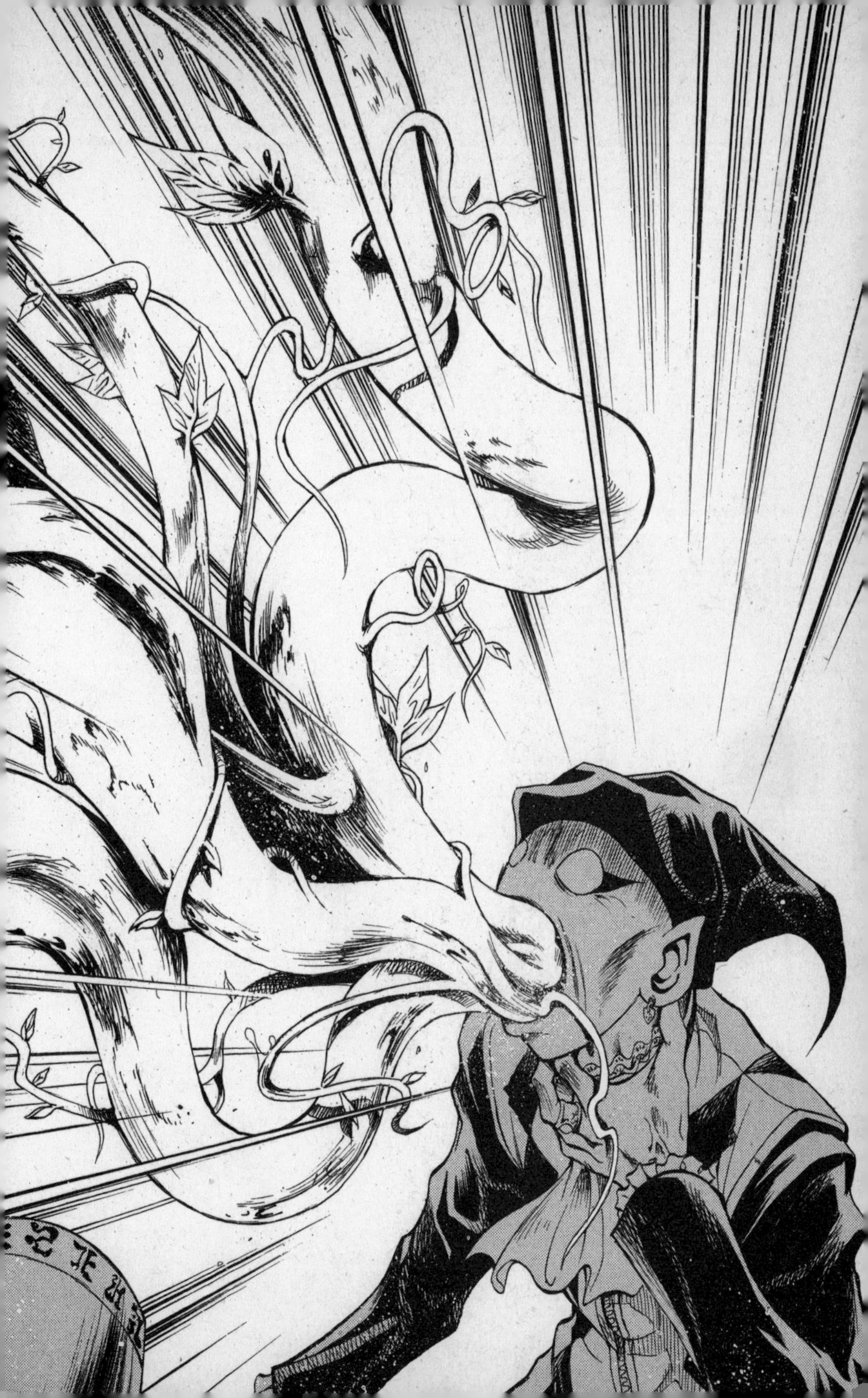

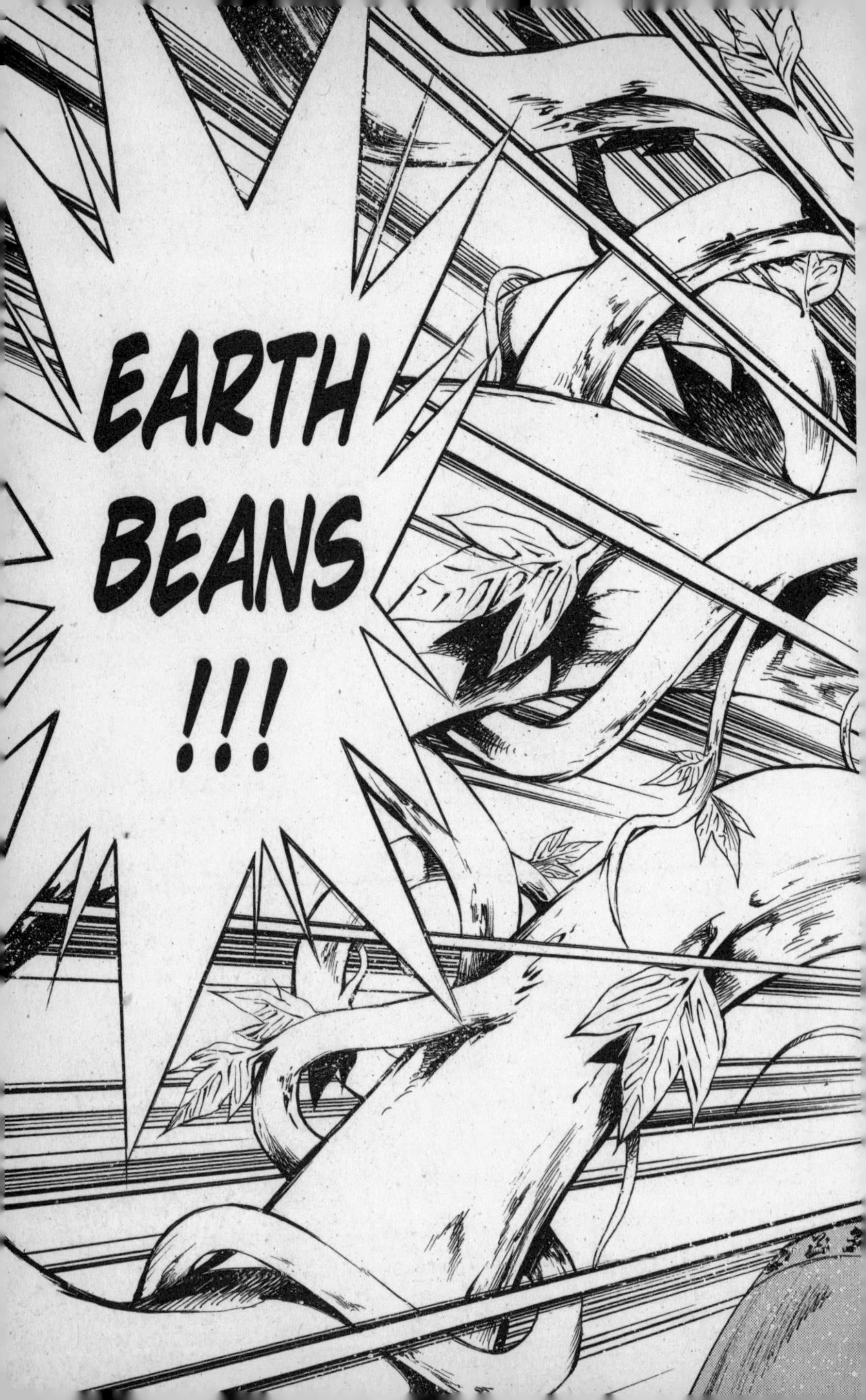
EARTH BEANS !!!

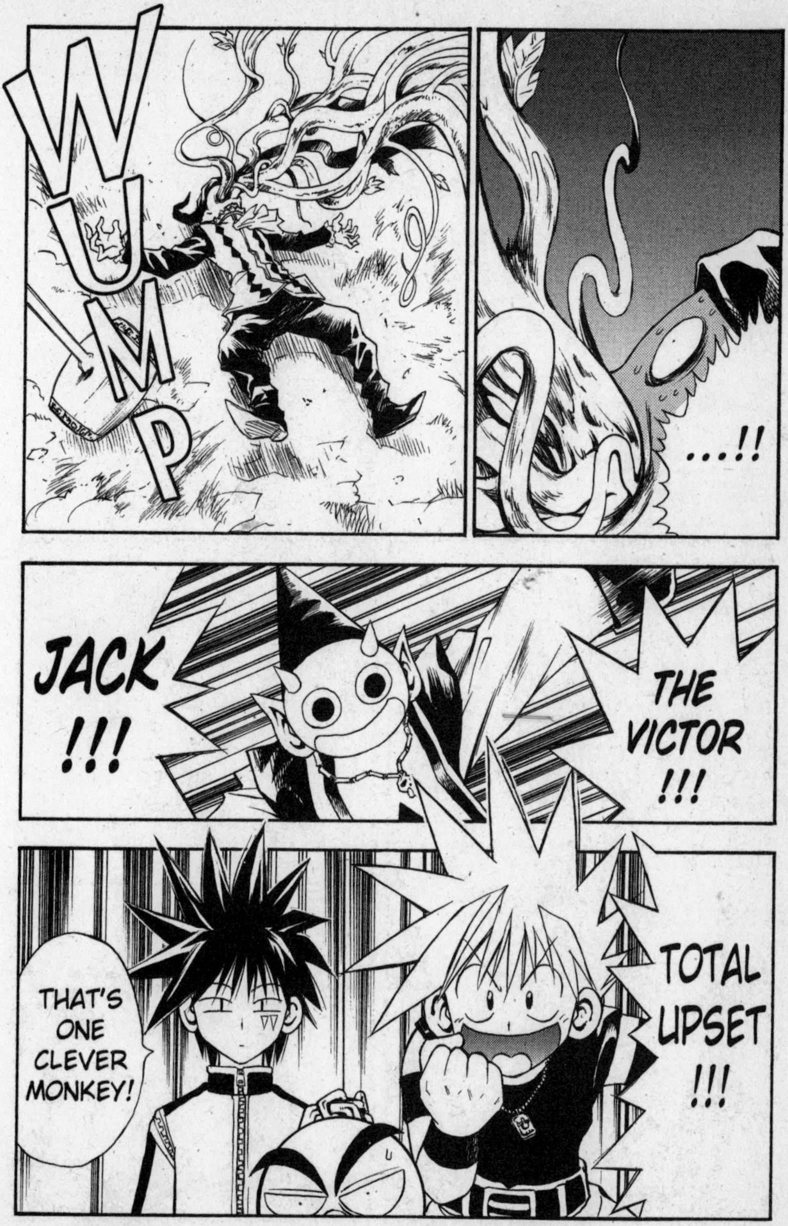
...!!
WUMP
THE VICTOR !!!
JACK !!!
TOTAL UPSET !!!
THAT'S ONE CLEVER MONKEY!

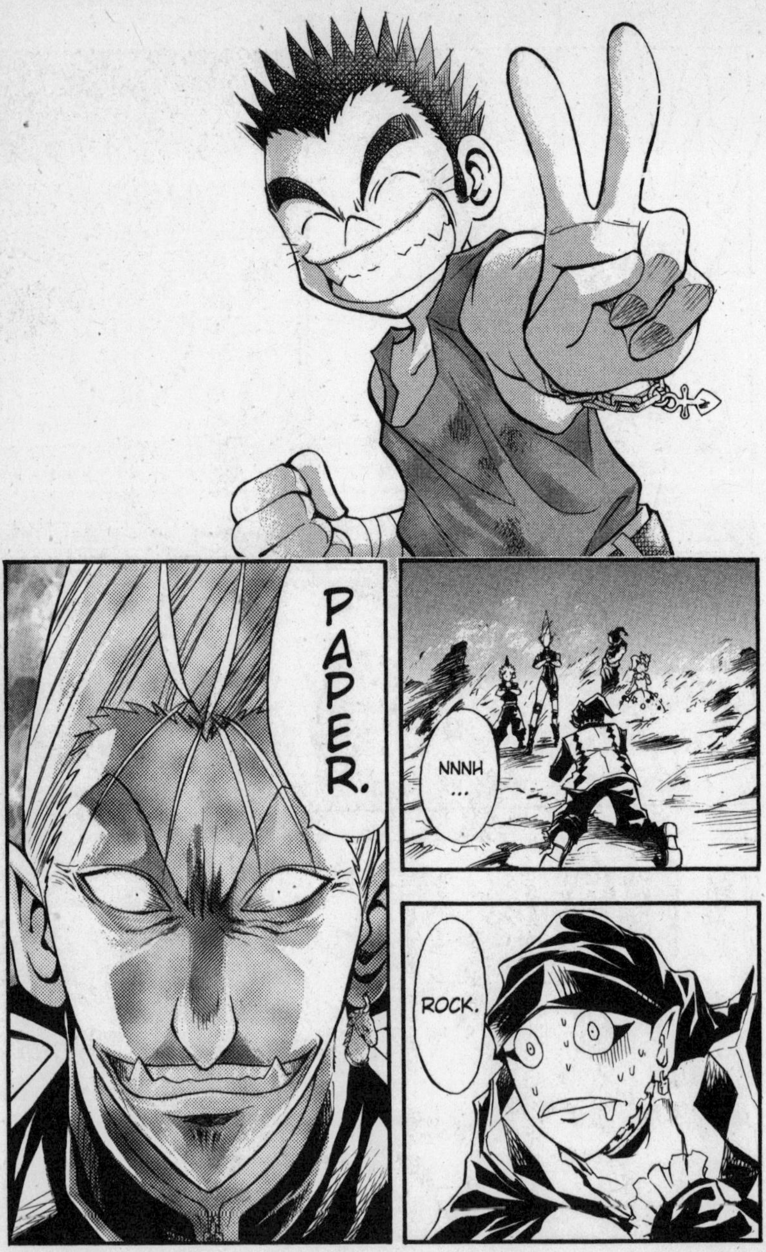
NNNH ...
PAPER.
ROCK.

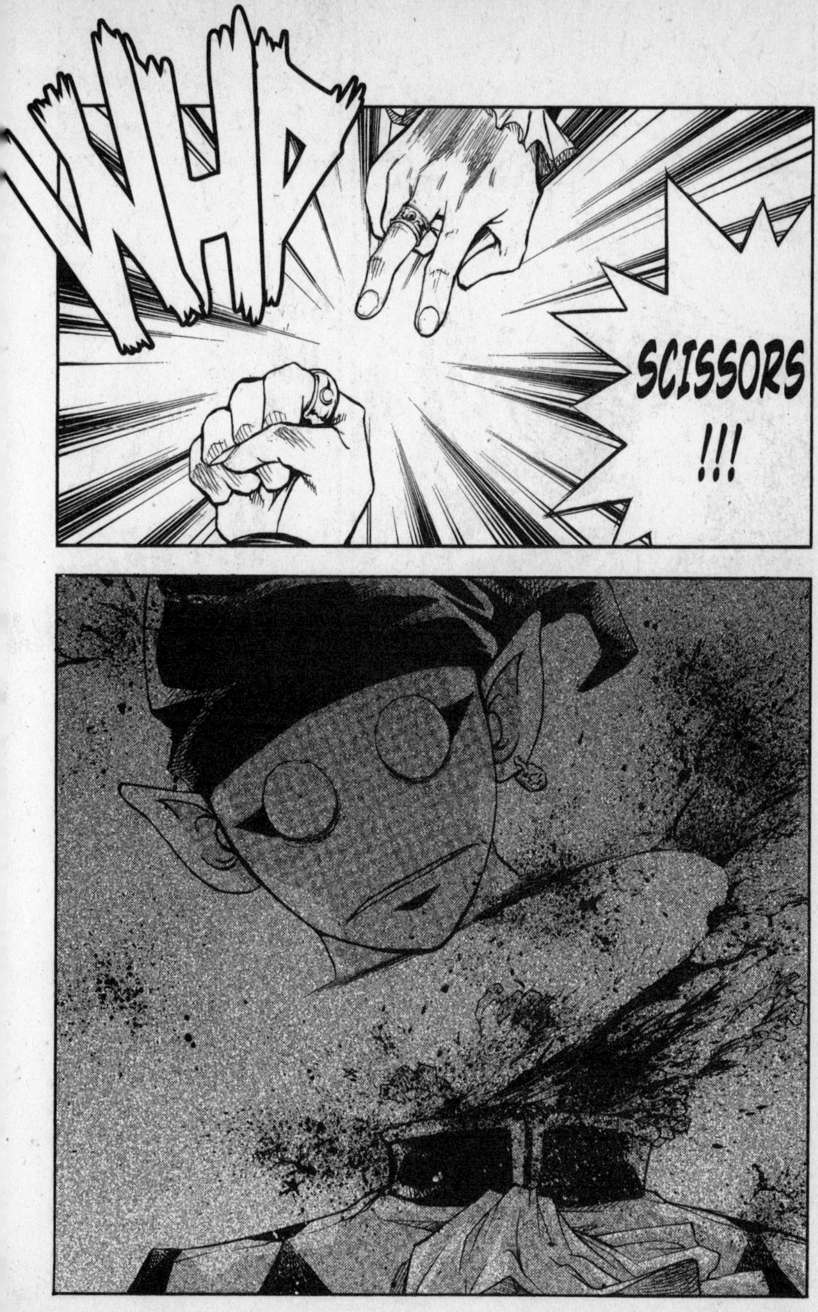
WHAP
SCISSORS
!!!

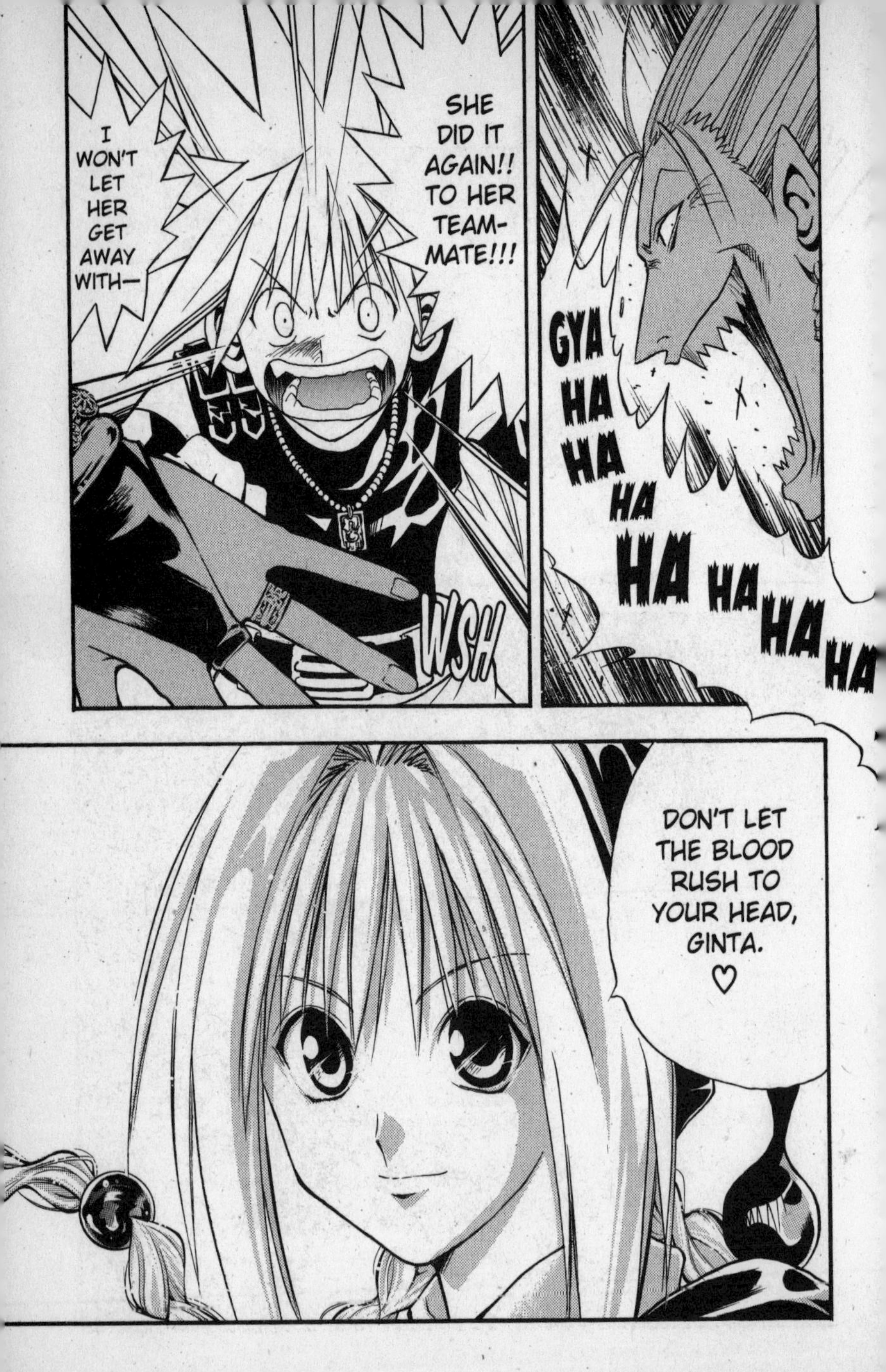
GYA HA HA HA HA HA HA HA
SHE DID IT AGAIN!! TO HER TEAM-MATE!!!
I WON'T LET HER GET AWAY WITH—
WSH
DON'T LET THE BLOOD RUSH TO YOUR HEAD, GINTA. ♡

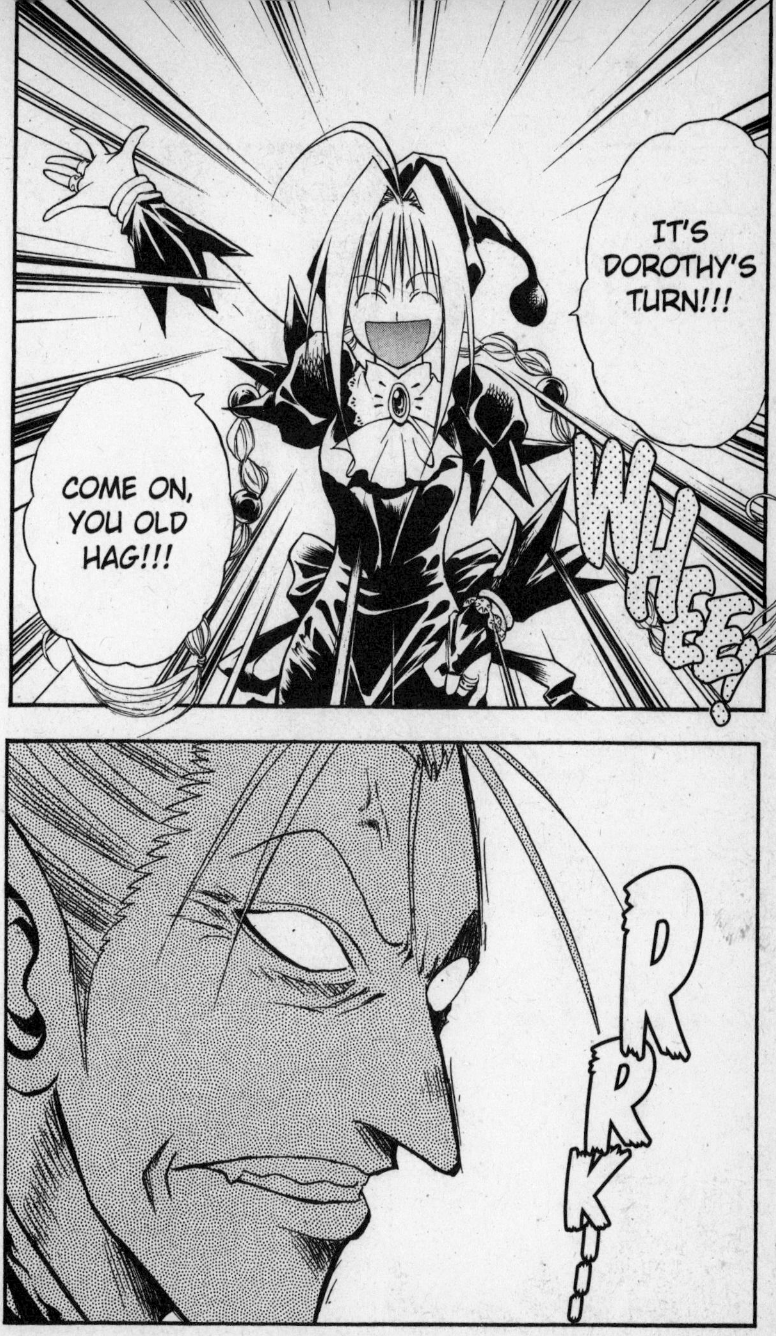
IT'S DOROTHY'S TURN!!!
COME ON, YOU OLD HAG!!!
WHEEE!
RRK

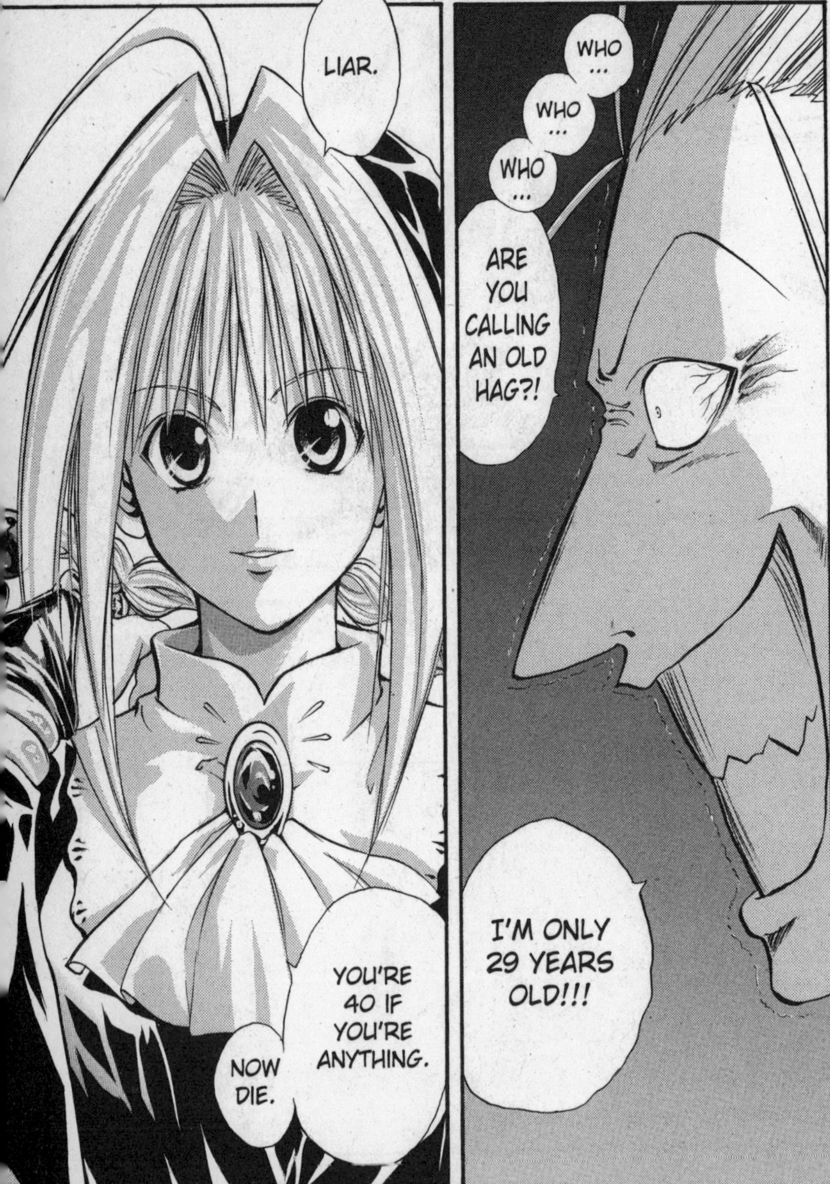
WHO ...
WHO ...
WHO ...
ARE YOU CALLING AN OLD HAG?!
I'M ONLY 29 YEARS OLD!!!
LIAR.
YOU'RE 40 IF YOU'RE ANYTHING.
NOW DIE.

AKT.77/ DOROTHY VS. AVRUTE

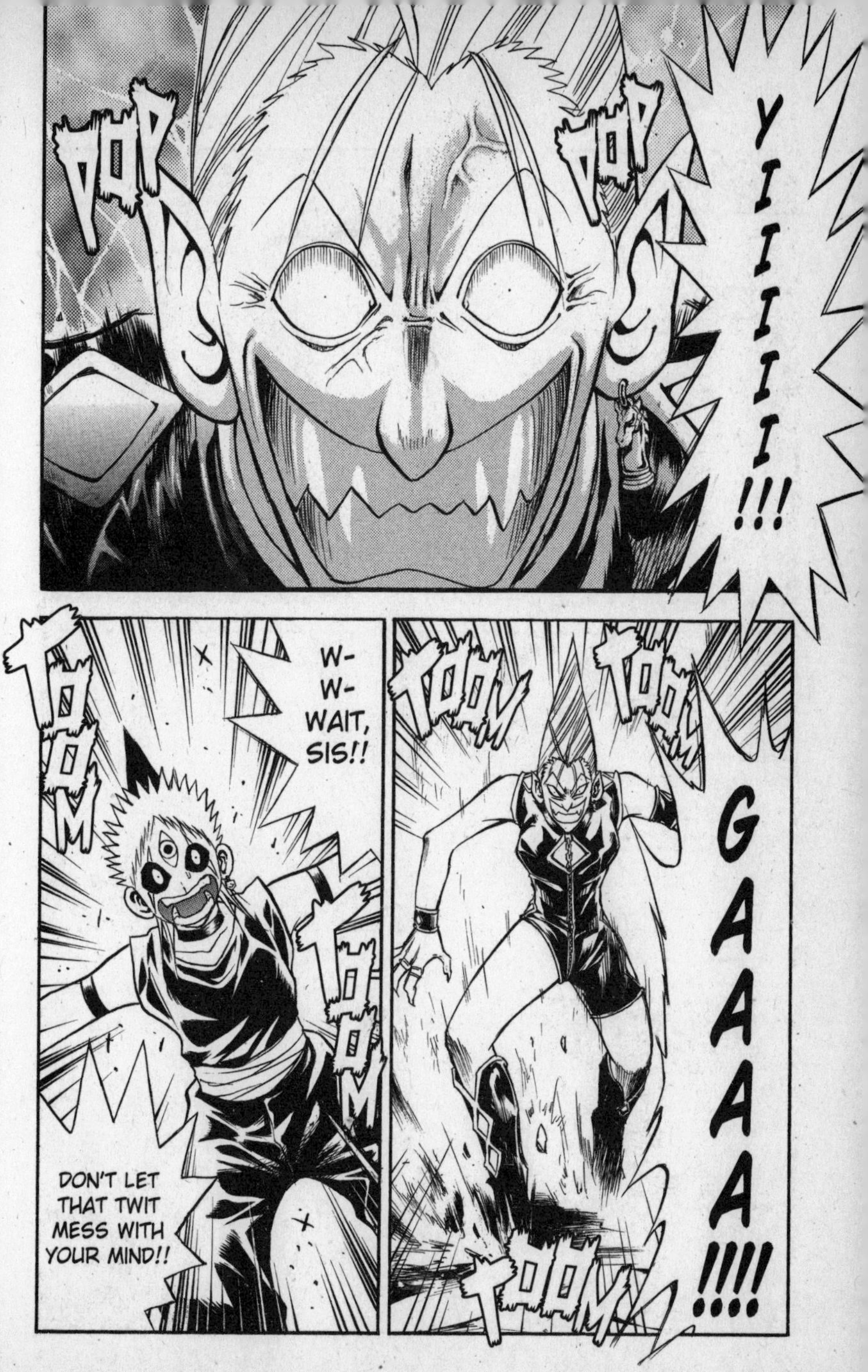
YIIIII!!!
TOOM
TOOM
GAAAA!!!!
TOOM
W-W-WAIT, SIS!!
TOOM
TOOM
DON'T LET THAT TWIT MESS WITH YOUR MIND!!

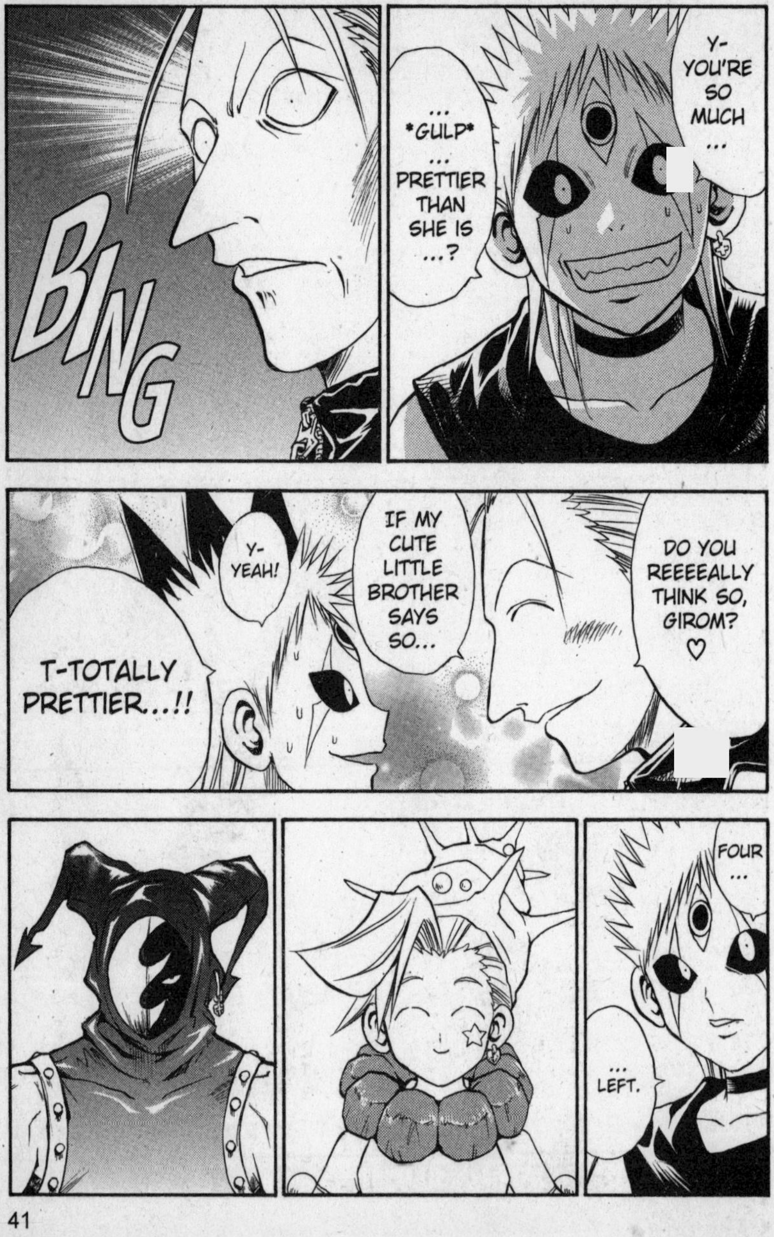
Y- YOU'RE SO MUCH ...
... *GULP* ... PRETTIER THAN SHE IS ...?
BING
DO YOU REEEEALLY THINK SO, GIROM? ♡
IF MY CUTE LITTLE BROTHER SAYS SO...
Y- YEAH!
T-TOTALLY PRETTIER...!!
FOUR ...
... LEFT.

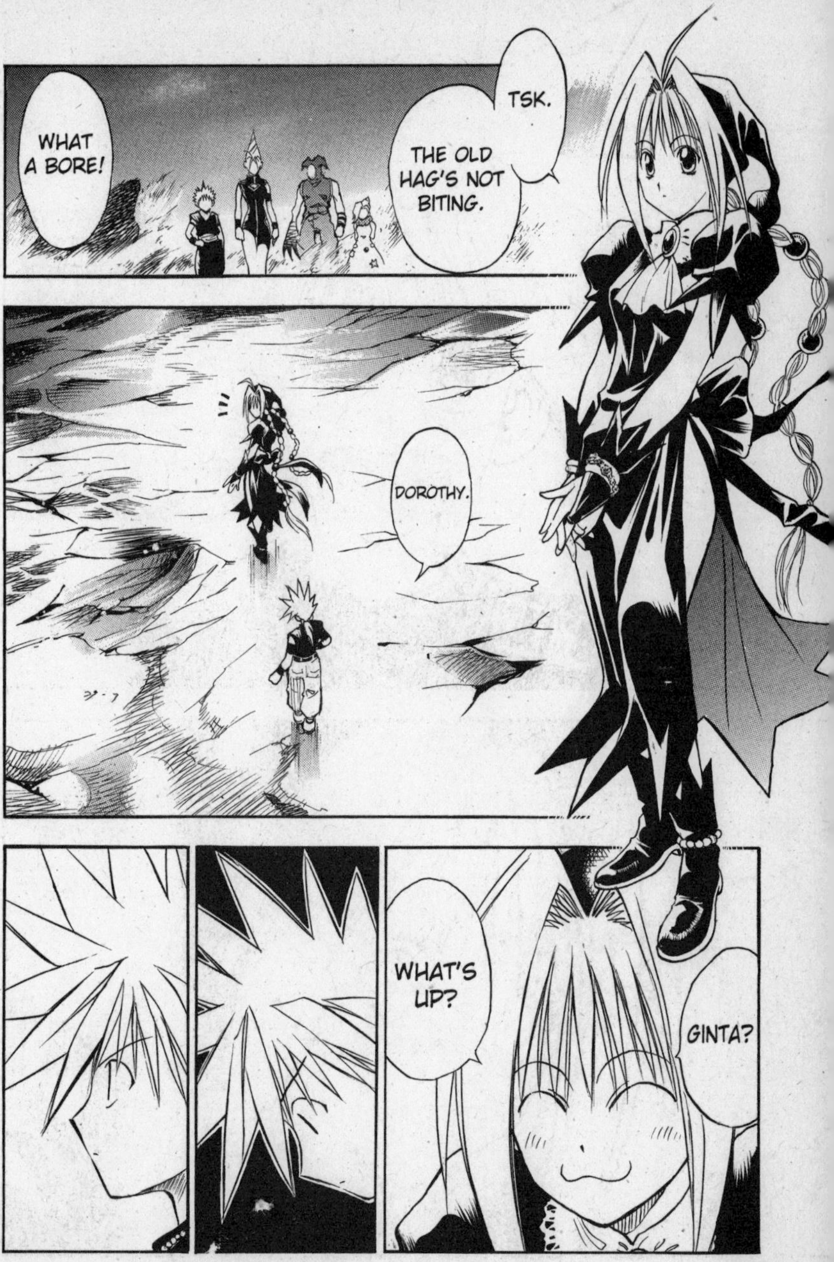
TSK.
THE OLD HAG'S NOT BITING.
WHAT A BORE!
DOROTHY.
GINTA?
WHAT'S UP?

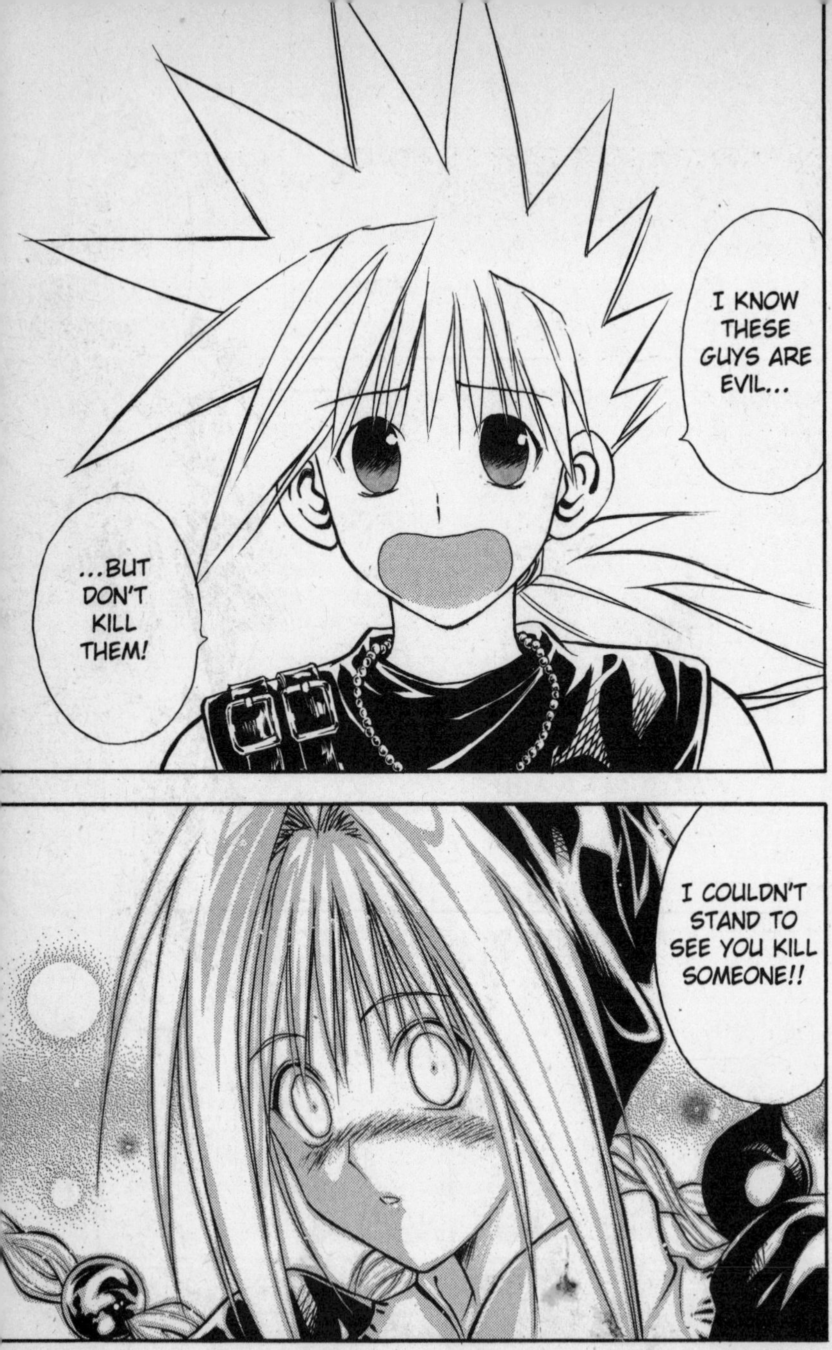
I KNOW THESE GUYS ARE EVIL...
...BUT DON'T KILL THEM!
I COULDN'T STAND TO SEE YOU KILL SOMEONE!!

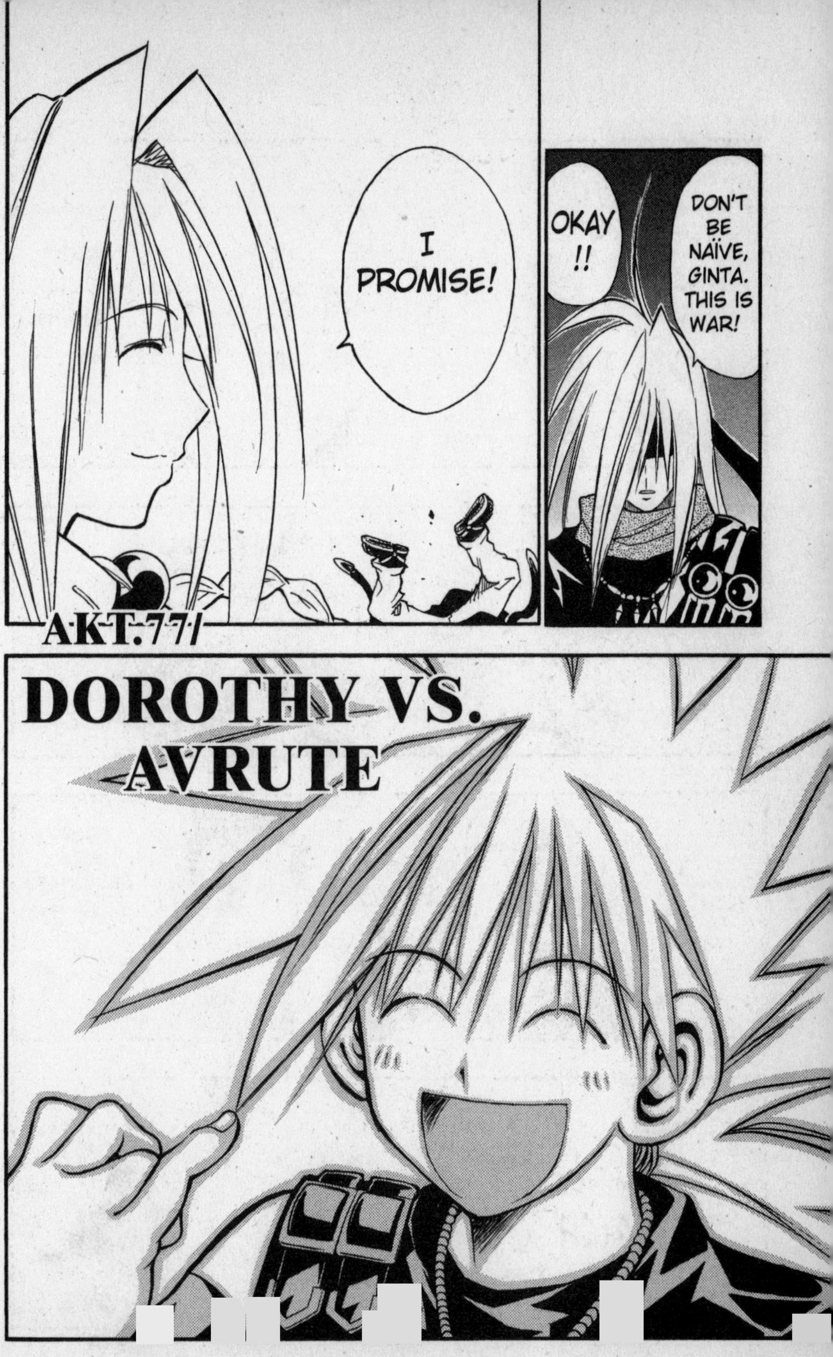
DON'T BE NAÏVE, GINTA. THIS IS WAR!
OKAY !!
I PROMISE!
AKT.77
DOROTHY VS. AVRUTE

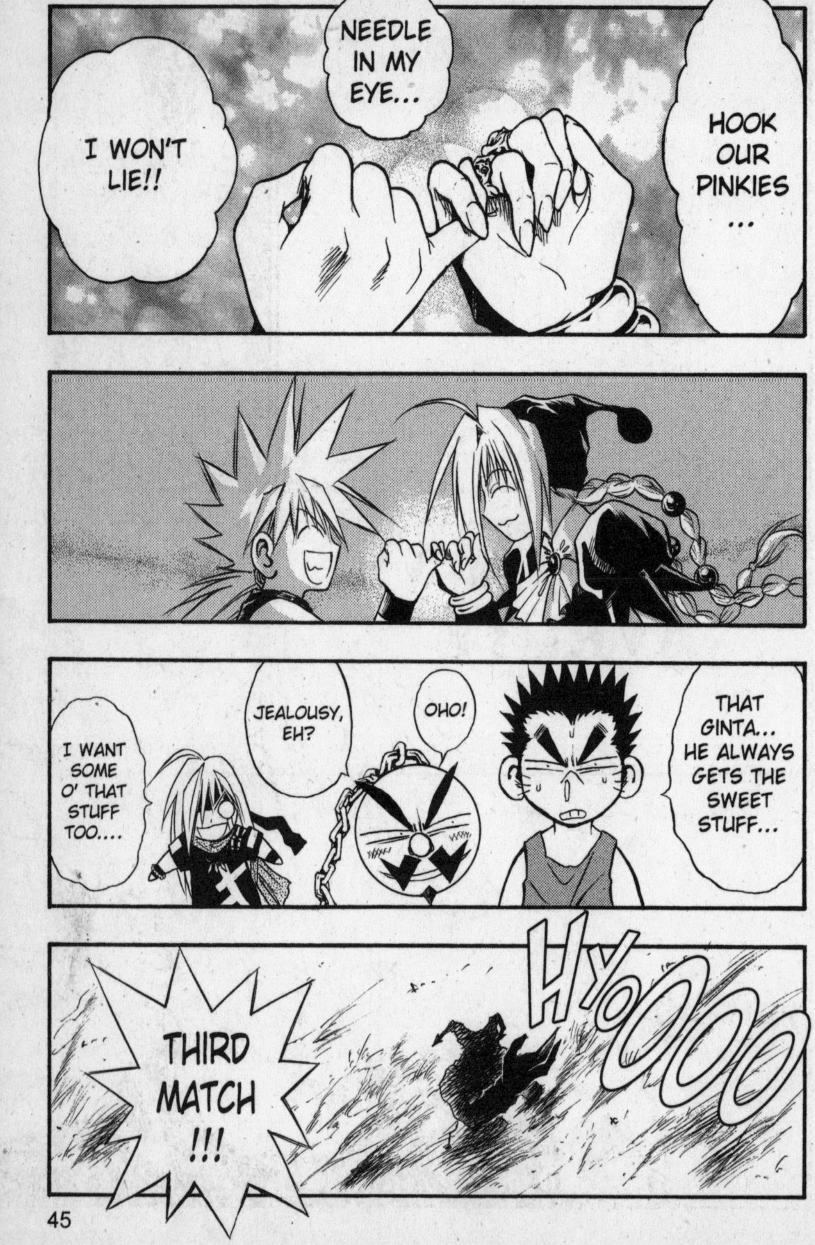
HOOK OUR PINKIES ...
NEEDLE IN MY EYE...
I WON'T LIE!!
THAT GINTA... HE ALWAYS GETS THE SWEET STUFF...
OHO!
JEALOUSY, EH?
I WANT SOME O' THAT STUFF TOO....
HYOOOO
THIRD MATCH !!!

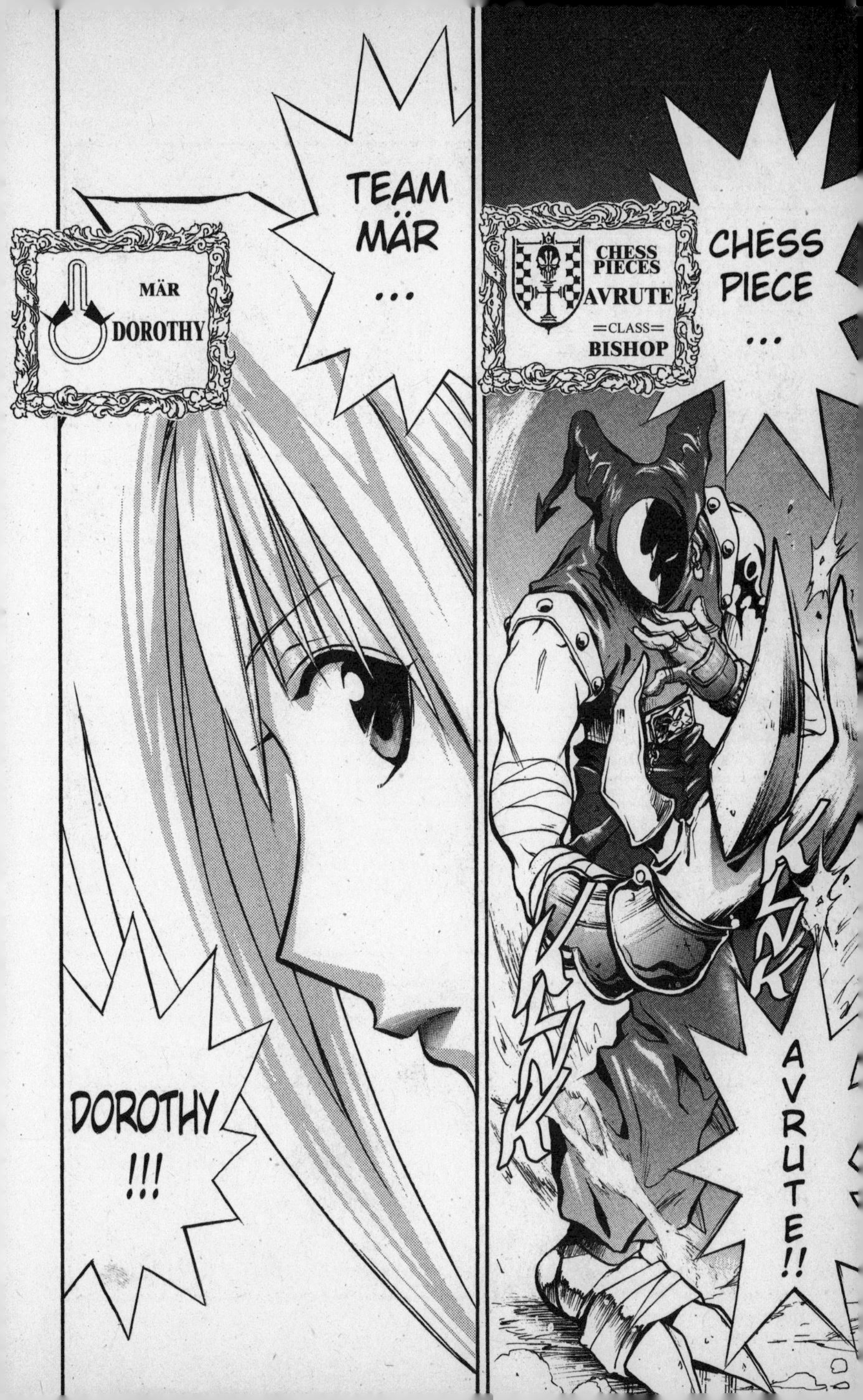
CHESS PIECES
AVRUTE
=CLASS=
BISHOP
CHESS PIECE ...
AVRUTE!!
MÄR
DOROTHY
TEAM MÄR ...
DOROTHY !!!

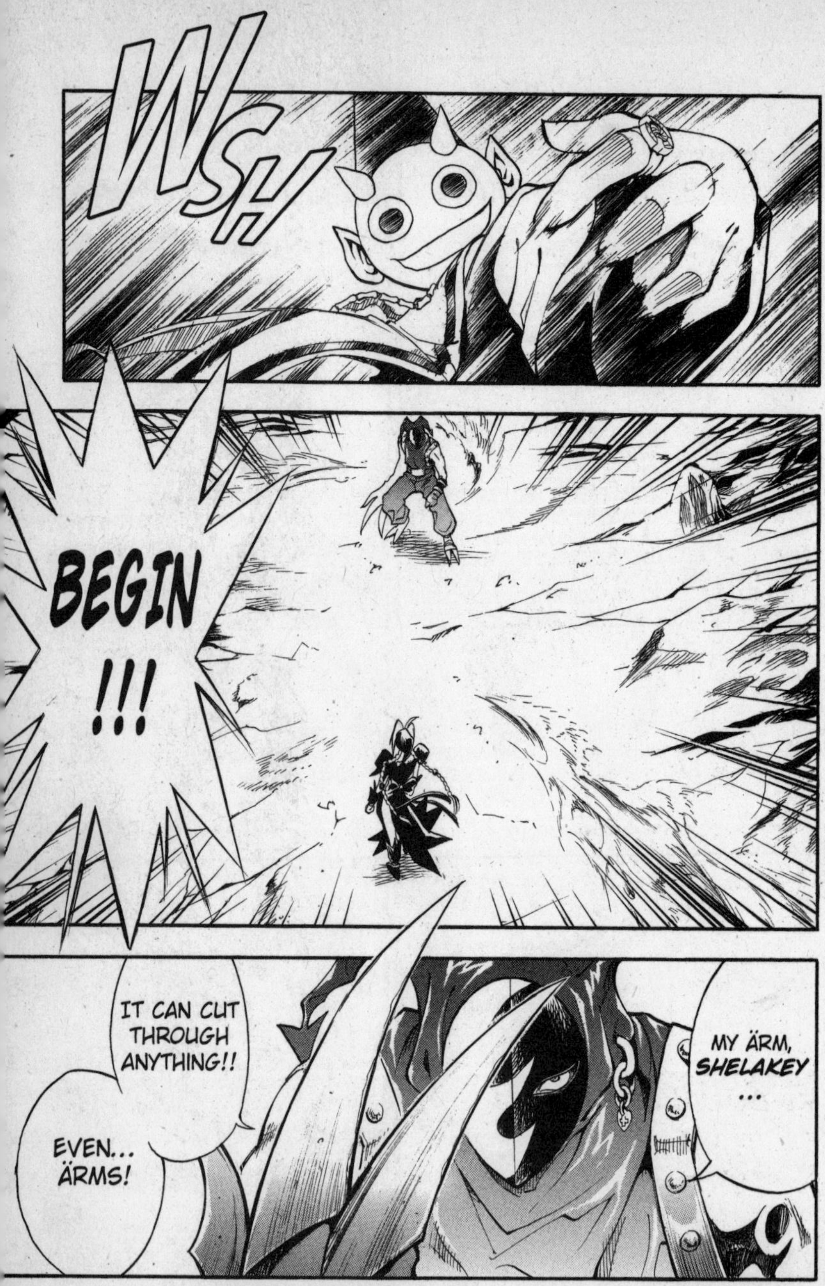
WSH
BEGIN!!!
MY ÄRM, SHELAKEY...
IT CAN CUT THROUGH ANYTHING!!
EVEN... ÄRMS!

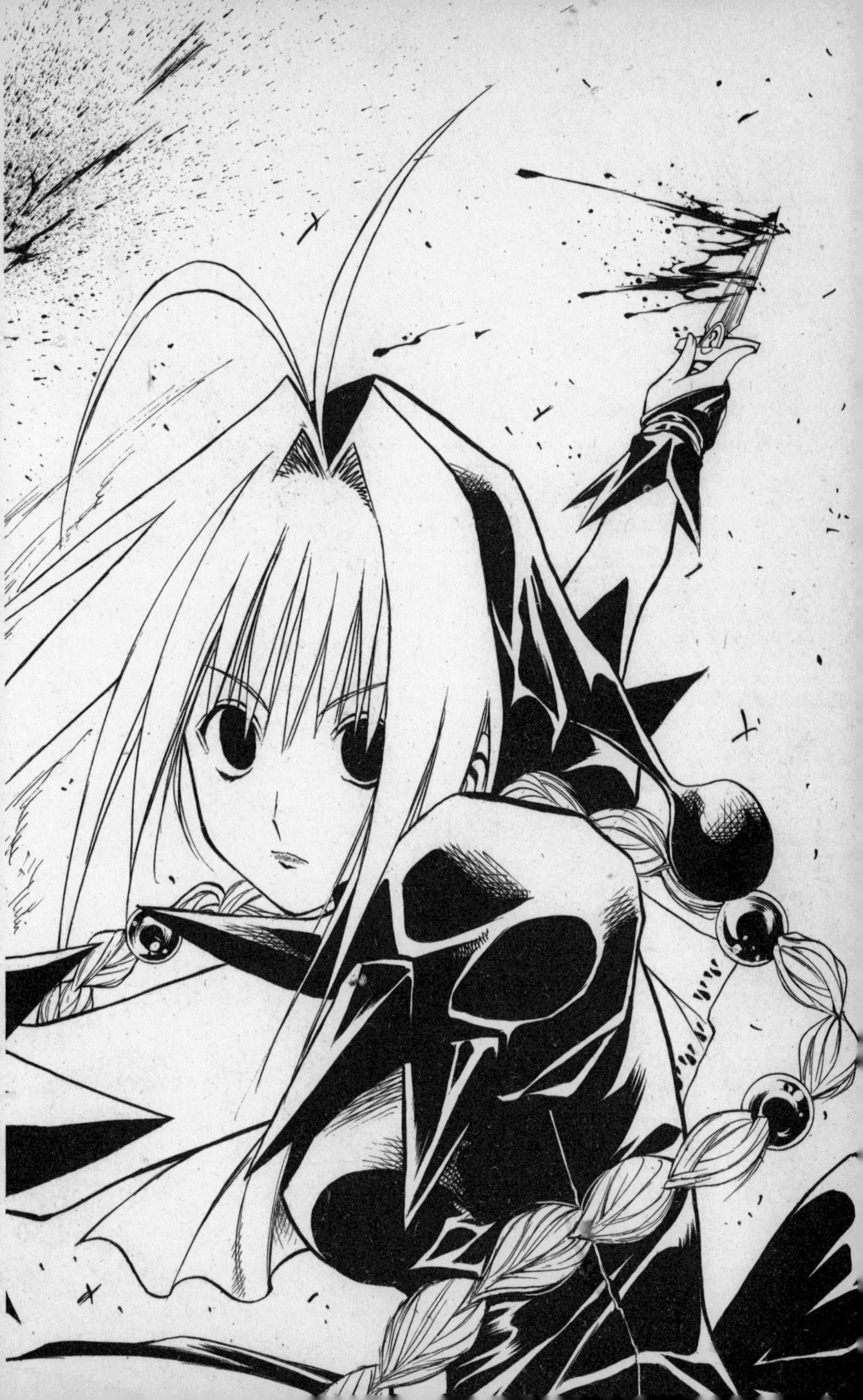

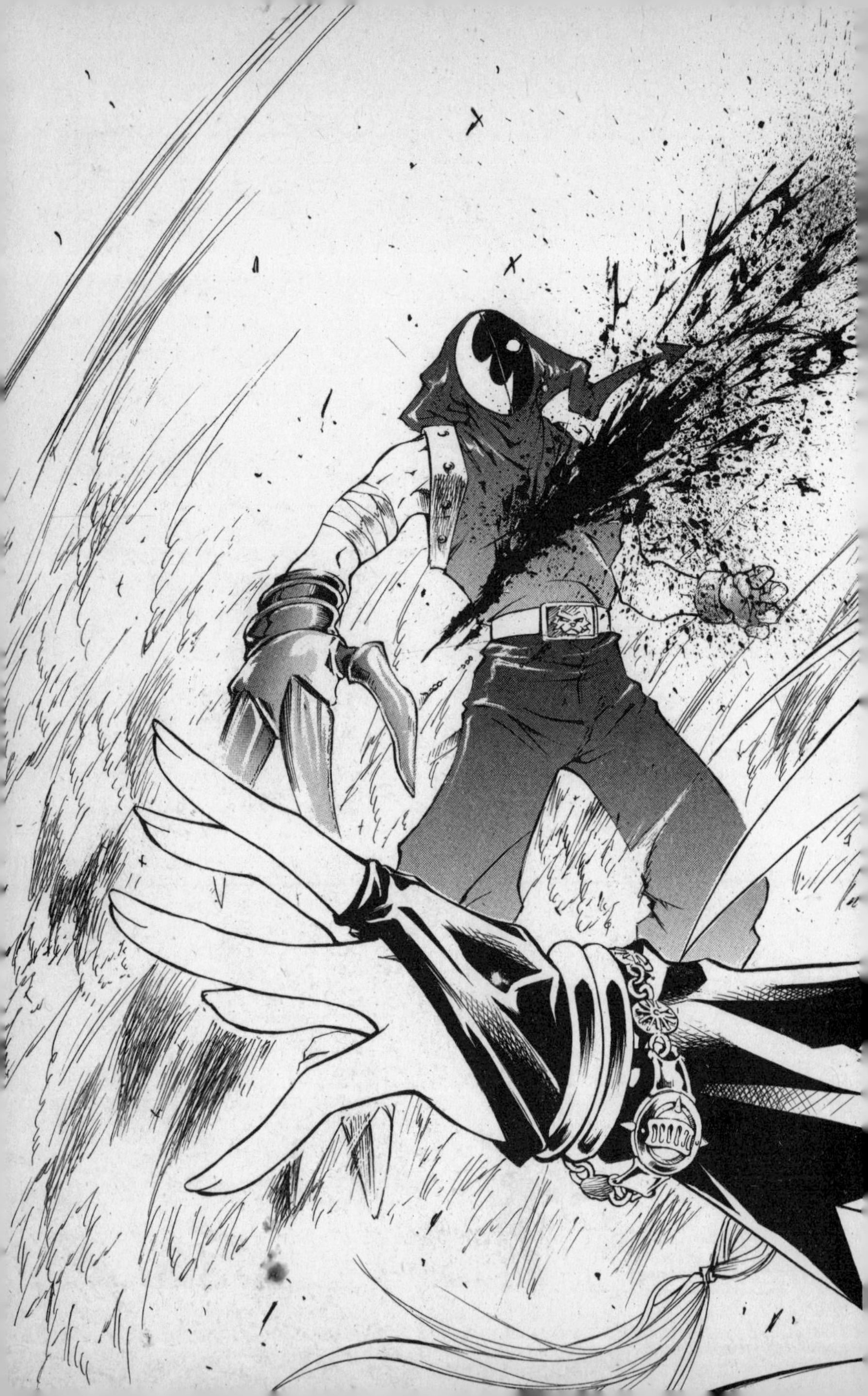

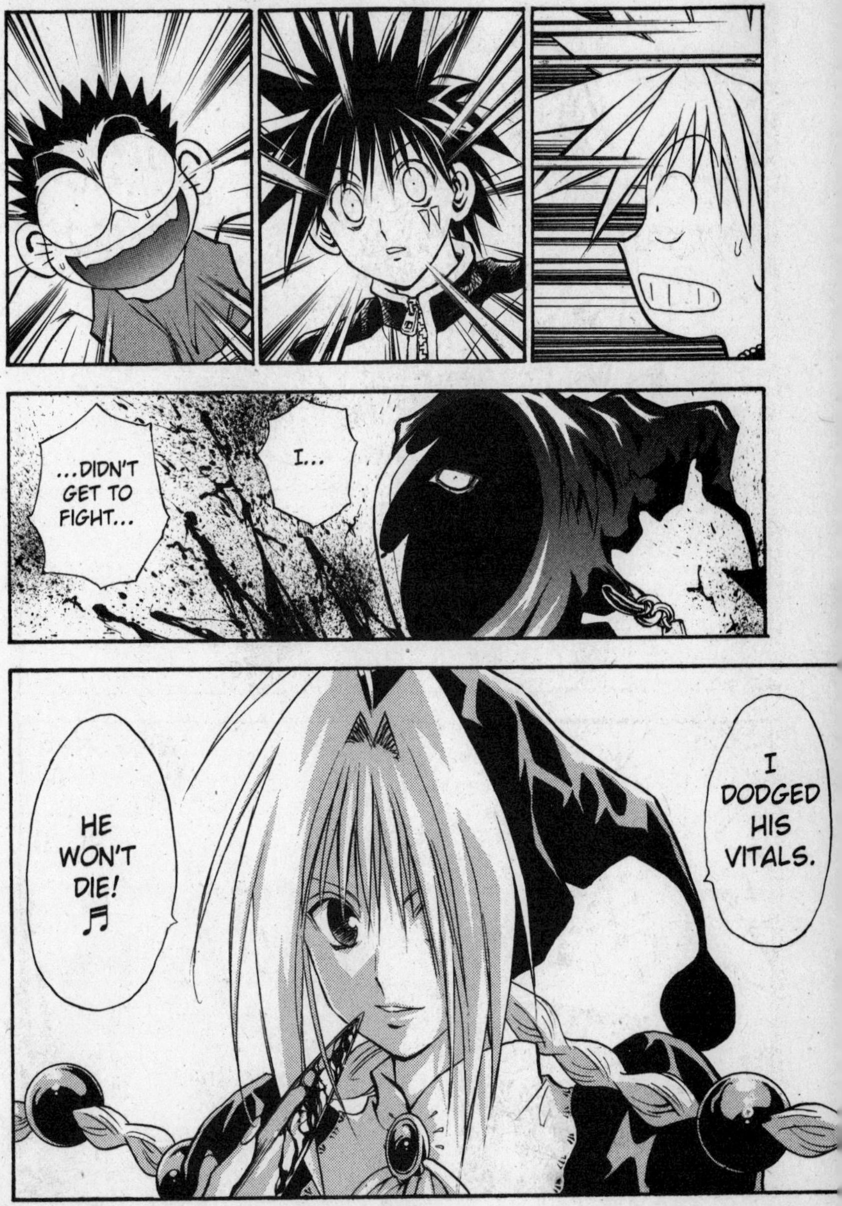
I...
...DIDN'T GET TO FIGHT...
I DODGED HIS VITALS.
HE WON'T DIE! ♬

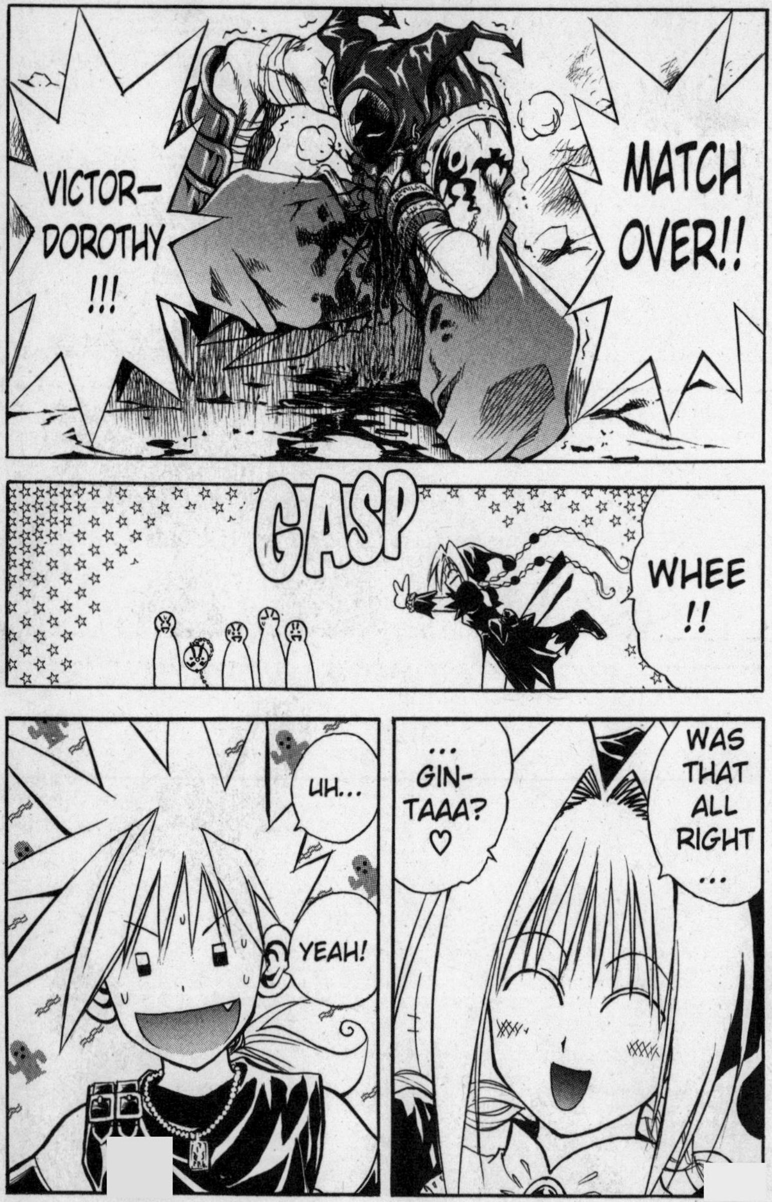
MATCH OVER!!
VICTOR— DOROTHY !!!
WHEE !!
GASP
WAS THAT ALL RIGHT ...
... GIN- TAAA? ♡
UH...
YEAH!

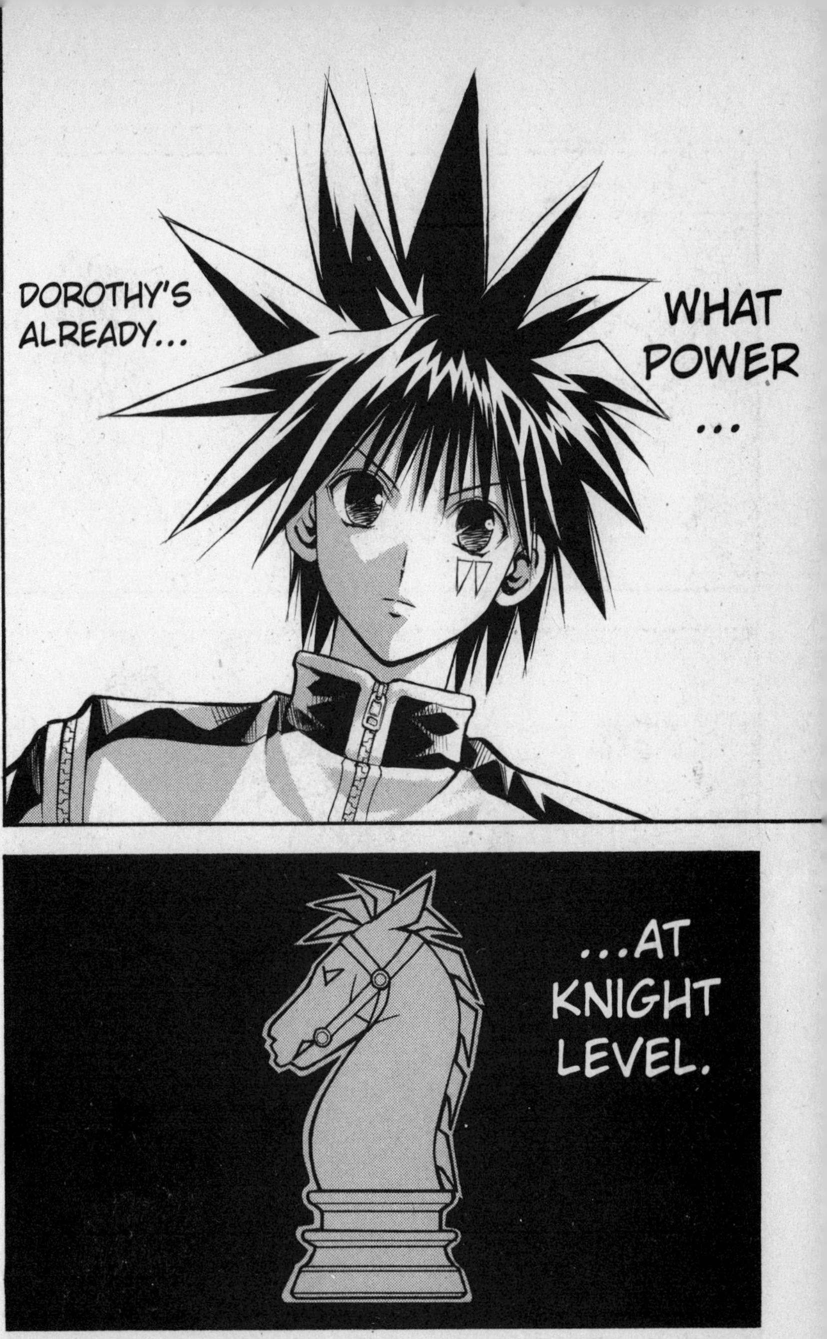
WHAT POWER ...
DOROTHY'S ALREADY...
...AT KNIGHT LEVEL.

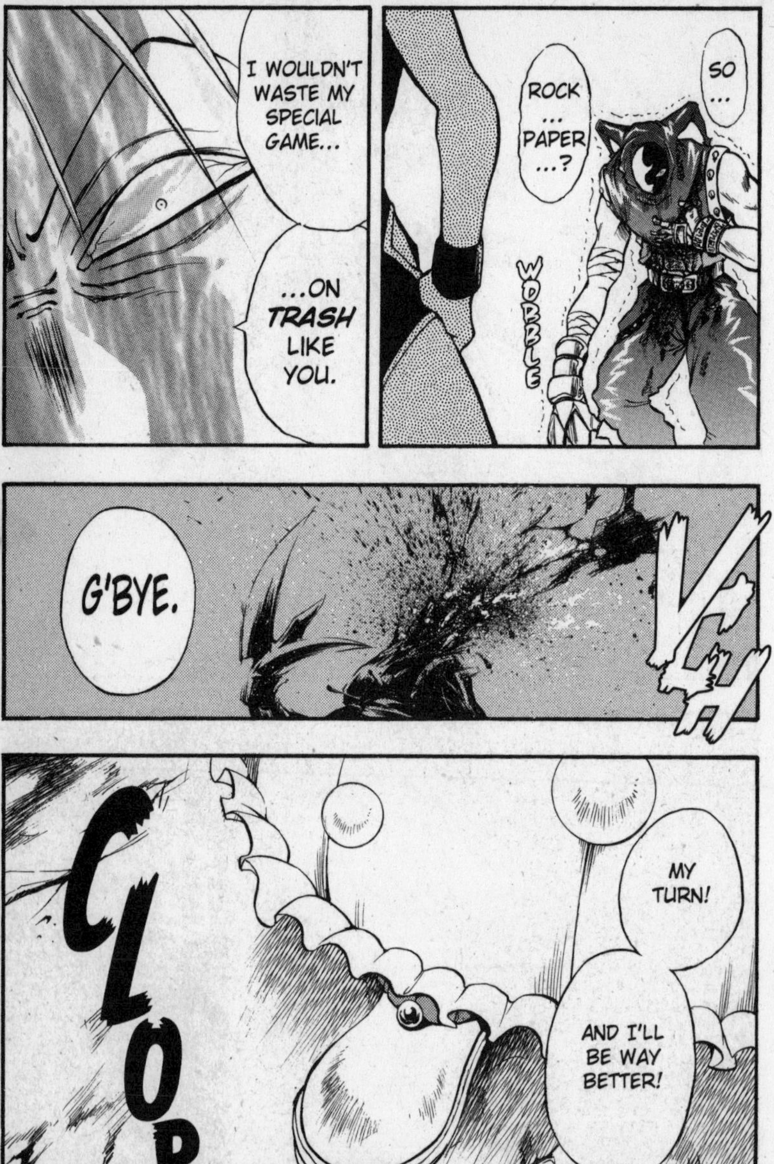
SO ...
ROCK ... PAPER ...?
WOBBLE
I WOULDN'T WASTE MY SPECIAL GAME...
...ON TRASH LIKE YOU.
G'BYE.
MY TURN!
AND I'LL BE WAY BETTER!
CLOP

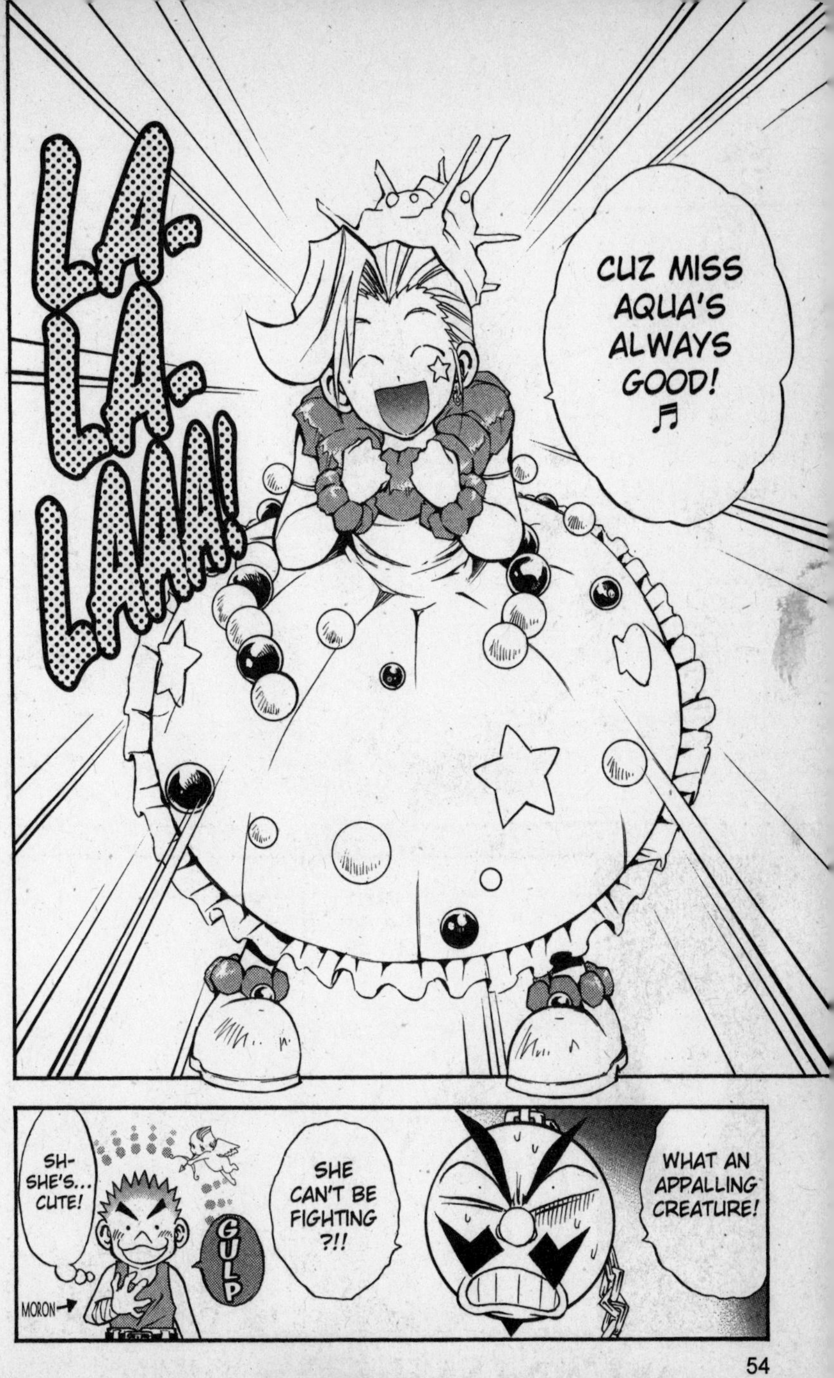
CUZ MISS AQUA'S ALWAYS GOOD! ♬
LA-LA-LAAA!
WHAT AN APPALLING CREATURE!
SHE CAN'T BE FIGHTING ?!!
GULP
SH- SHE'S... CUTE!
MORON

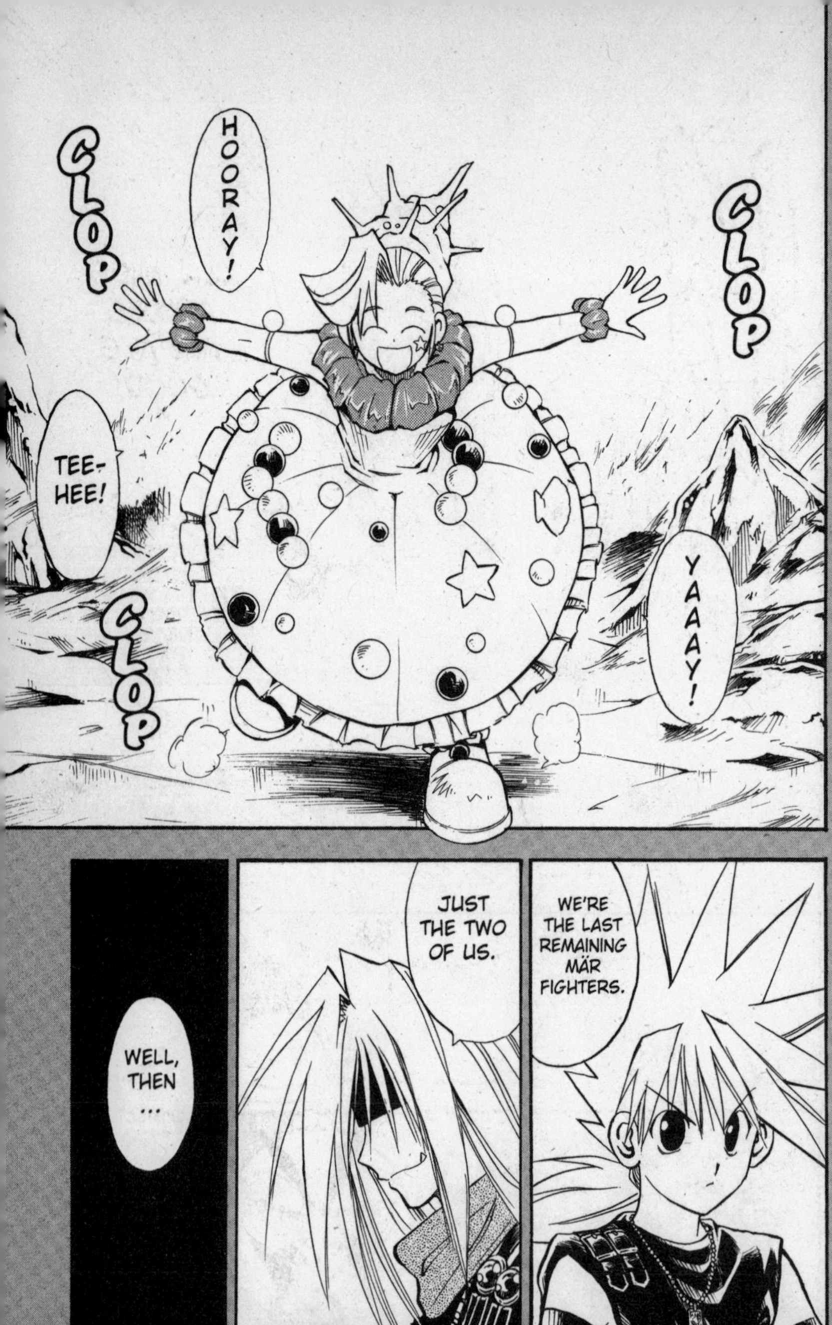
CLOP
HOORAY!
YAAAAY!
CLOP
TEE-HEE!
CLOP
CLOP
WE'RE THE LAST REMAINING MÄR FIGHTERS.
JUST THE TWO OF US.
WELL, THEN ...

AKT.78/NANASHI VS. AQUA ①

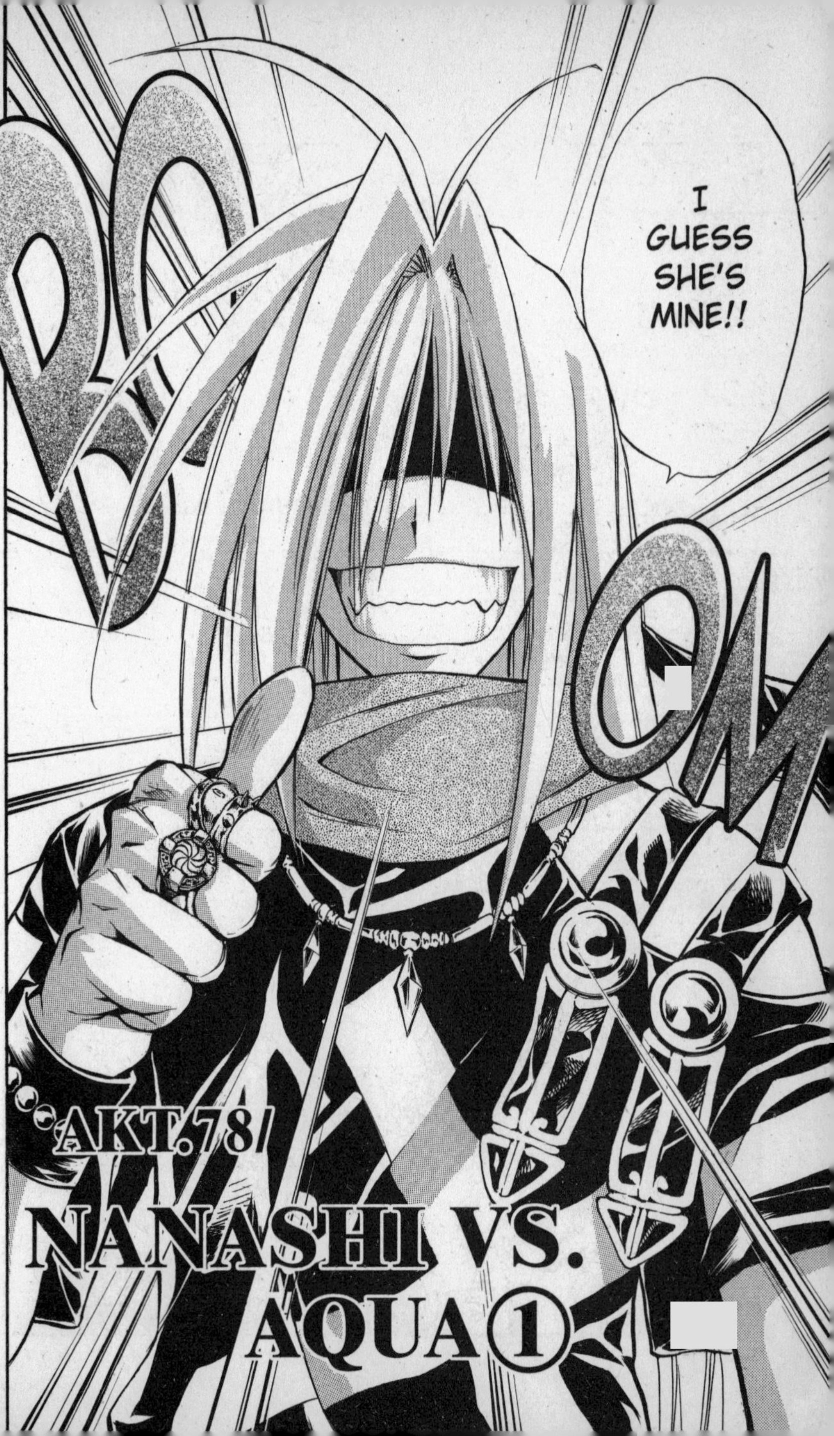

I GUESS SHE'S MINE!!
DOOOM
AKT.78/
NANASHI VS. AQUA ①

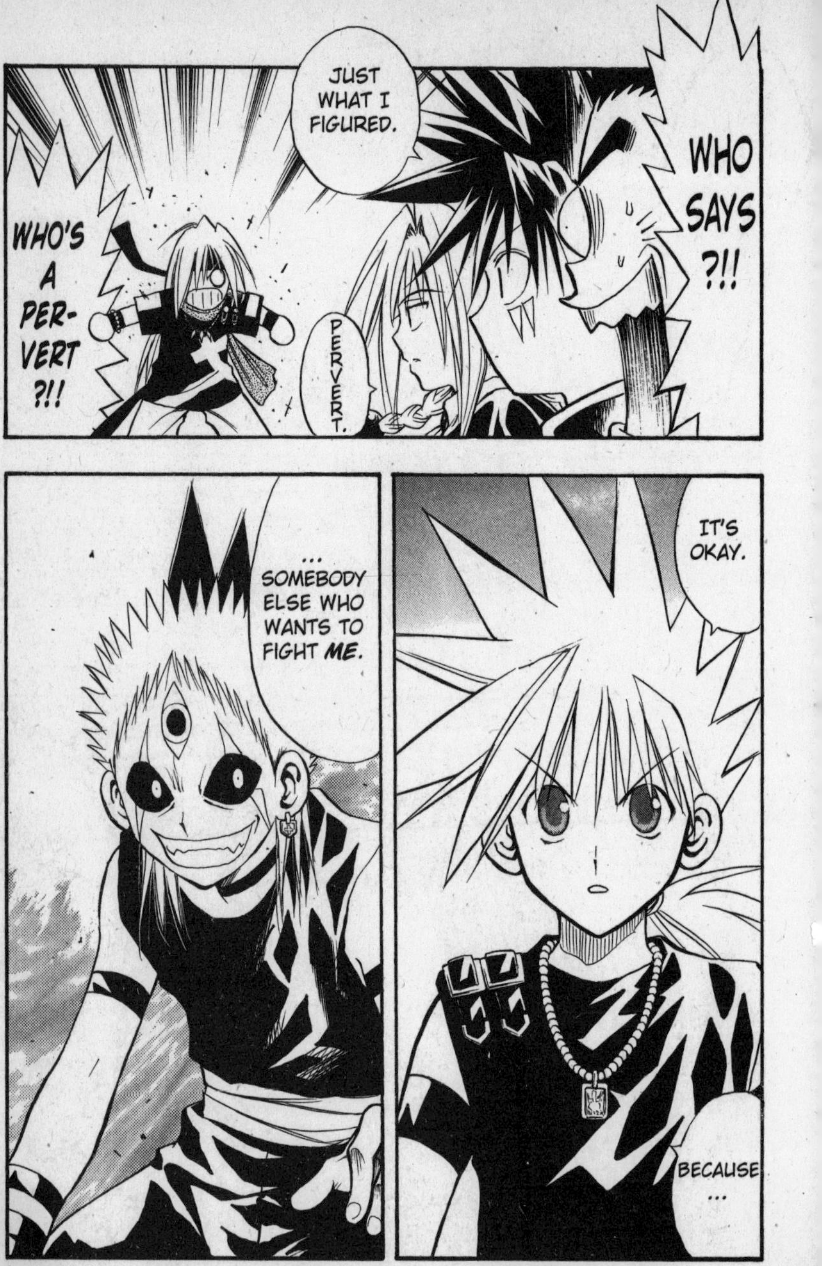
JUST WHAT I FIGURED.
PERVERT.
WHO'S A PER-VERT ?!!
WHO SAYS ?!!
IT'S OKAY.
BECAUSE ...
... SOMEBODY ELSE WHO WANTS TO FIGHT *ME*.

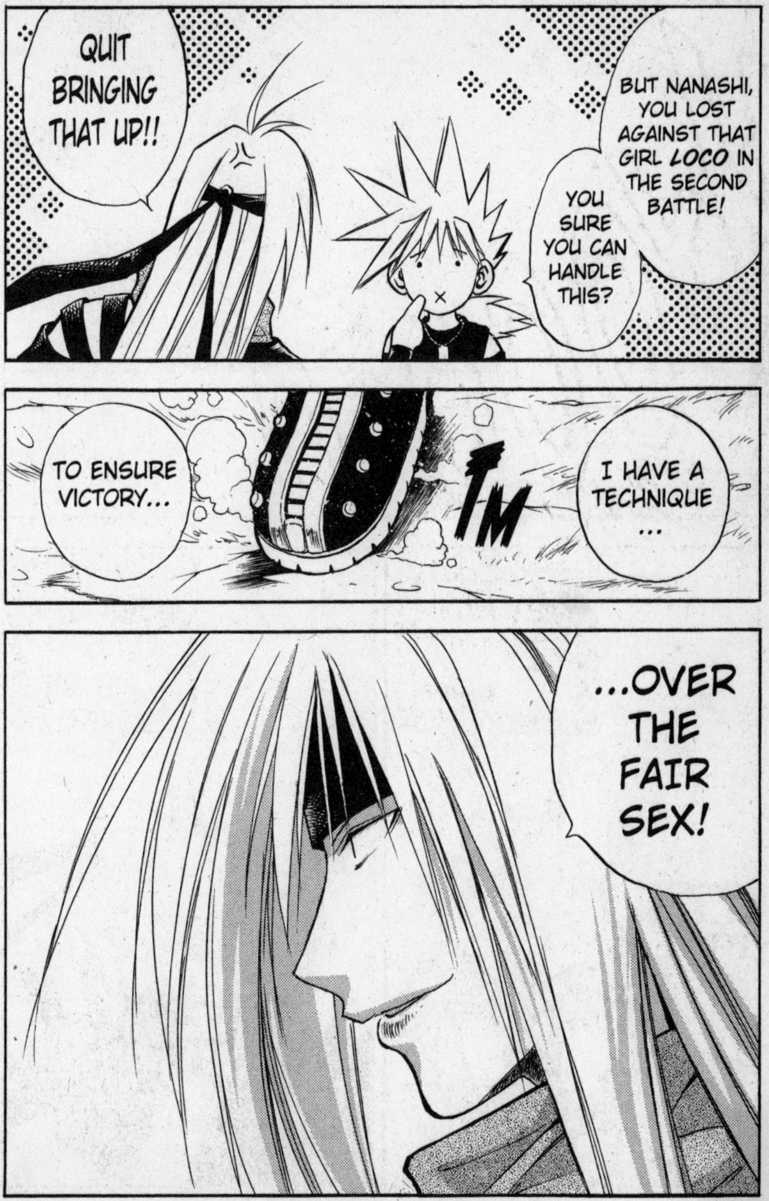
BUT NANASHI, YOU LOST AGAINST THAT GIRL LOCO IN THE SECOND BATTLE!
YOU SURE YOU CAN HANDLE THIS?
QUIT BRINGING THAT UP!!
I HAVE A TECHNIQUE ...
TM
TO ENSURE VICTORY...
...OVER THE FAIR SEX!

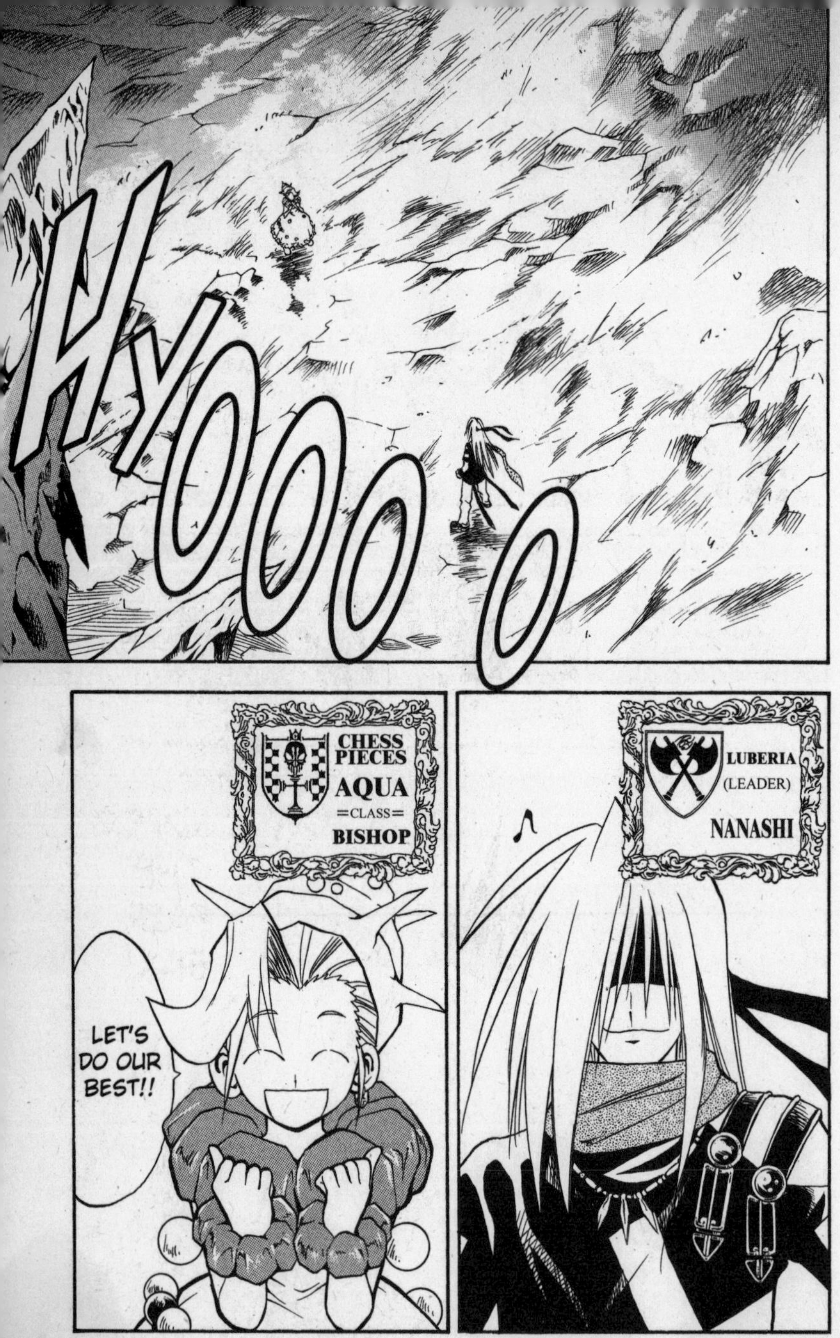
HYOOOO O
LUBERIA (LEADER) NANASHI
CHESS PIECES AQUA =CLASS= BISHOP
LET'S DO OUR BEST!!

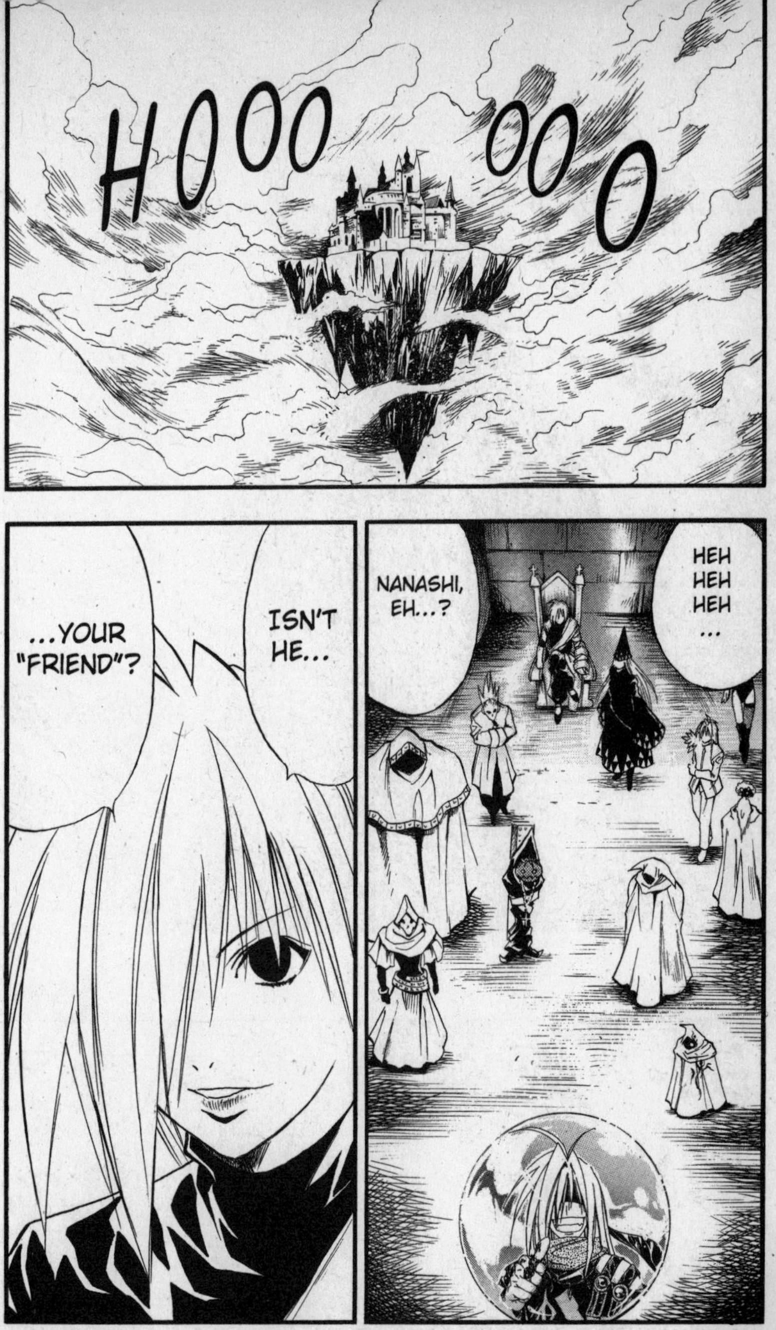
HOOO OOOO
HEH HEH HEH ...
NANASHI, EH...?
ISN'T HE...
...YOUR "FRIEND"?

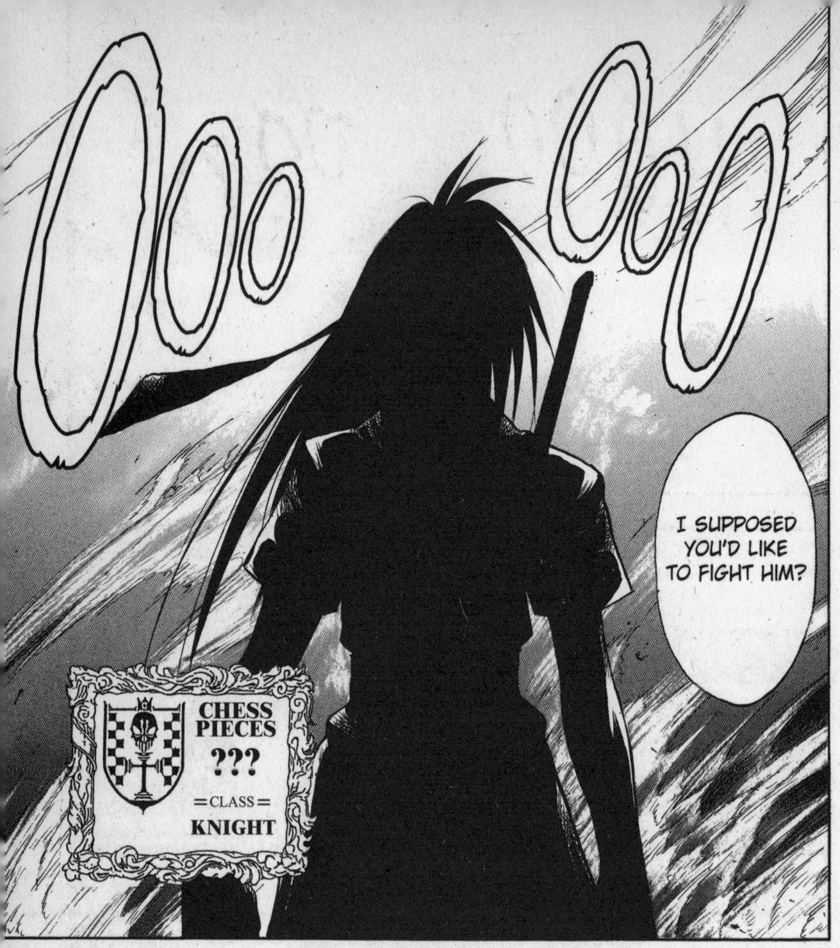
OOOOOOO
I SUPPOSED YOU'D LIKE TO FIGHT HIM?
CHESS PIECES
???
=CLASS=
KNIGHT

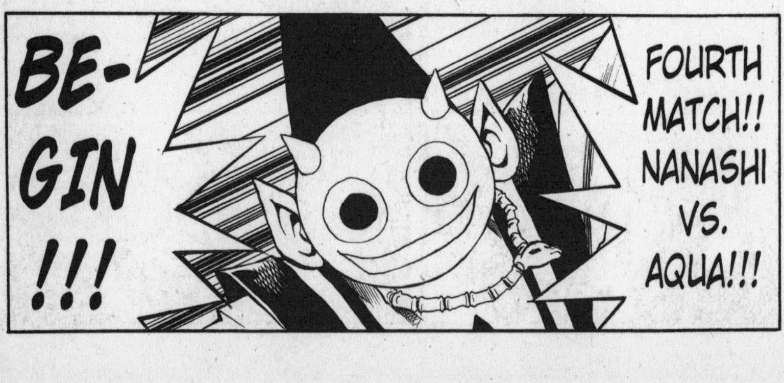
FOURTH MATCH!! NANASHI VS. AQUA!!!
BE-GIN!!!

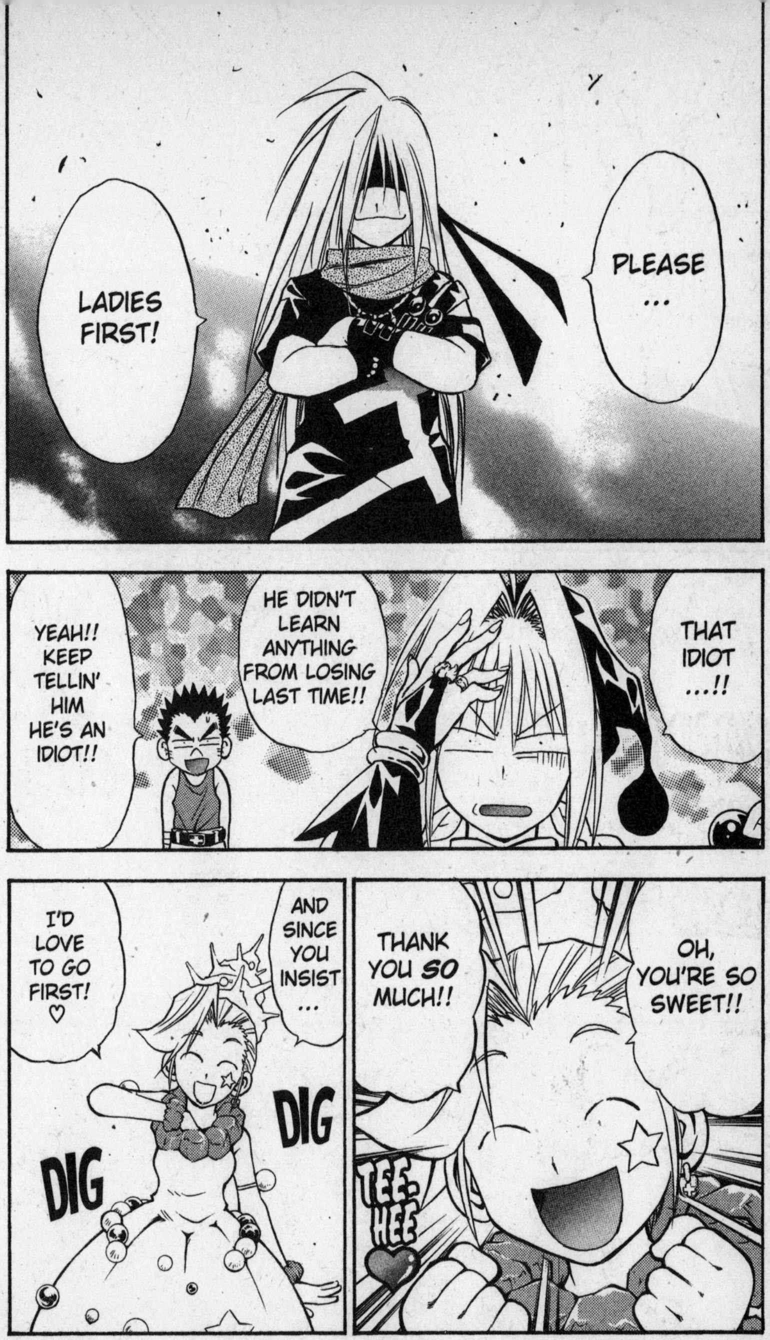
PLEASE...
LADIES FIRST!
THAT IDIOT...!!
HE DIDN'T LEARN ANYTHING FROM LOSING LAST TIME!!
YEAH!! KEEP TELLIN' HIM HE'S AN IDIOT!!
OH, YOU'RE SO SWEET!!
THANK YOU SO MUCH!!
TEE-HEE
AND SINCE YOU INSIST...
I'D LOVE TO GO FIRST! ♡
DIG
DIG

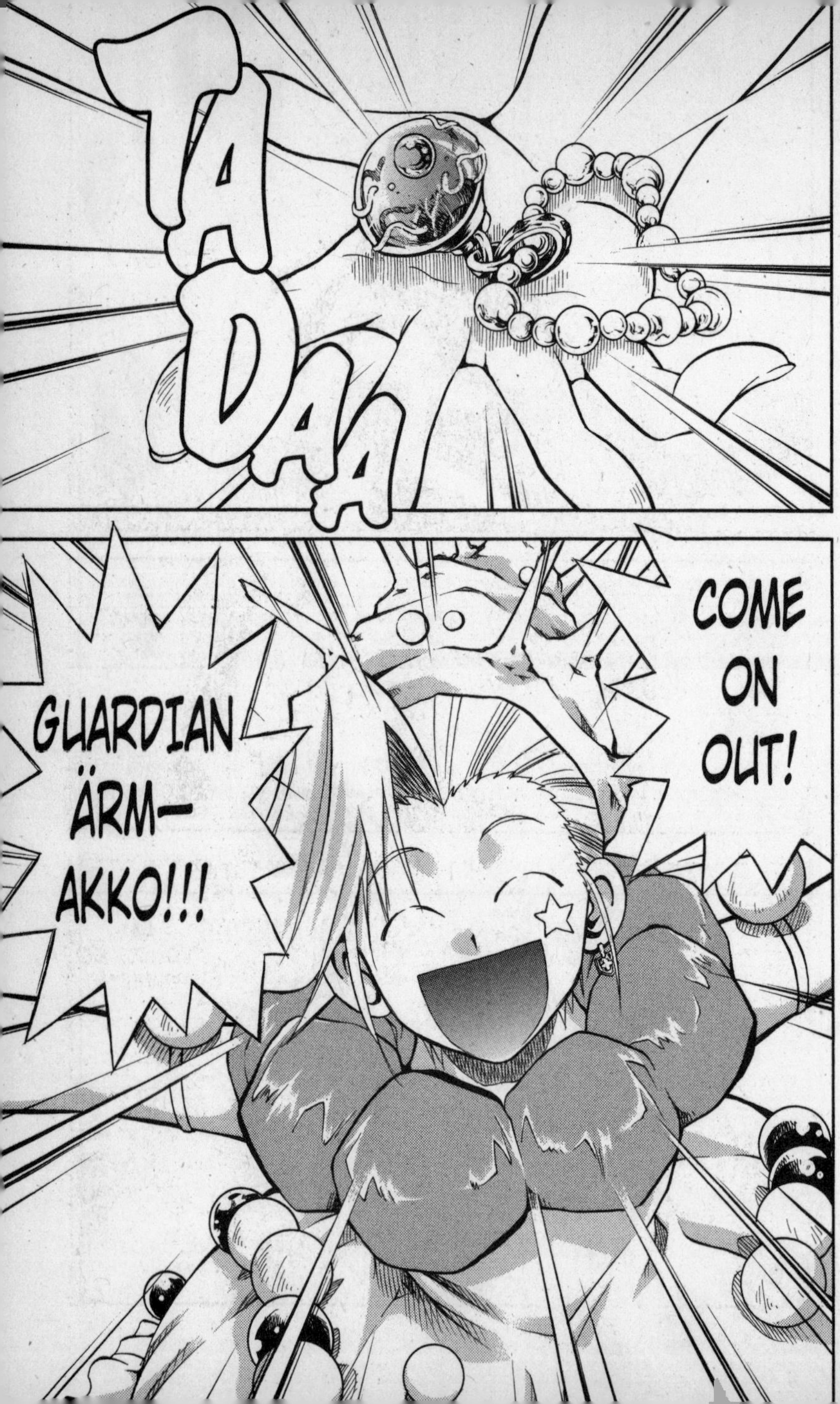
TA DAA
COME ON OUT!
GUARDIAN ÄRM— AKKO!!!

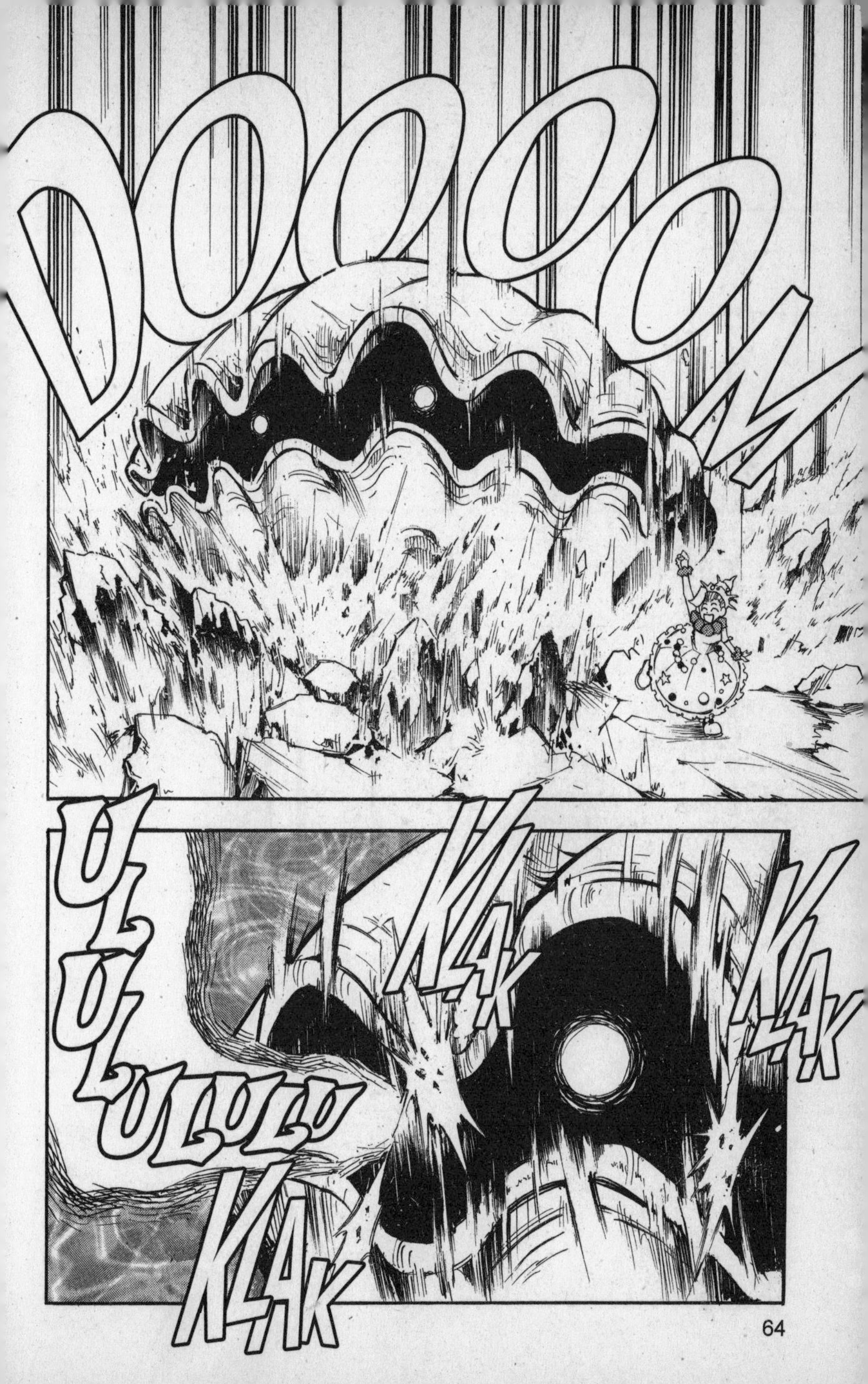
DOOOOM
KLAK
KLAK
ULULULOLO
KLAK

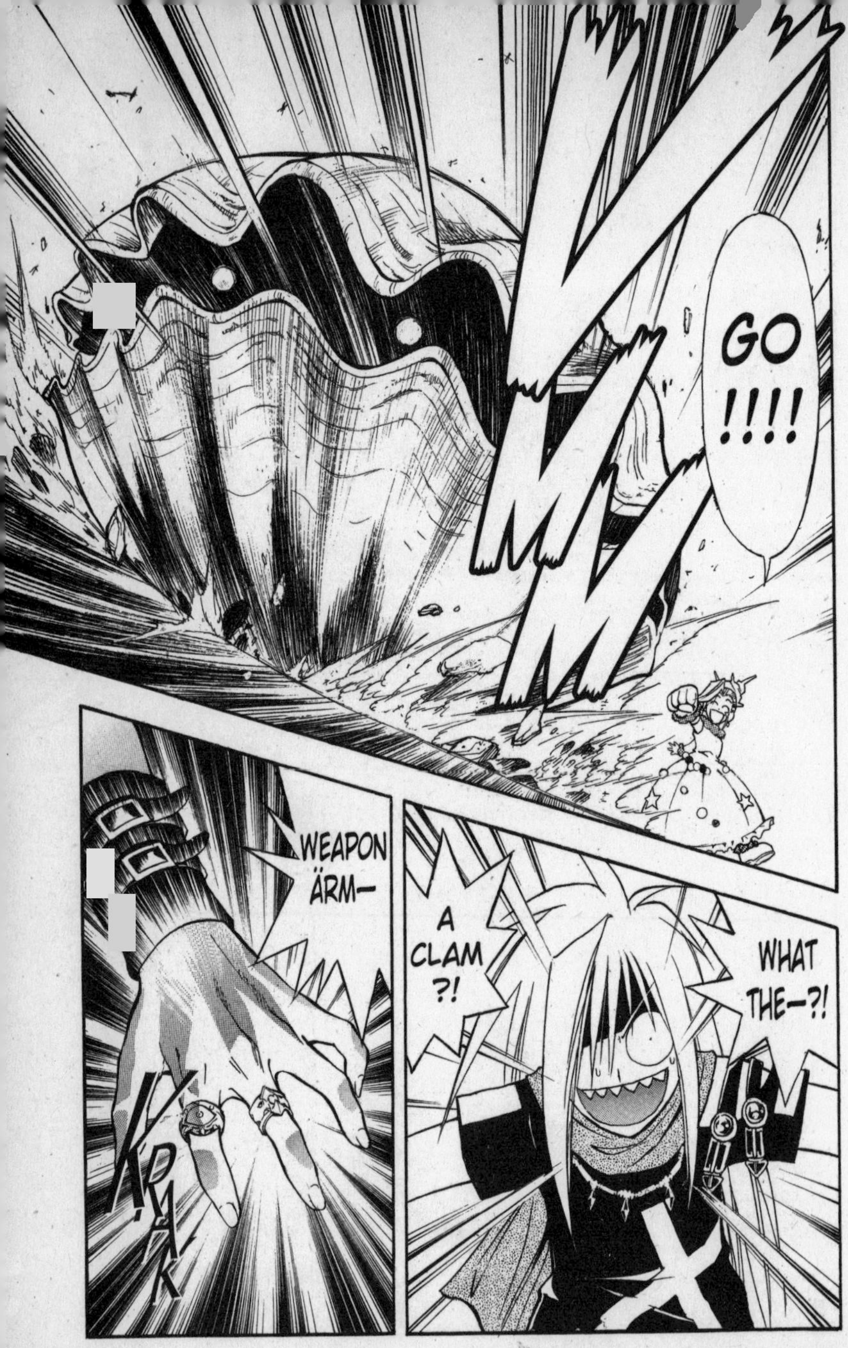
GO !!!!
WHAT THE–?!
A CLAM ?!
WEAPON ÄRM–

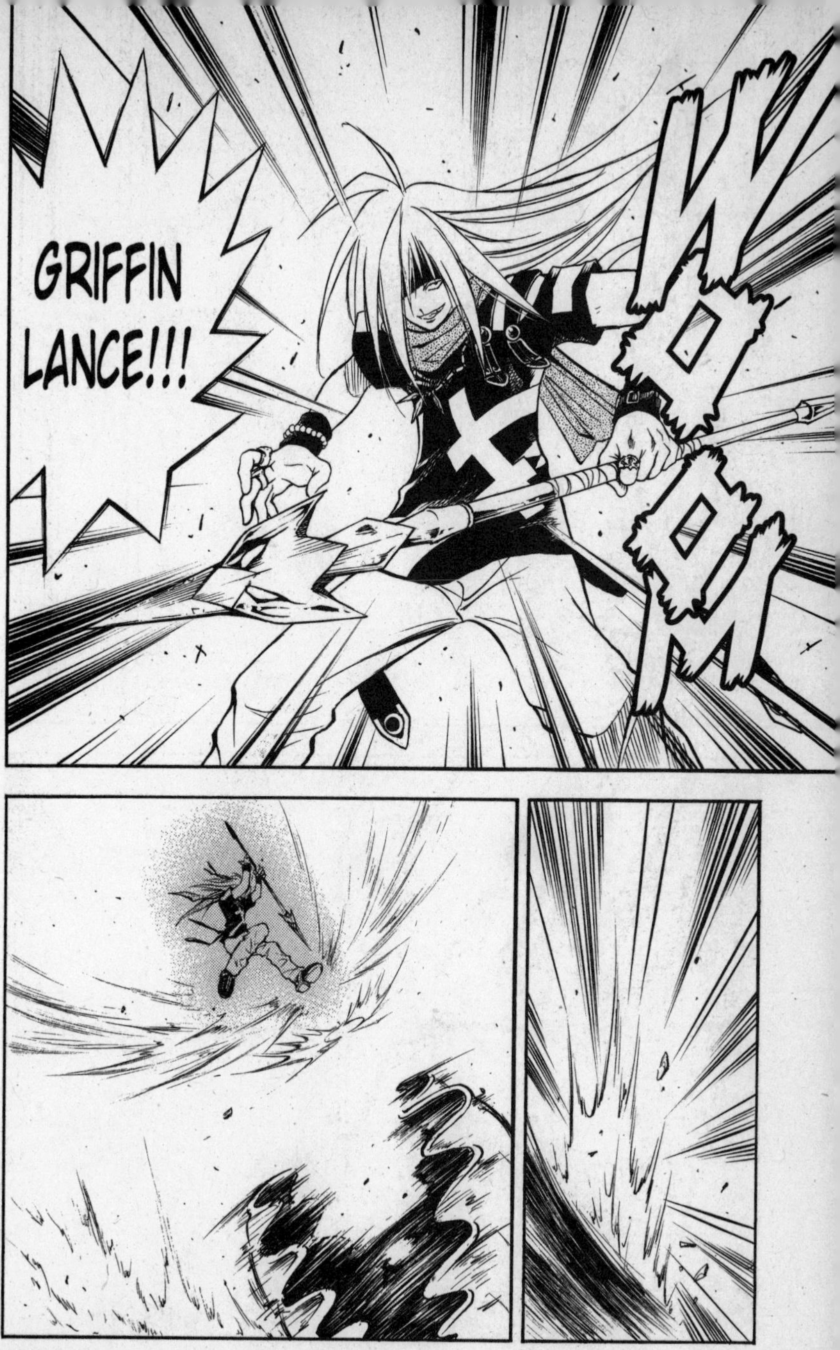
GRIFFIN LANCE!!!
WOOM

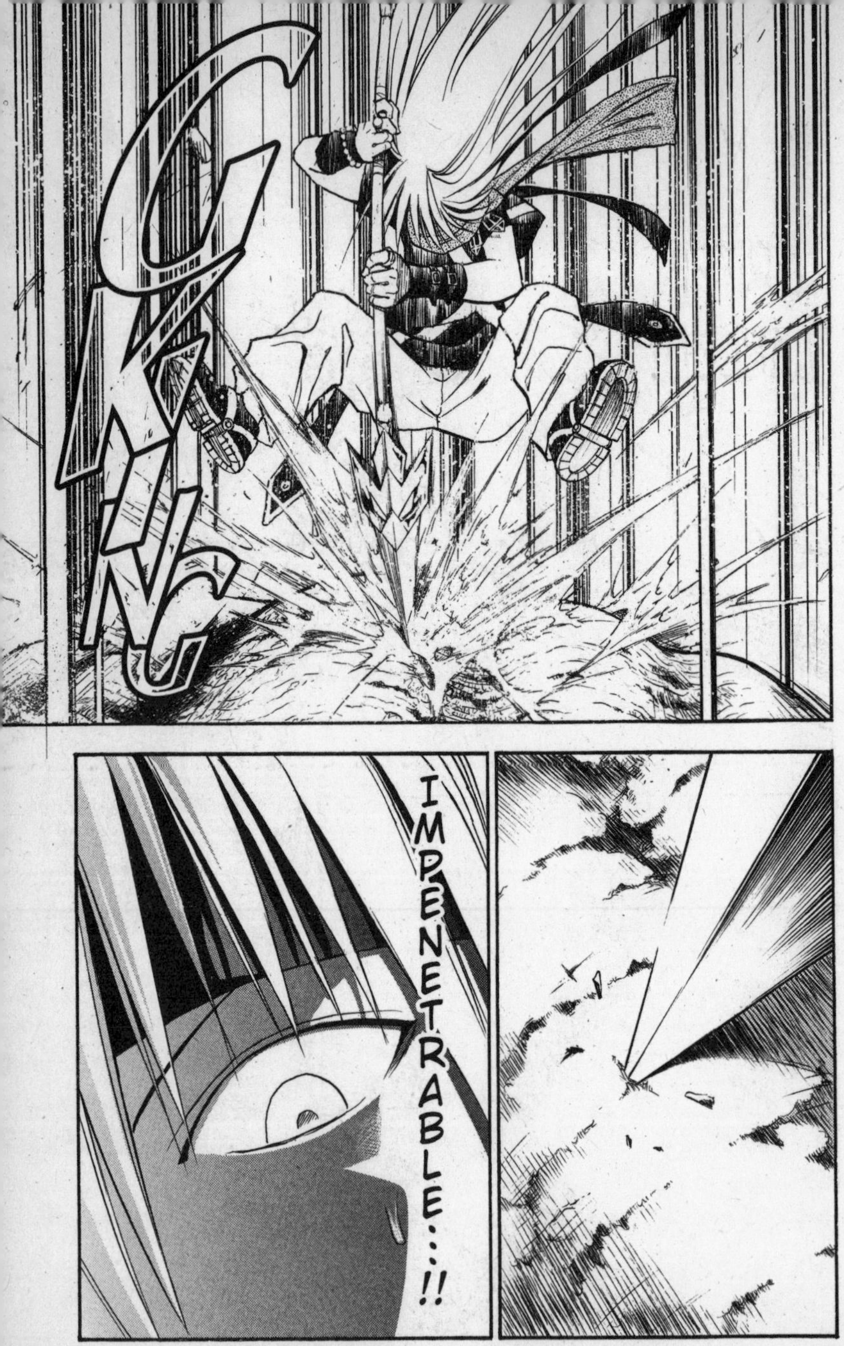
IMPENETRABLE...!!

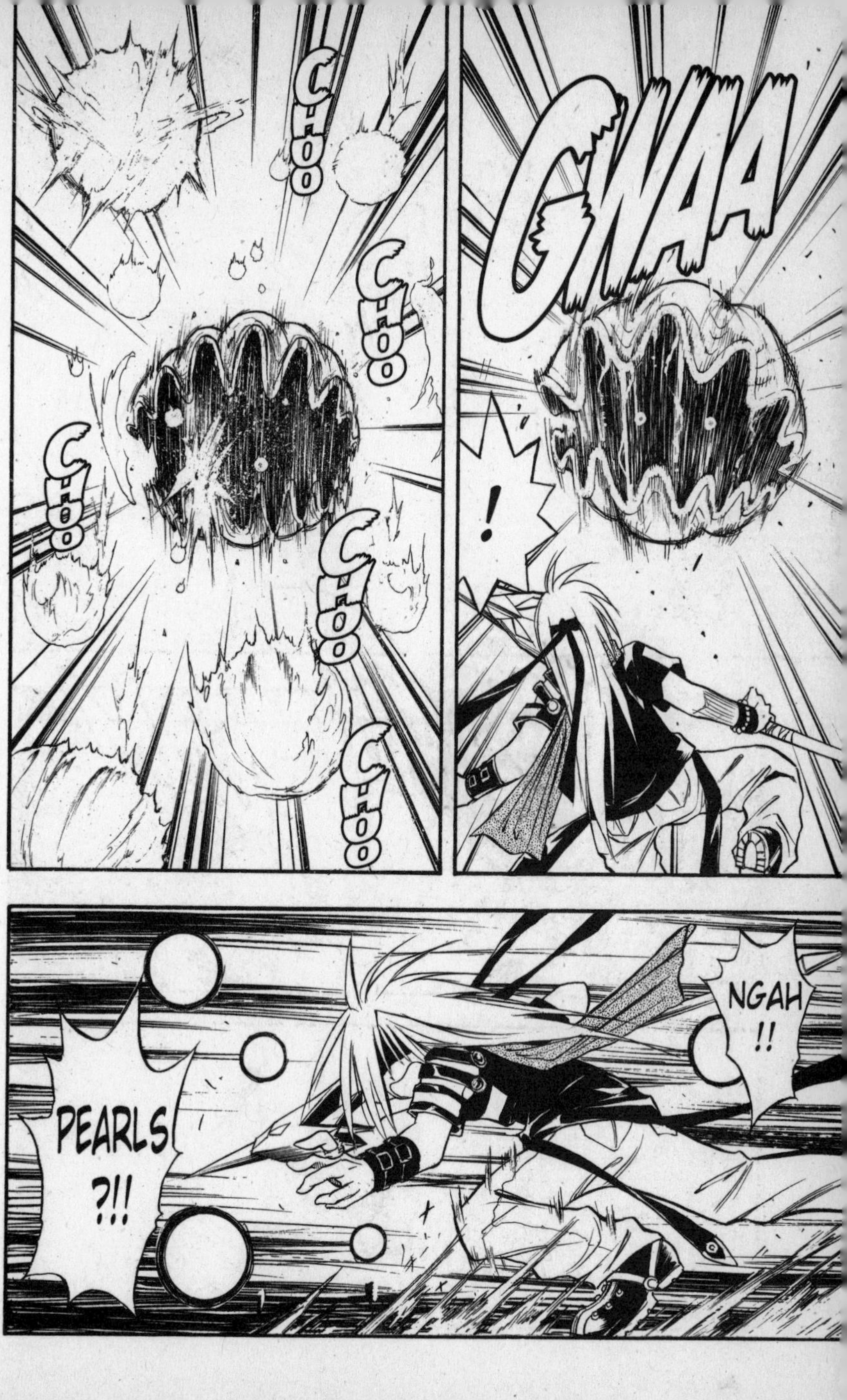
GNAA
!
CHOO
CHOO
CHOO
CHOO
CHOO
NGAH !!
PEARLS ?!!

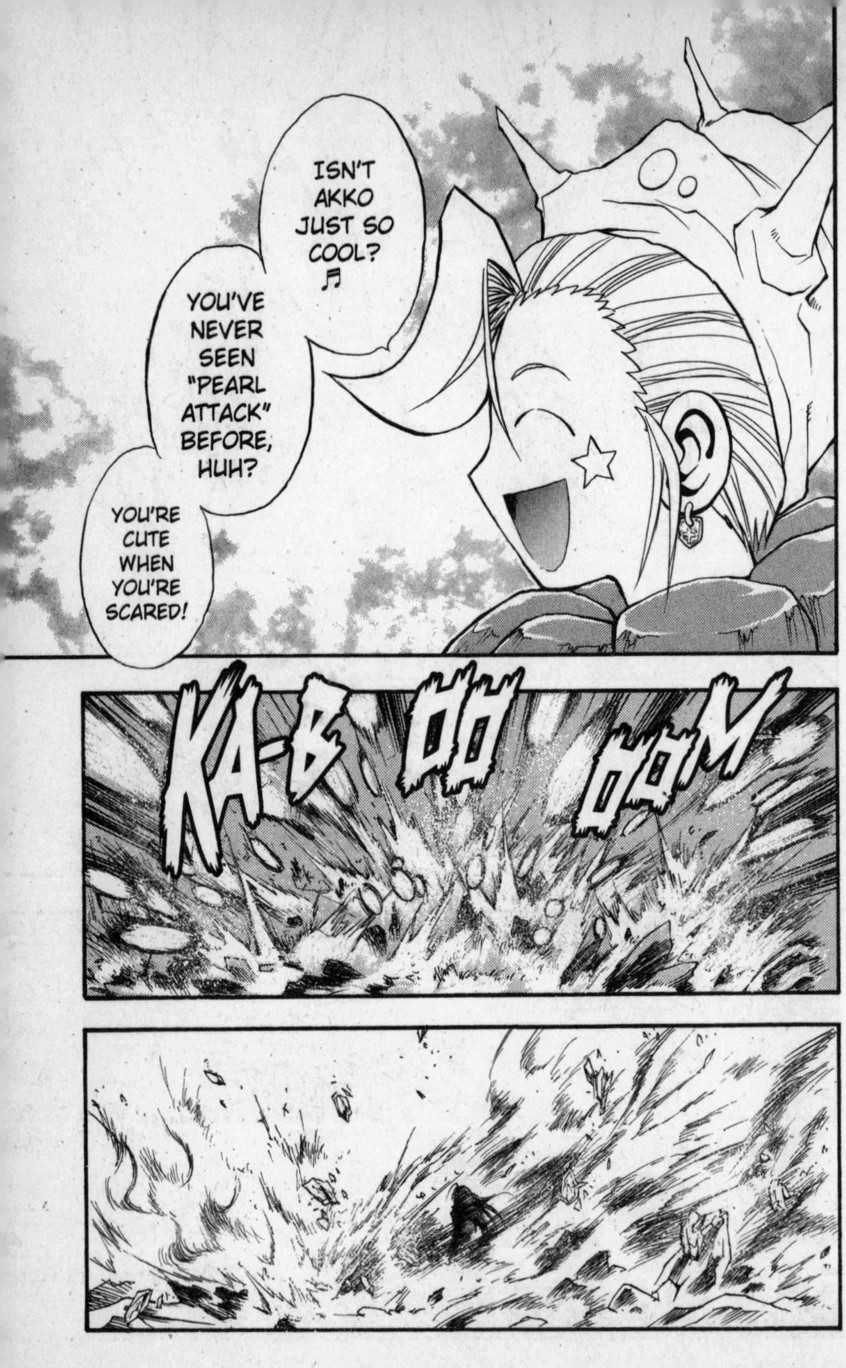
ISN'T AKKO JUST SO COOL? ♬
YOU'VE NEVER SEEN "PEARL ATTACK" BEFORE, HUH?
YOU'RE CUTE WHEN YOU'RE SCARED!
KA-BOOOOM

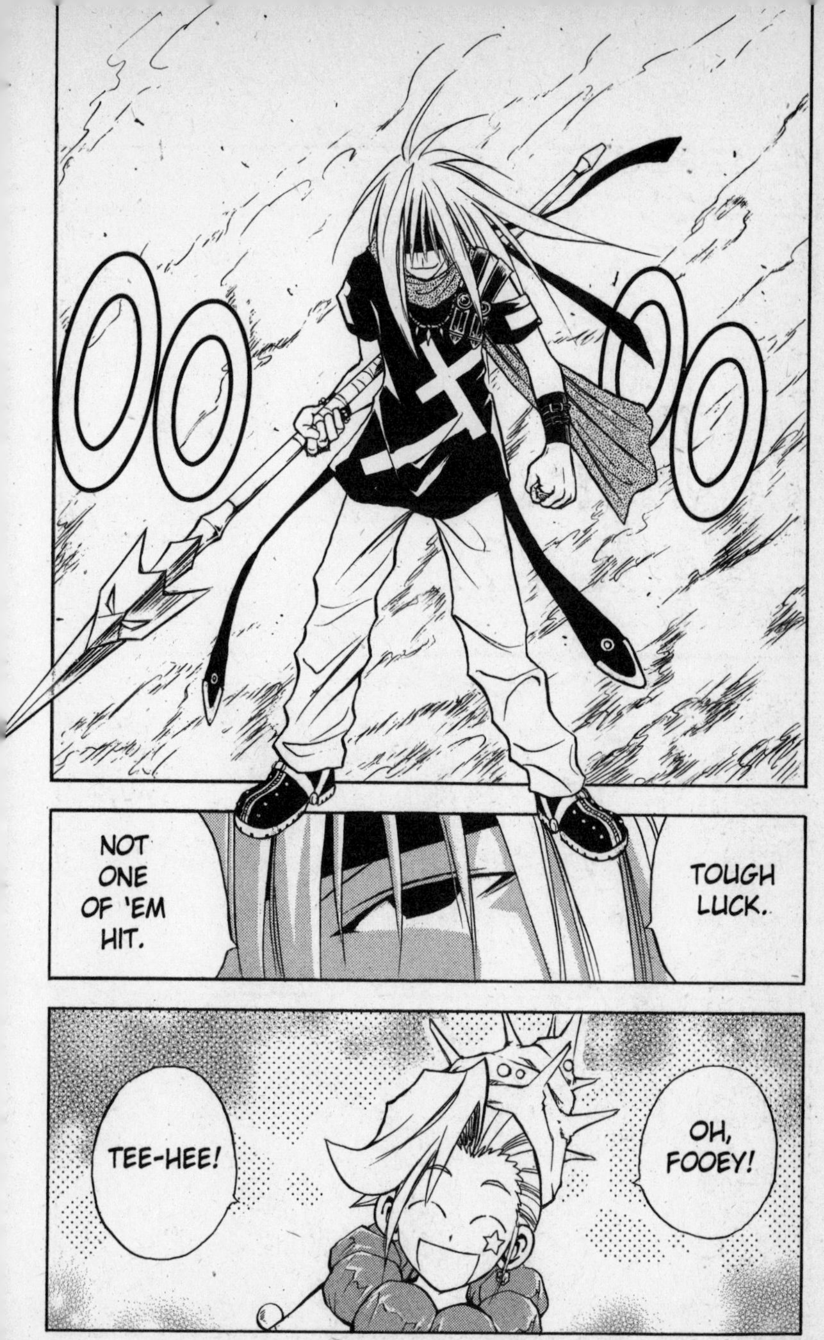
TOUGH LUCK.
NOT ONE OF 'EM HIT.
OH, FOOEY!
TEE-HEE!

AKT.79/ NANASHI VS. AQUA ②

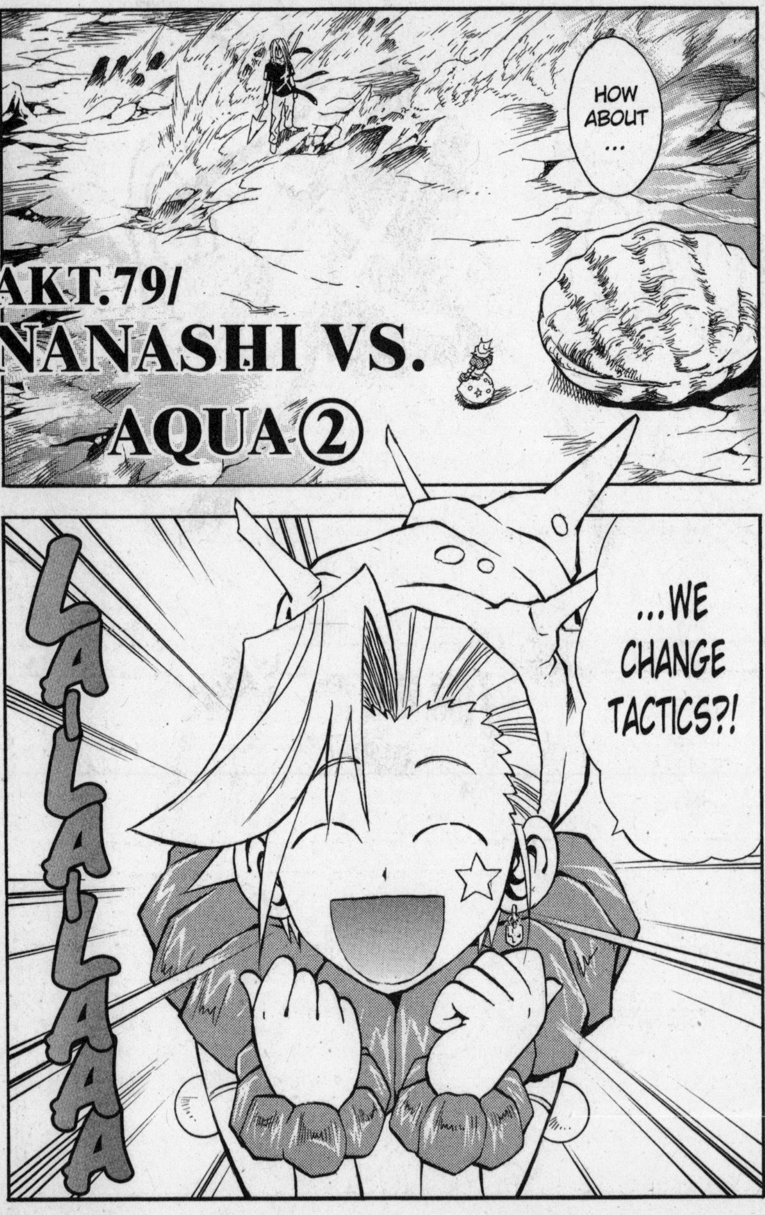
HOW ABOUT ...
...WE CHANGE TACTICS?!
LA-LA-LA-LAAAA

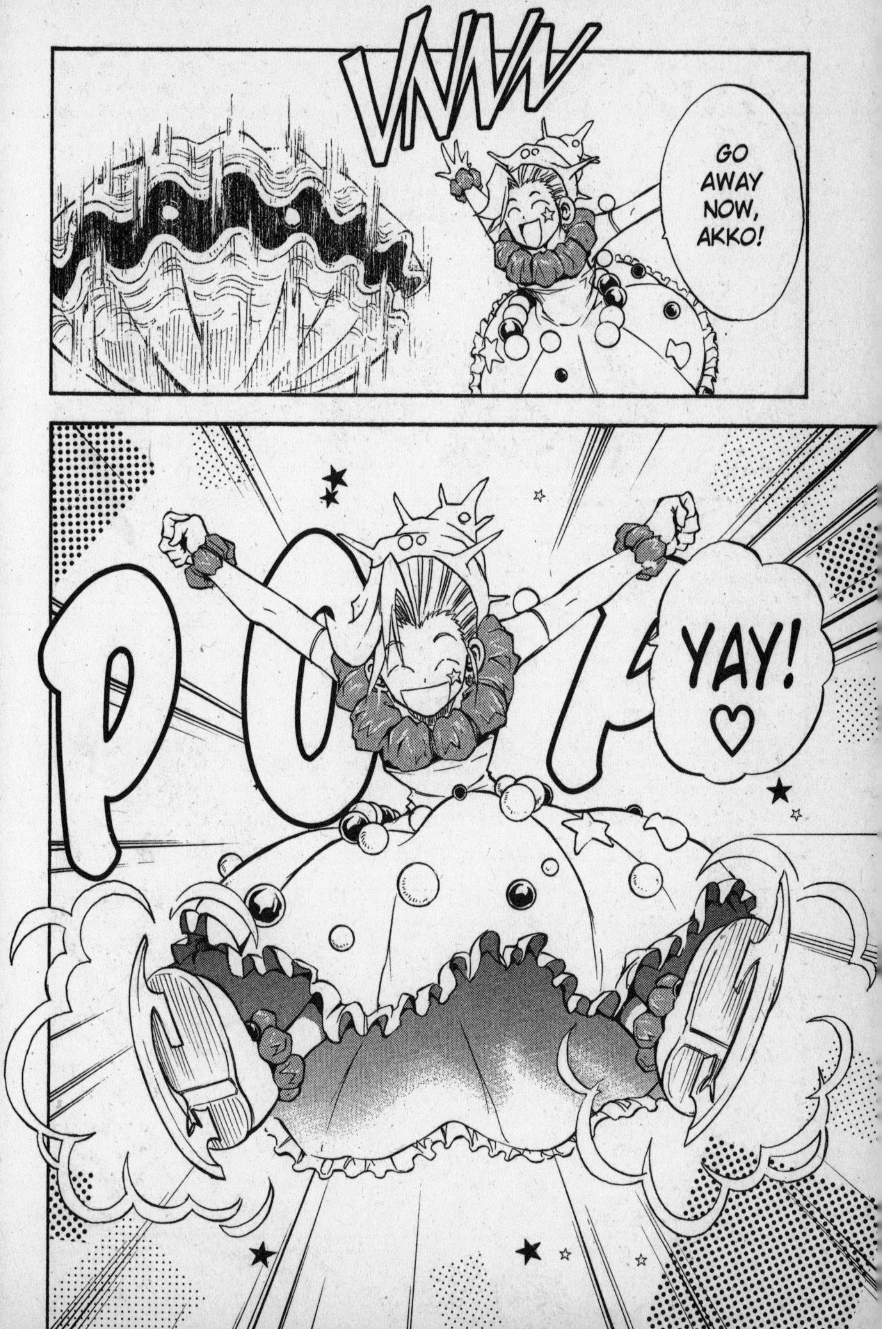
VWW
GO AWAY NOW, AKKO!
PO
YAY! ♥

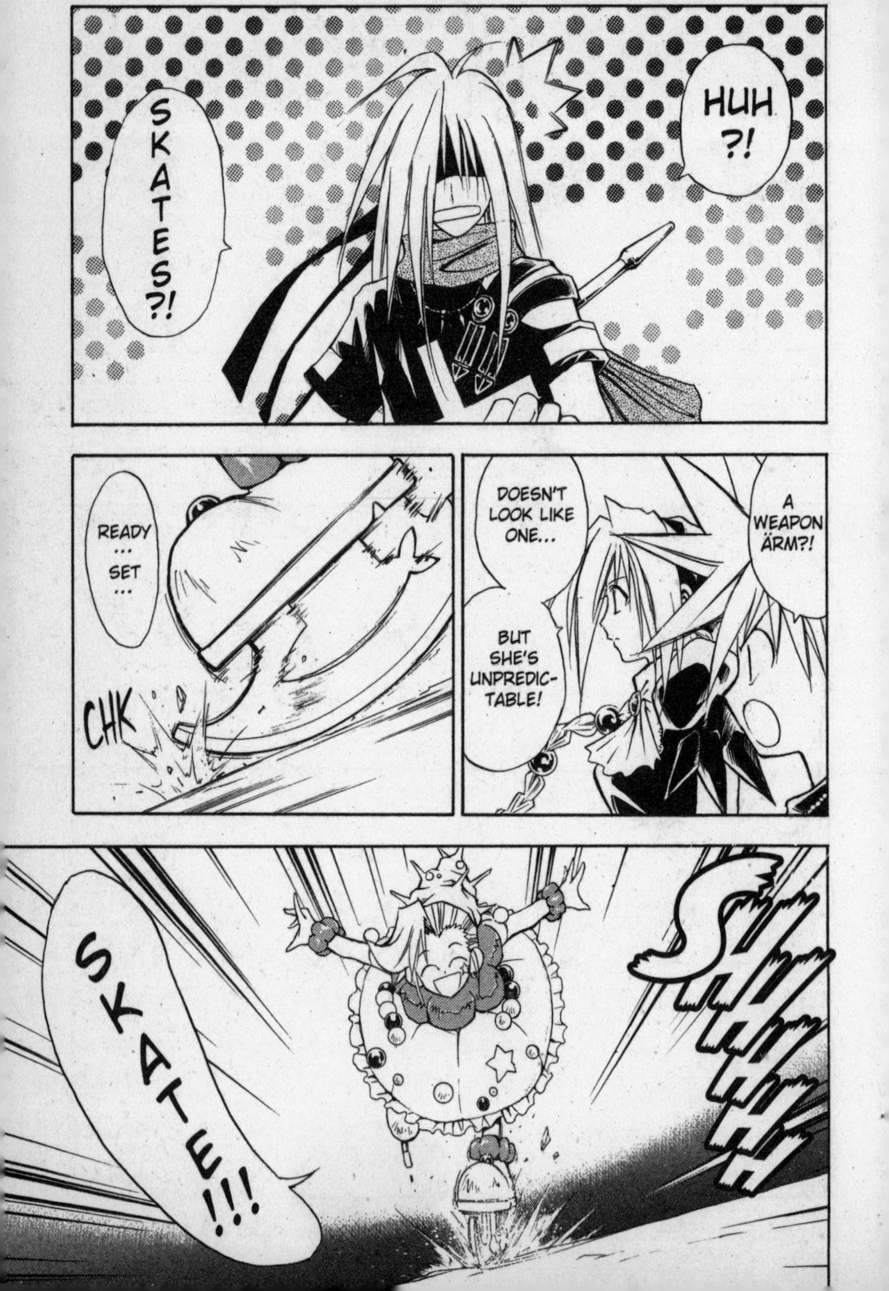
HUH?!
SKATES?!
A WEAPON ÄRM?!
DOESN'T LOOK LIKE ONE...
BUT SHE'S UNPREDIC-TABLE!
READY... SET...
CHK
SKATE!!!

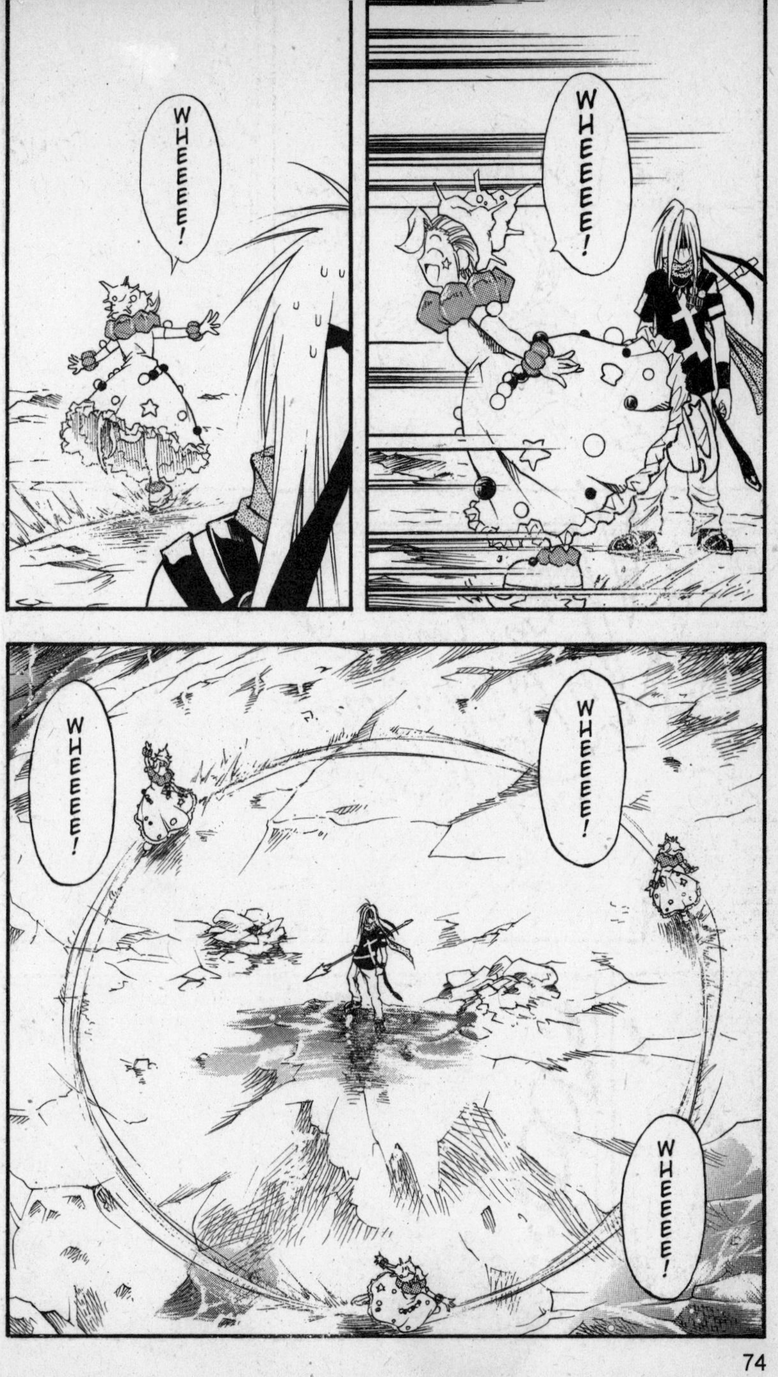
WHEEEEE!
WHEEEEE!
WHEEEEE!
WHEEEE!
WHEEEEE!

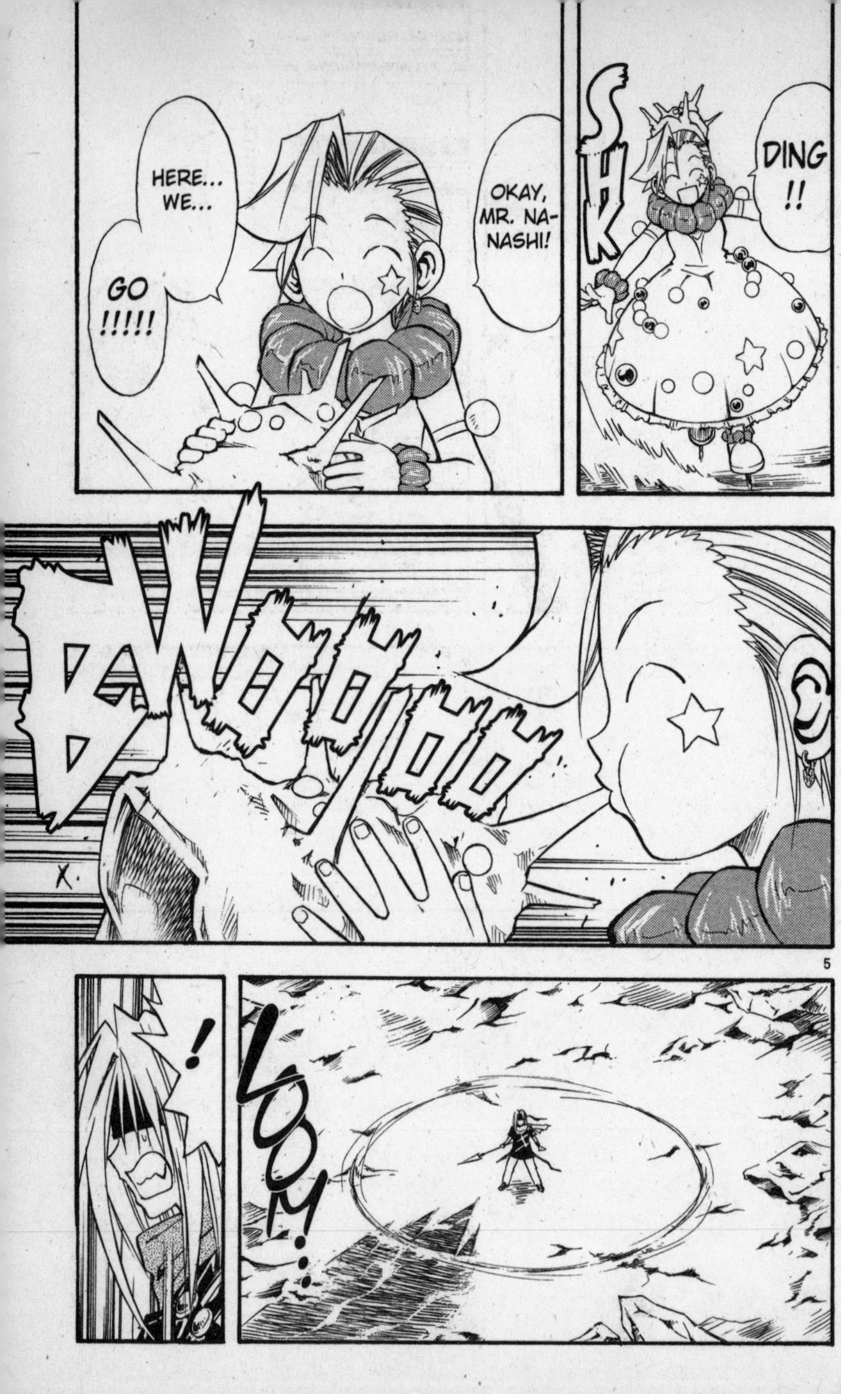
SHK
DING!!
OKAY, MR. NA-NASHI!
HERE... WE...
GO!!!!!
BWOOOO
VOOM!...
!

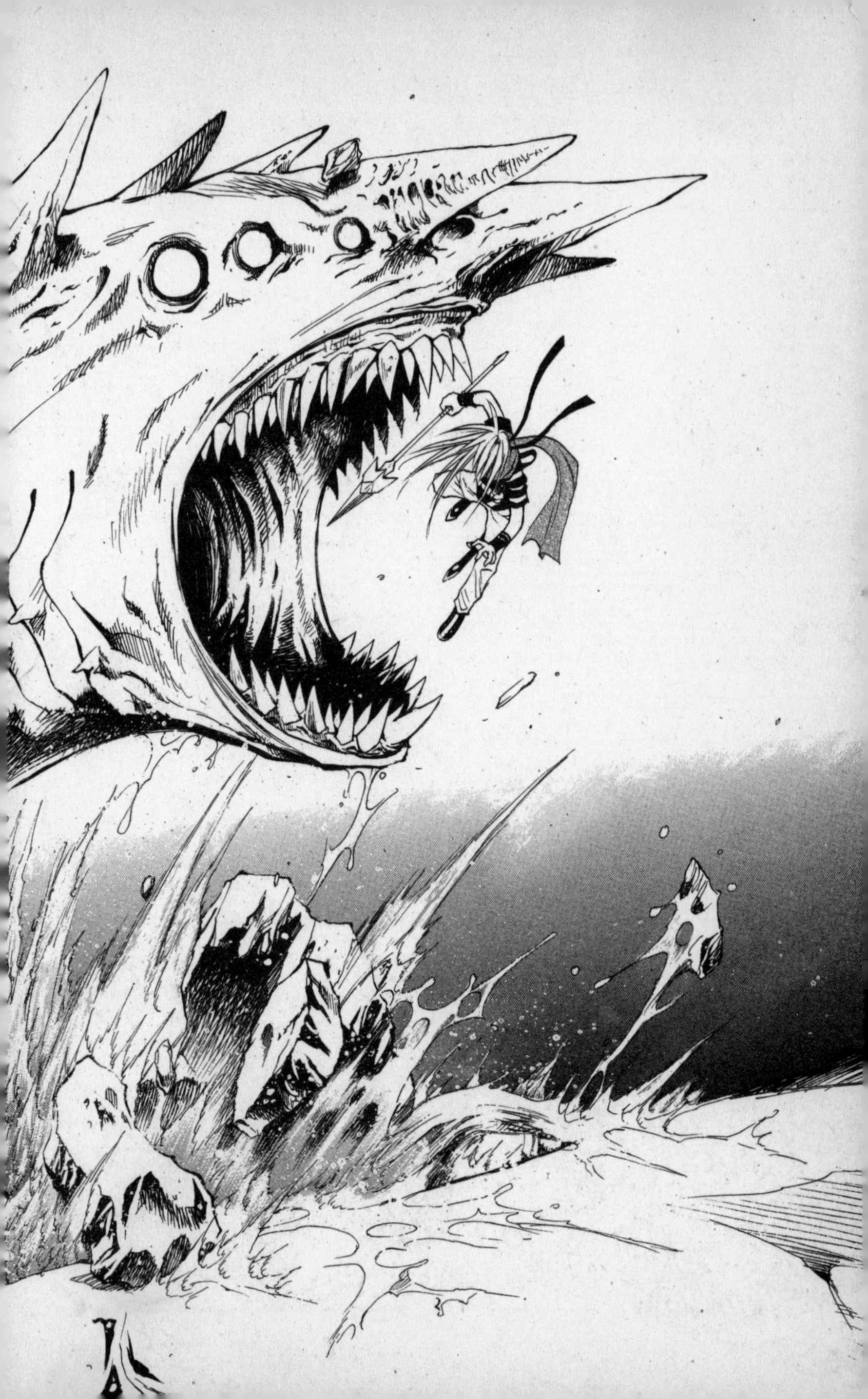

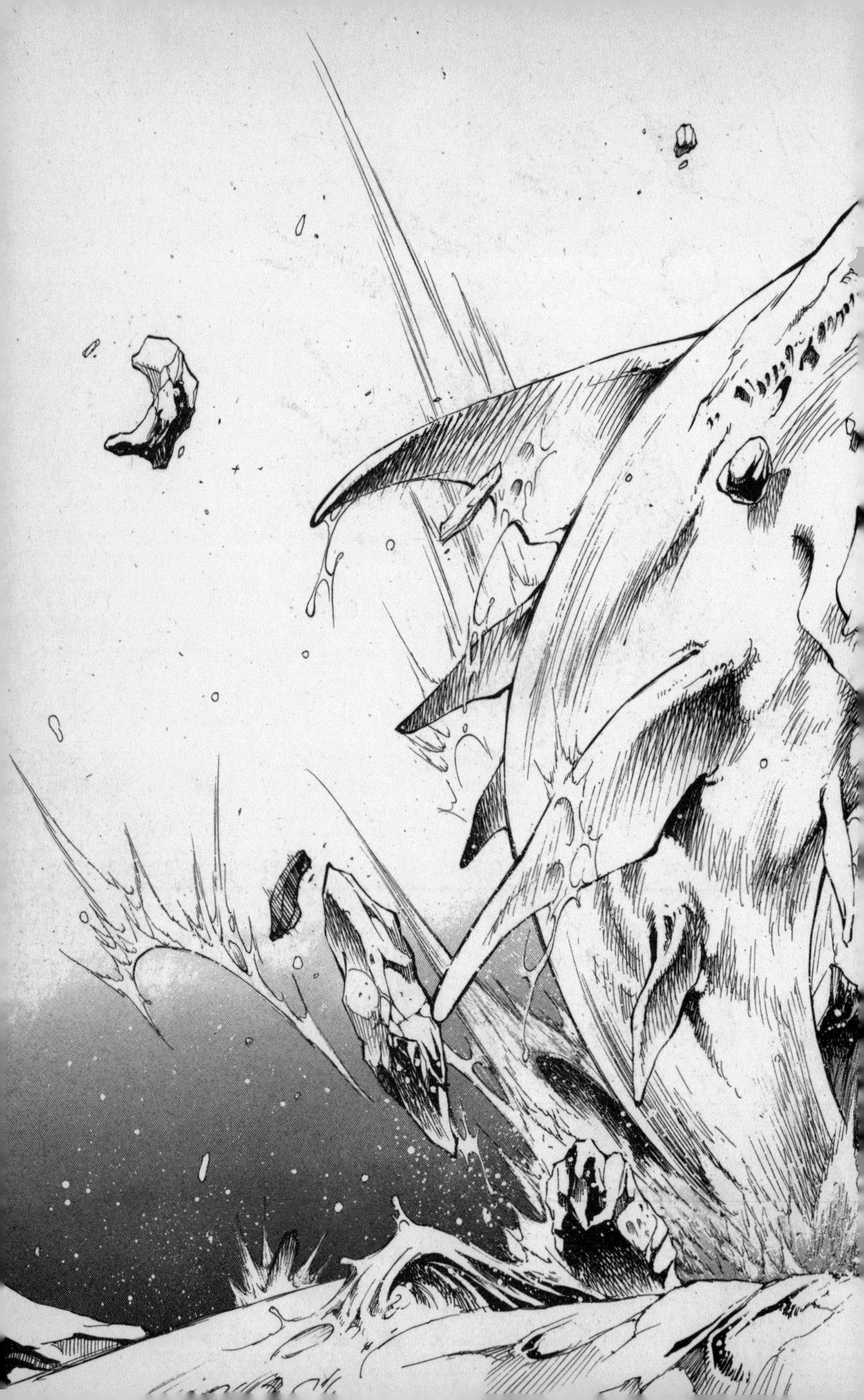

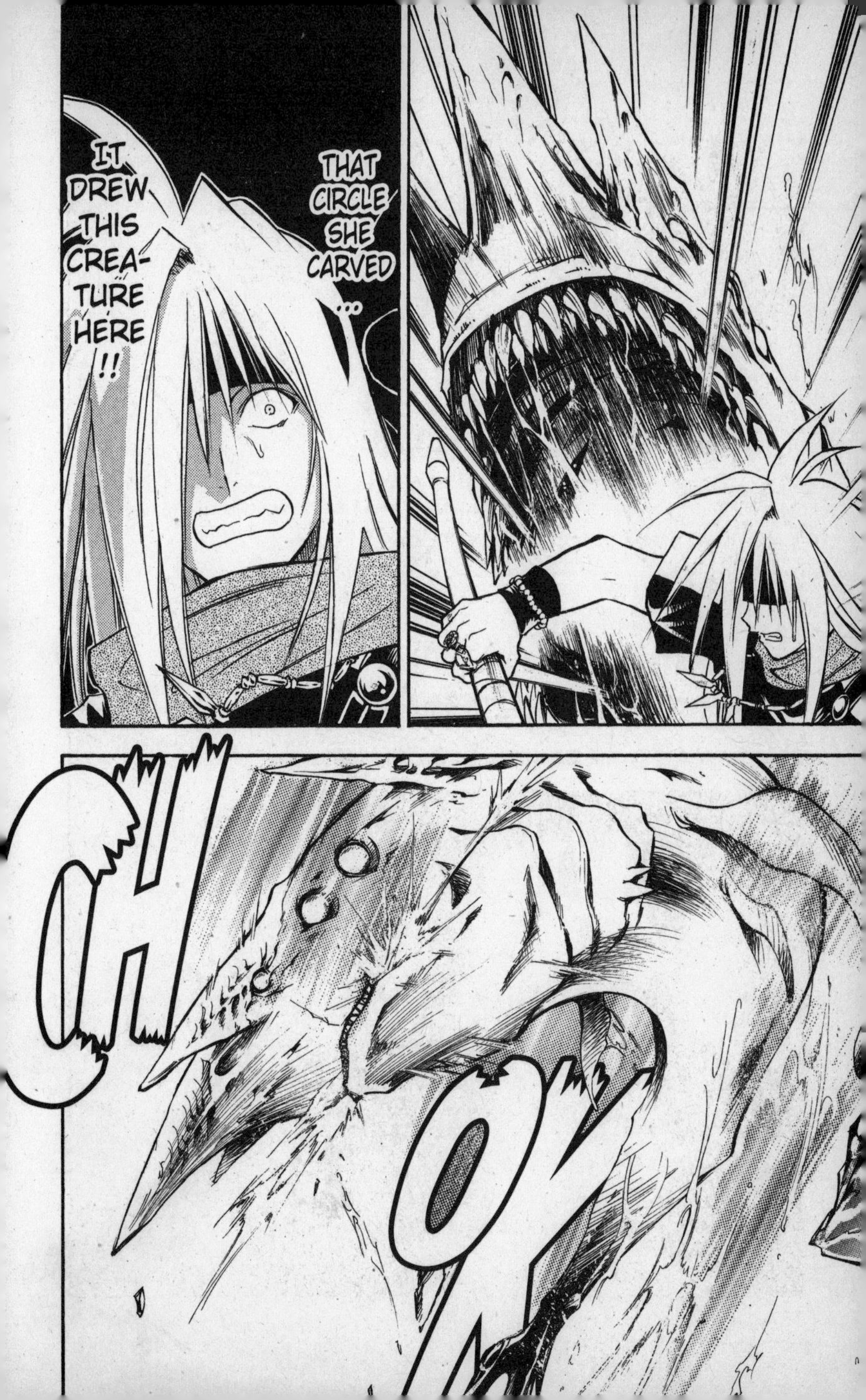
THAT CIRCLE SHE CARVED...
IT DREW THIS CREA-TURE HERE!!
CHO

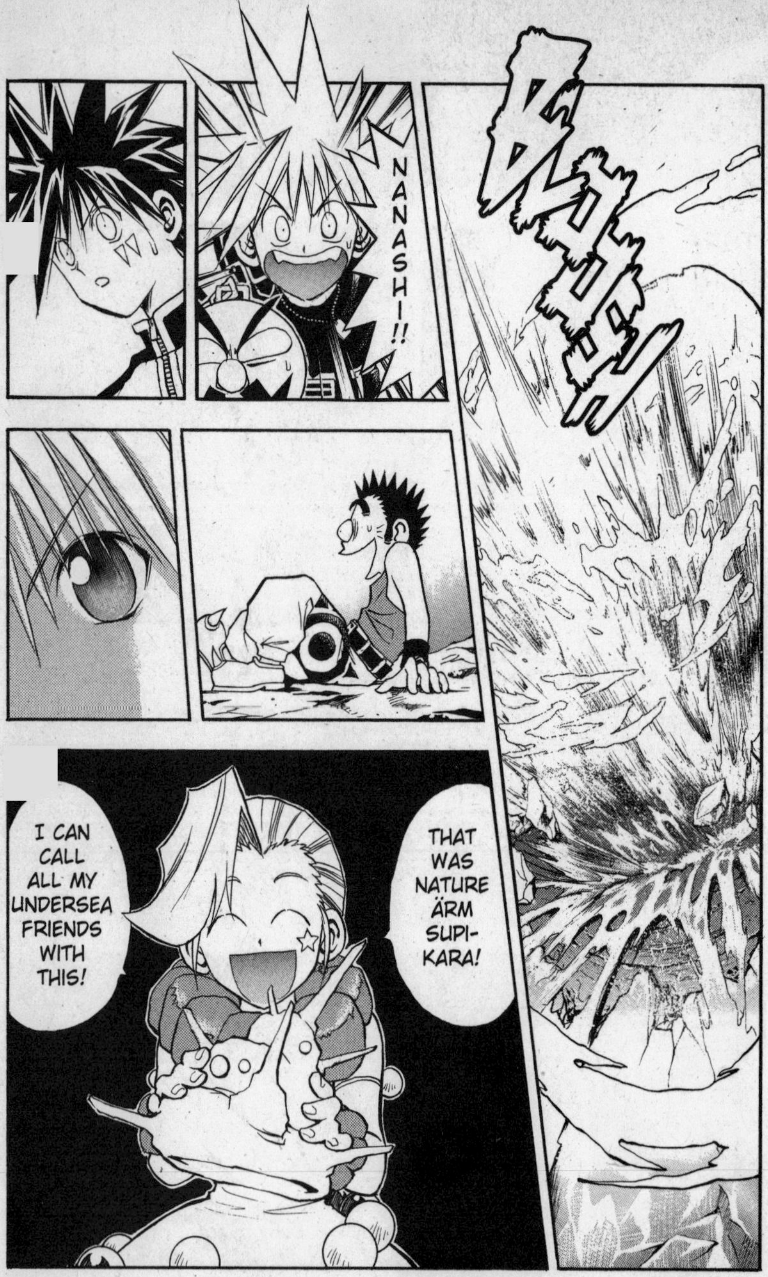
NANASHI!!
THAT WAS NATURE ÄRM SUPI-KARA!
I CAN CALL ALL MY UNDERSEA FRIENDS WITH THIS!

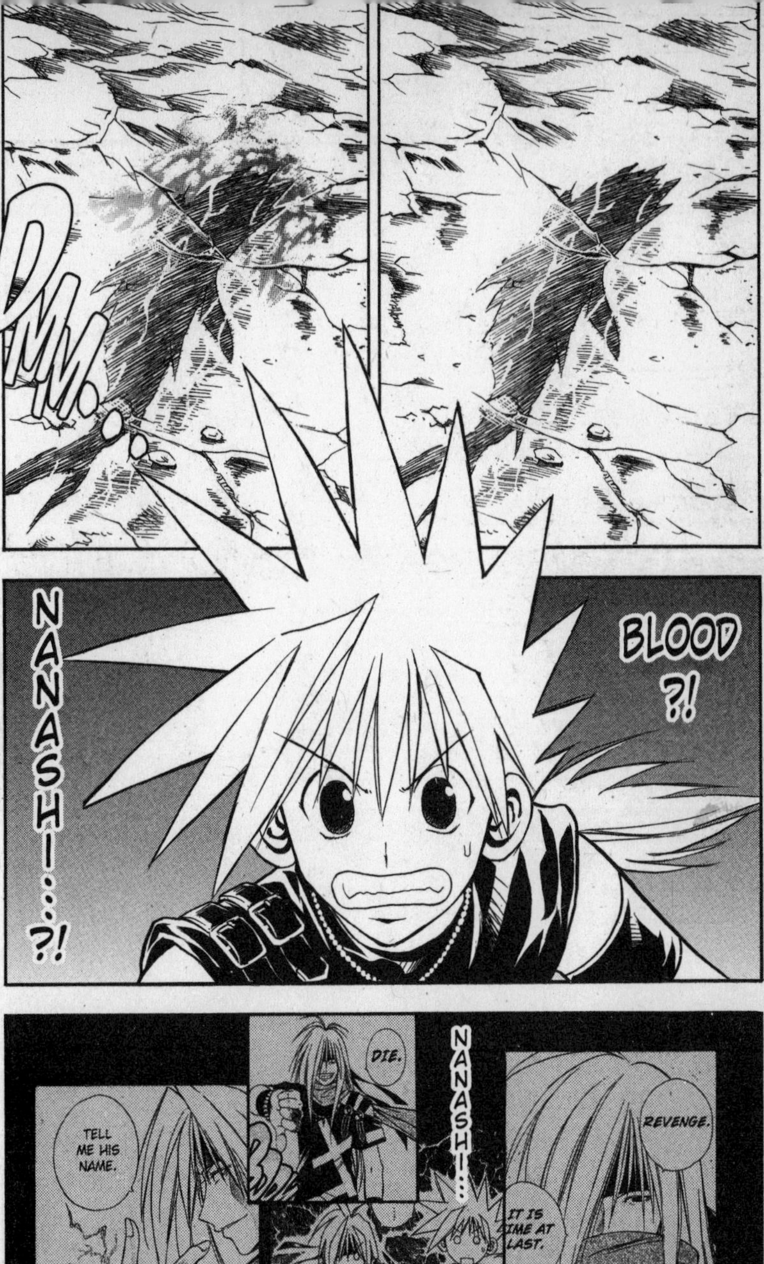
DMMM...
BLOOD ?!
NANASHI...?!
REVENGE.
IT IS TIME AT LAST.
NANASHI...!
DIE.
TELL ME HIS NAME.

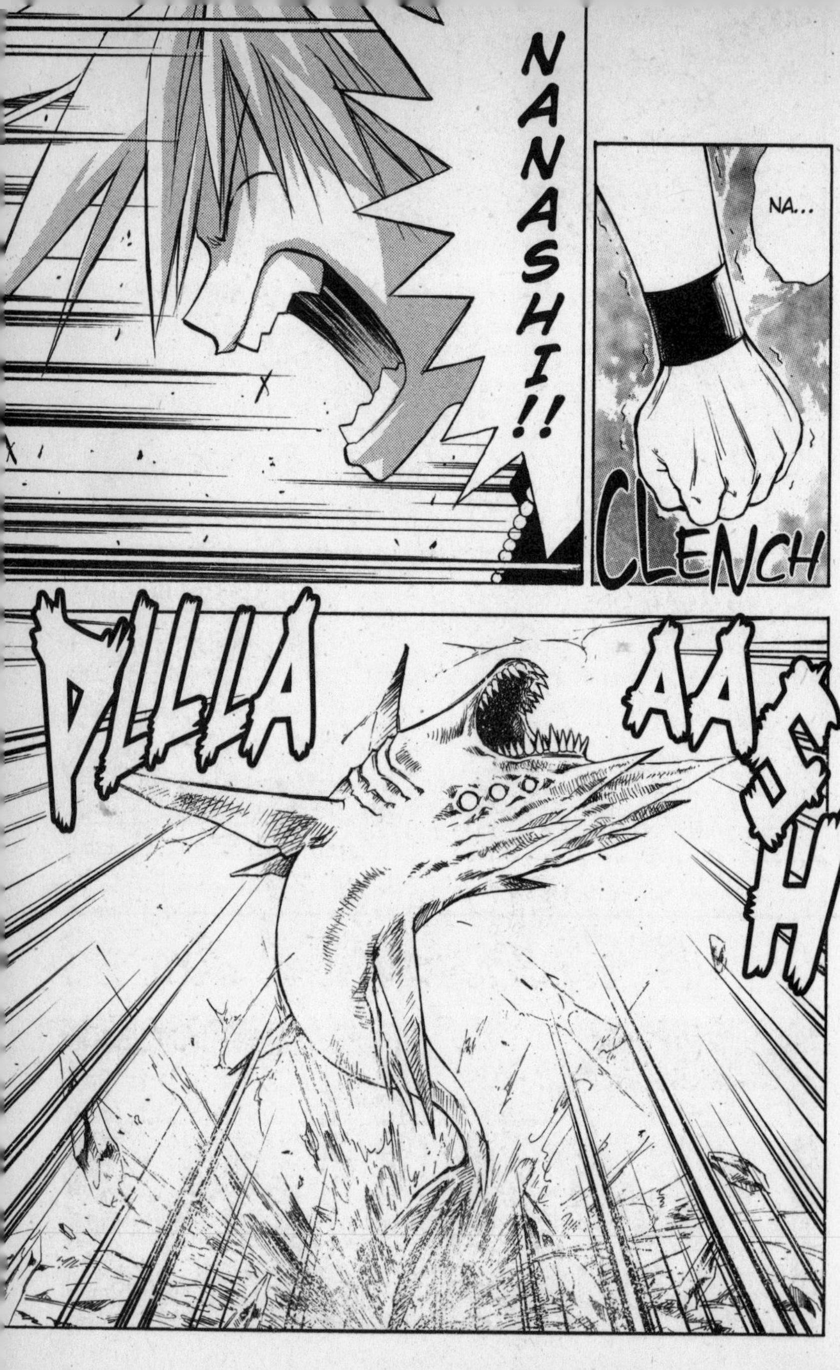

NA...
CLENCH
NANASHI!!
DLLA
AASH

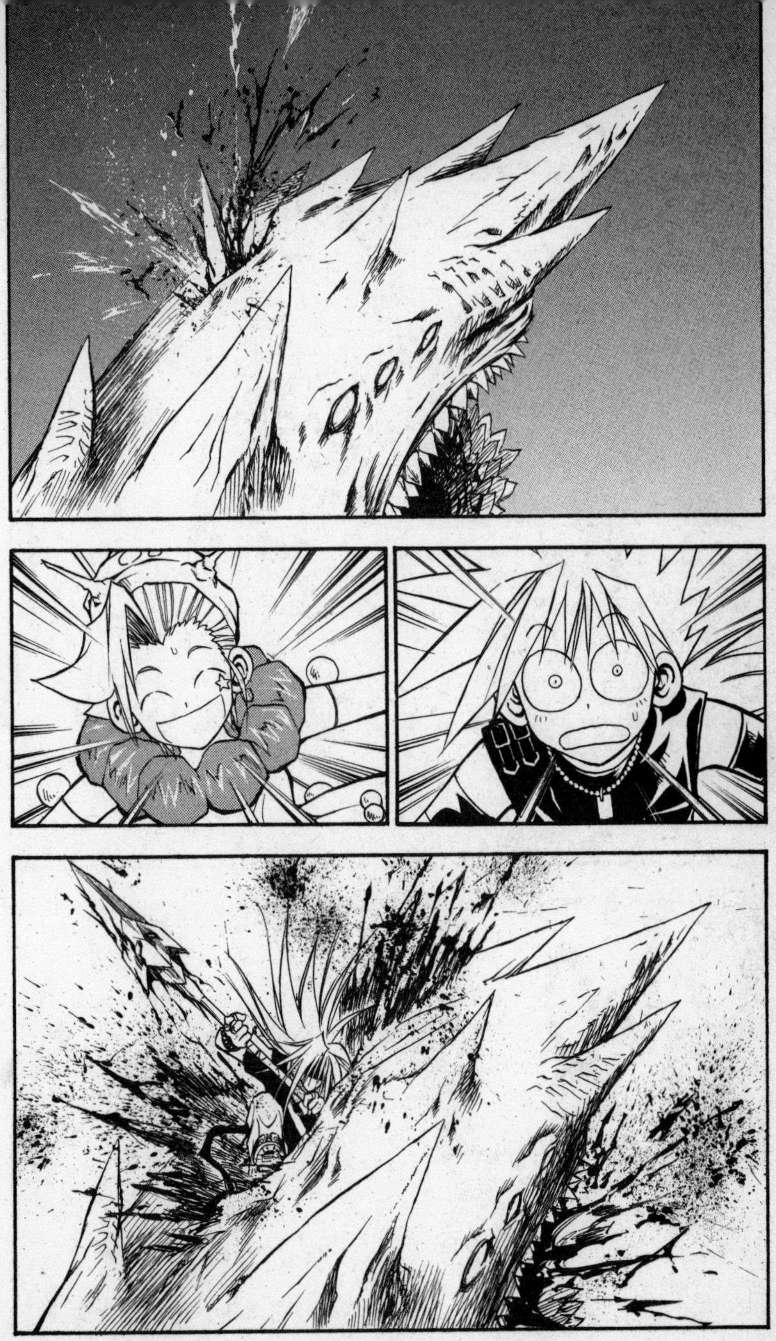

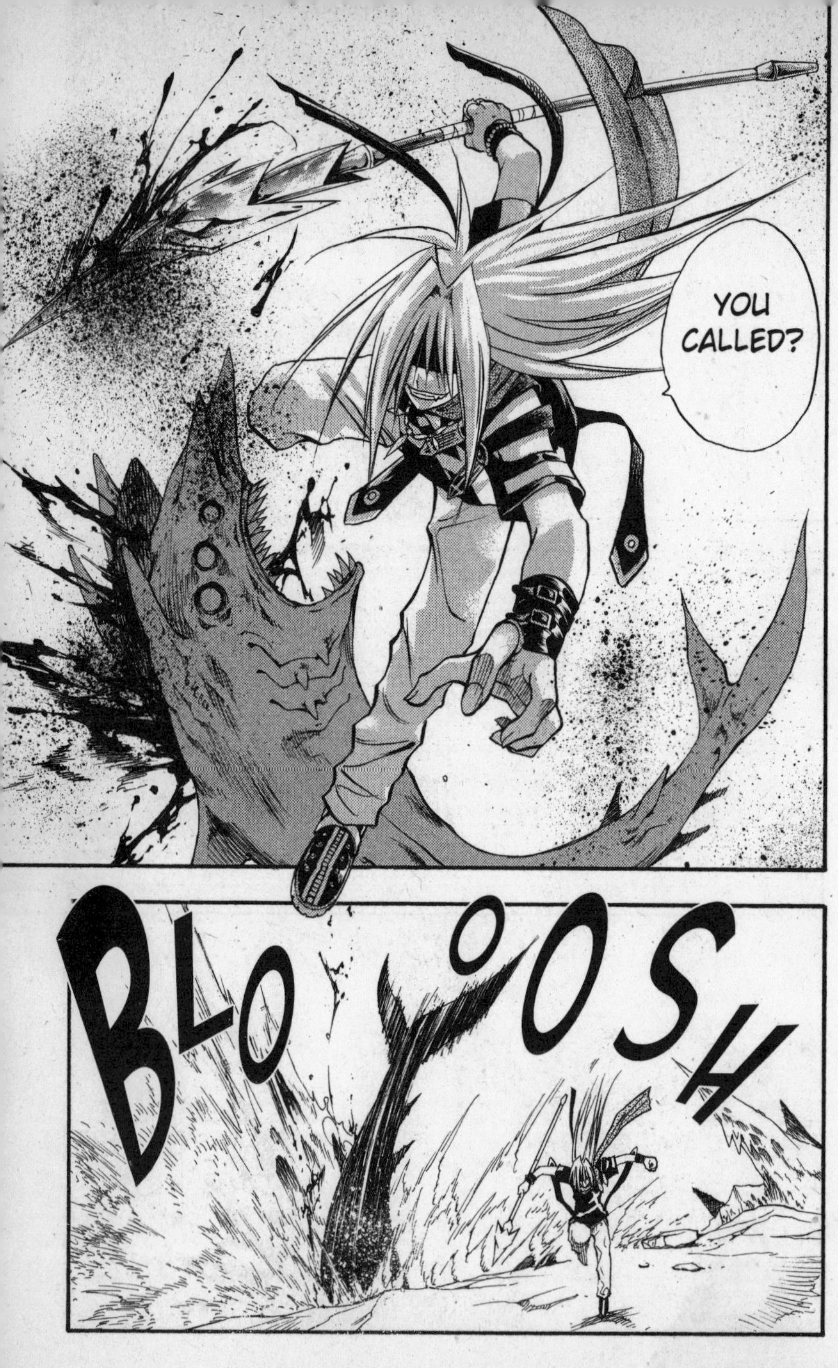
YOU CALLED?
BLOOOSH

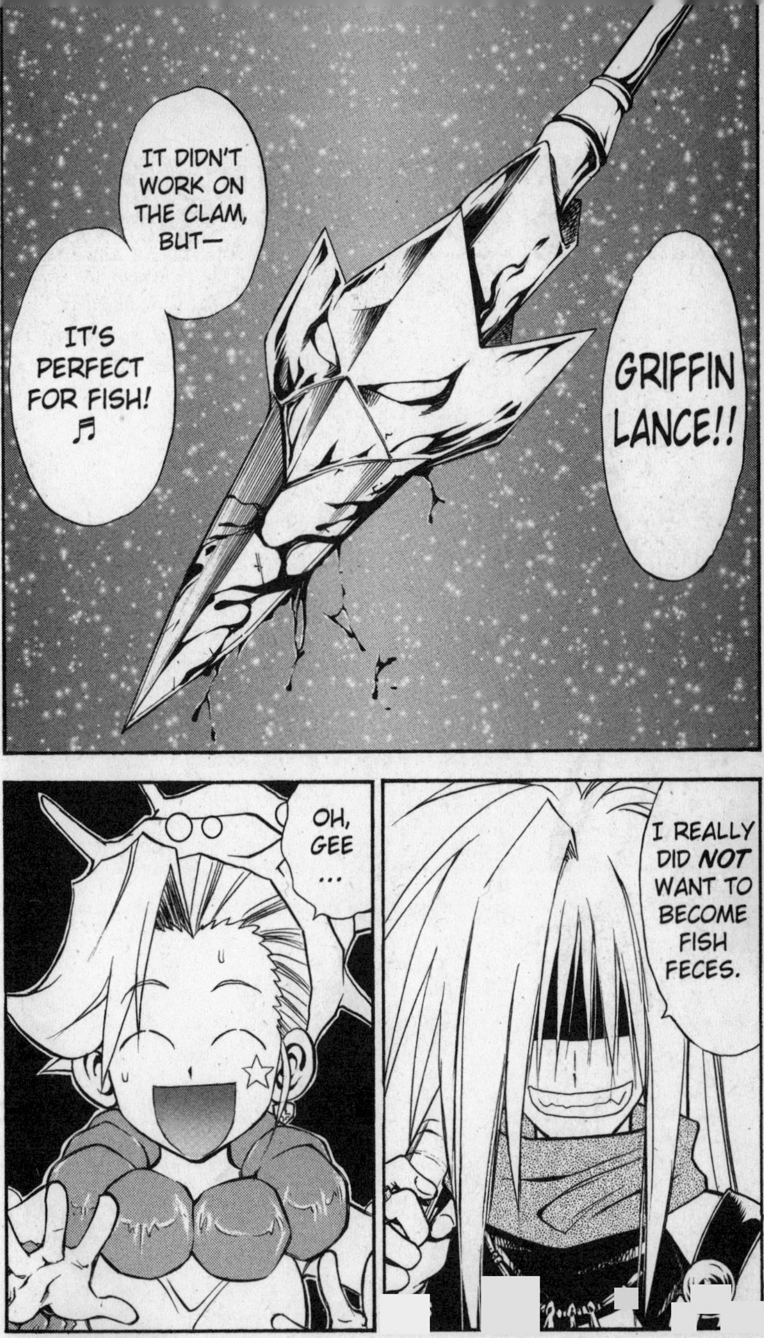
GRIFFIN LANCE!!
IT DIDN'T WORK ON THE CLAM, BUT—
IT'S PERFECT FOR FISH! ♬
I REALLY DID ***NOT*** WANT TO BECOME FISH FECES.
OH, GEE ...

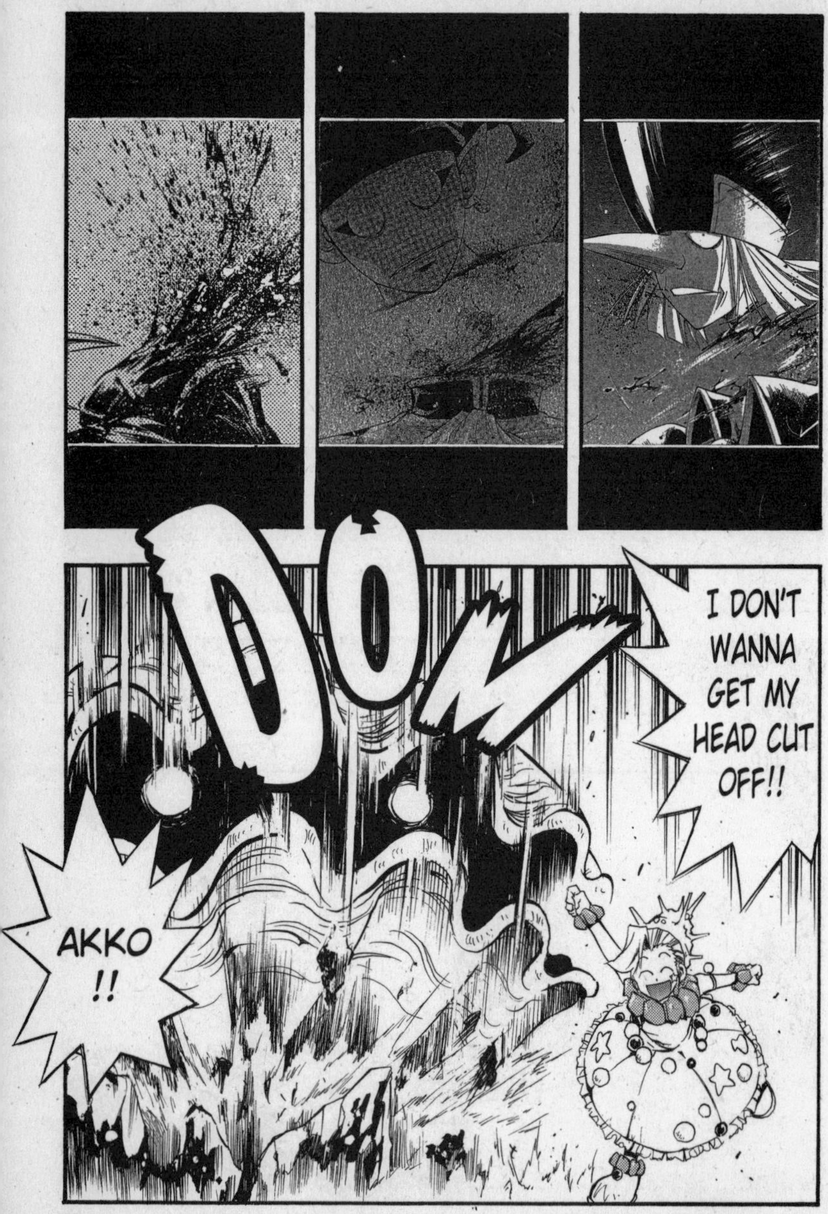
I DON'T WANNA GET MY HEAD CUT OFF!!
DOM
AKKO !!

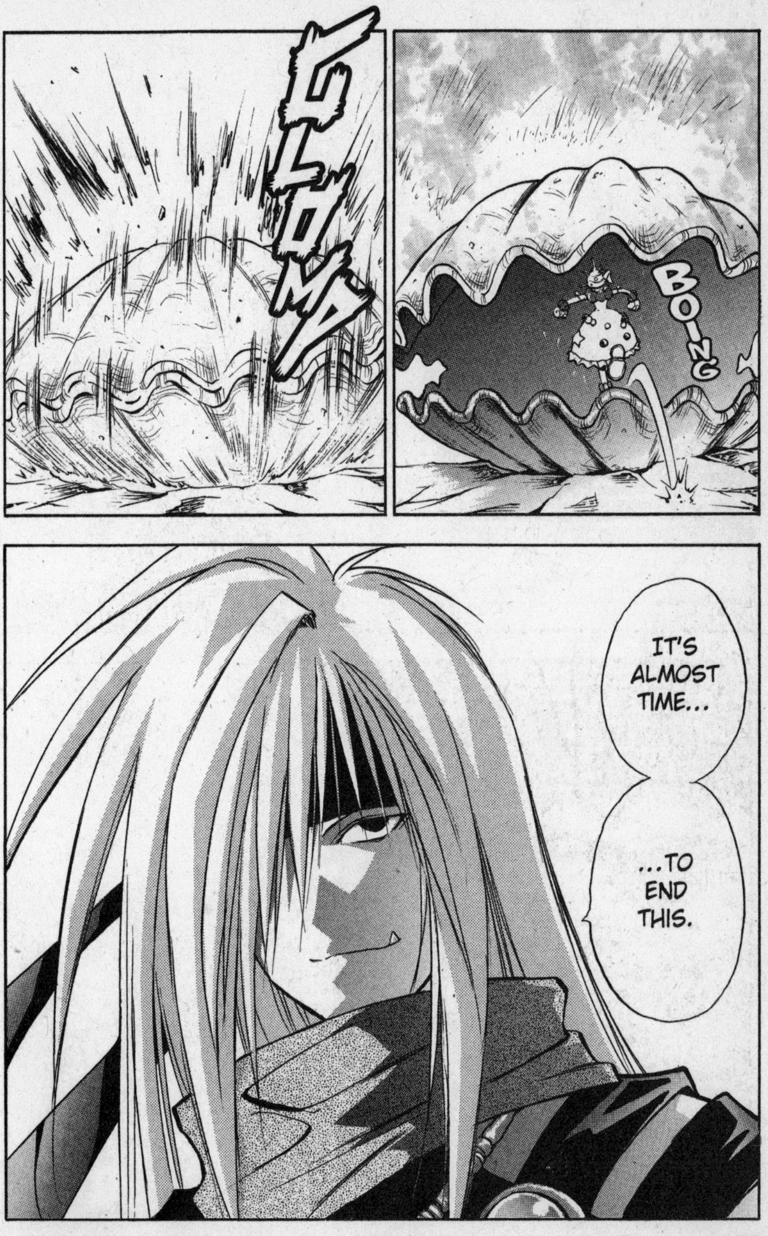
BOING
GLOMP
IT'S ALMOST TIME...
...TO END THIS.

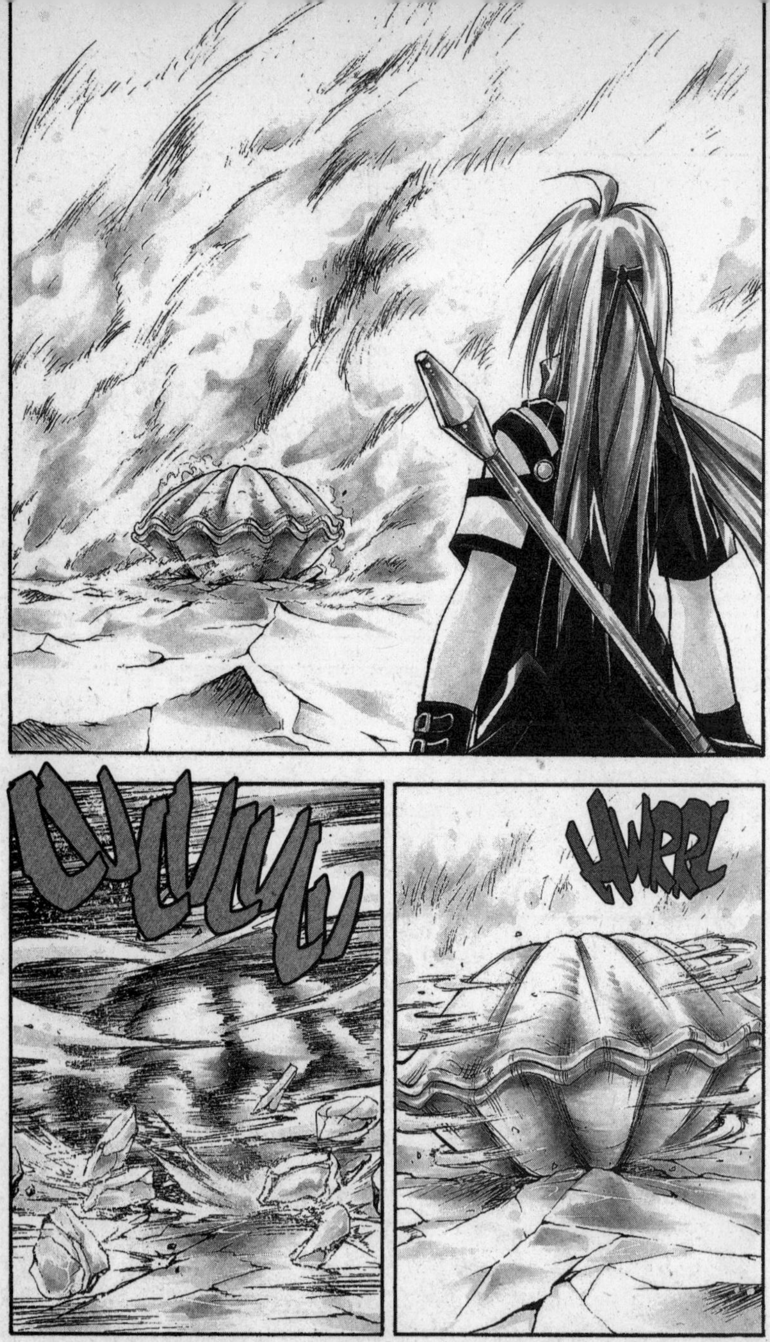
HWRRL

AKT.80/NANASHI VS. AQUA③

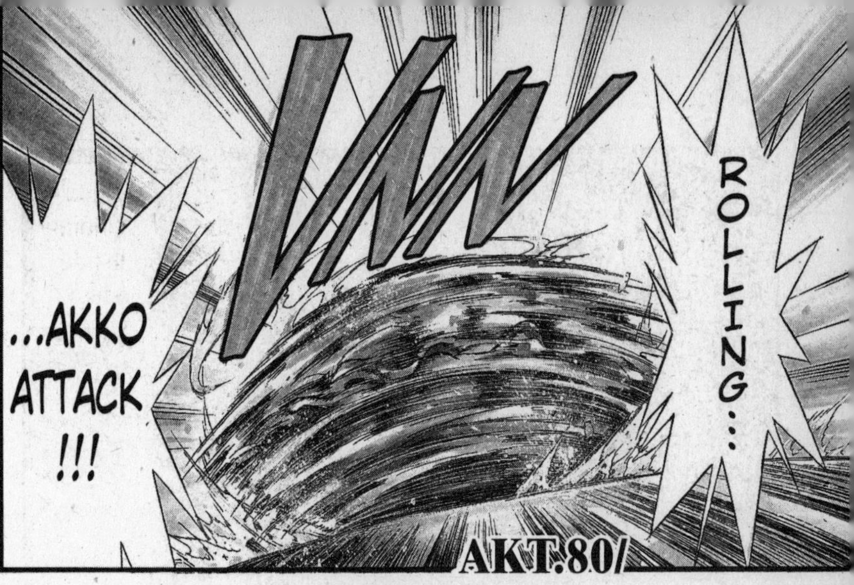
ROLLING...
...AKKO ATTACK!!!

AKT.80/ NANASHI VS. AQUA③

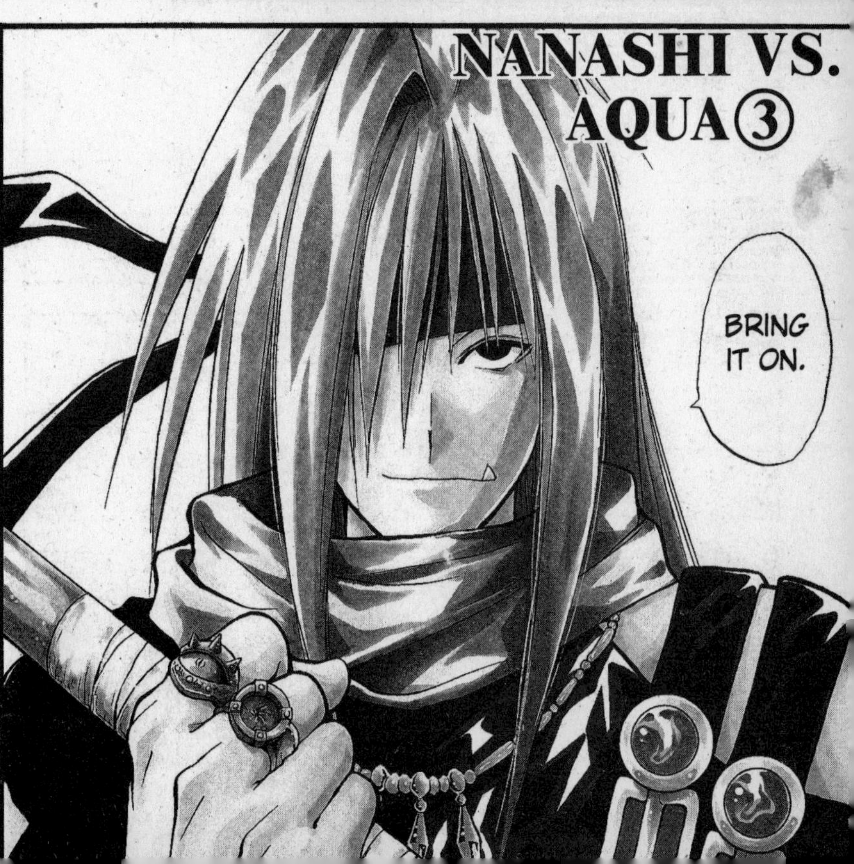
BRING IT ON.

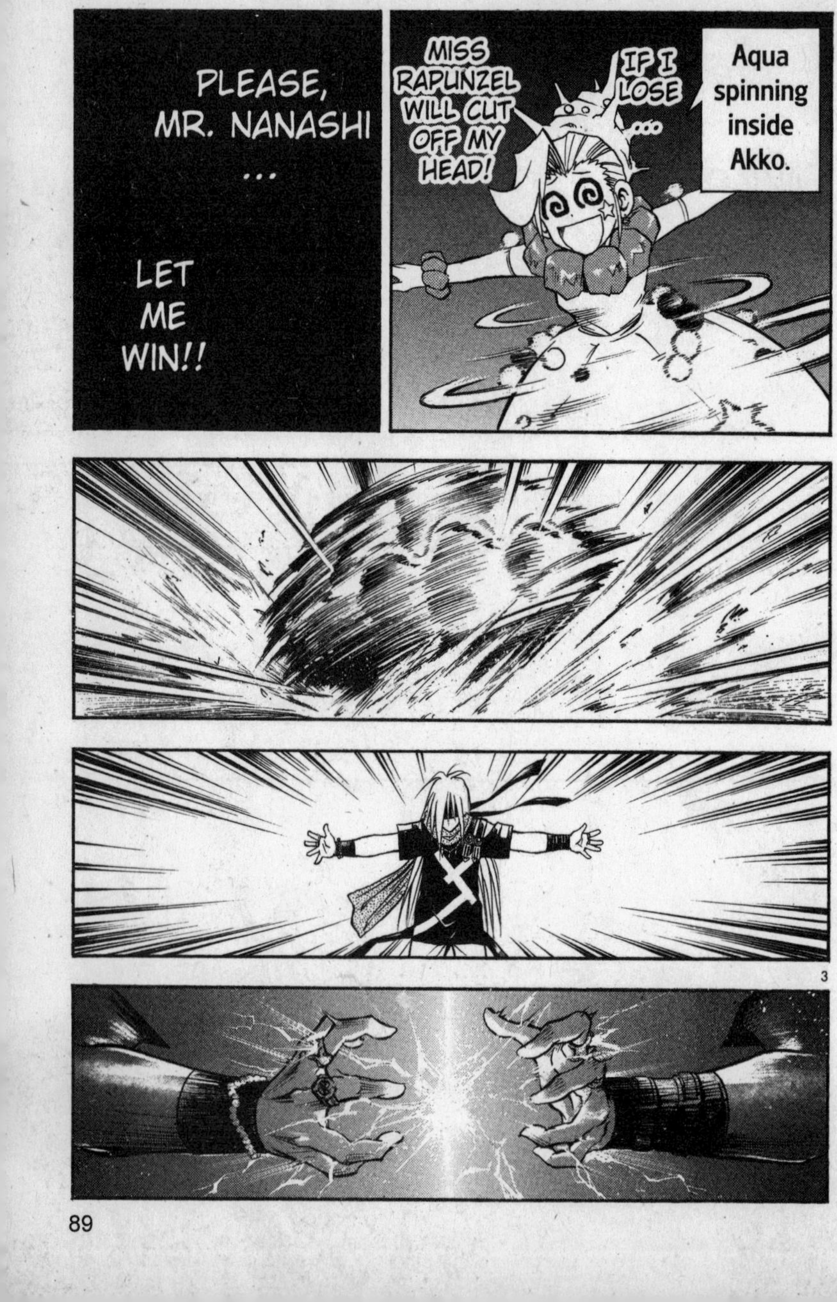

Aqua spinning inside Akko.
IF I LOSE...
MISS RAPUNZEL WILL CUT OFF MY HEAD!
PLEASE, MR. NANASHI...
LET ME WIN!!

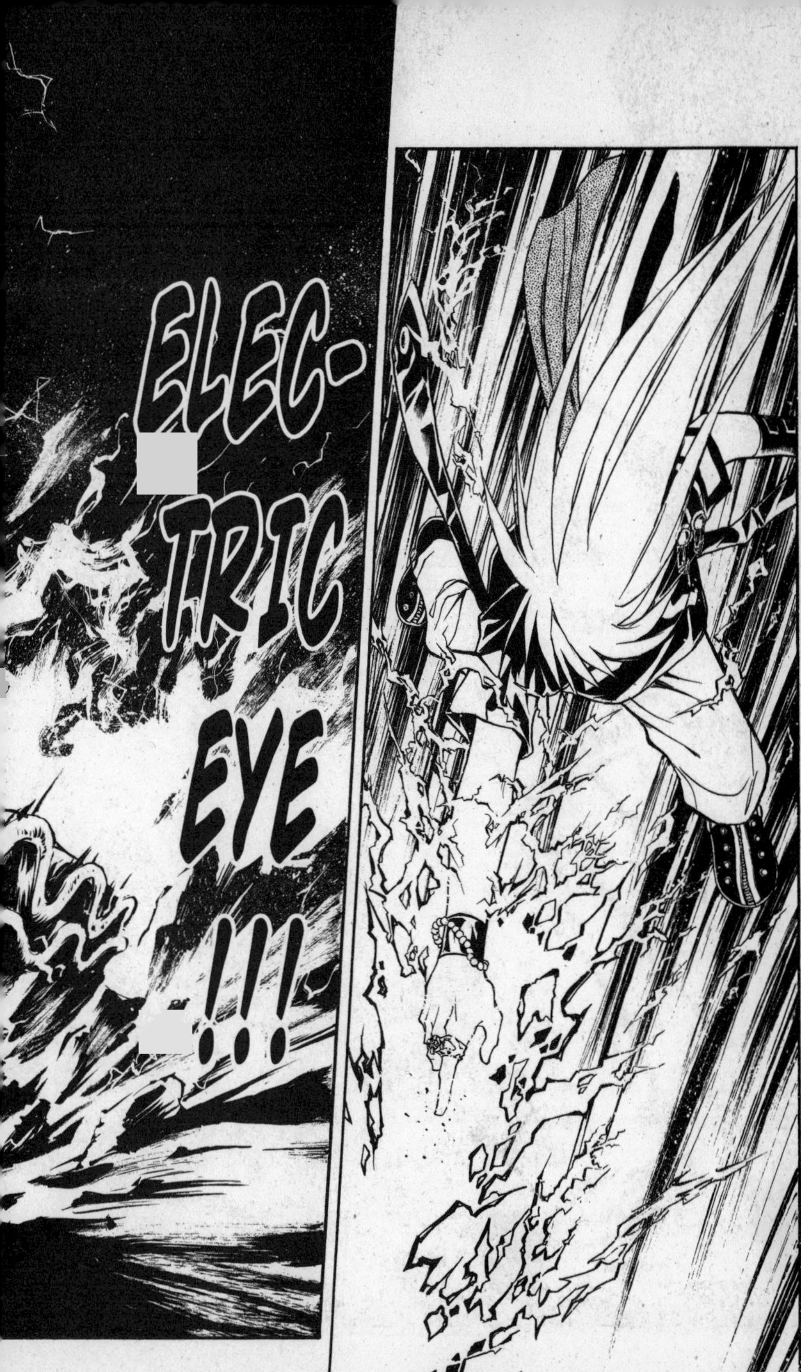
ELEC-TRIC EYE!!!

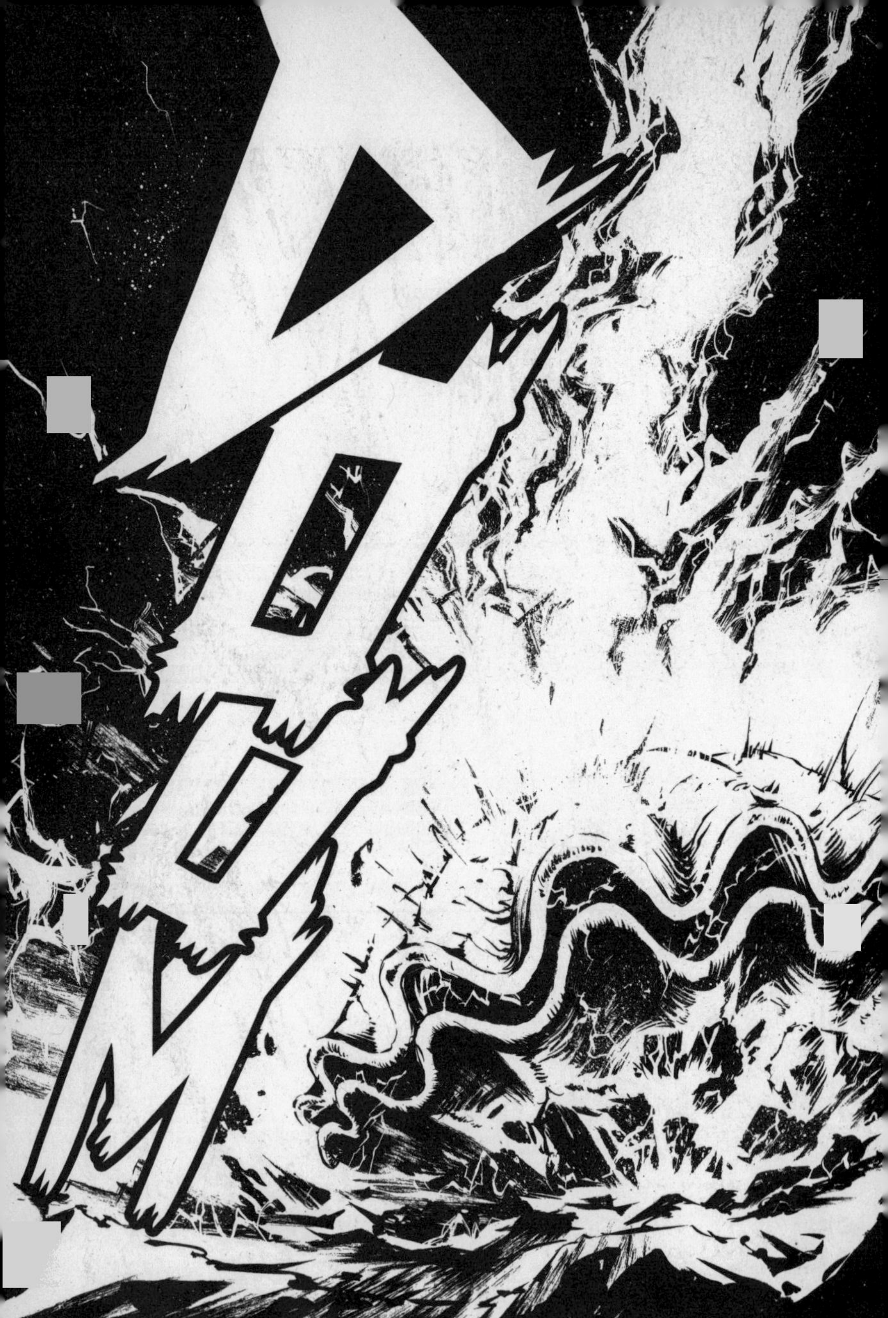

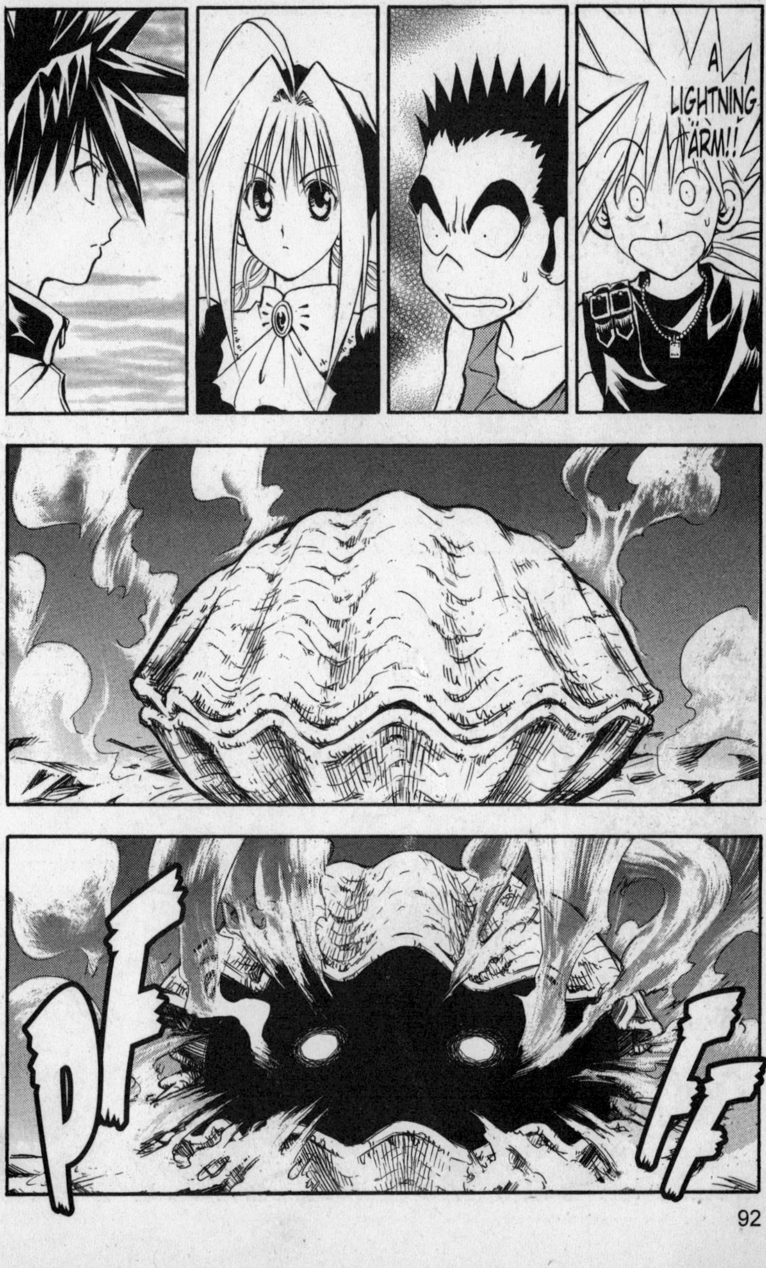
A LIGHTNING ARM!!
PFFF

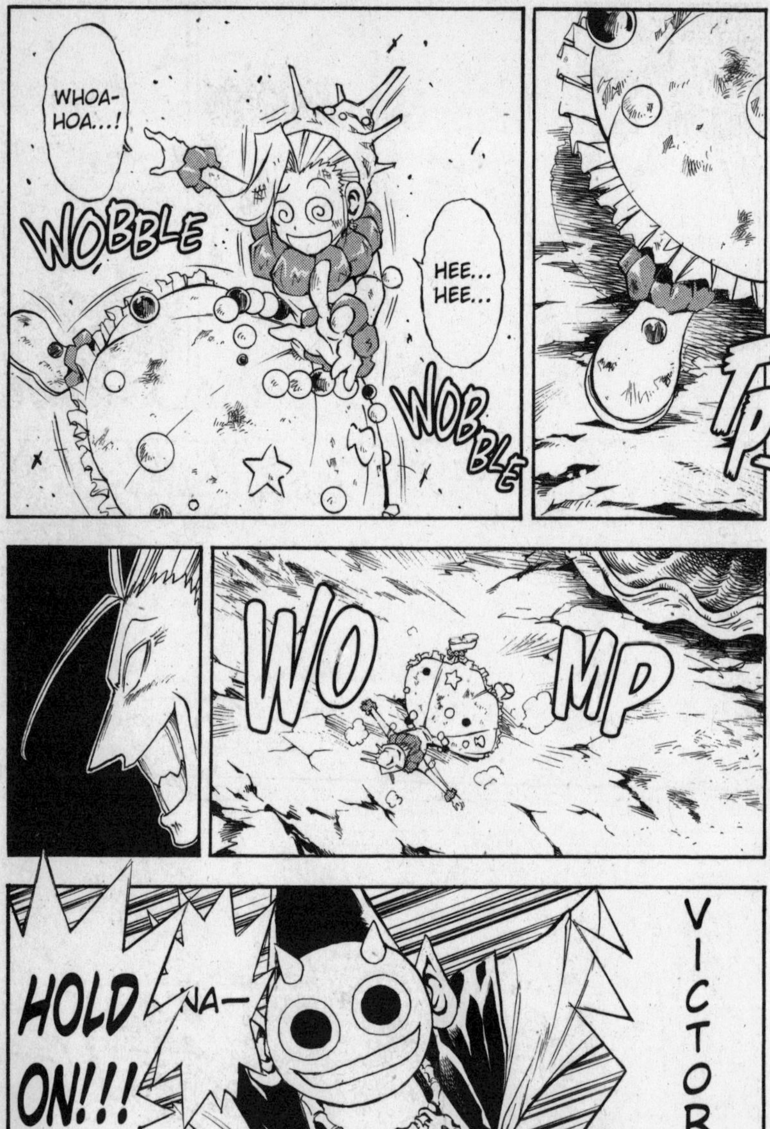
TP-
WHOA-HOA...!
HEE... HEE...
WOBBLE
WOBBLE
WO MP
VICTOR...
NA-
HOLD ON!!!

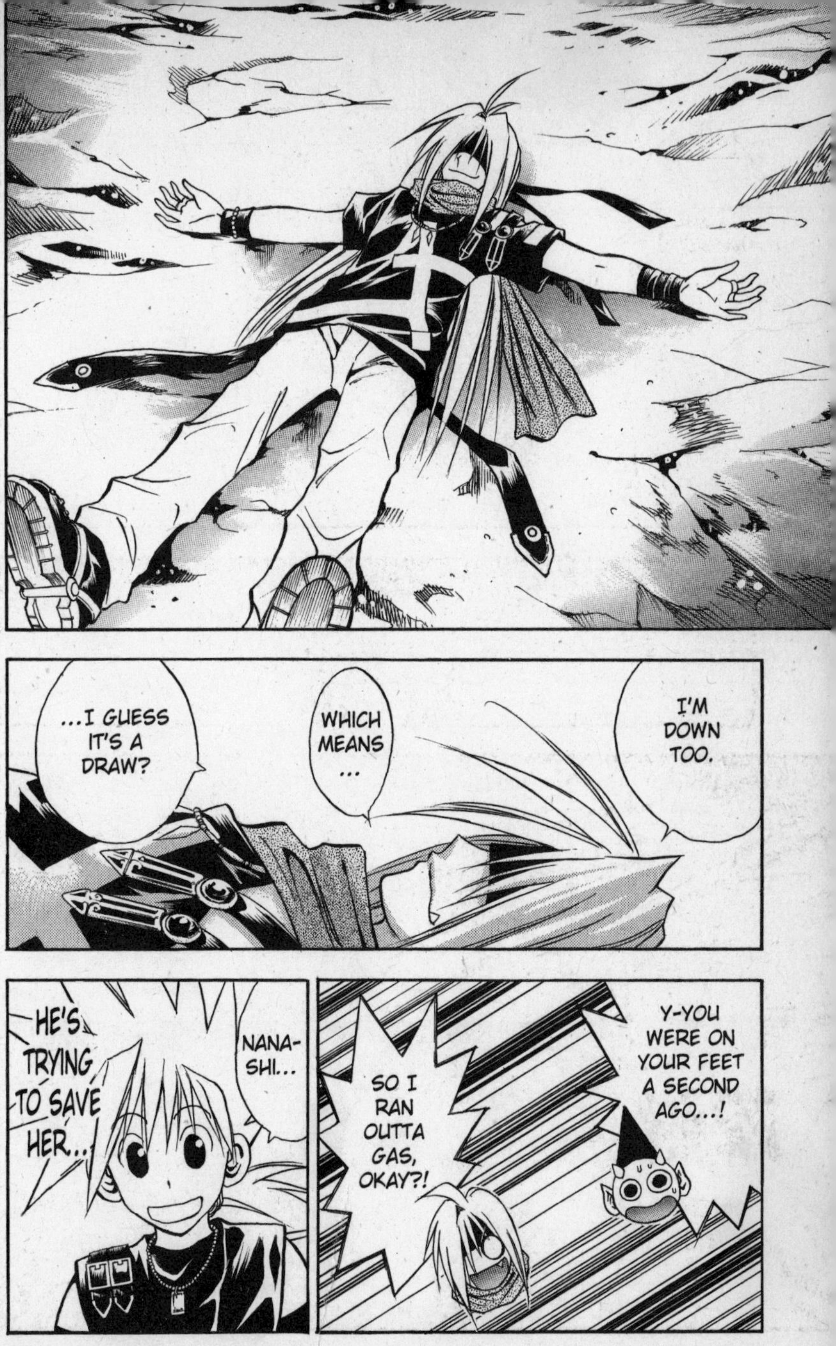
I'M DOWN TOO.
WHICH MEANS ...
...I GUESS IT'S A DRAW?
Y-YOU WERE ON YOUR FEET A SECOND AGO...!
SO I RAN OUTTA GAS, OKAY?!
NANA-SHI...
HE'S TRYING TO SAVE HER...

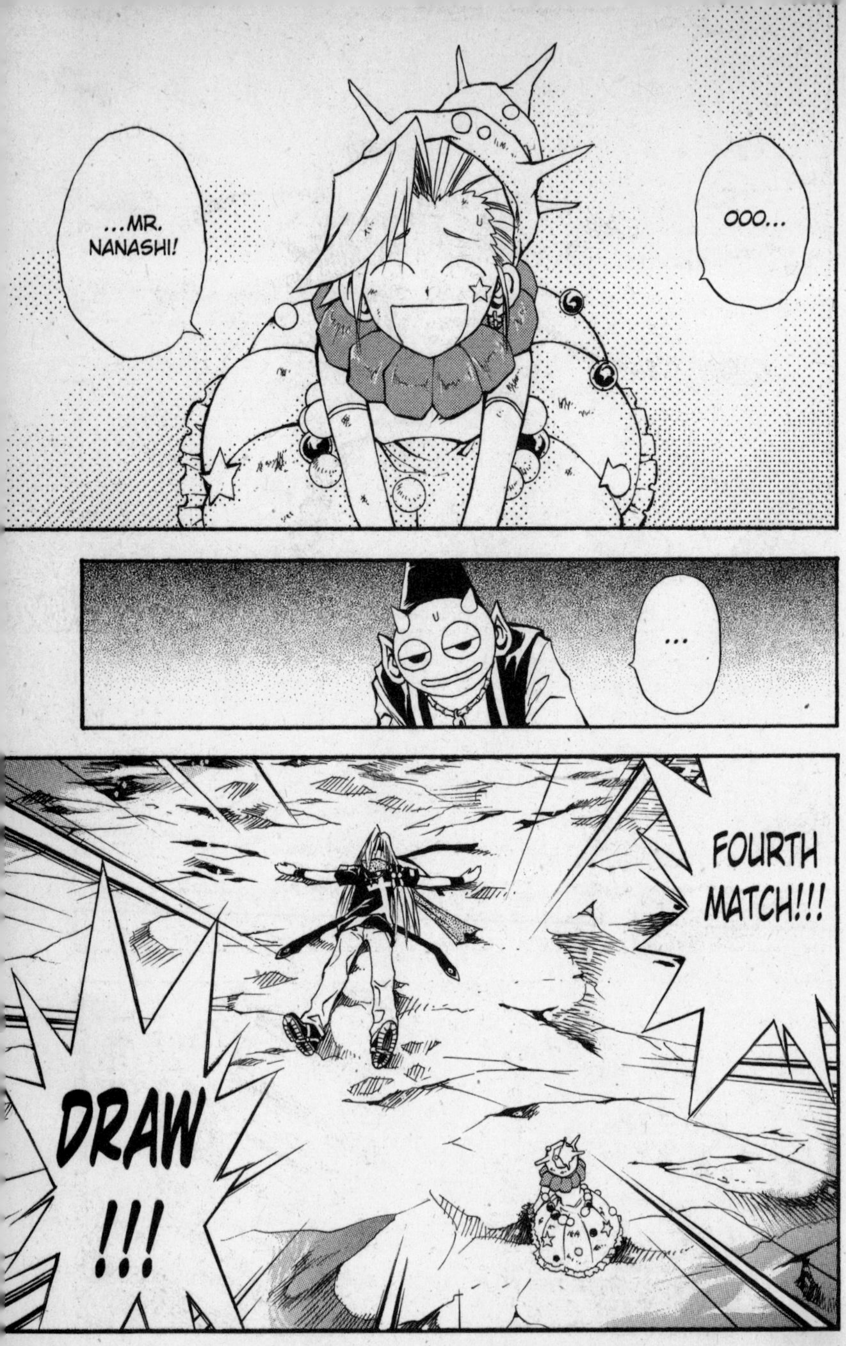
OOO...
...MR. NANASHI!
...
FOURTH MATCH!!!
DRAW !!!

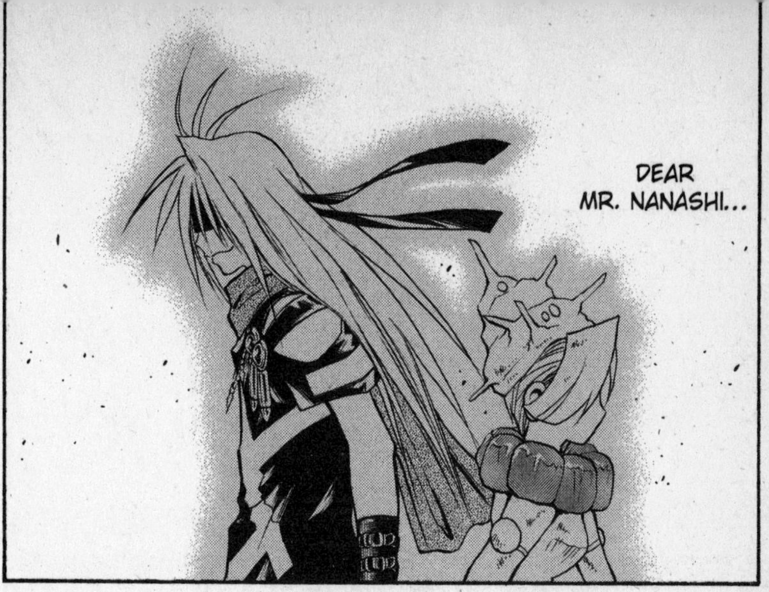
DEAR MR. NANASHI...

...THANK YOU...

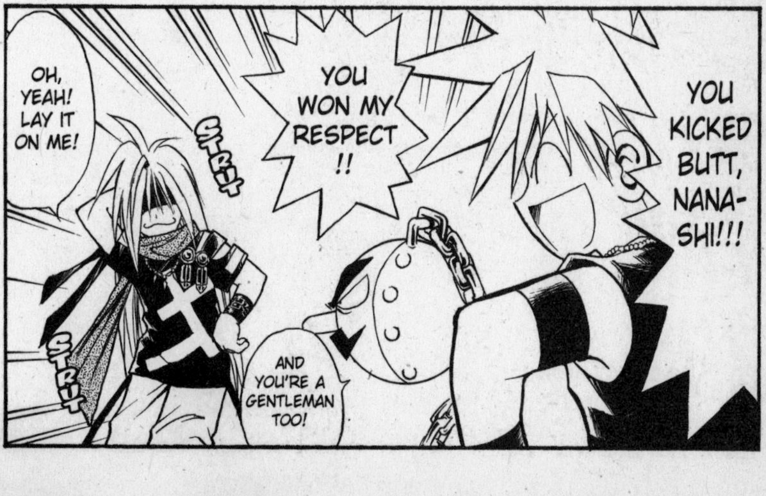
YOU KICKED BUTT, NANA-SHI!!!
YOU WON MY RESPECT !!
AND YOU'RE A GENTLEMAN TOO!
OH, YEAH! LAY IT ON ME!
STRUT
STRUT

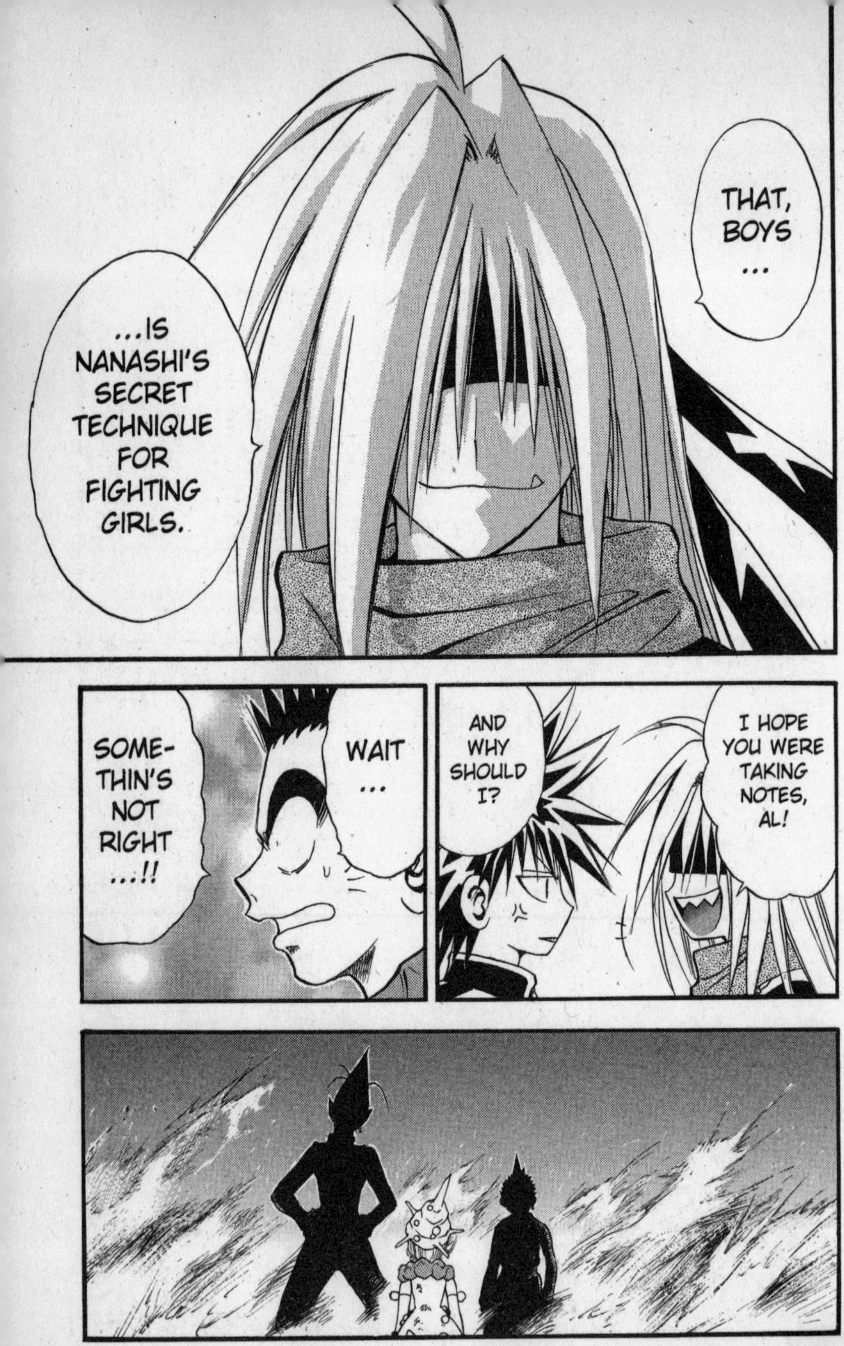
THAT, BOYS ...
...IS NANASHI'S SECRET TECHNIQUE FOR FIGHTING GIRLS.
I HOPE YOU WERE TAKING NOTES, AL!
AND WHY SHOULD I?
WAIT ...
SOME-THIN'S NOT RIGHT ...!!

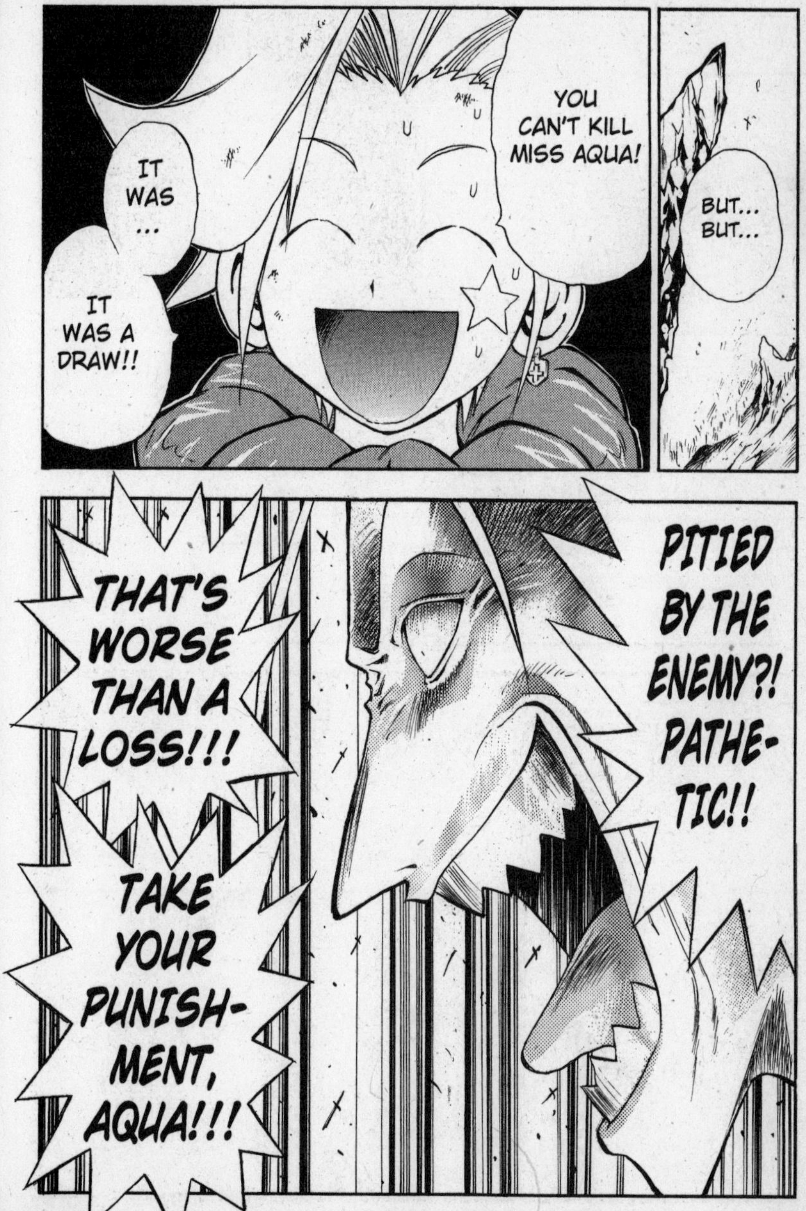
BUT... BUT...
YOU CAN'T KILL MISS AQUA!
IT WAS ...
IT WAS A DRAW!!
PITIED BY THE ENEMY?! PATHE-TIC!!
THAT'S WORSE THAN A LOSS!!!
TAKE YOUR PUNISH-MENT, AQUA!!!

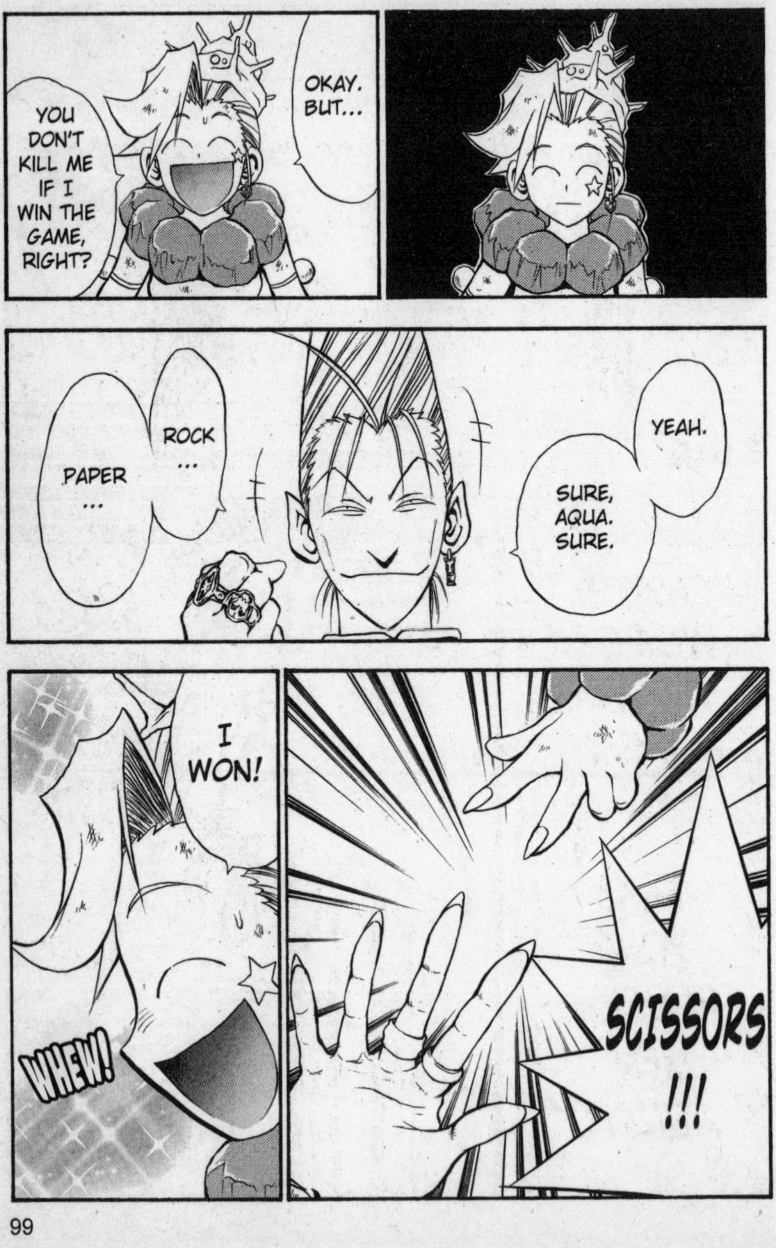

OKAY. BUT...
YOU DON'T KILL ME IF I WIN THE GAME, RIGHT?
YEAH.
SURE, AQUA. SURE.
ROCK ...
PAPER ...
SCISSORS !!!
I WON!
WHEW!

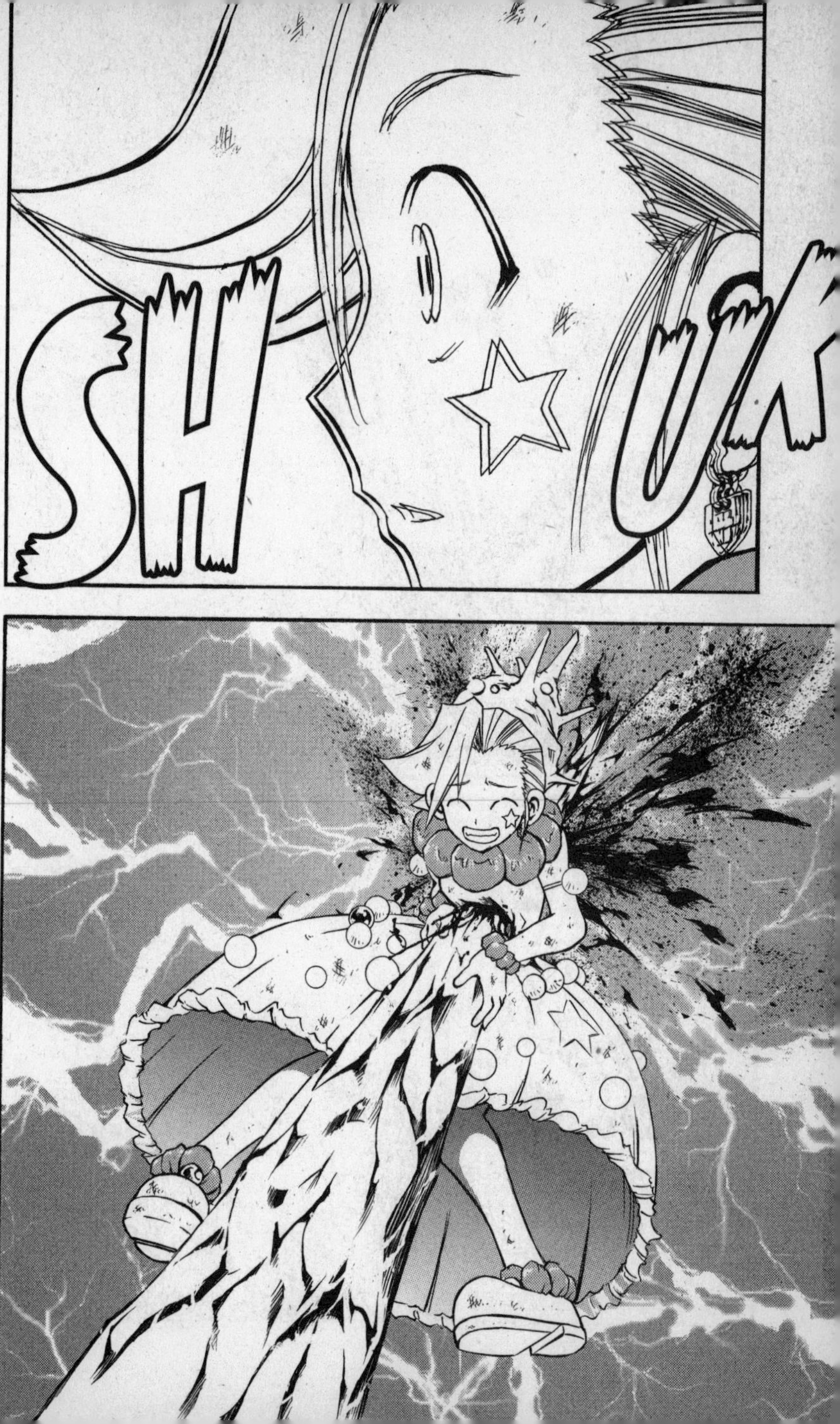
SHUK

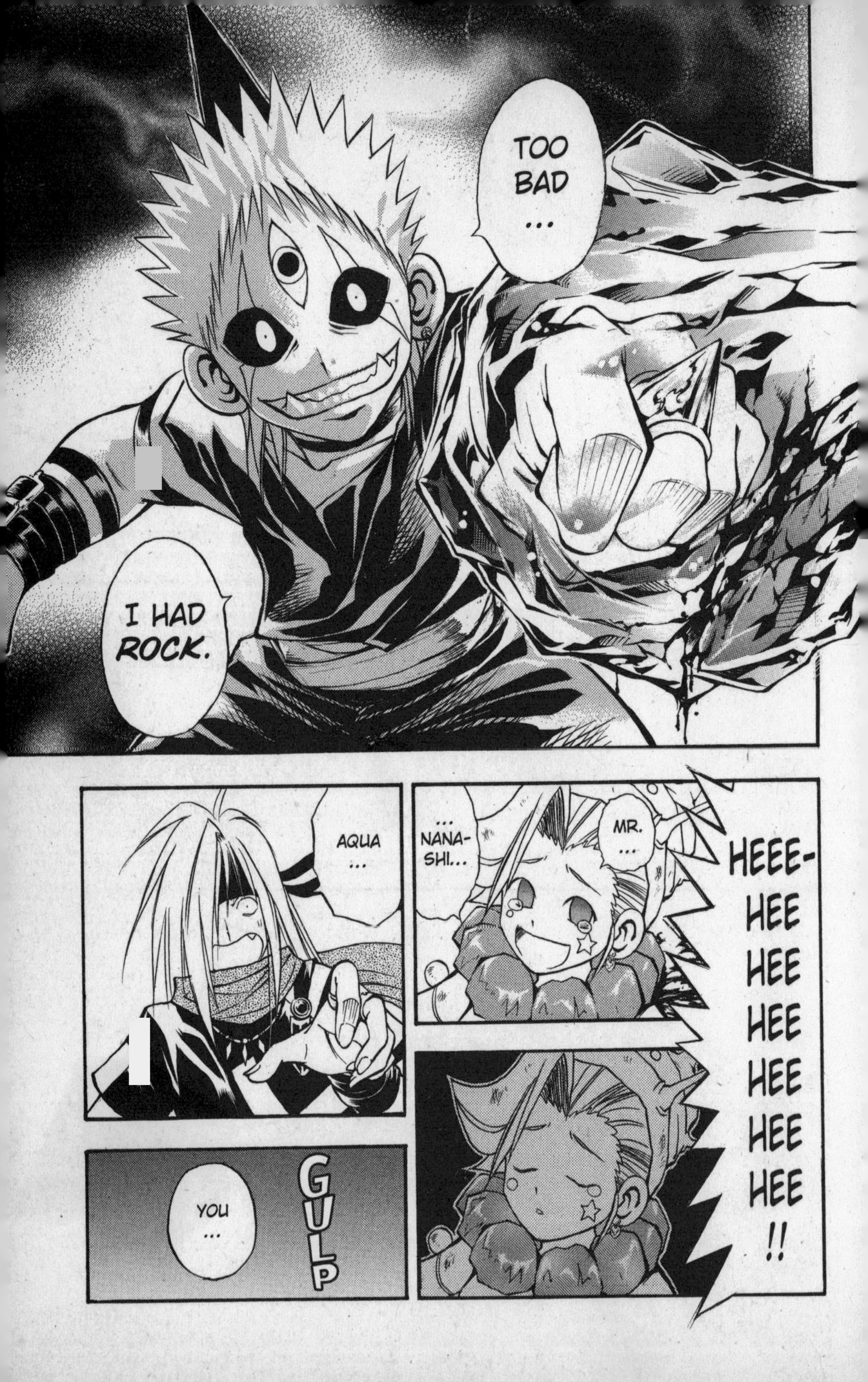
TOO BAD ...
I HAD ROCK.
MR. ...
... NANA-SHI...
AQUA ...
HEEE-HEE HEE HEE HEE HEE HEE!!
YOU ...
GULP

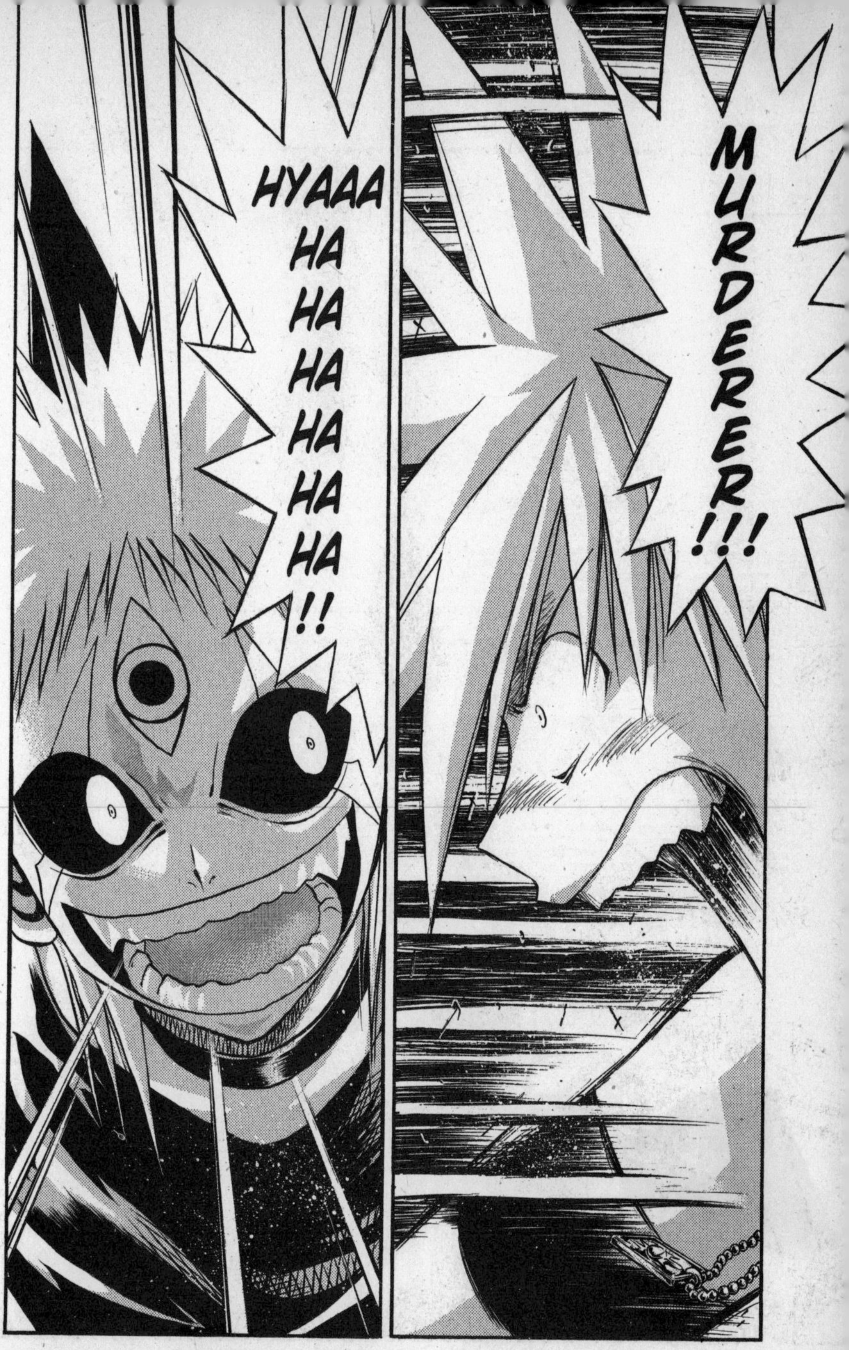
MURDERER!!!
HYAAA HA HA HA HA HA HA!!

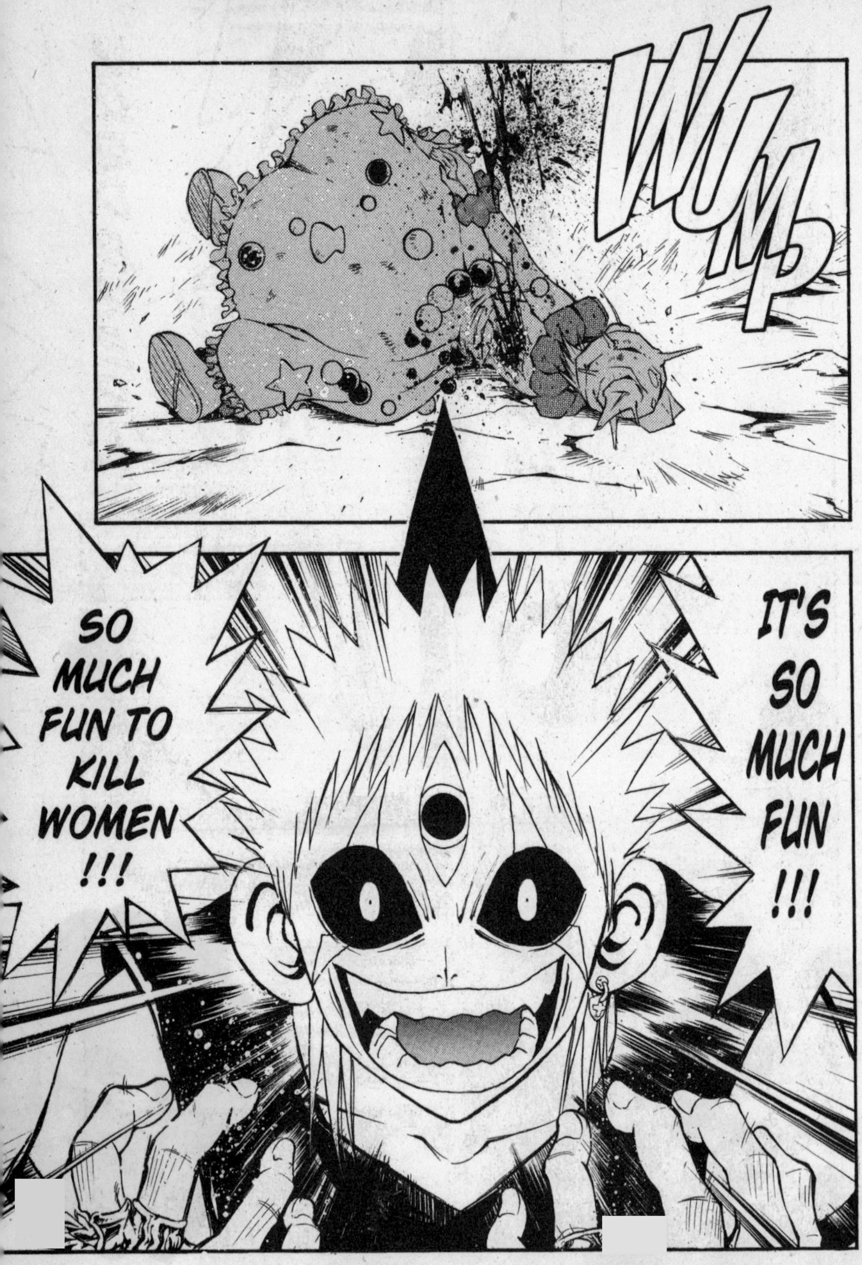
WUMP
IT'S SO MUCH FUN!!!
SO MUCH FUN TO KILL WOMEN!!!

AKT.81/GINTA VS. GIROM①

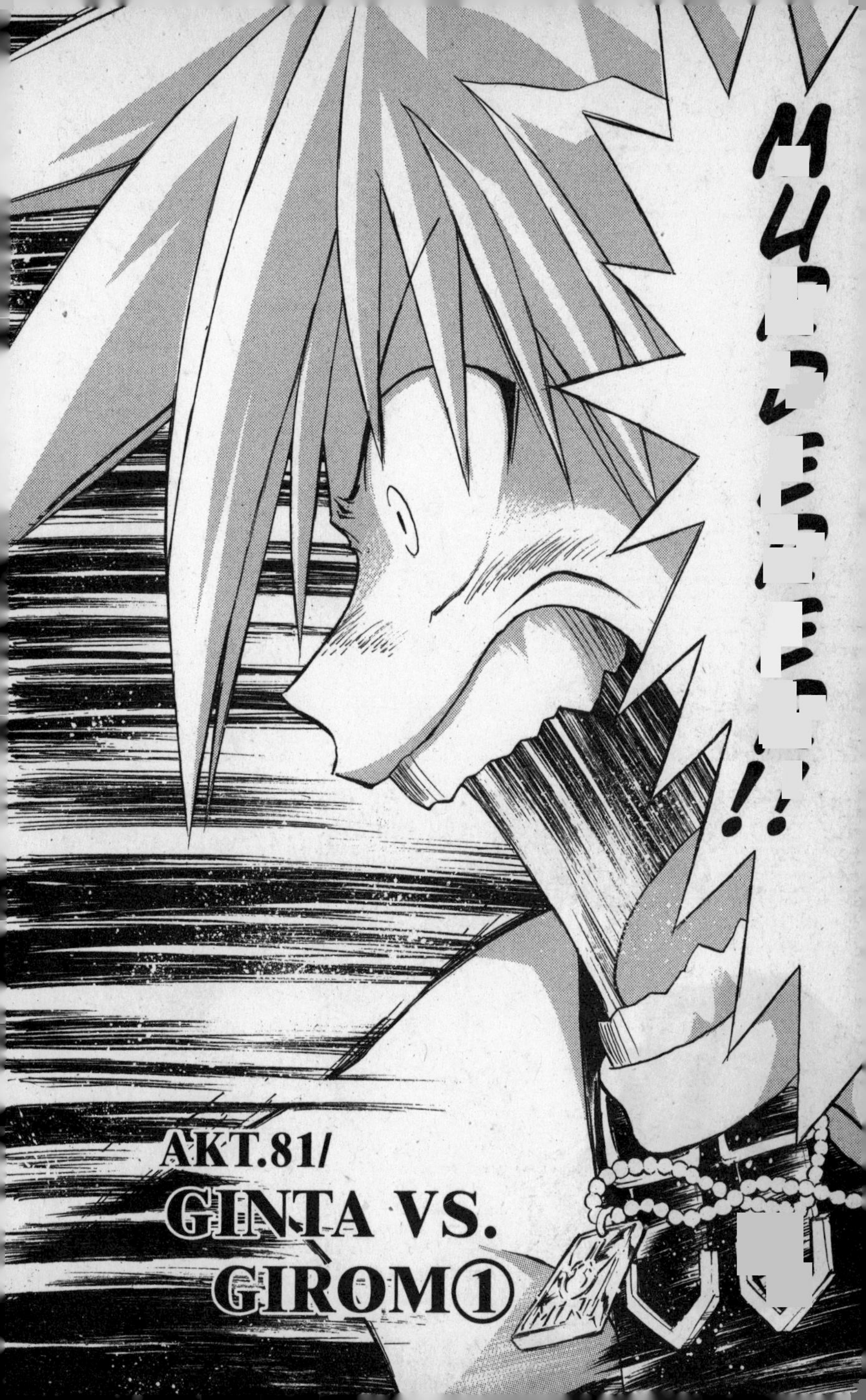

AKT.81/ GINTA VS. GIROM①

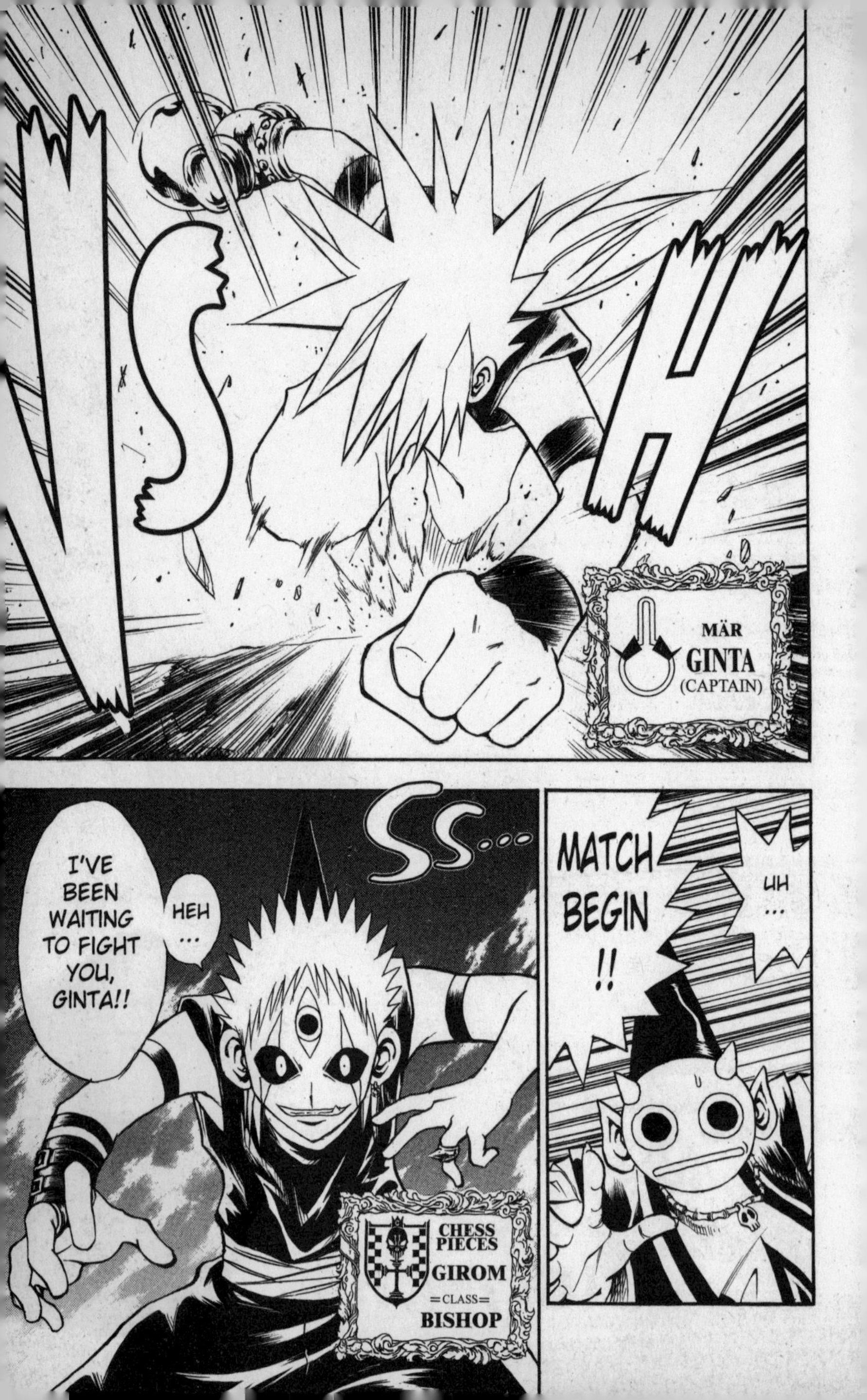
MÄR
GINTA
(CAPTAIN)
MATCH BEGIN!!
UH ...
SS...
HEH ...
I'VE BEEN WAITING TO FIGHT YOU, GINTA!!
CHESS PIECES
GIROM
=CLASS=
BISHOP

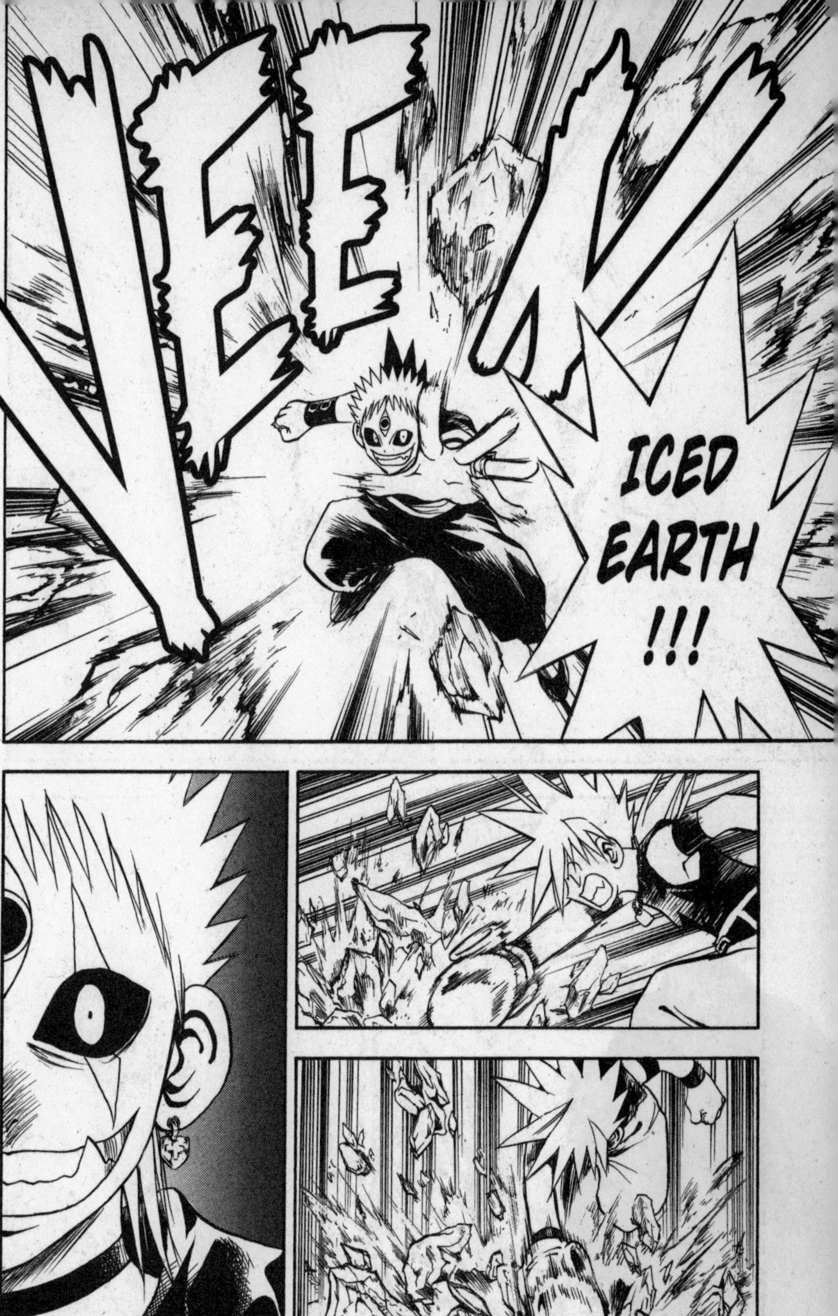
ICED EARTH !!!

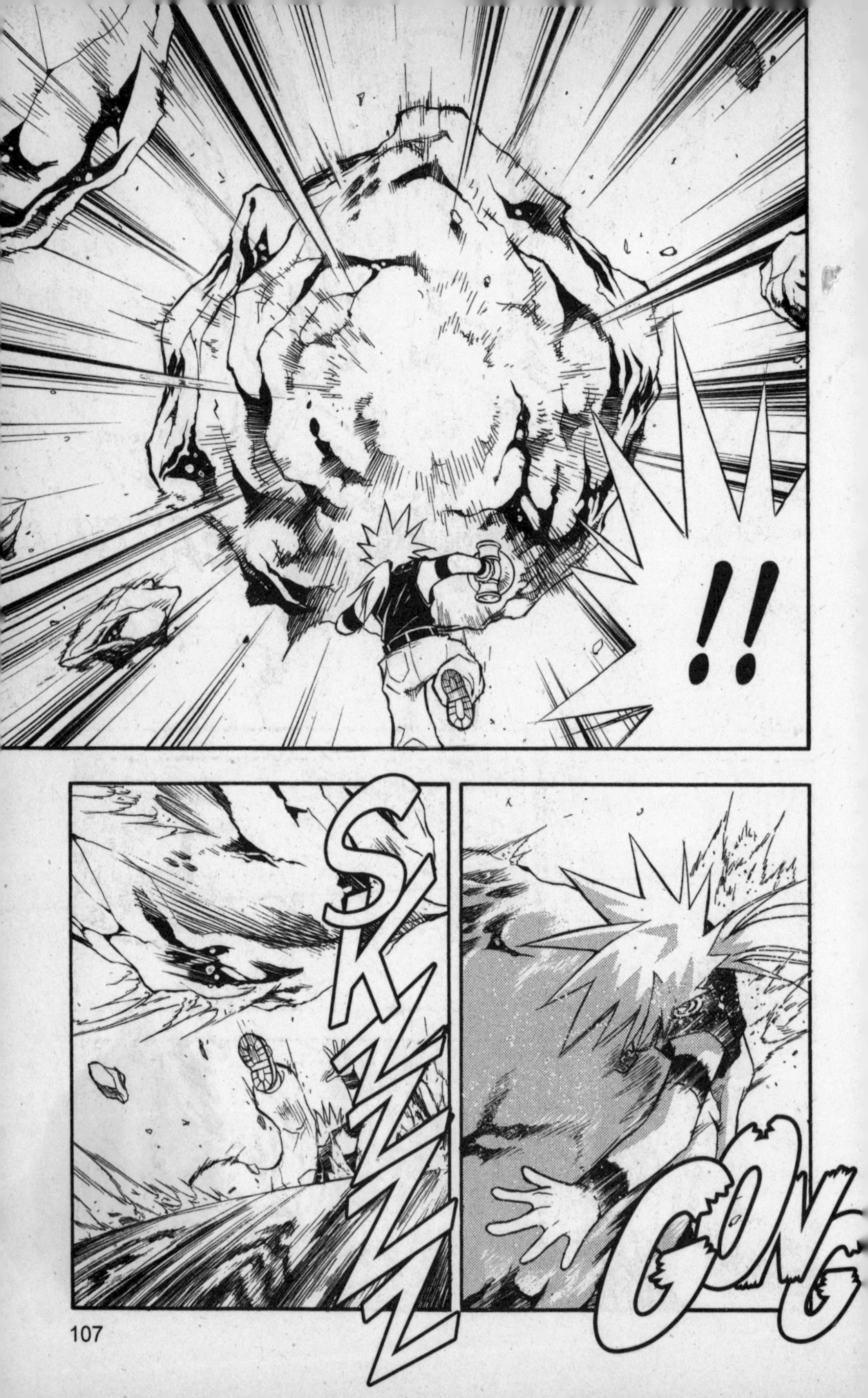
!!
GONG
SKZZZZ

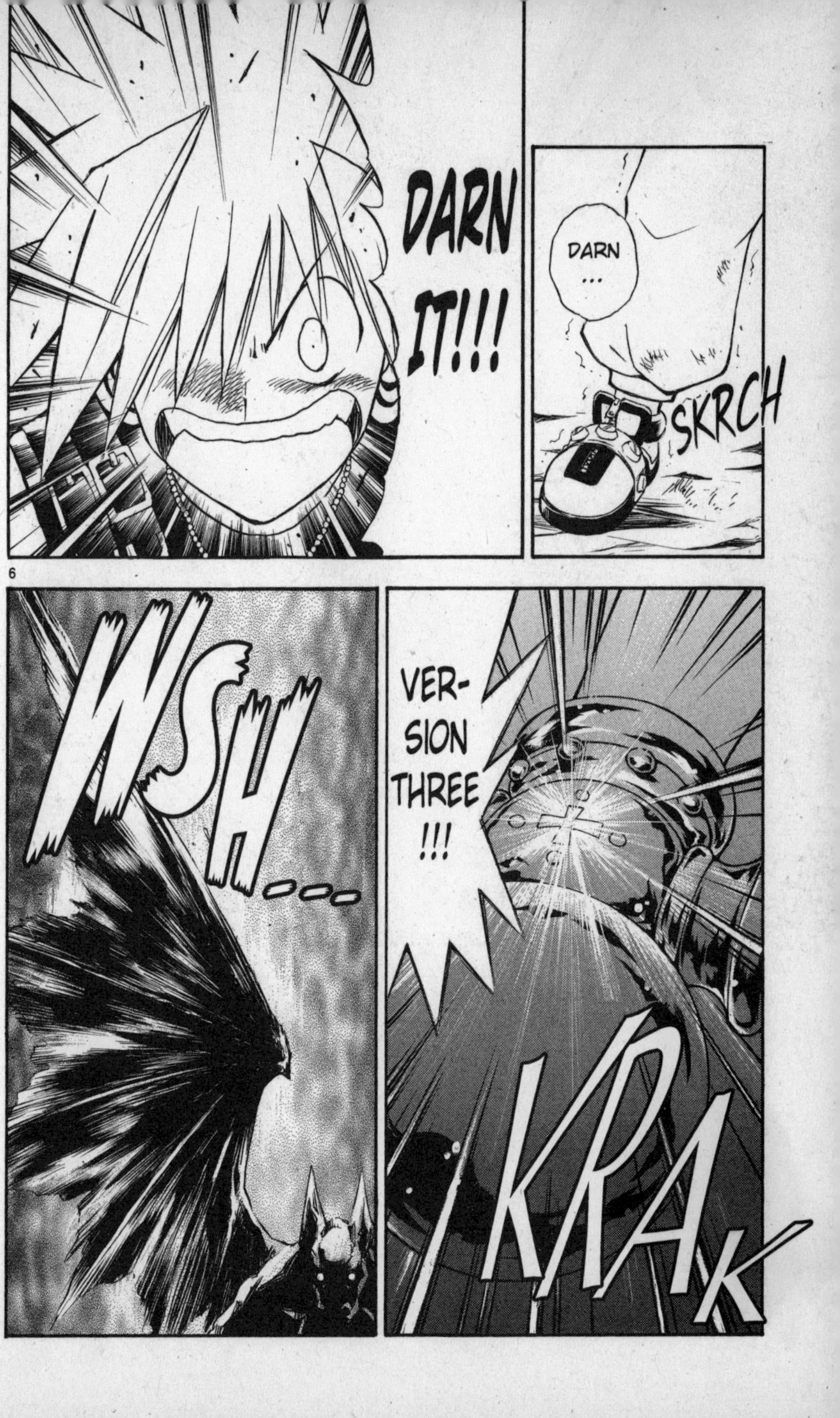

DARN ...
SKRCH
DARN IT!!!
VER-SION THREE !!!
KRAK
WSH...

6

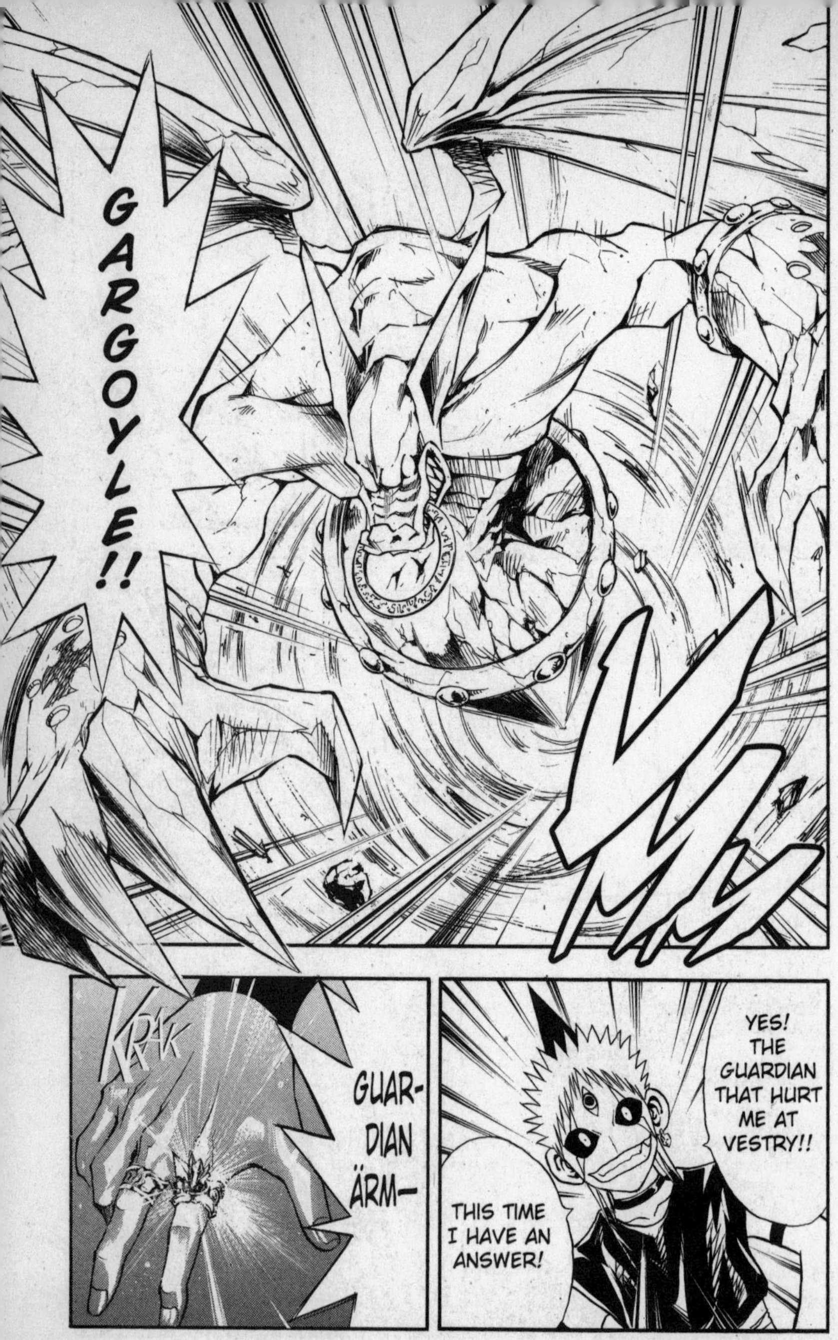
GARGOYLE!!
YES! THE GUARDIAN THAT HURT ME AT VESTRY!!
THIS TIME I HAVE AN ANSWER!
KRAK
GUAR-DIAN ÄRM-

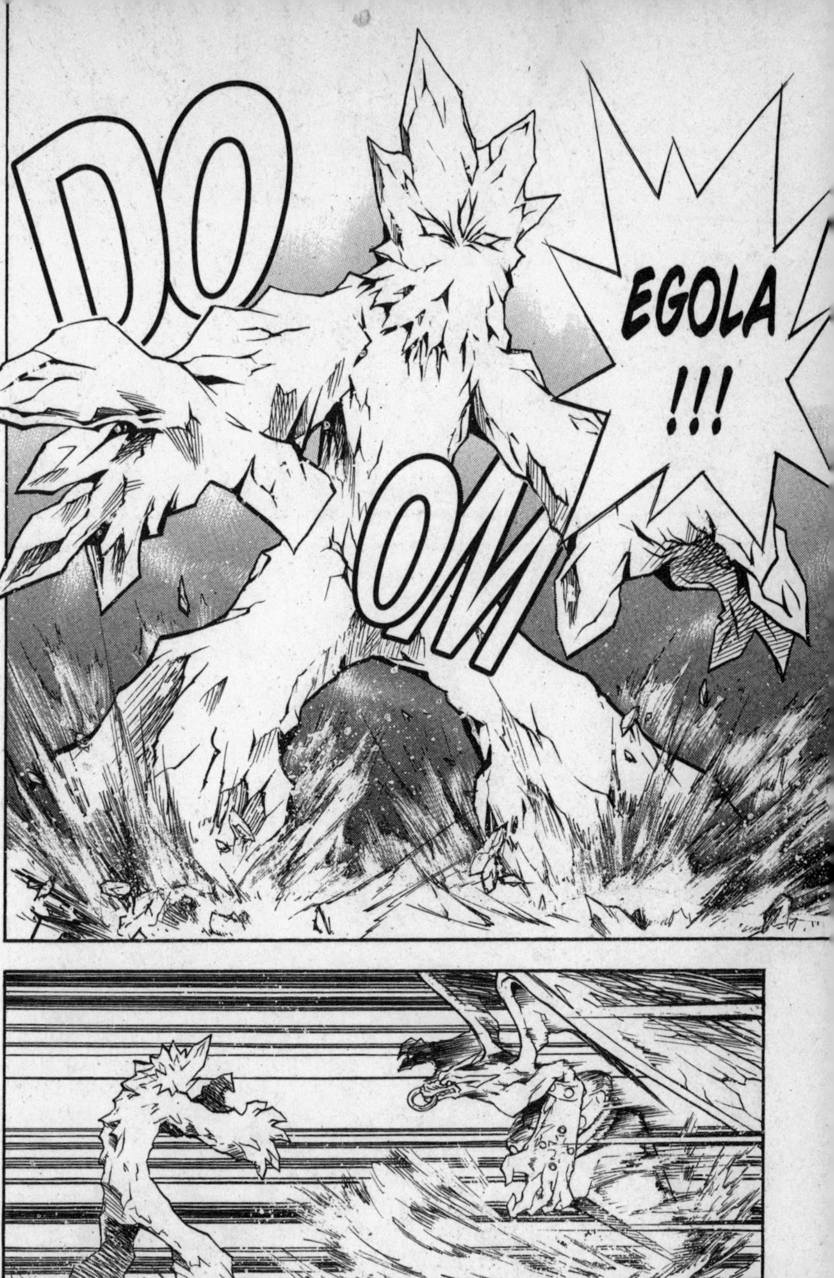
EGOLA !!!
DO
OM

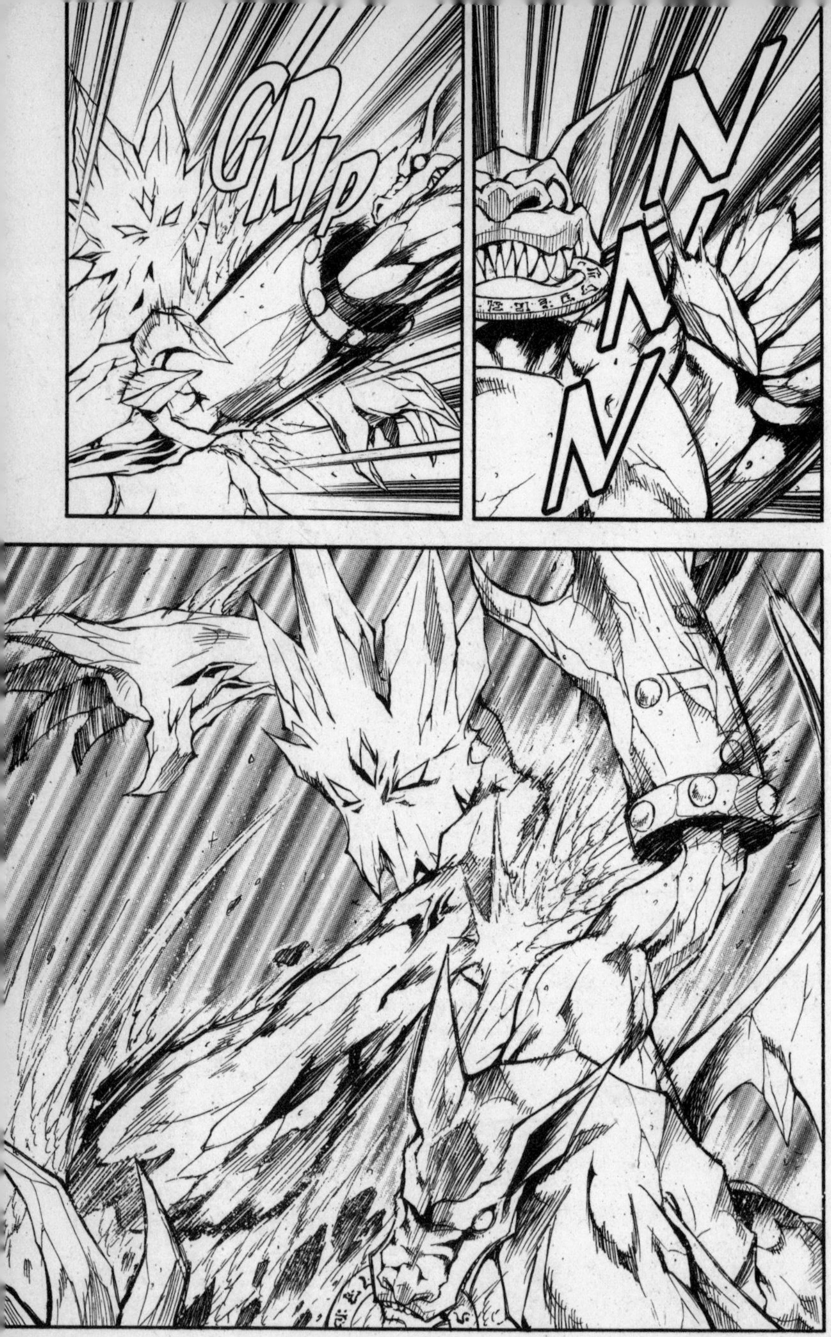
NNNN
GRIP

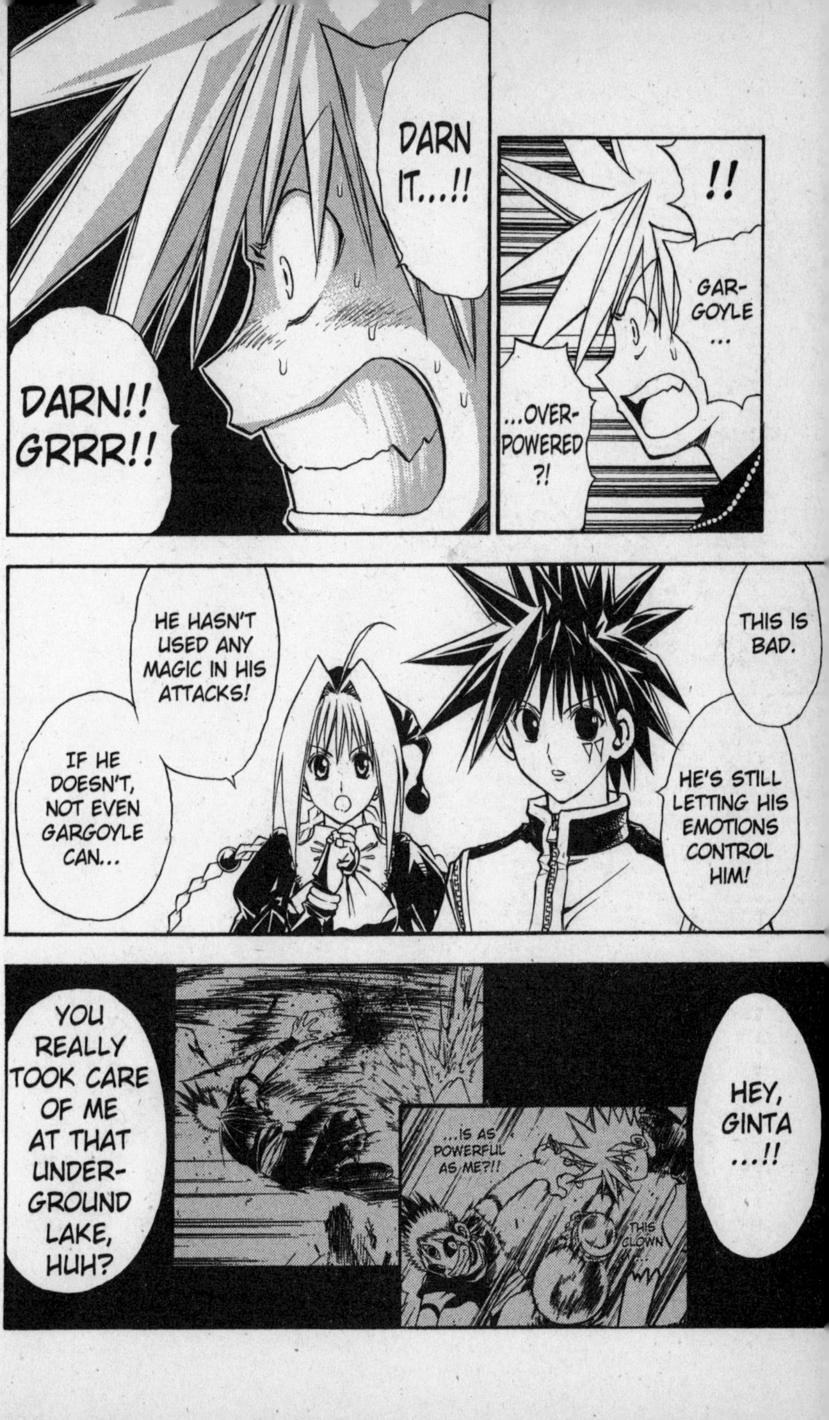
!!
GAR-GOYLE ...
...OVER-POWERED ?!
DARN IT...!!
DARN!! GRRR!!
THIS IS BAD.
HE'S STILL LETTING HIS EMOTIONS CONTROL HIM!
HE HASN'T USED ANY MAGIC IN HIS ATTACKS!
IF HE DOESN'T, NOT EVEN GARGOYLE CAN...
HEY, GINTA ...!!
THIS CLOWN ...
...IS AS POWERFUL AS ME?!!
YOU REALLY TOOK CARE OF ME AT THAT UNDER-GROUND LAKE, HUH?

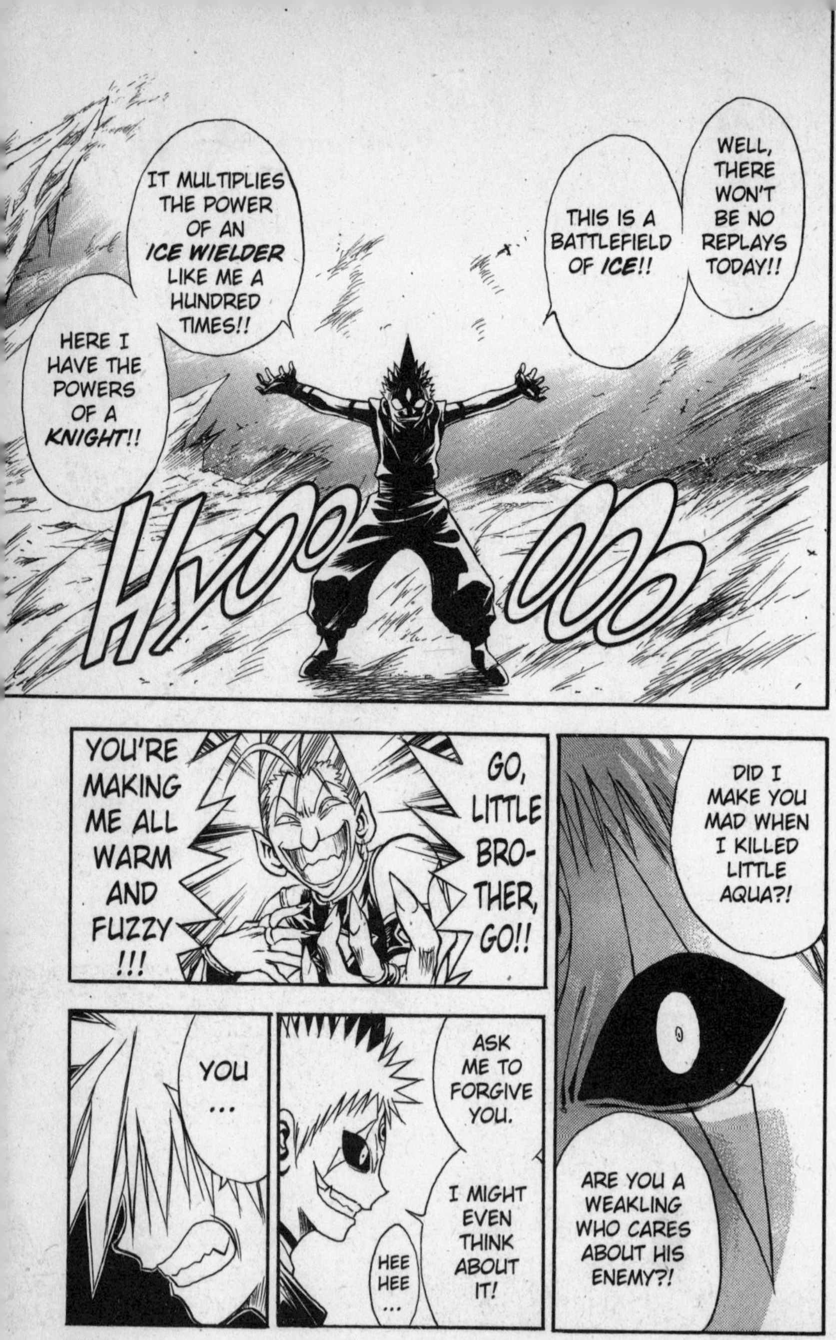
WELL, THERE WON'T BE NO REPLAYS TODAY!!
THIS IS A BATTLEFIELD OF *ICE*!!
IT MULTIPLIES THE POWER OF AN *ICE WIELDER* LIKE ME A HUNDRED TIMES!!
HERE I HAVE THE POWERS OF A *KNIGHT*!!
HYOOOOOO
DID I MAKE YOU MAD WHEN I KILLED LITTLE AQUA?!
ARE YOU A WEAKLING WHO CARES ABOUT HIS ENEMY?!
GO, LITTLE BRO-THER, GO!!
YOU'RE MAKING ME ALL WARM AND FUZZY!!!
ASK ME TO FORGIVE YOU.
I MIGHT EVEN THINK ABOUT IT!
HEE HEE...
YOU...

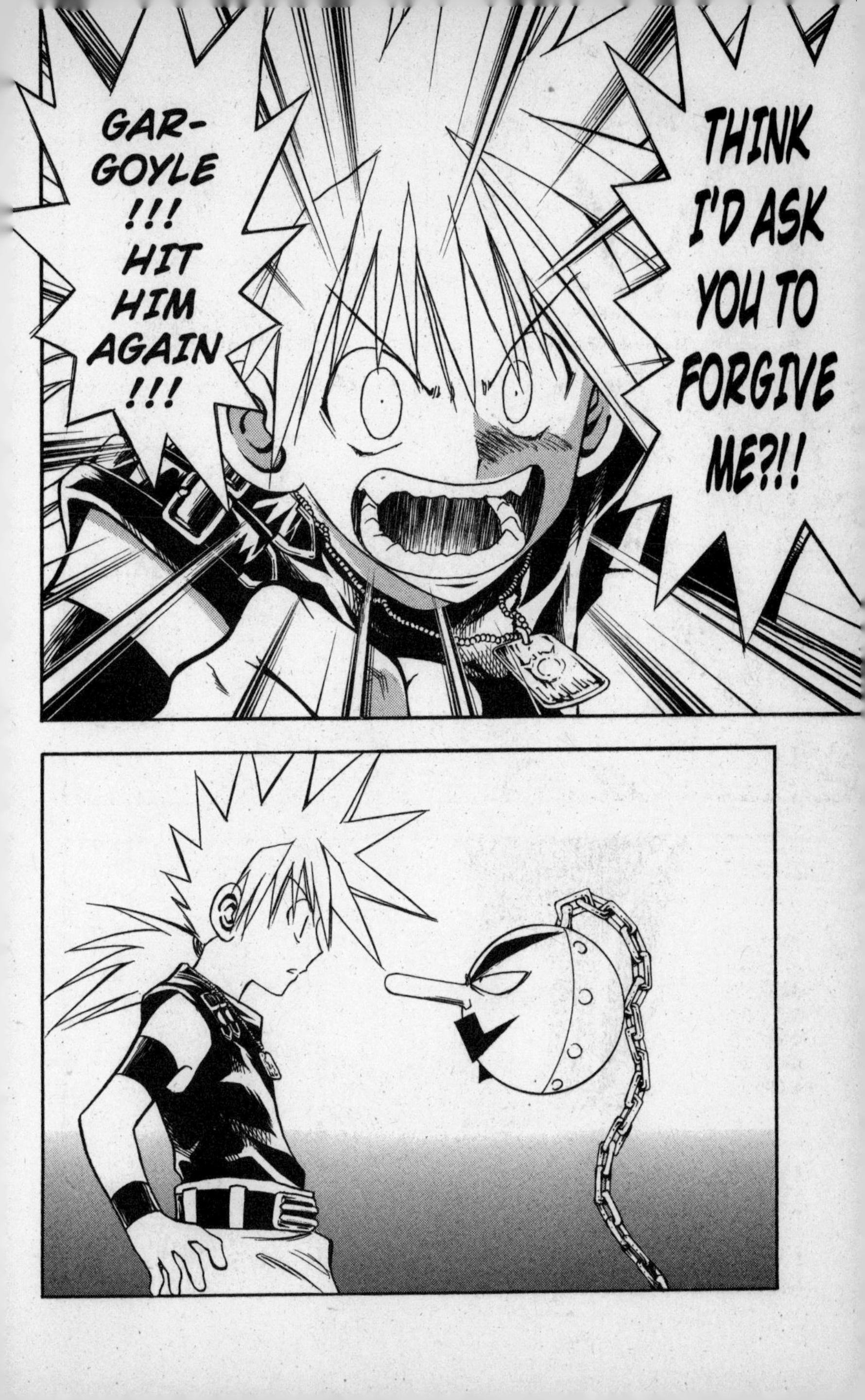
THINK I'D ASK YOU TO FORGIVE ME?!!
GAR-GOYLE!!! HIT HIM AGAIN!!!

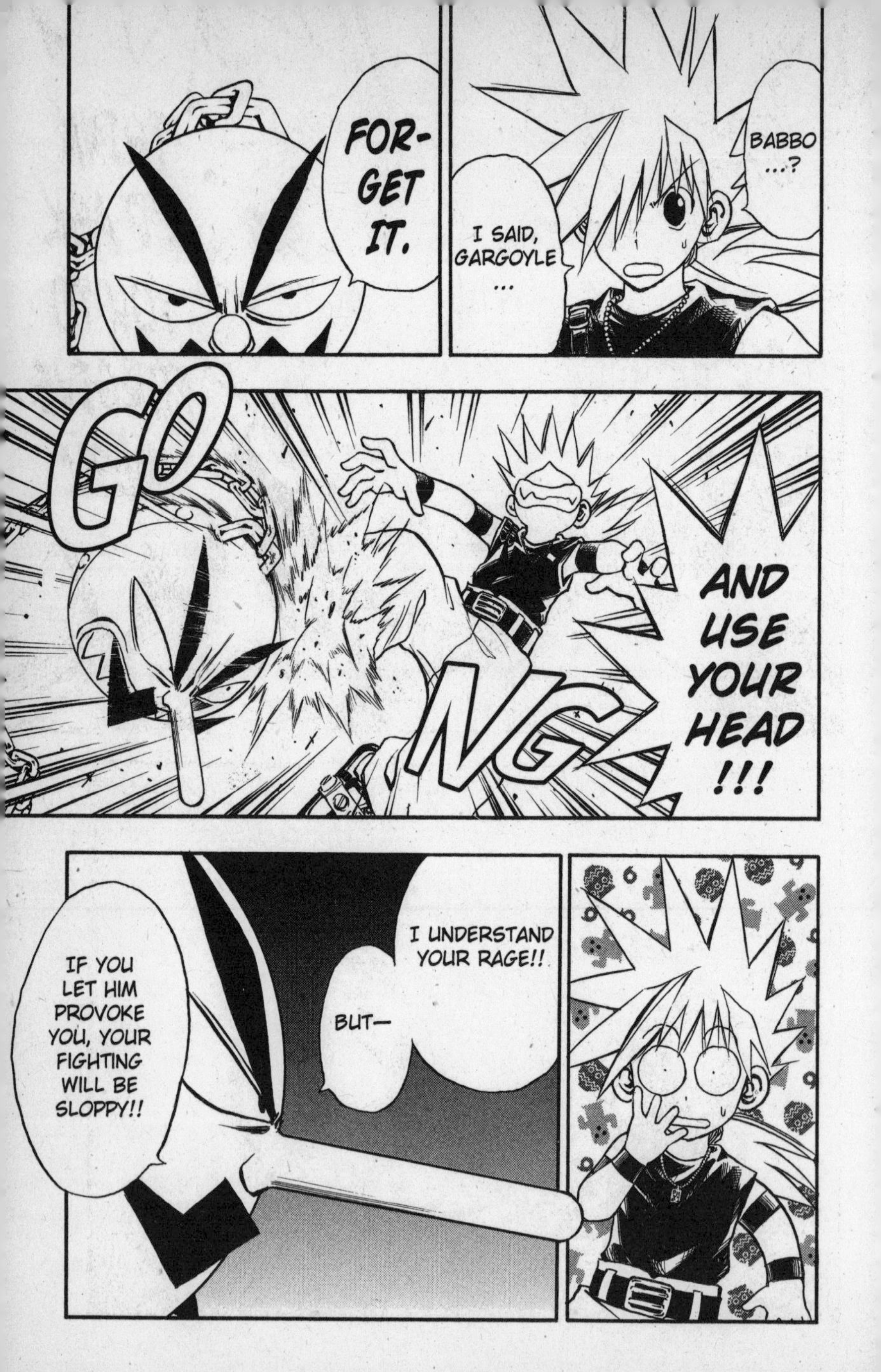
BABBO ...?
I SAID, GARGOYLE ...
FOR-GET IT.
AND USE YOUR HEAD!!!
GO
NG
I UNDERSTAND YOUR RAGE!!
BUT—
IF YOU LET HIM PROVOKE YOU, YOUR FIGHTING WILL BE SLOPPY!!

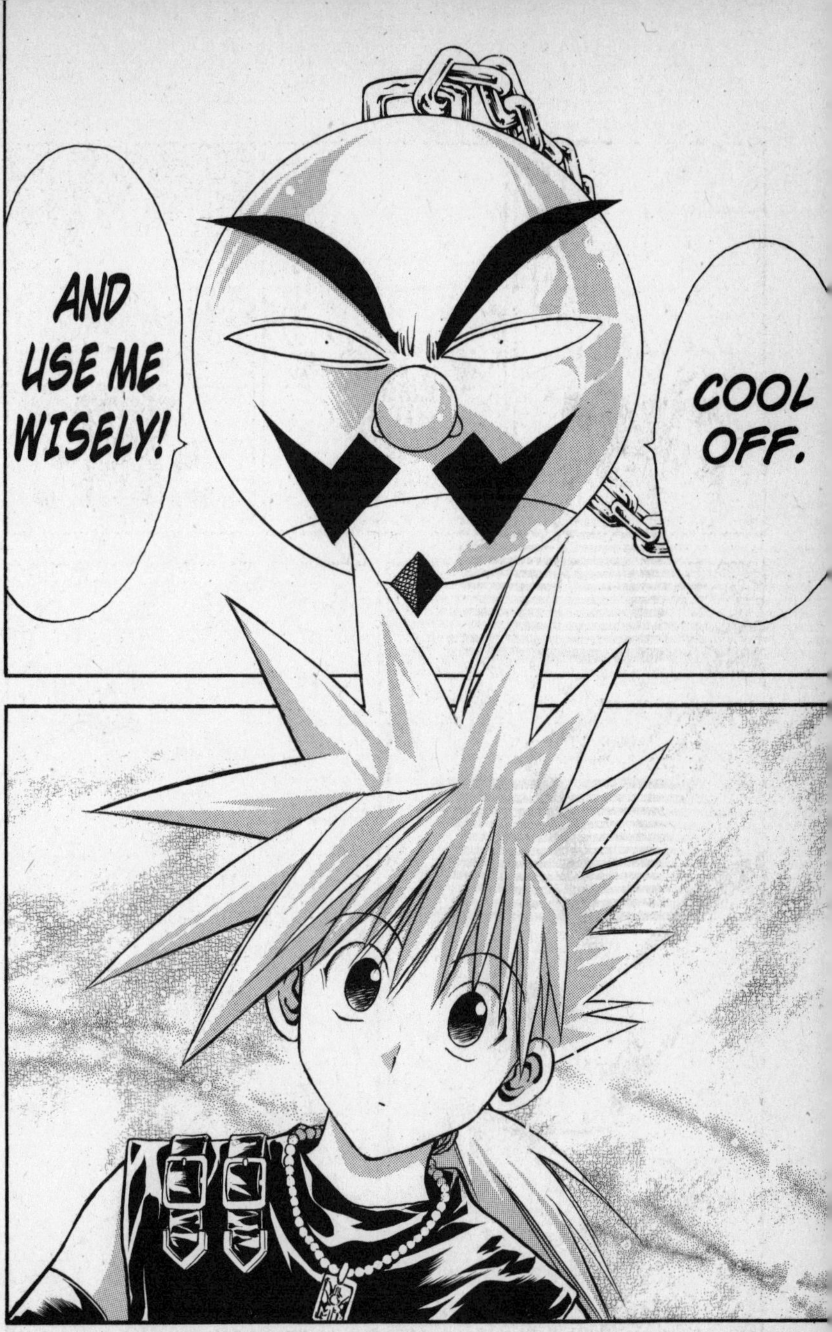
COOL OFF.
AND USE ME WISELY!

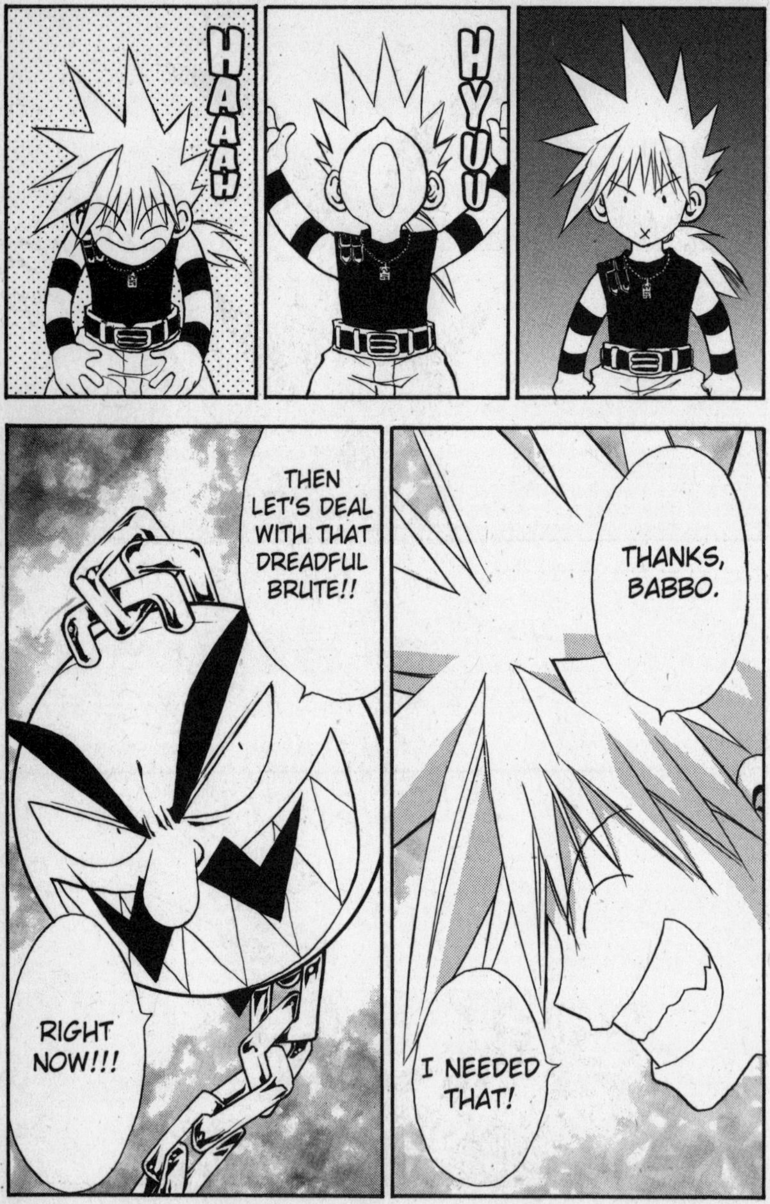
HYUUU
HAAAAH
THANKS, BABBO.
I NEEDED THAT!
THEN LET'S DEAL WITH THAT DREADFUL BRUTE!!
RIGHT NOW!!!

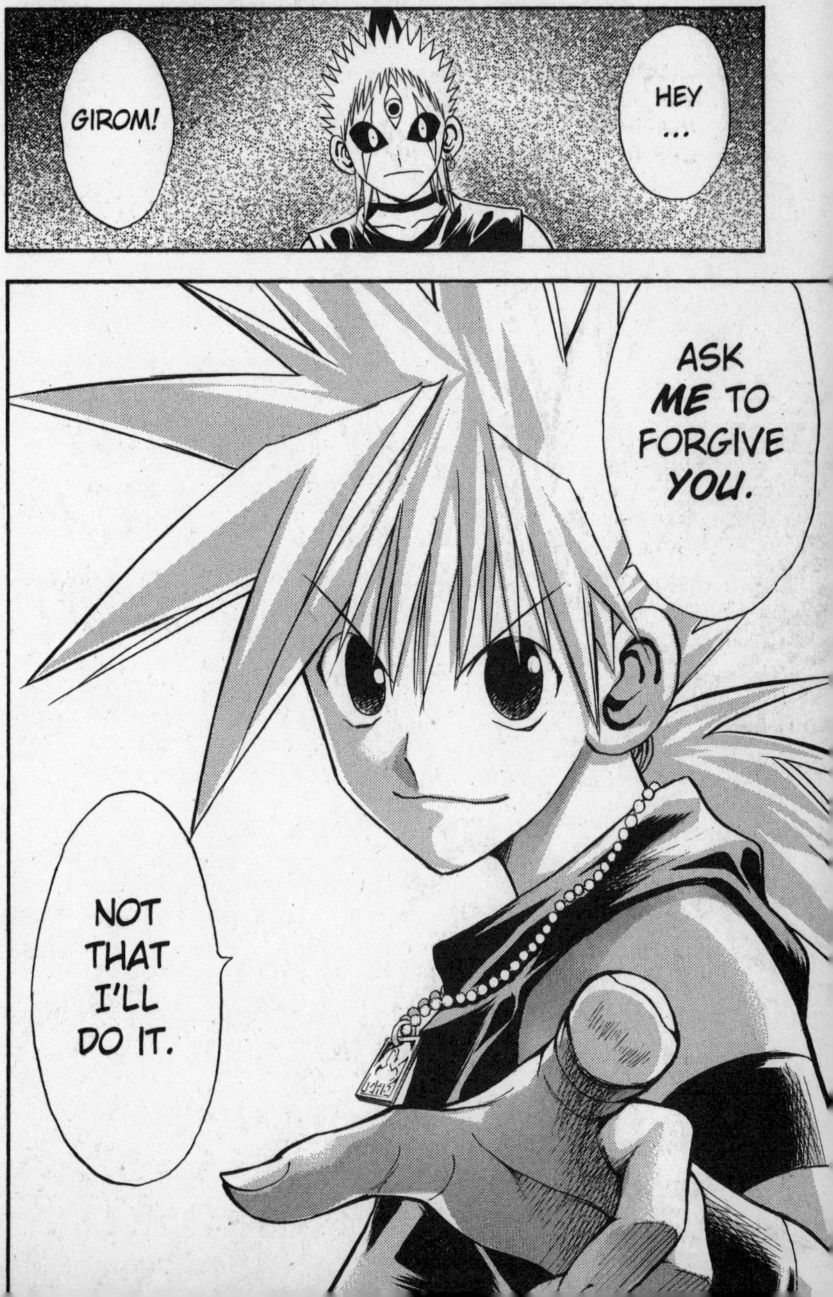
HEY ...
GIROM!
ASK *ME* TO FORGIVE *YOU*.
NOT THAT I'LL DO IT.

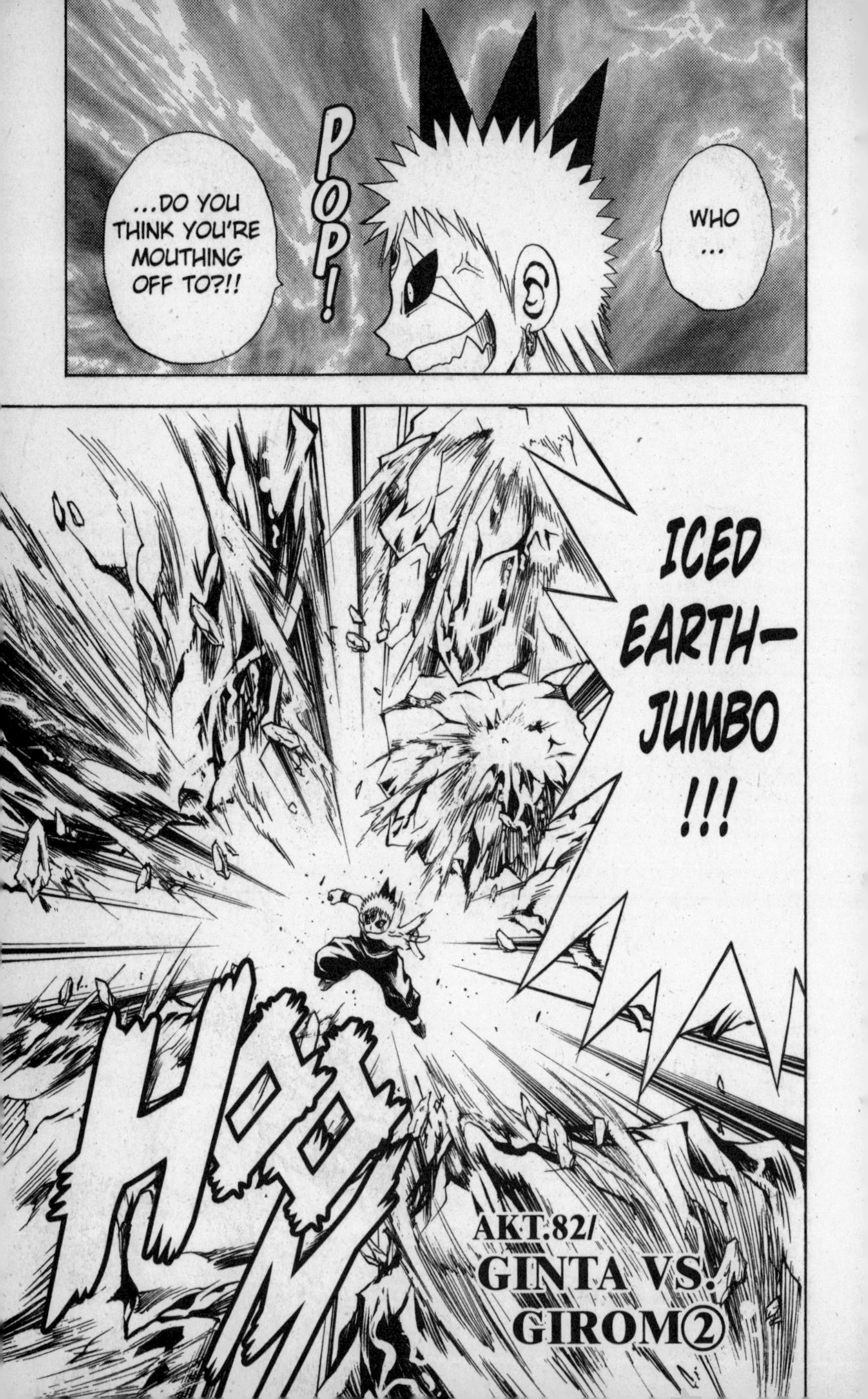
WHO ...
POP!
...DO YOU THINK YOU'RE MOUTHING OFF TO?!!
ICED EARTH-JUMBO !!!
AKT.82/
GINTA VS.
GIROM②

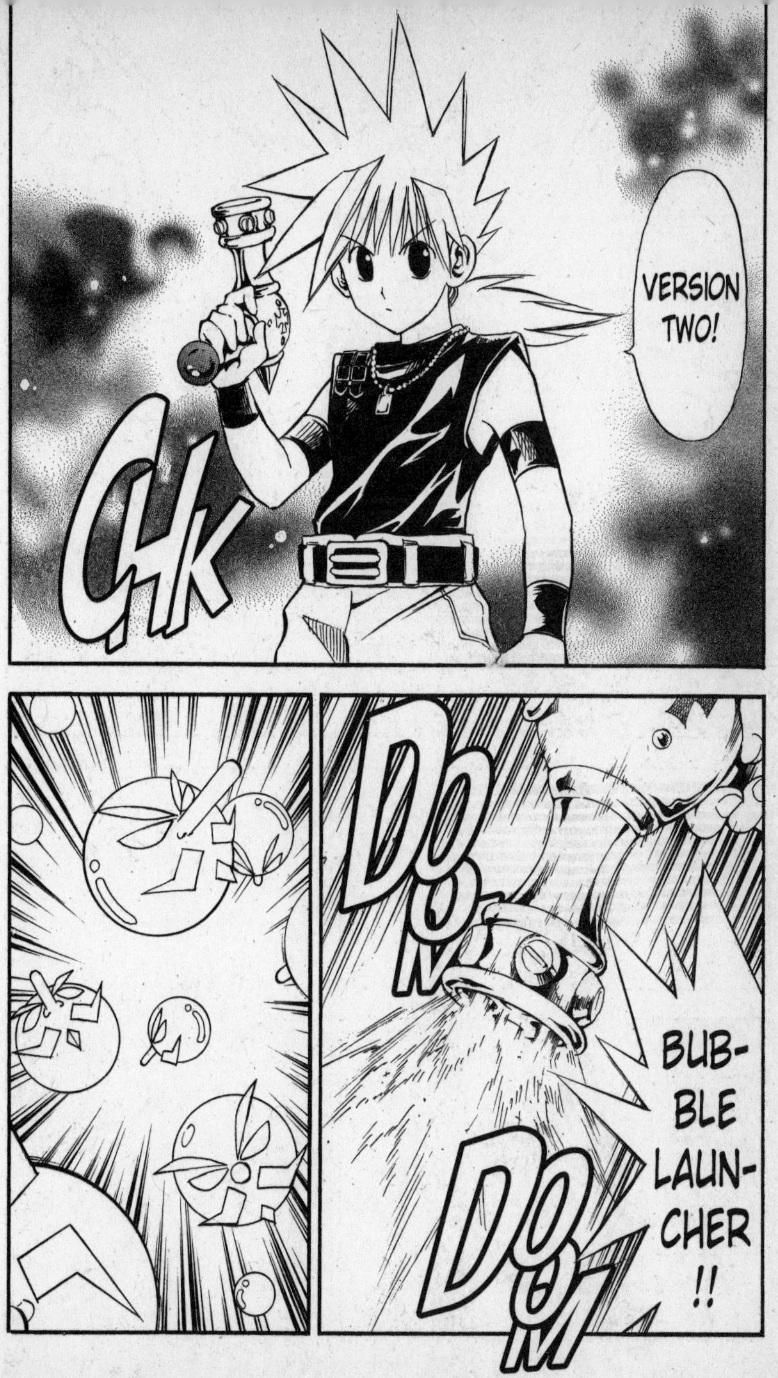
VERSION TWO!
CHK
DOON
BUB-BLE LAUN-CHER!!
DOOM

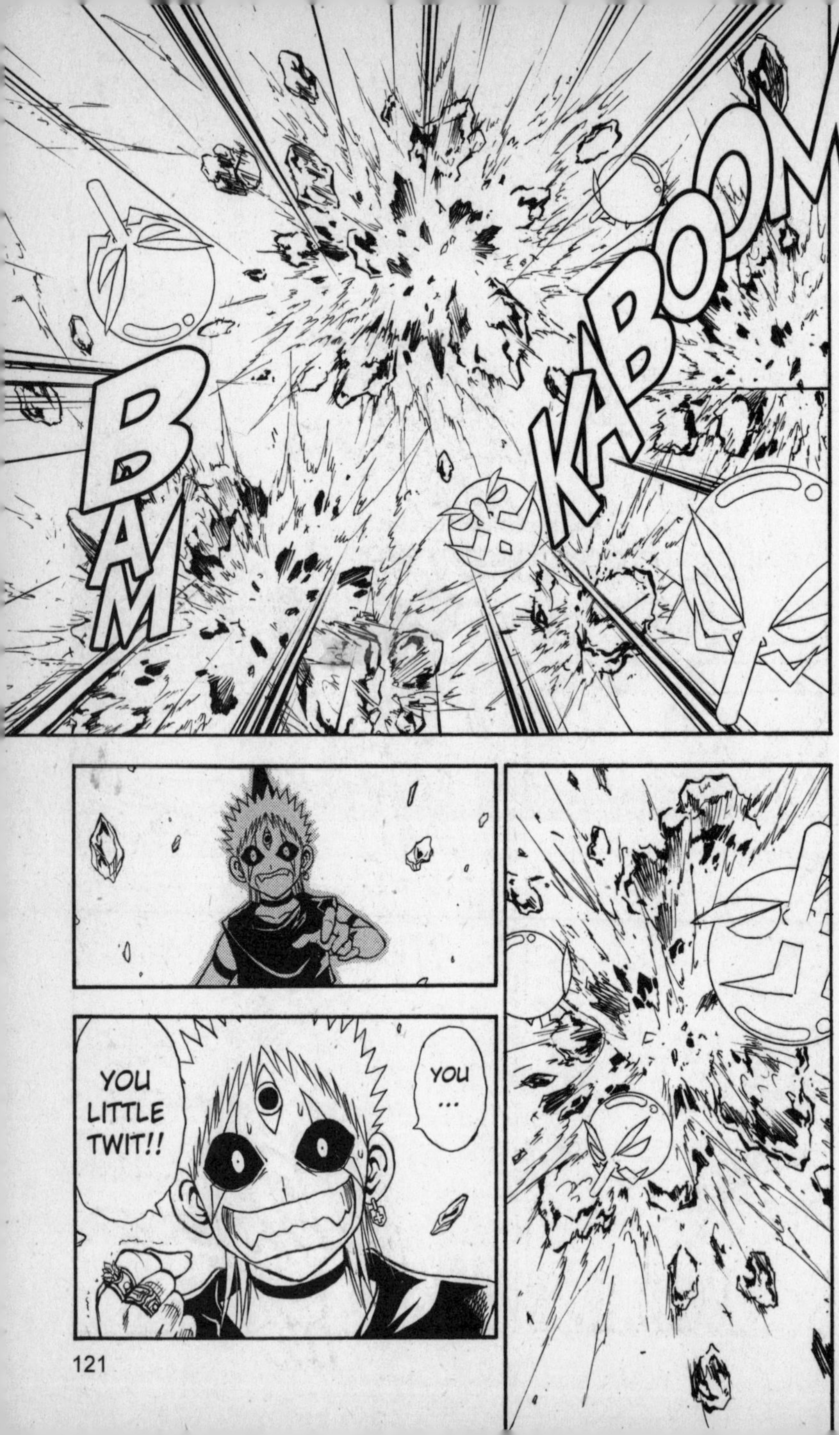
KABOOM
BAM
YOU ...
YOU LITTLE TWIT!!

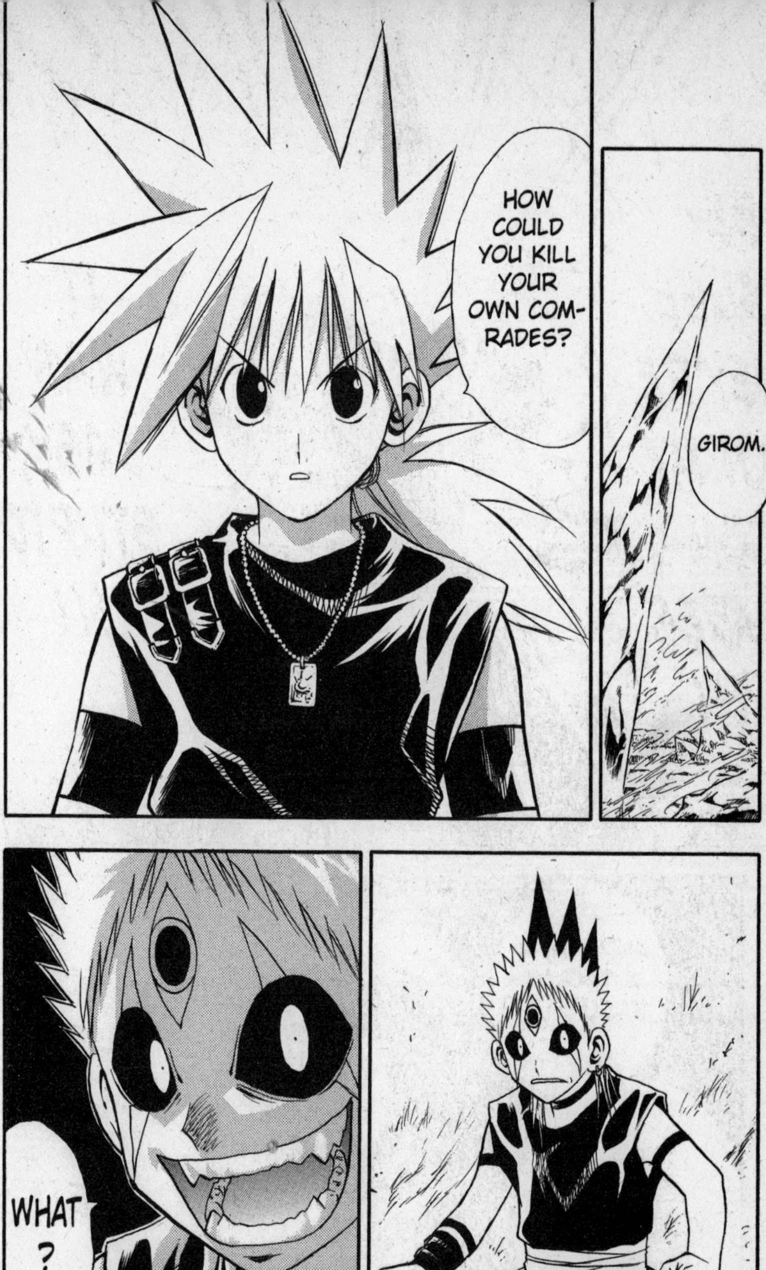
GIROM.
HOW COULD YOU KILL YOUR OWN COM-RADES?
WHAT ?

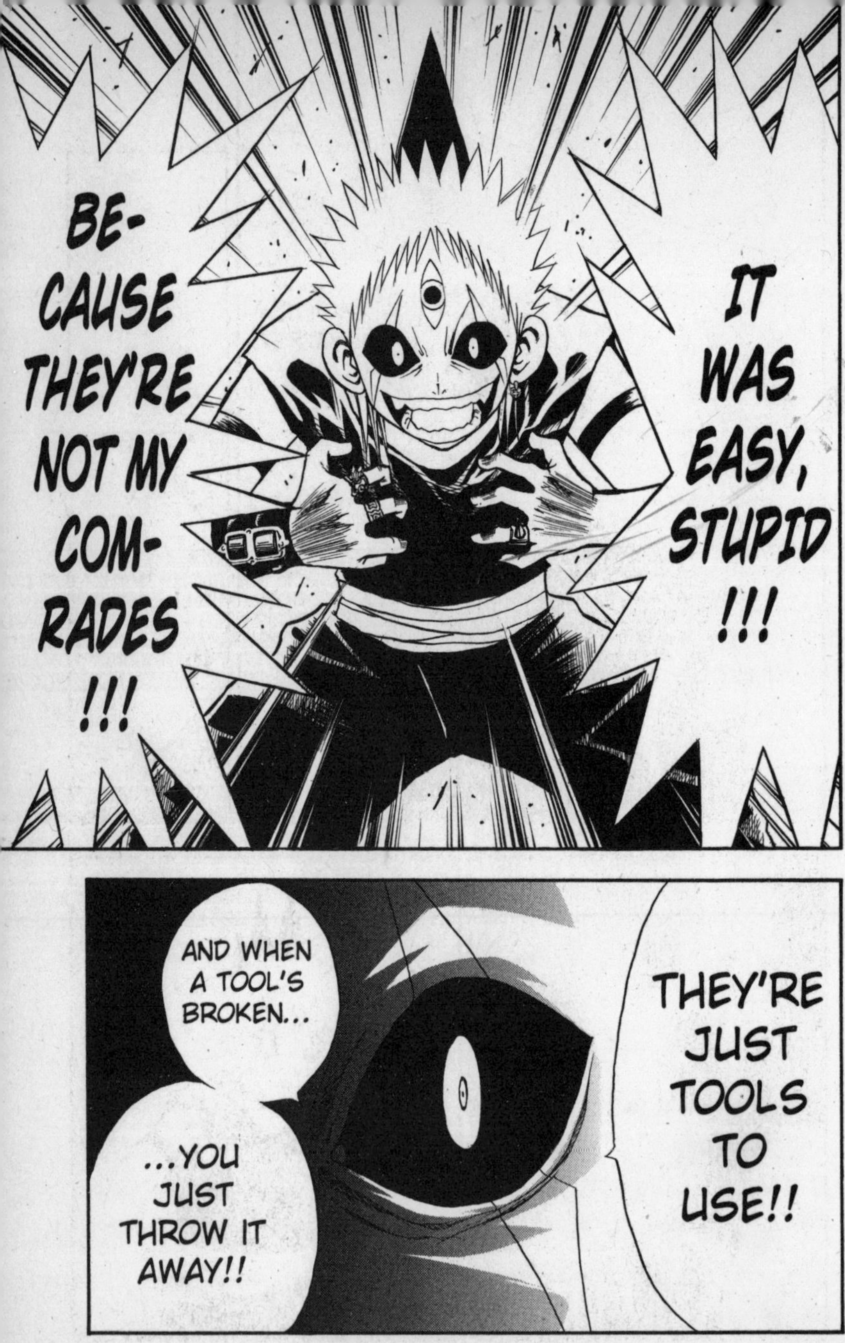
IT WAS EASY, STUPID!!!
BECAUSE THEY'RE NOT MY COMRADES!!!
THEY'RE JUST TOOLS TO USE!!
AND WHEN A TOOL'S BROKEN...
...YOU JUST THROW IT AWAY!!

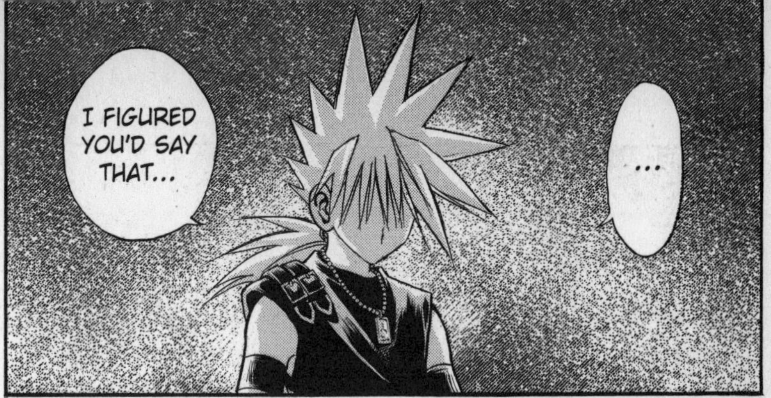
...
I FIGURED YOU'D SAY THAT...

AKT.82/ GINTA VS. GIROM②

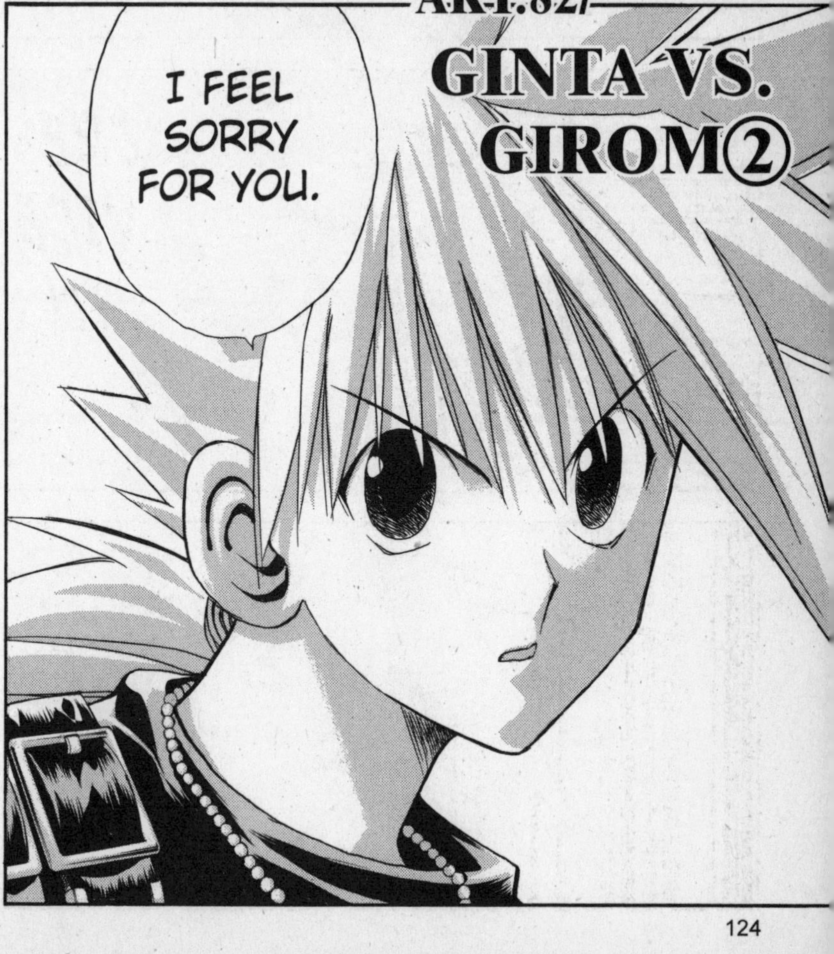
I FEEL SORRY FOR YOU.

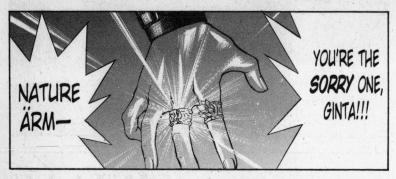

NATURE ÄRM—

YOU'RE THE **SORRY** ONE, GINTA!!!

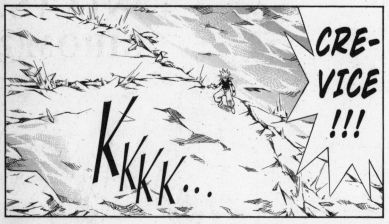

CRE- VICE !!!

K K K K...

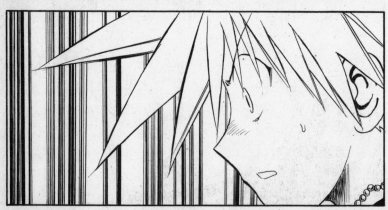

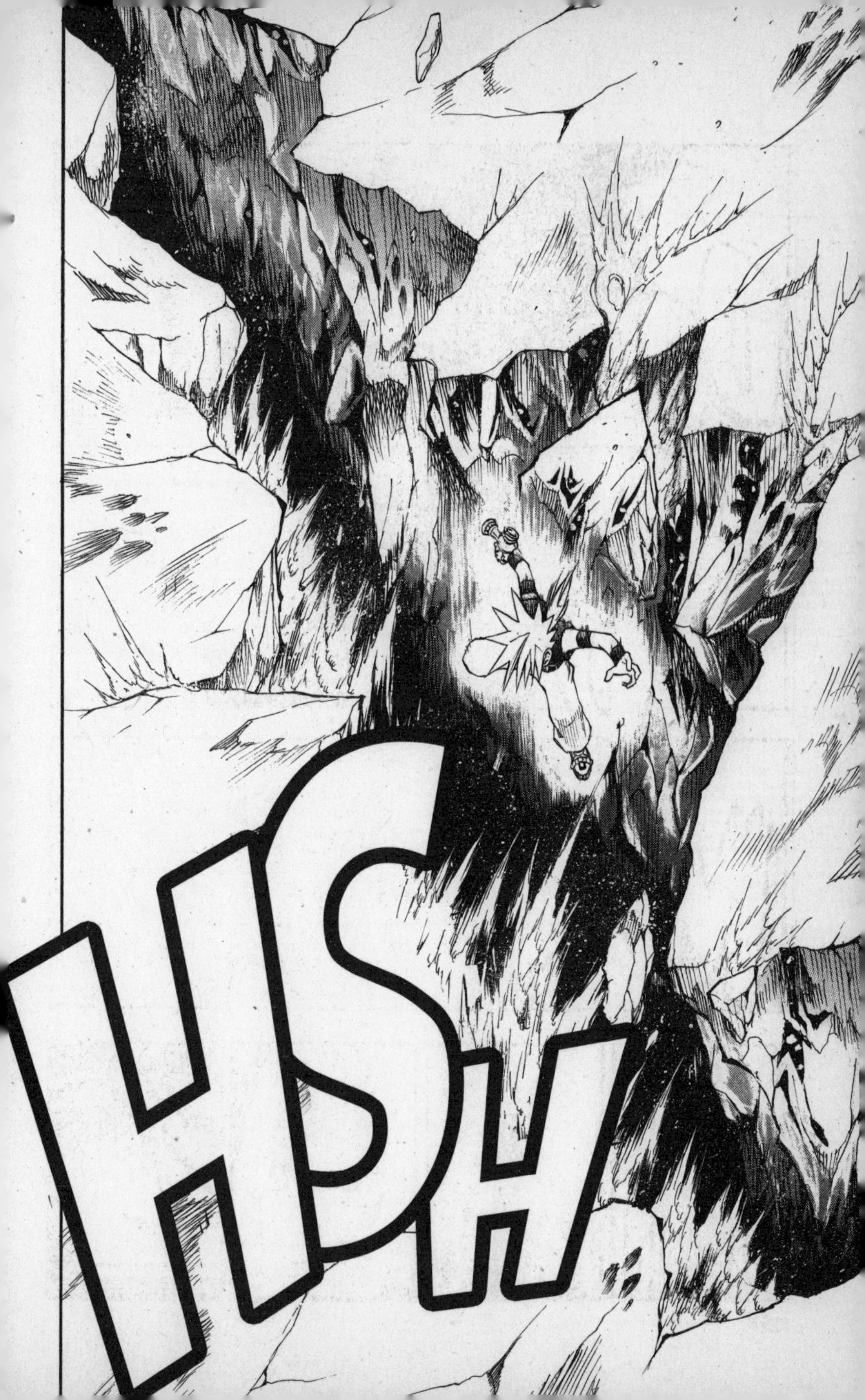
HSH

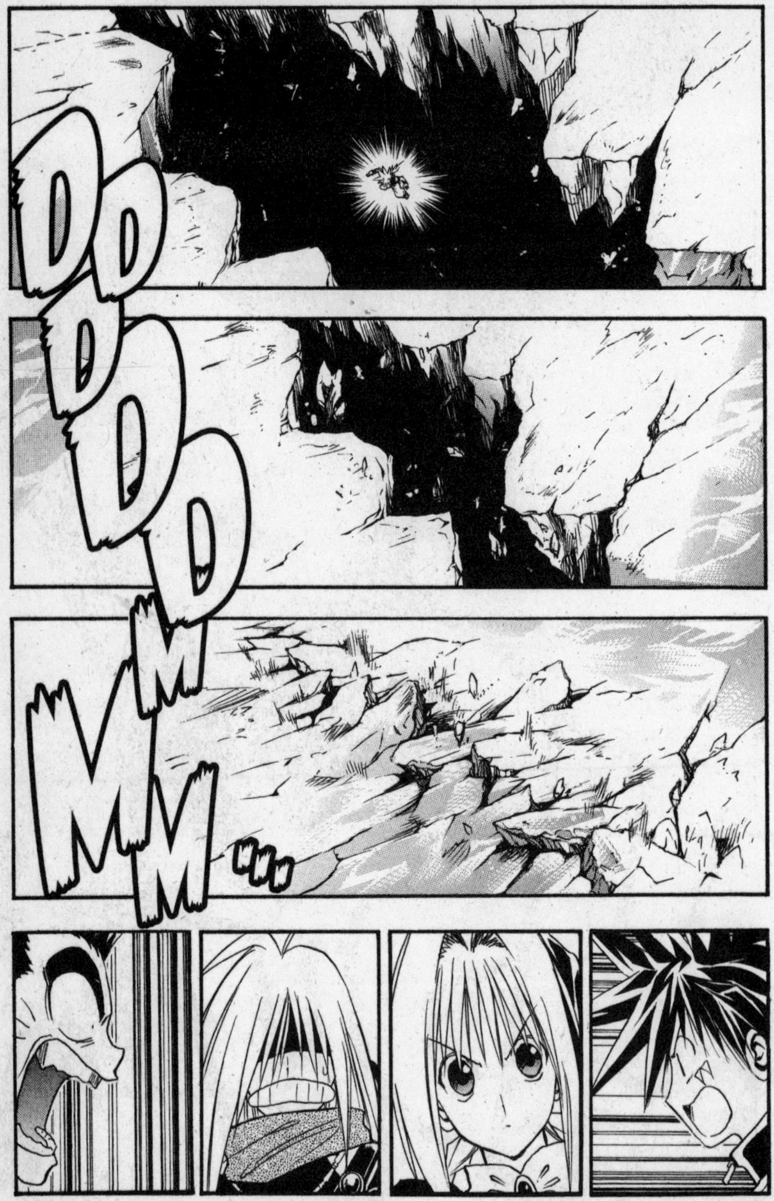
DDDDDMMMM...

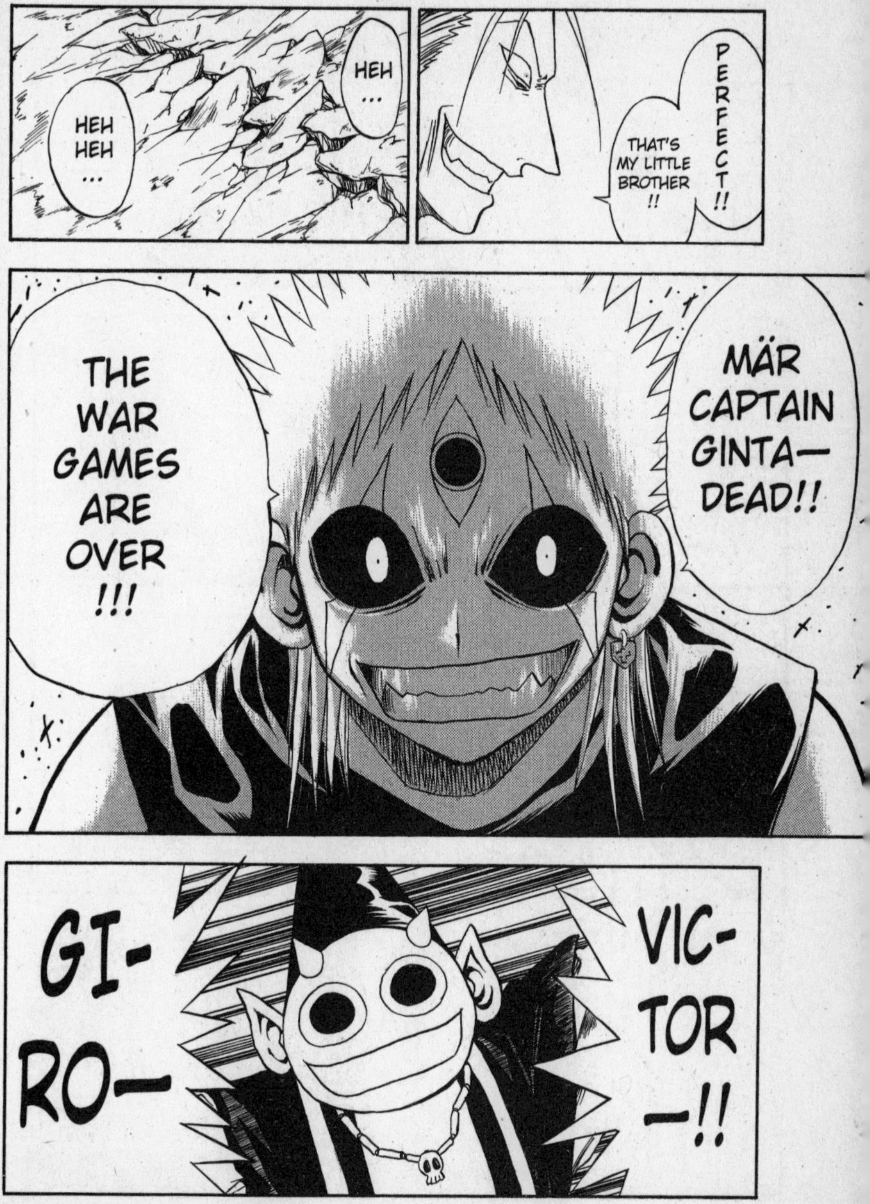
PERFECT!!
THAT'S MY LITTLE BROTHER!!
HEH ...
HEH HEH ...
MÄR CAPTAIN GINTA— DEAD!!
THE WAR GAMES ARE OVER!!!
VIC-TOR—!!
GI-RO—

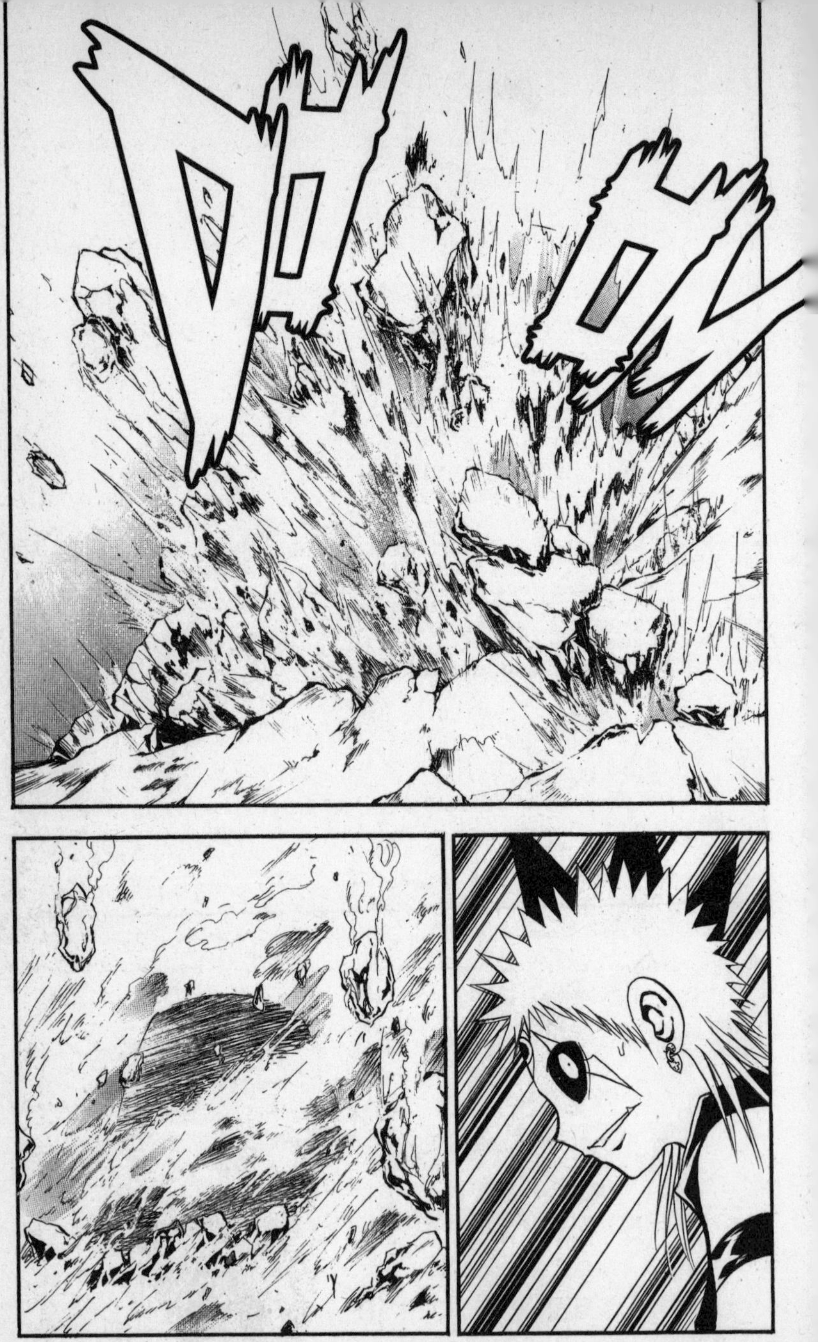
VOOM

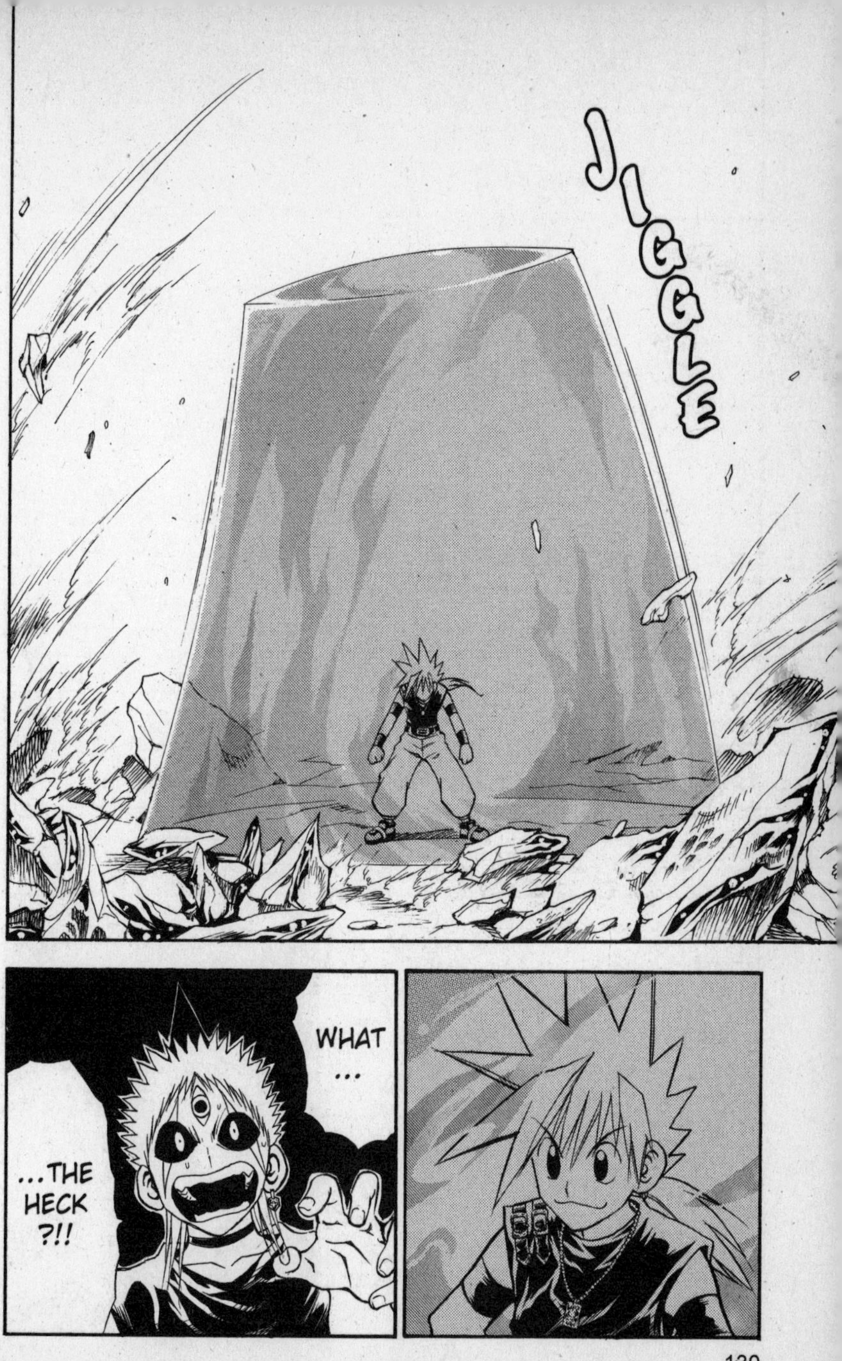
JIGGLE
WHAT ...
...THE HECK ?!!

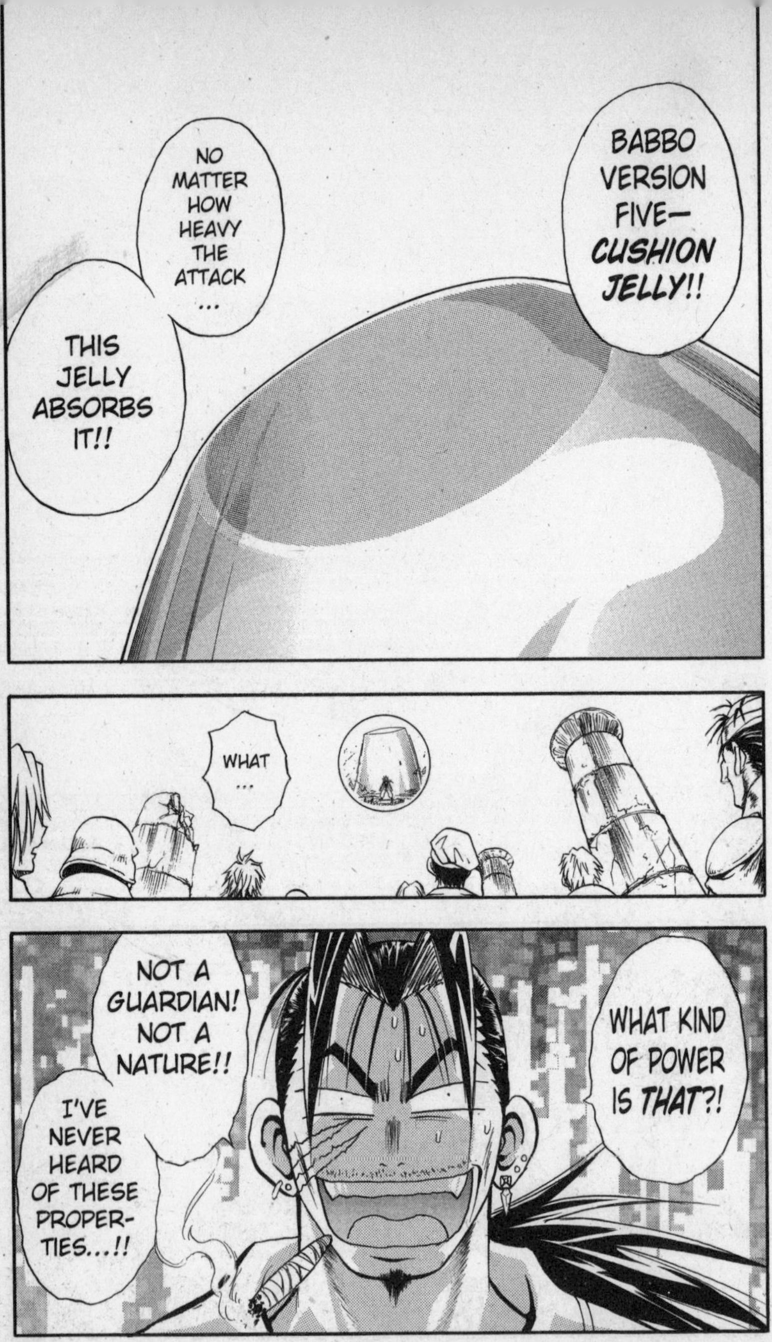
BABBO VERSION FIVE— CUSHION JELLY!!
NO MATTER HOW HEAVY THE ATTACK...
THIS JELLY ABSORBS IT!!
WHAT...
WHAT KIND OF POWER IS THAT?!
NOT A GUARDIAN! NOT A NATURE!!
I'VE NEVER HEARD OF THESE PROPER-TIES...!!

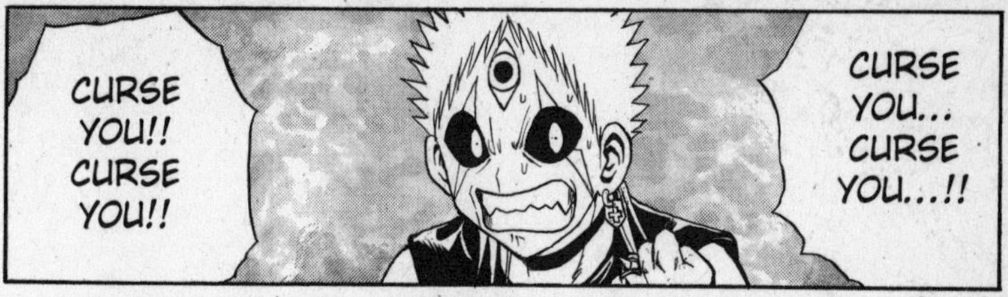
CURSE YOU... CURSE YOU...!!
CURSE YOU!! CURSE YOU!!

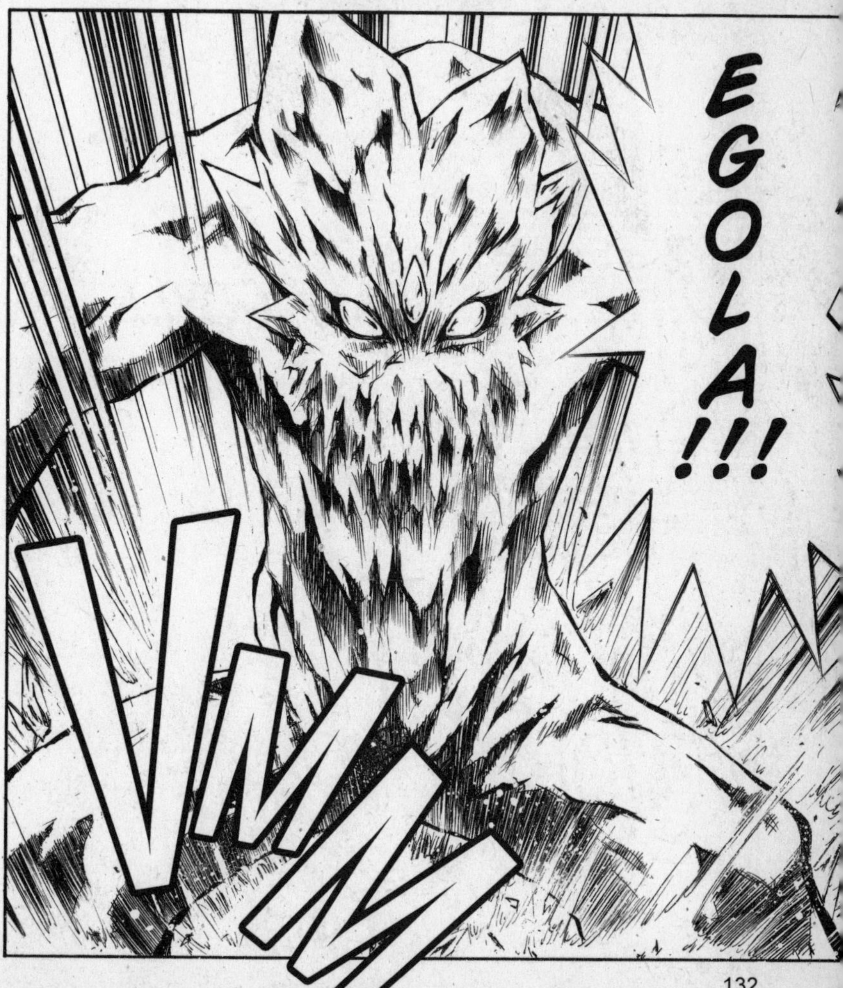
EGOLA!!!
VMMM

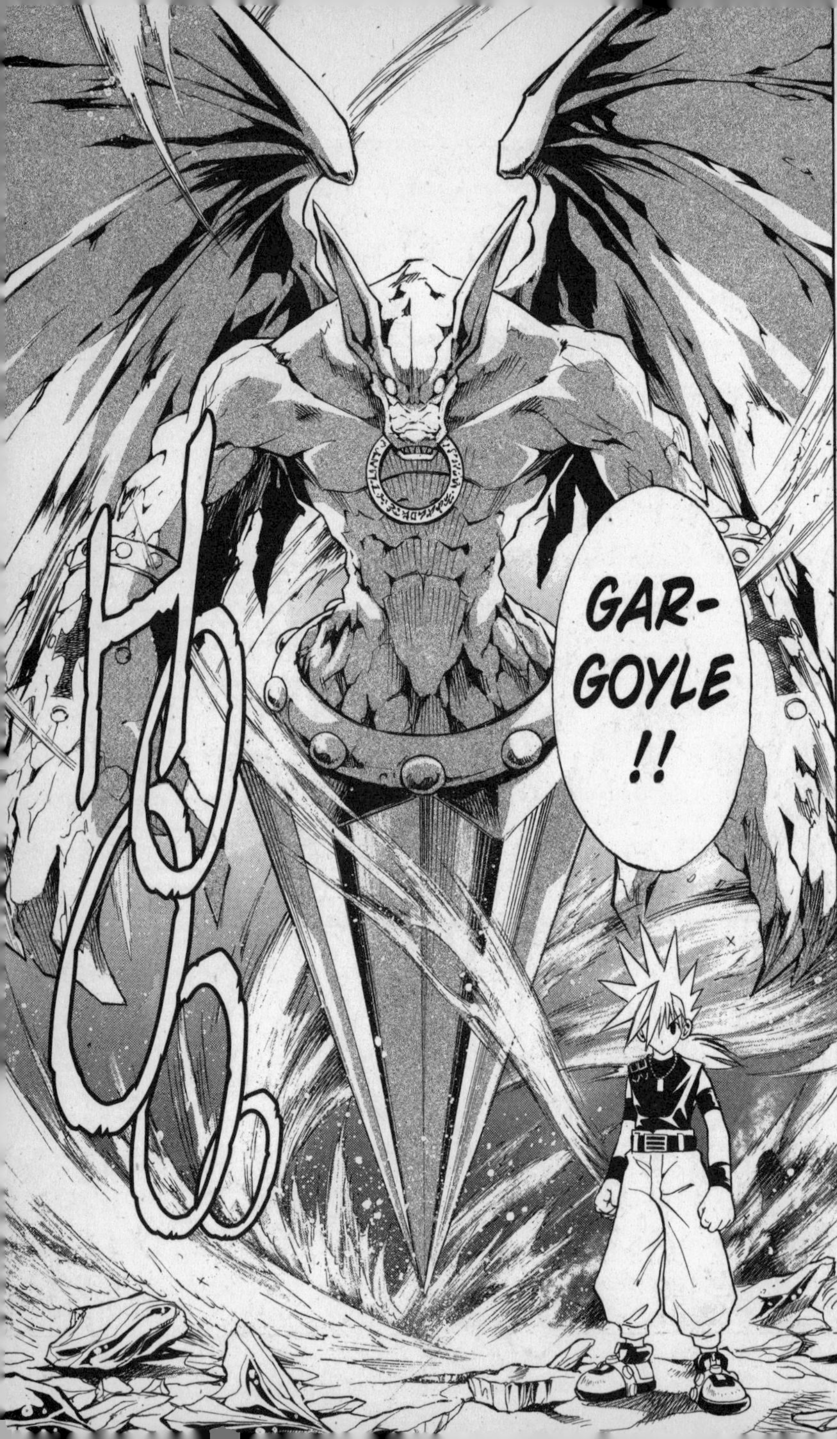
GAR-GOYLE !!

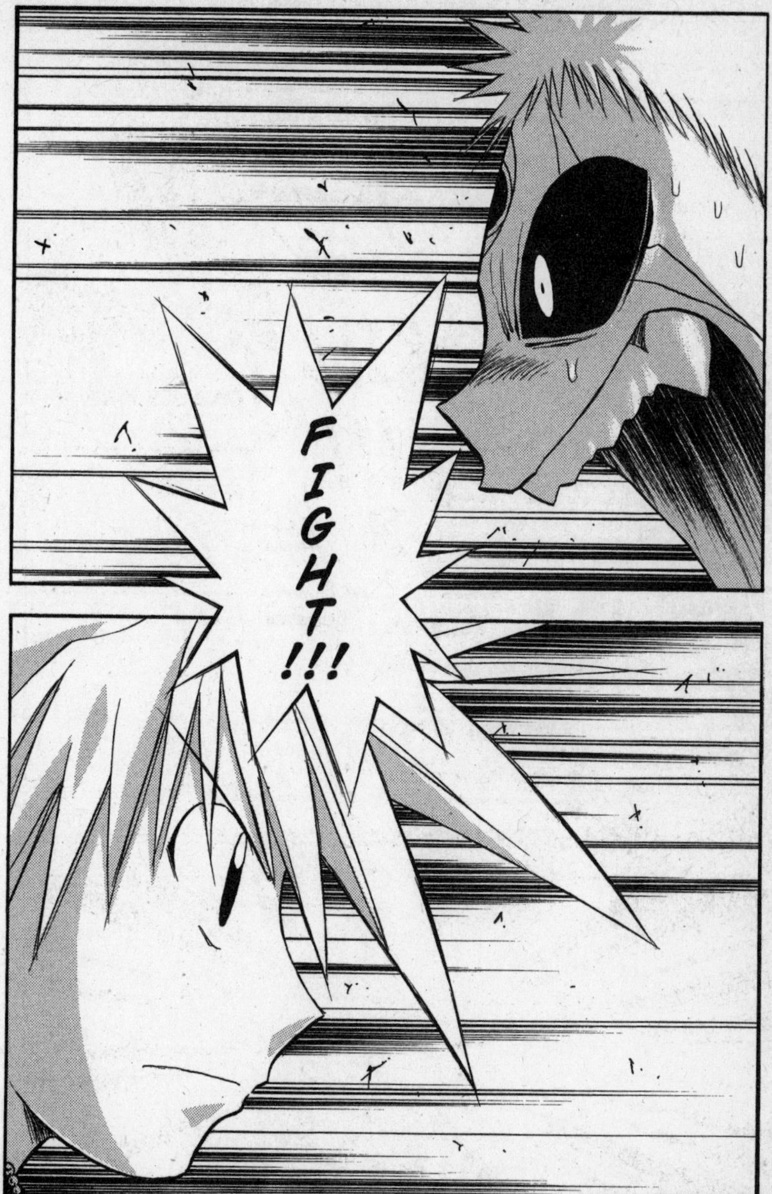
FIGHT!!!

AKT.83/GINTA VS. GIROM③

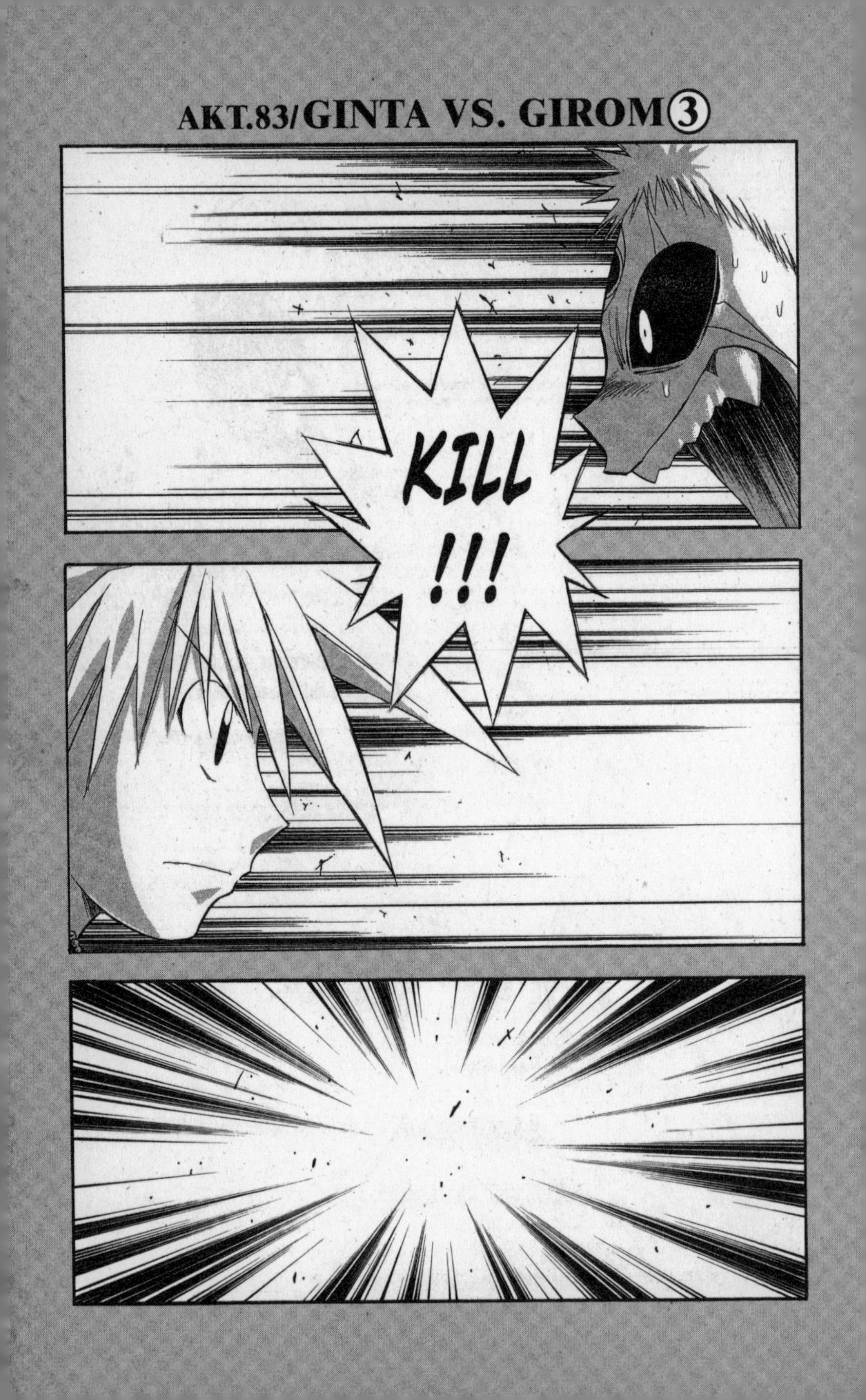
KILL !!!

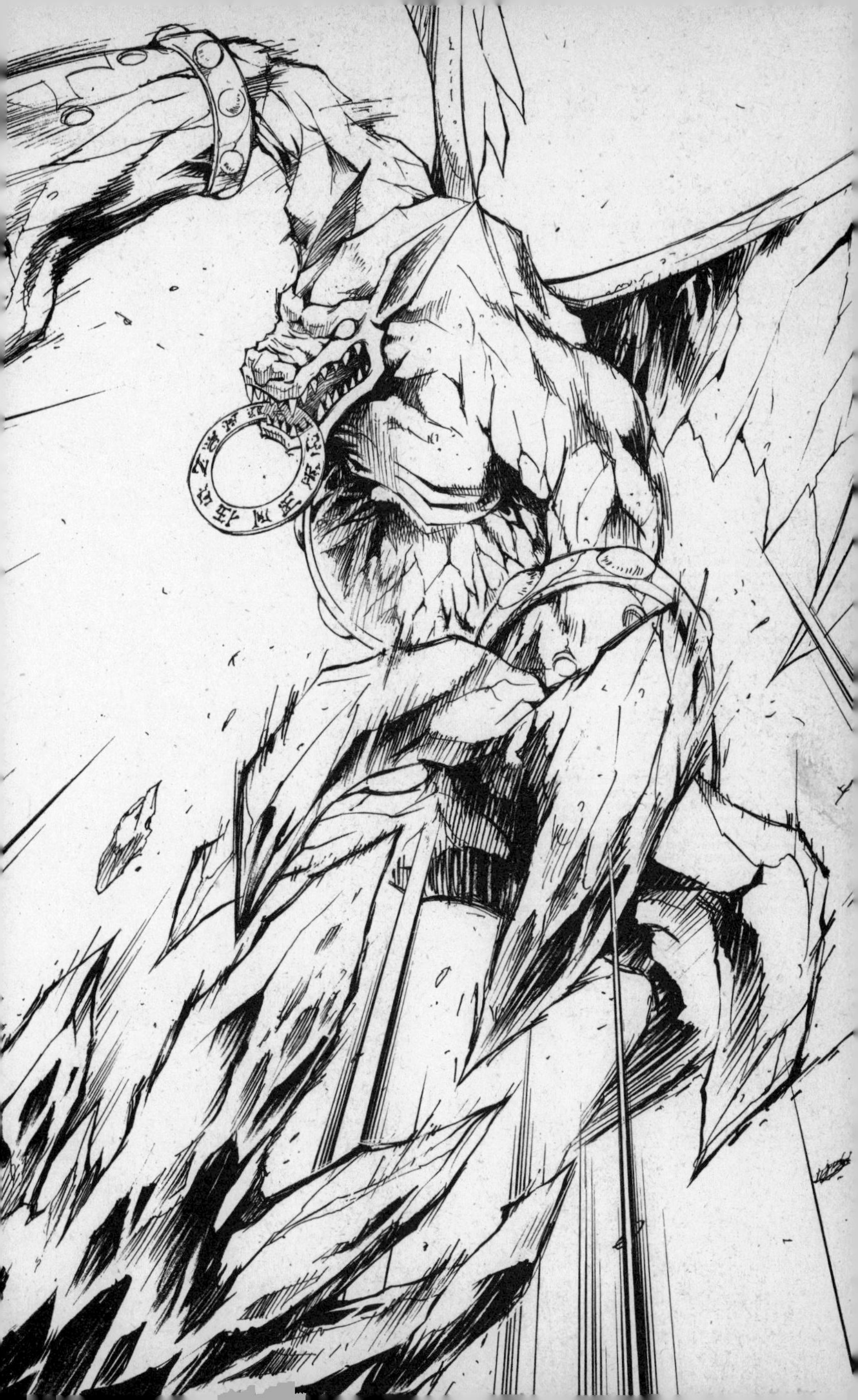

AKT.83/ GINTA VS. GIROM③

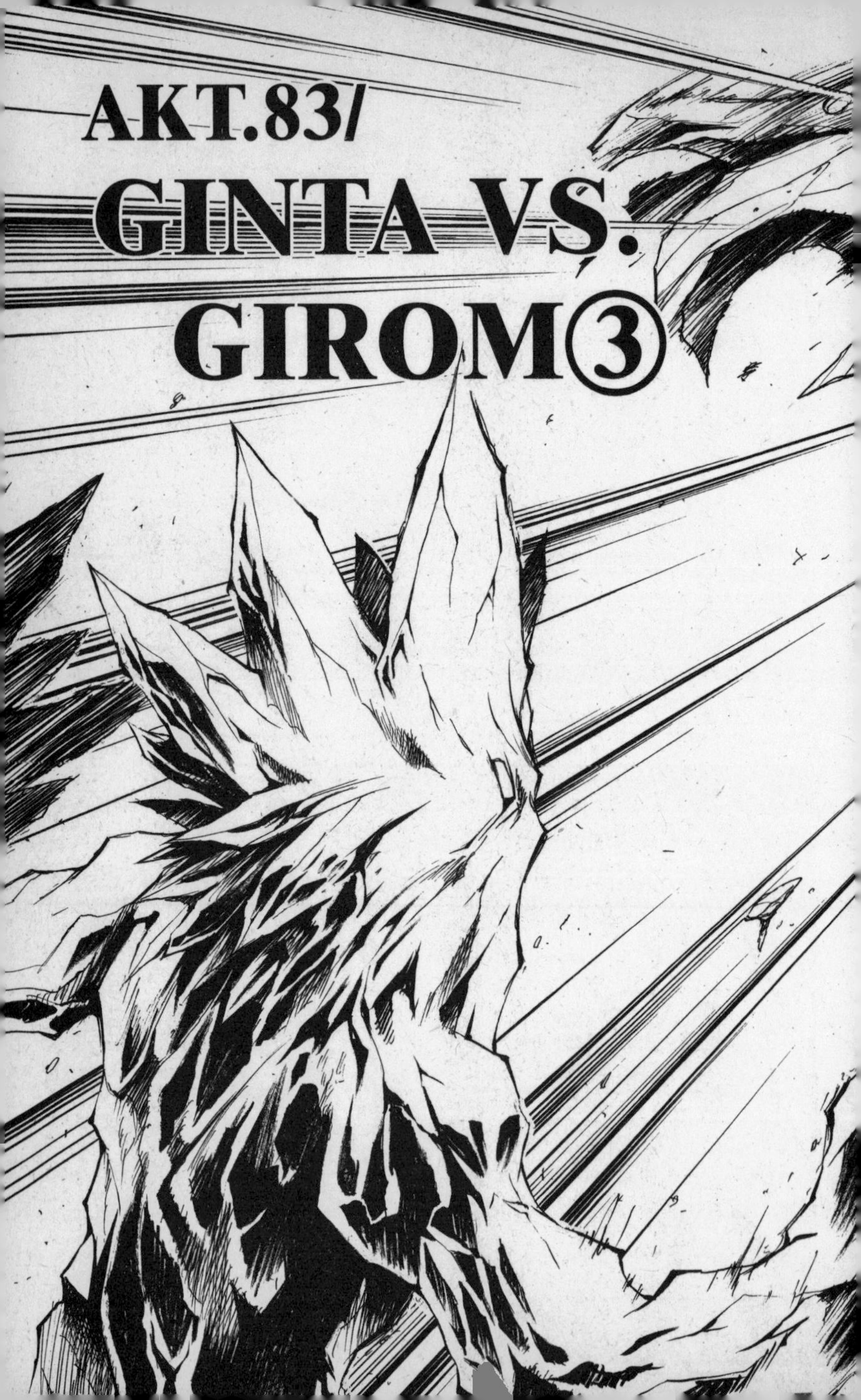

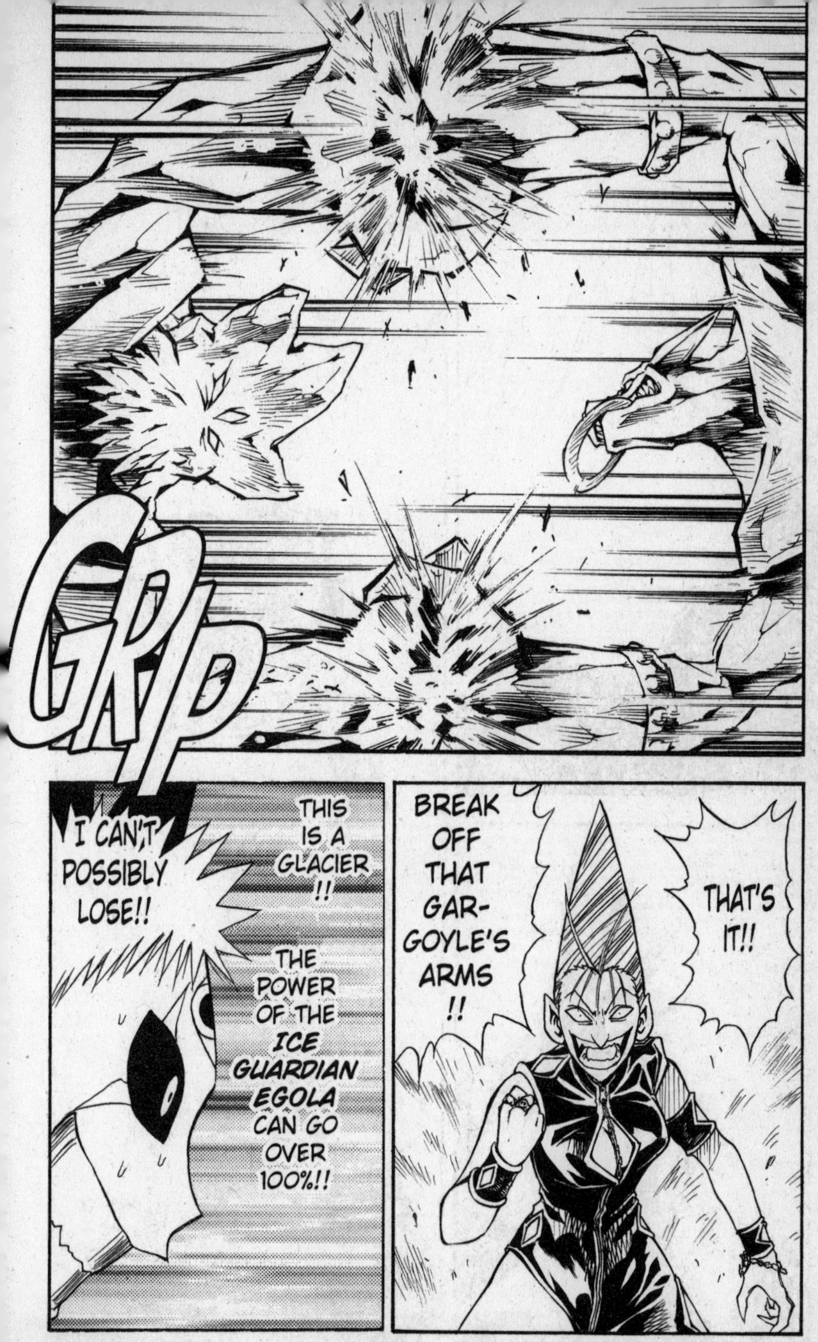
GRIP
THAT'S IT!!
BREAK OFF THAT GAR-GOYLE'S ARMS!!
THIS IS A GLACIER!!
THE POWER OF THE ICE GUARDIAN EGOLA CAN GO OVER 100%!!
I CAN'T POSSIBLY LOSE!!

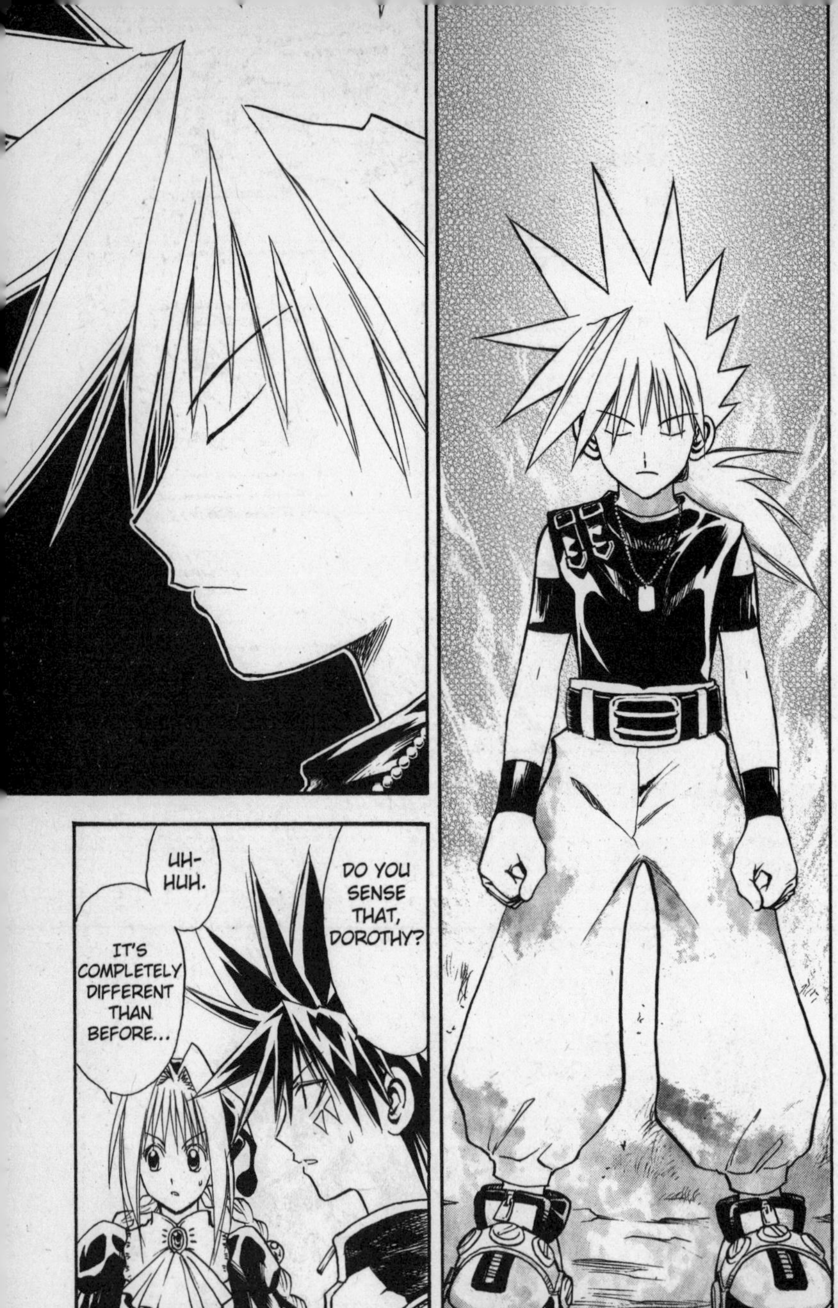
DO YOU SENSE THAT, DOROTHY?
UH-HUH.
IT'S COMPLETELY DIFFERENT THAN BEFORE...

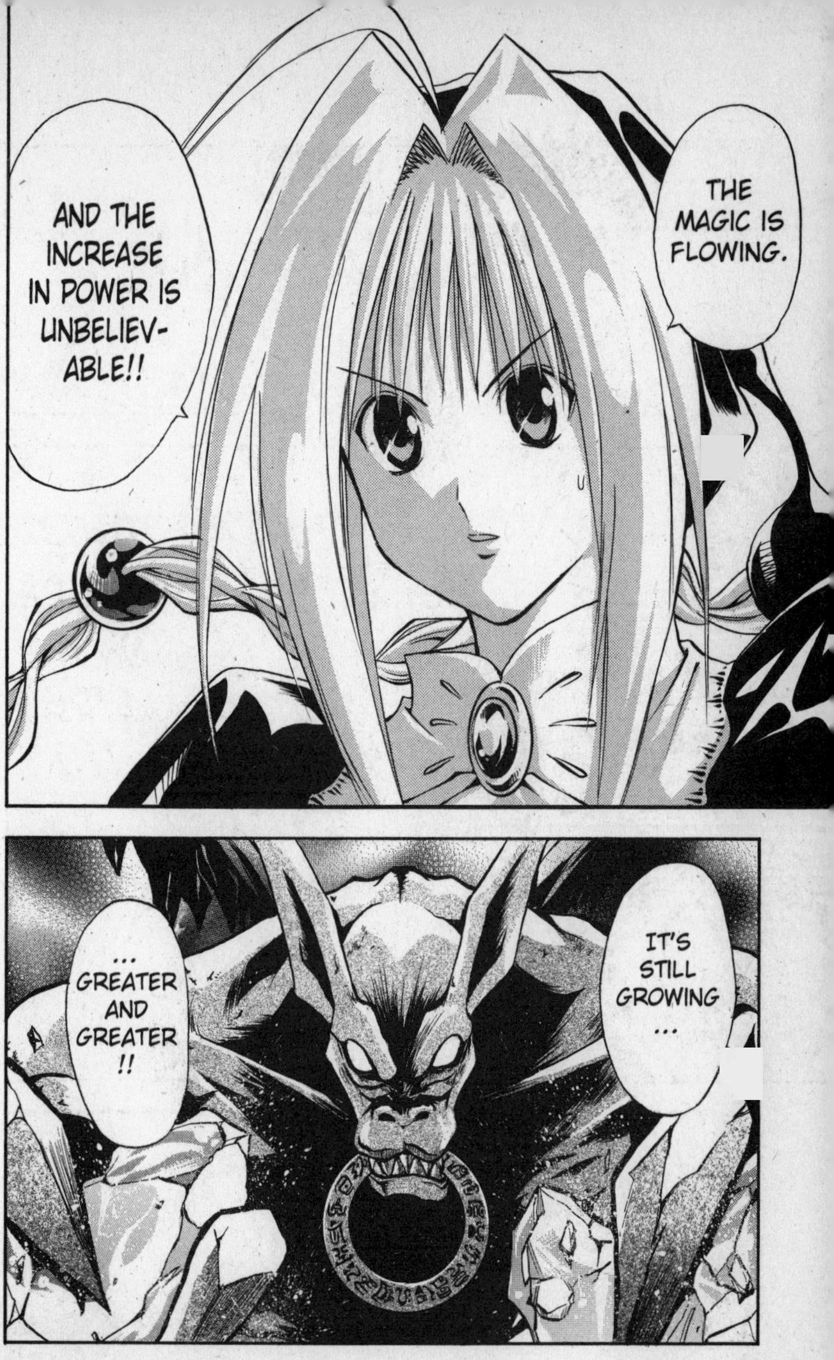
THE MAGIC IS FLOWING.
AND THE INCREASE IN POWER IS UNBELIEV-ABLE!!
IT'S STILL GROWING ...
... GREATER AND GREATER !!

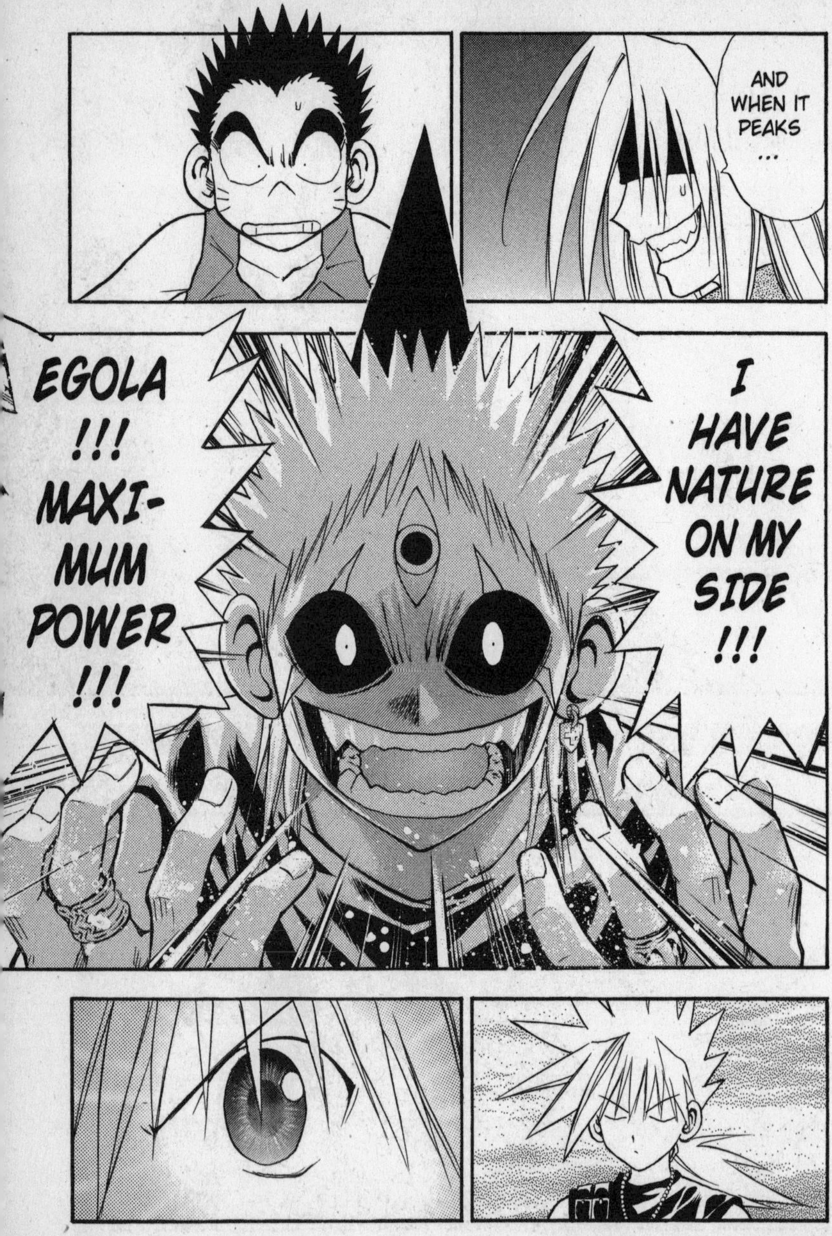
AND WHEN IT PEAKS ...
I HAVE NATURE ON MY SIDE !!!
EGOLA !!! MAXI-MUM POWER !!!

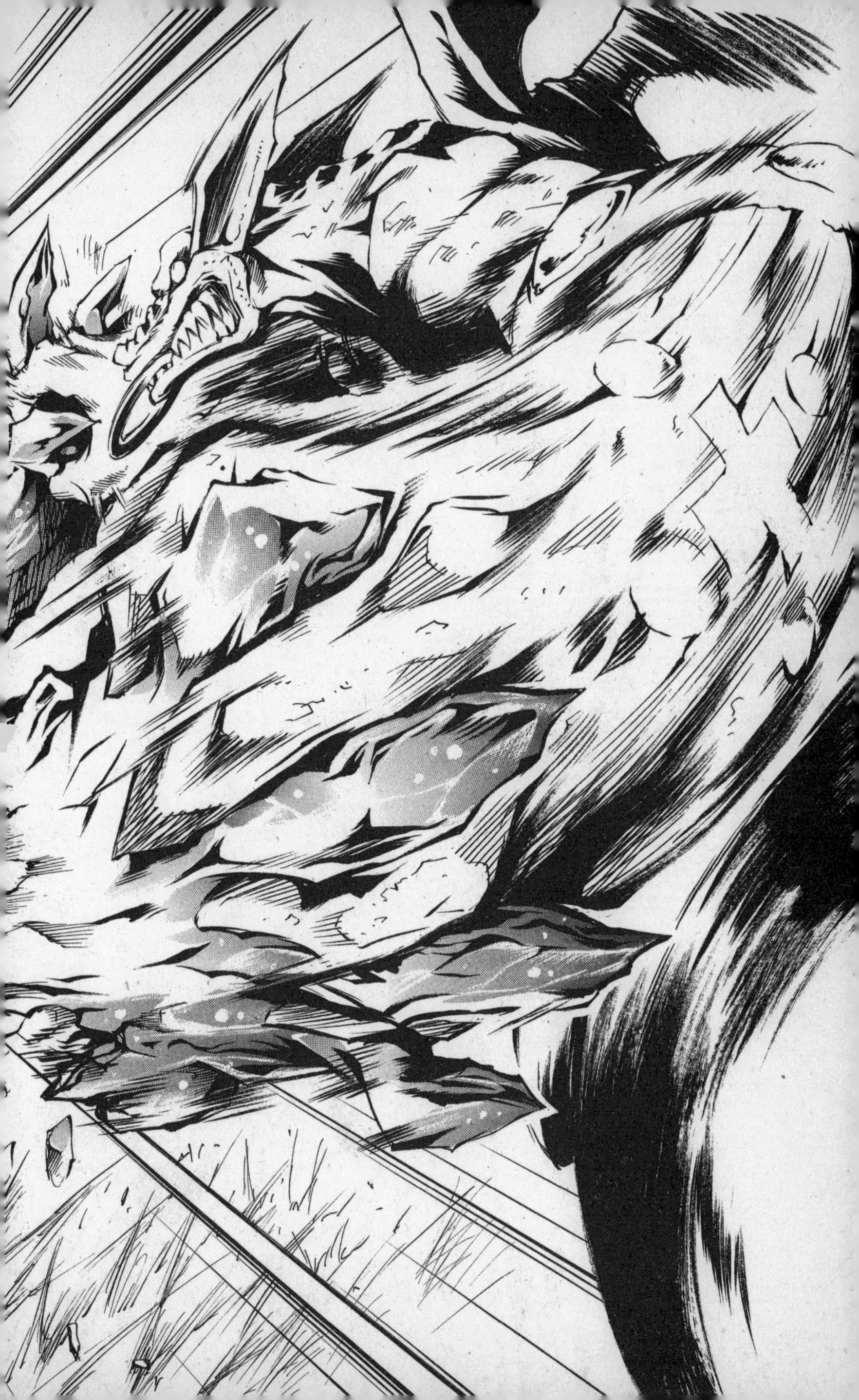

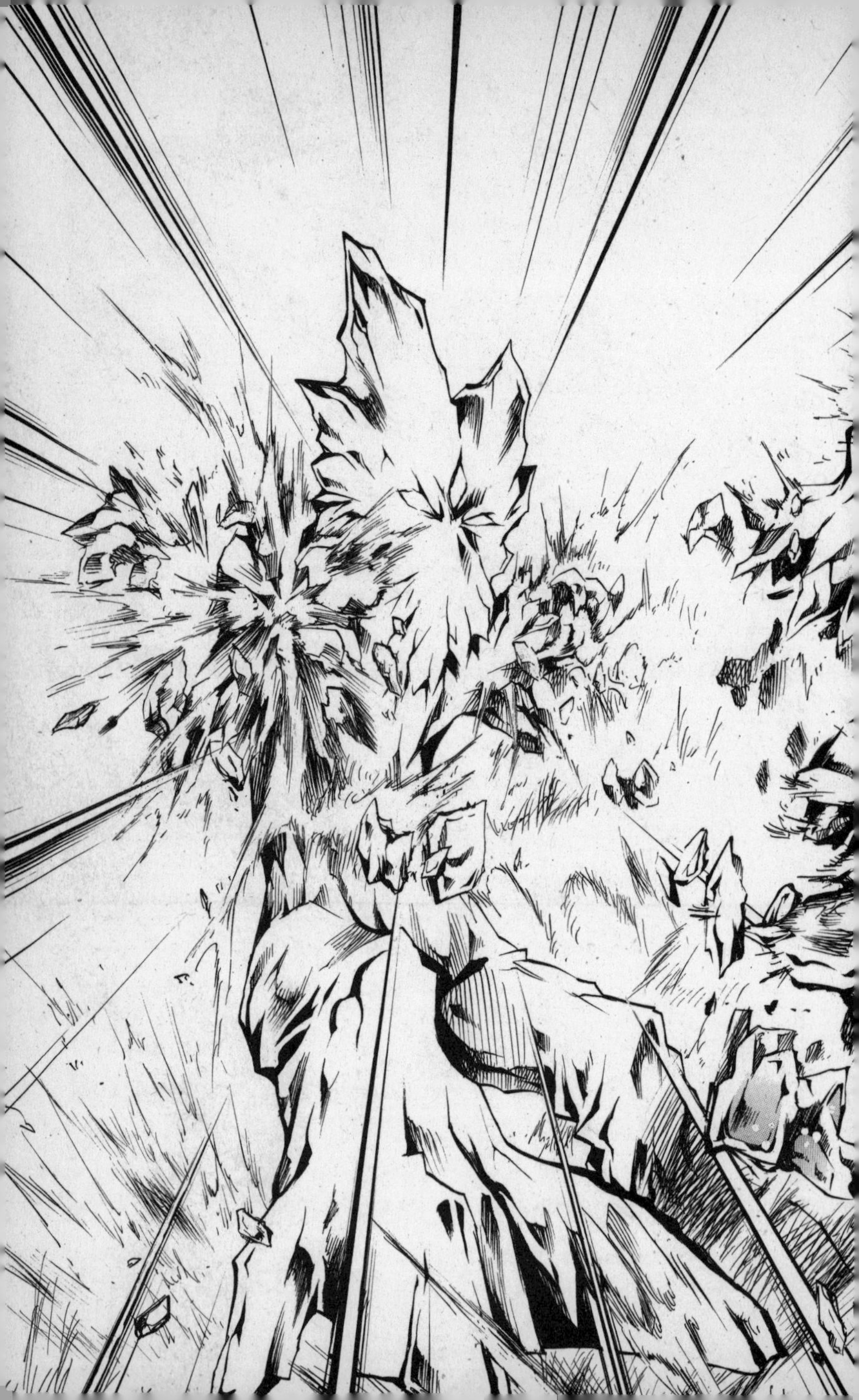

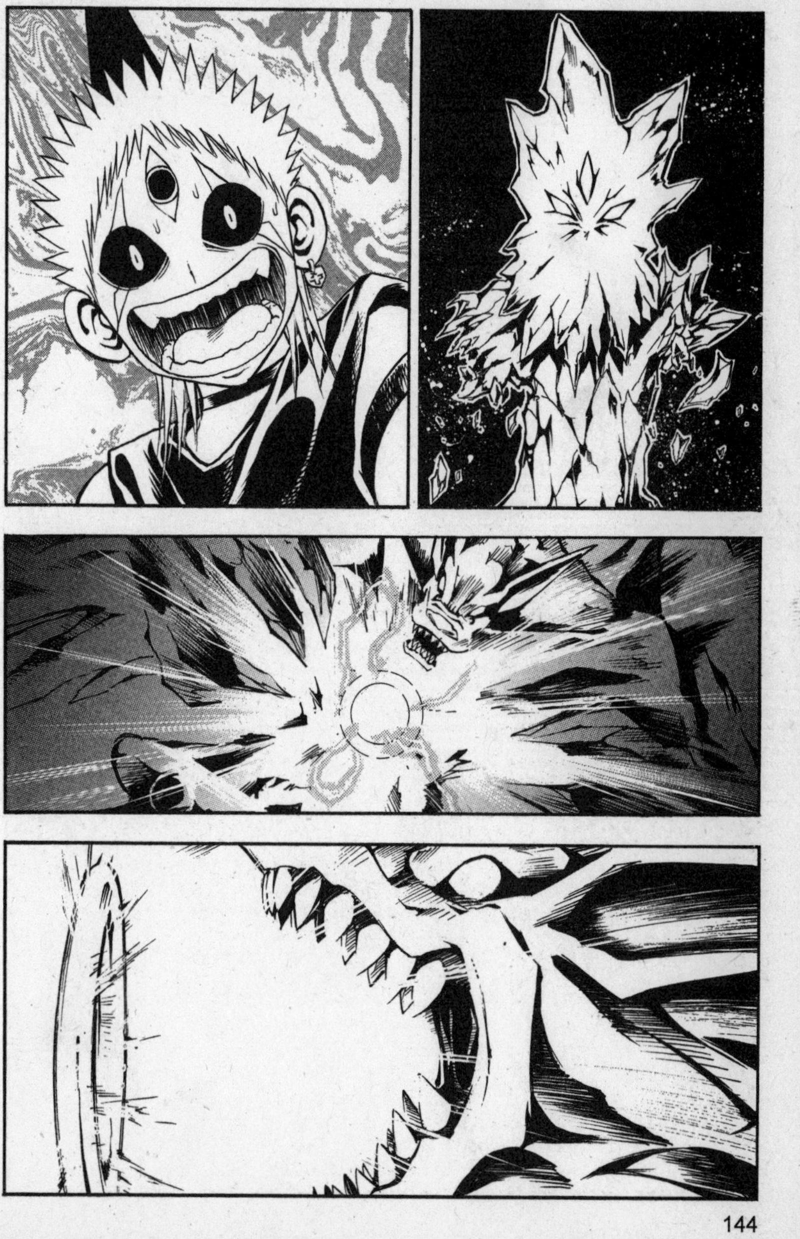

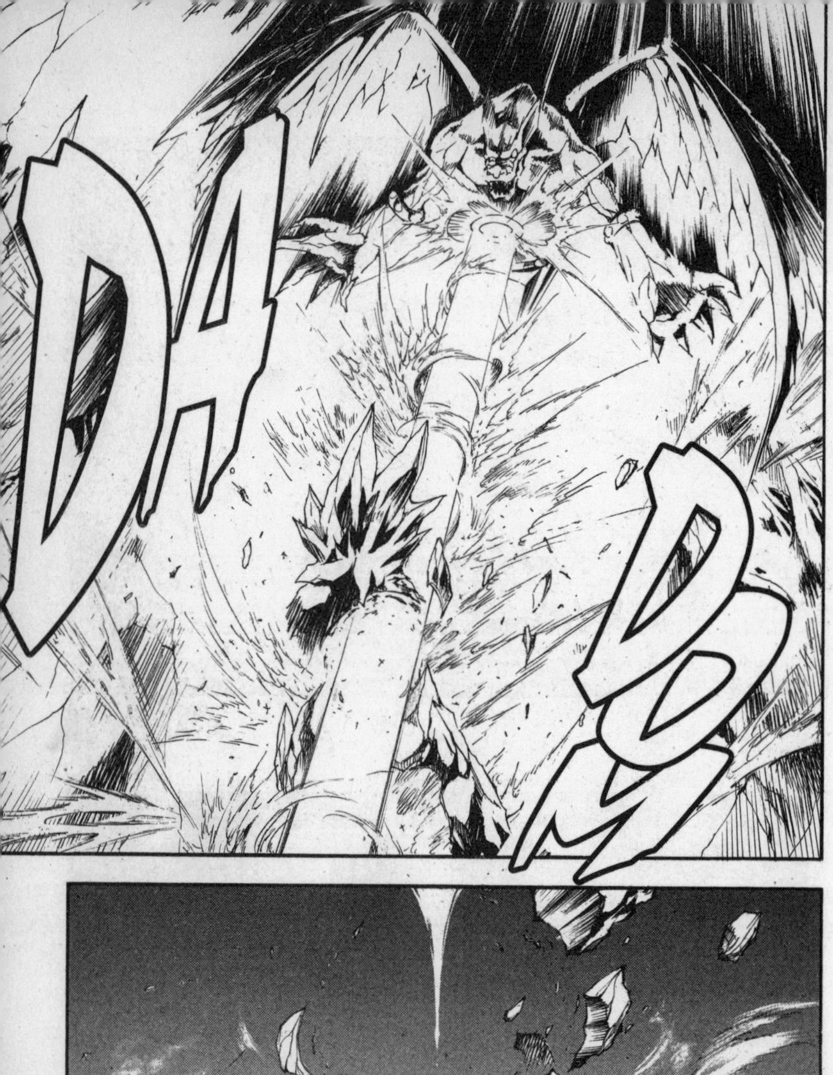
DOOM
DA

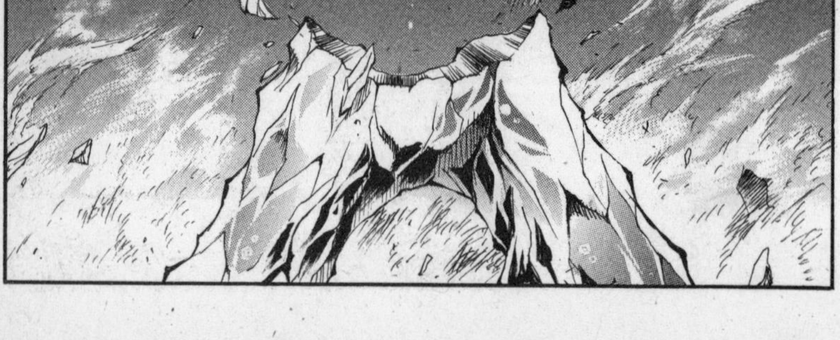

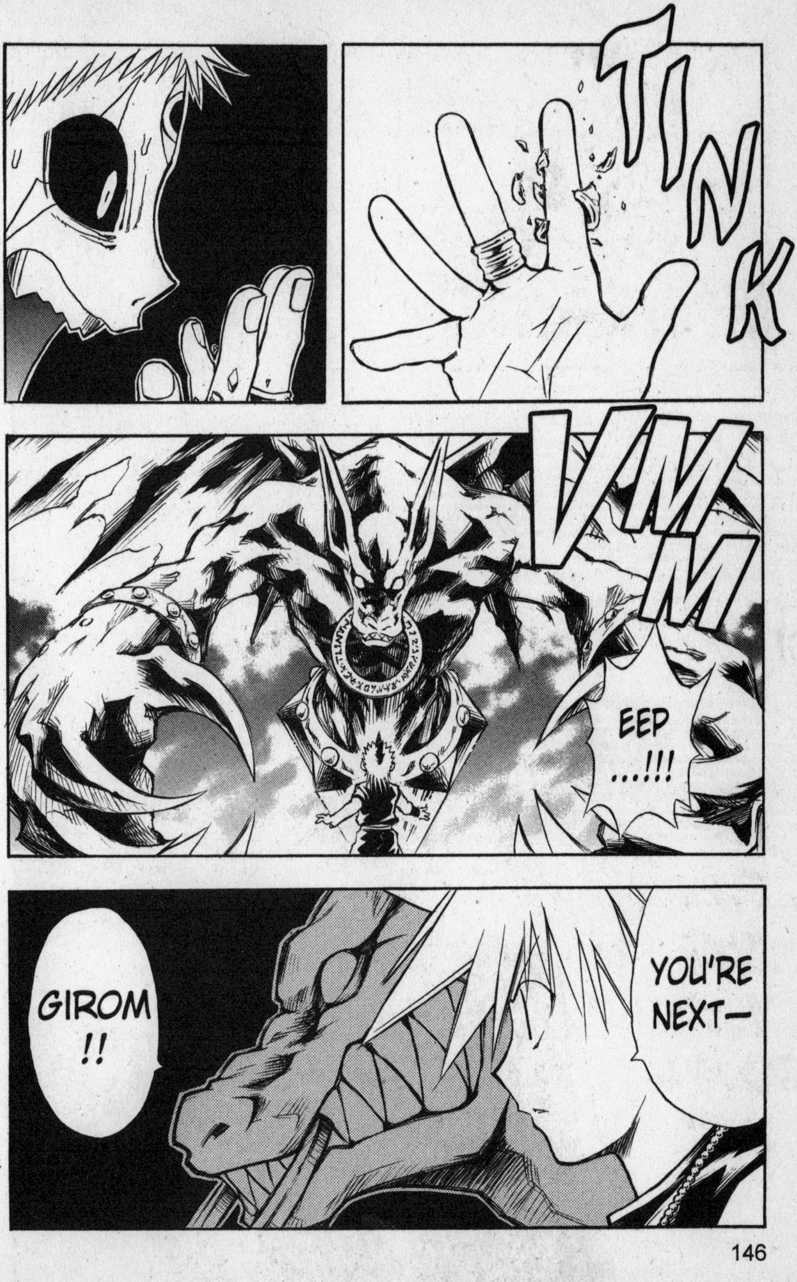
TINK
VMM
EEP ...!!!
YOU'RE NEXT—
GIROM !!

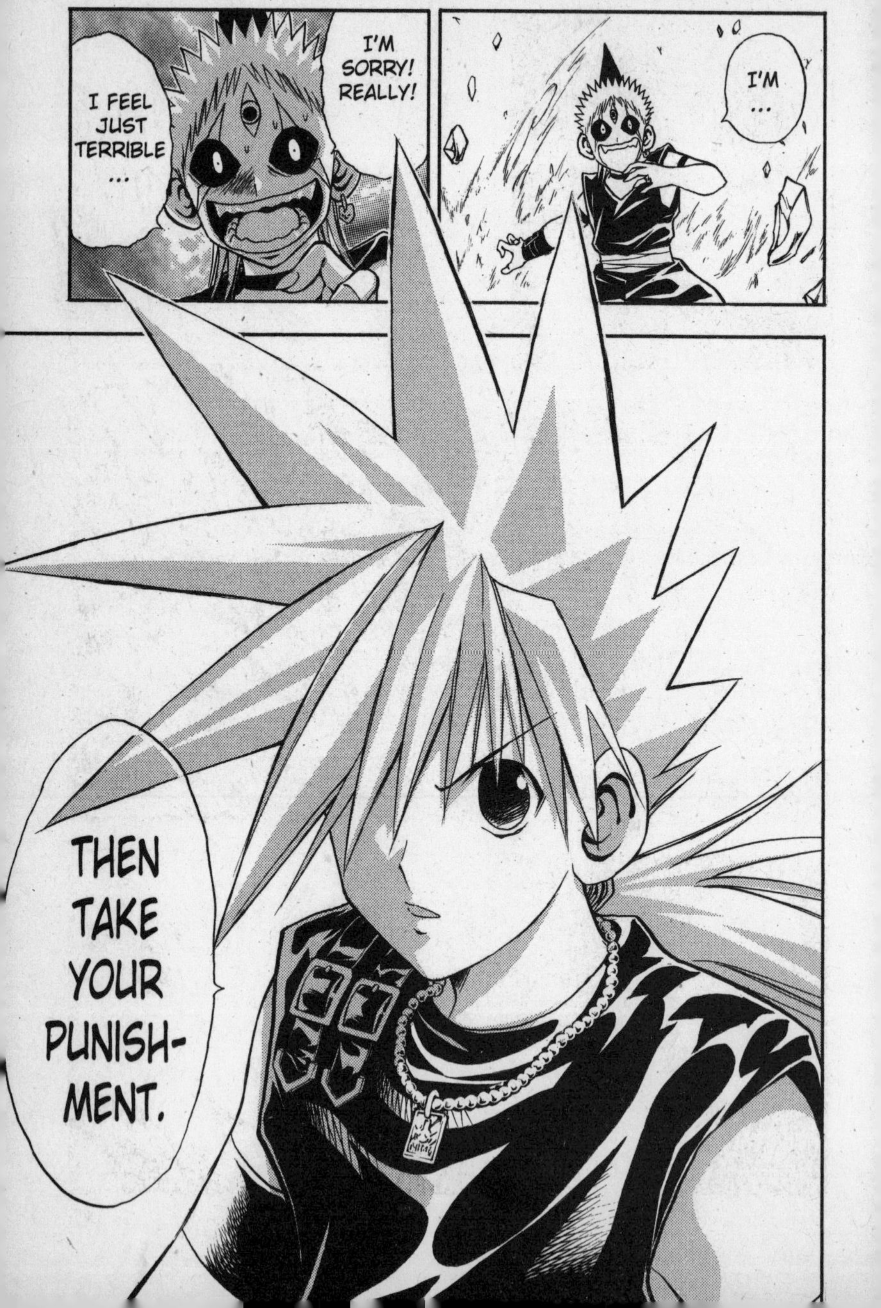
I'M ...
I'M SORRY! REALLY!
I FEEL JUST TERRIBLE ...
THEN TAKE YOUR PUNISH-MENT.

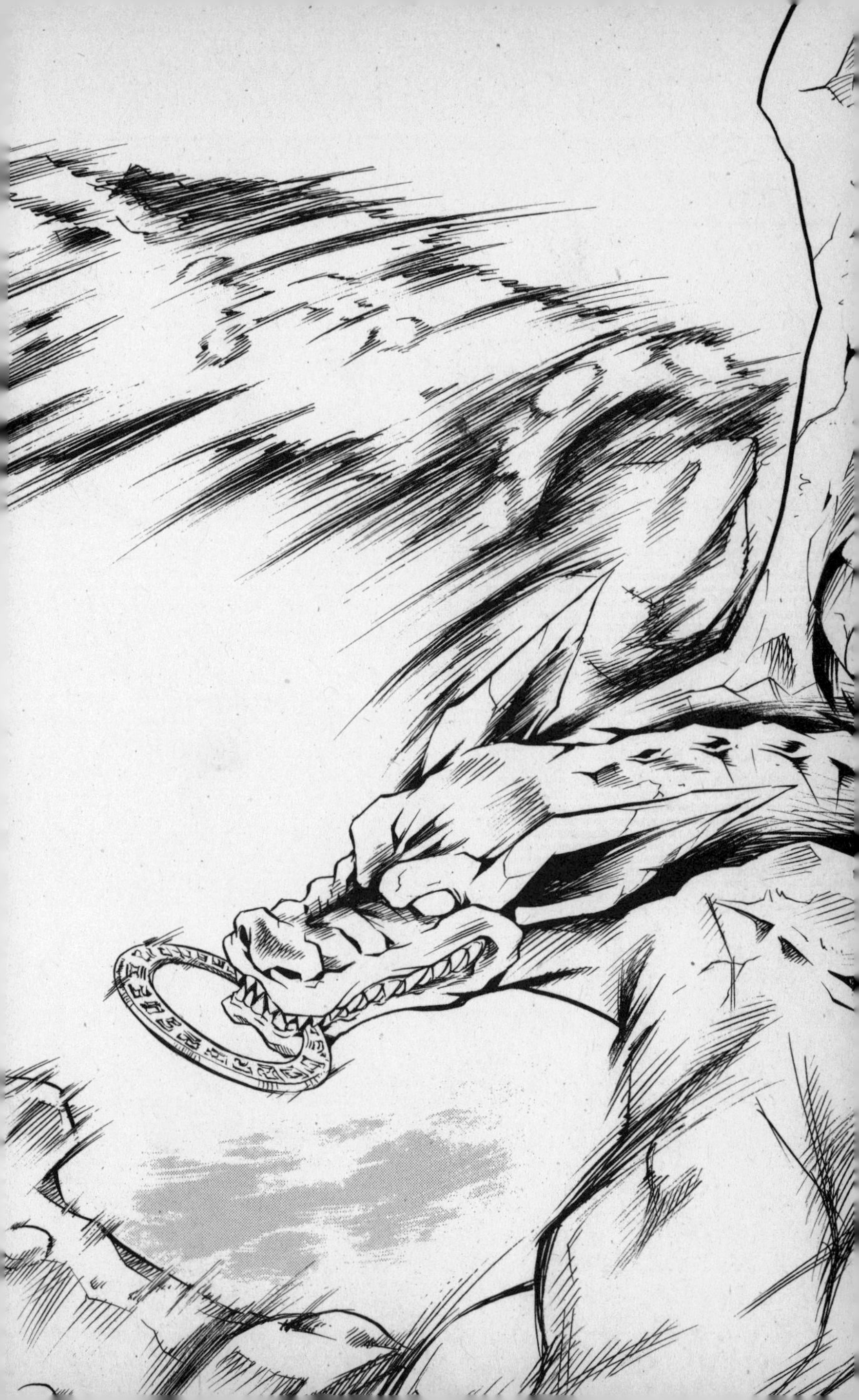

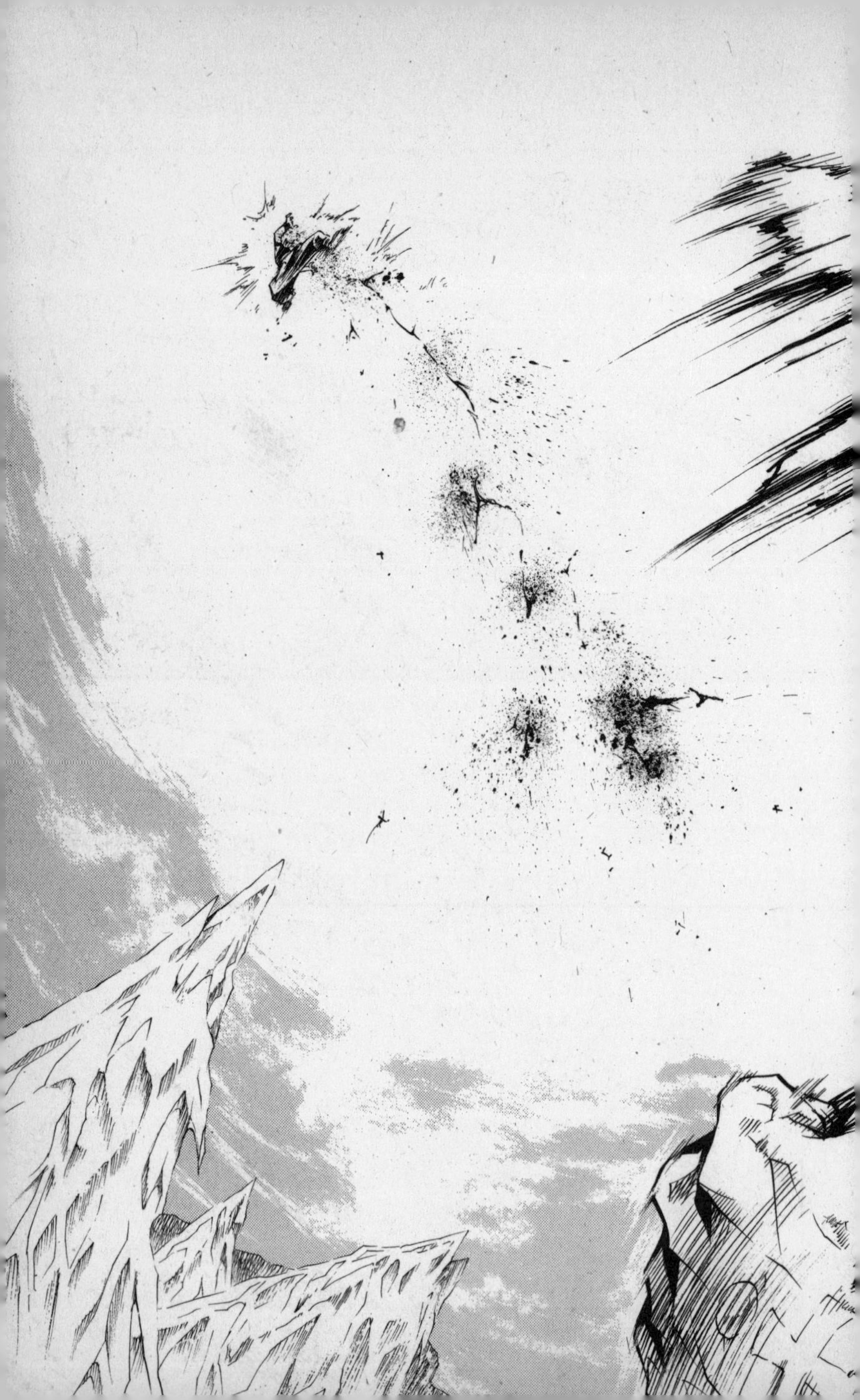

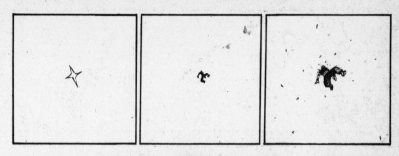

VICTOR-GINTA!!!

FIFTH MATCH!!! GINTA VS. GIROM!!!

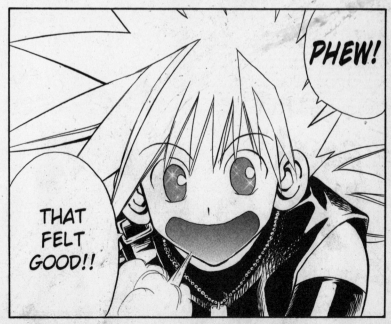

PHEW!

THAT FELT GOOD!!

AKT.84/DOROTHY VS. RAPUNZEL ①

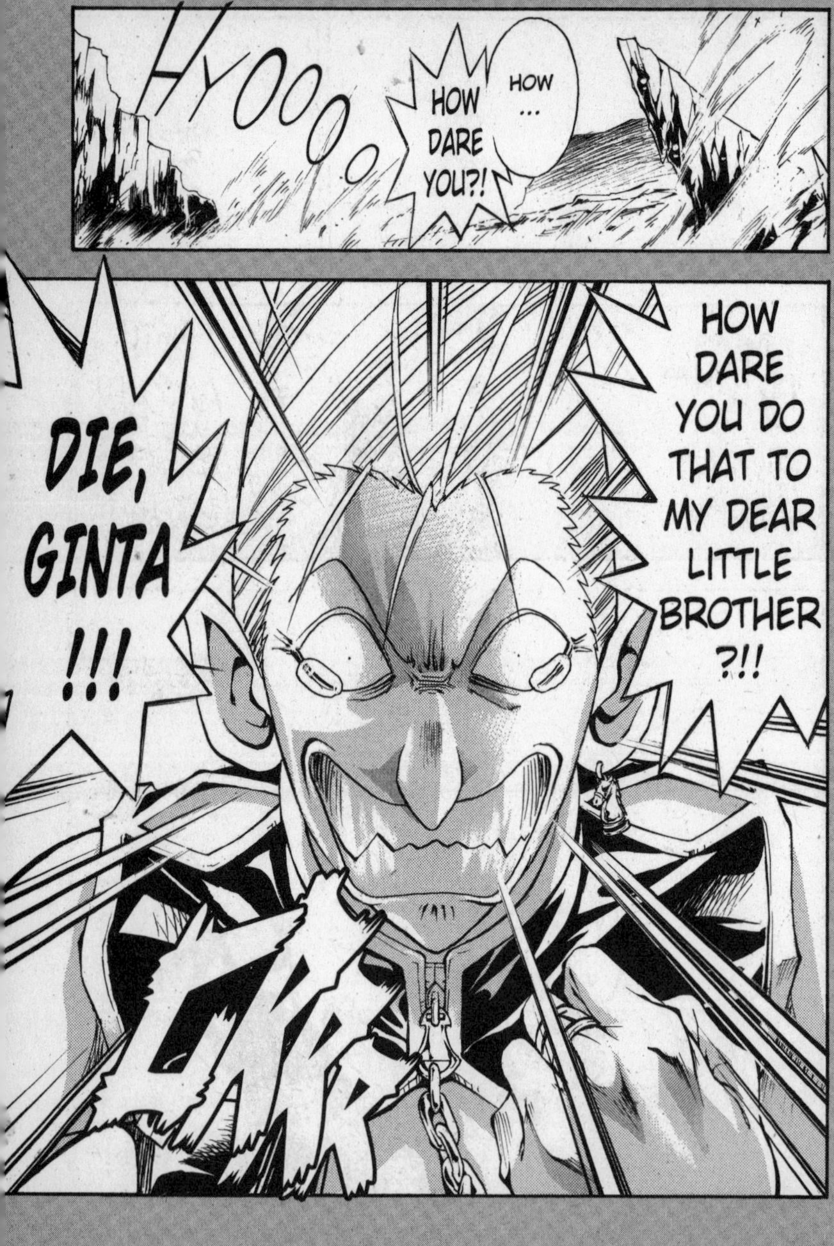
HOW ...
HOW DARE YOU?!
HYOOOO
HOW DARE YOU DO THAT TO MY DEAR LITTLE BROTHER ?!!
DIE, GINTA !!!

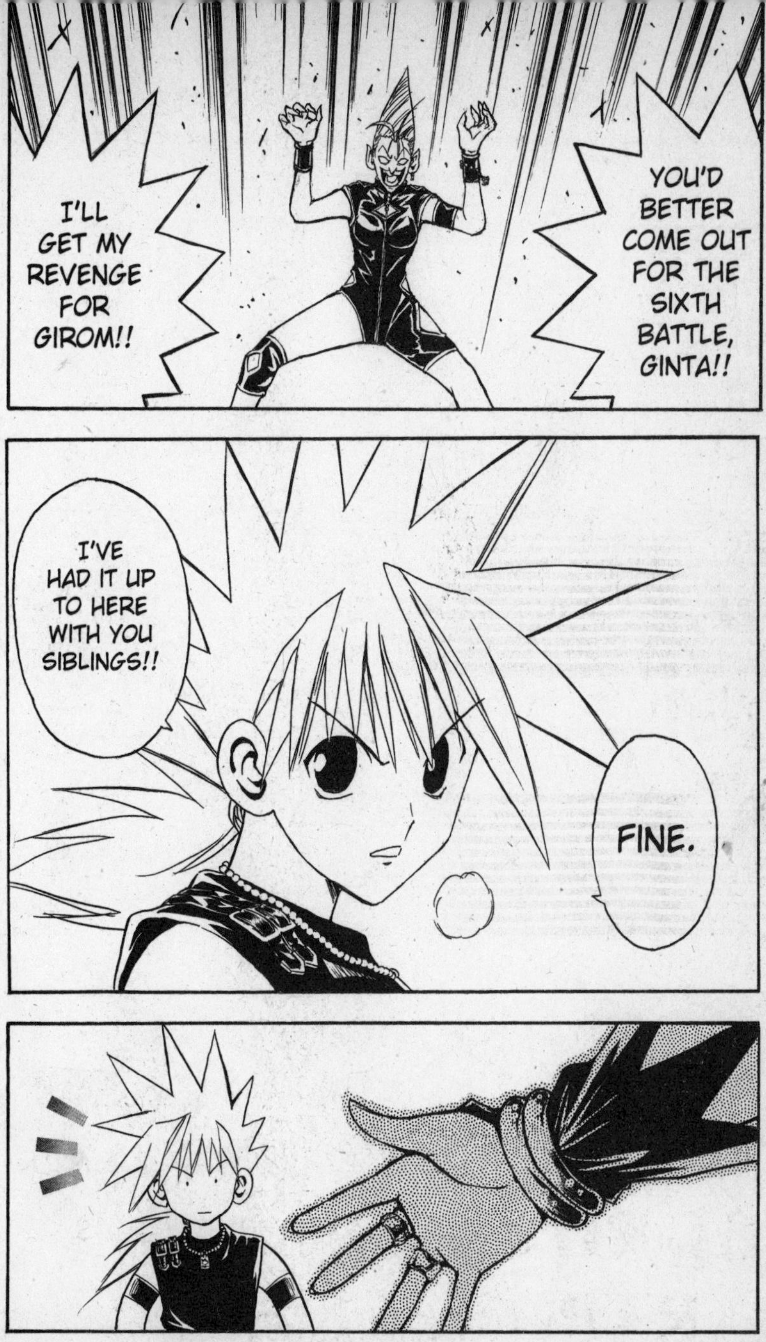
YOU'D BETTER COME OUT FOR THE SIXTH BATTLE, GINTA!!
I'LL GET MY REVENGE FOR GIROM!!
FINE.
I'VE HAD IT UP TO HERE WITH YOU SIBLINGS!!

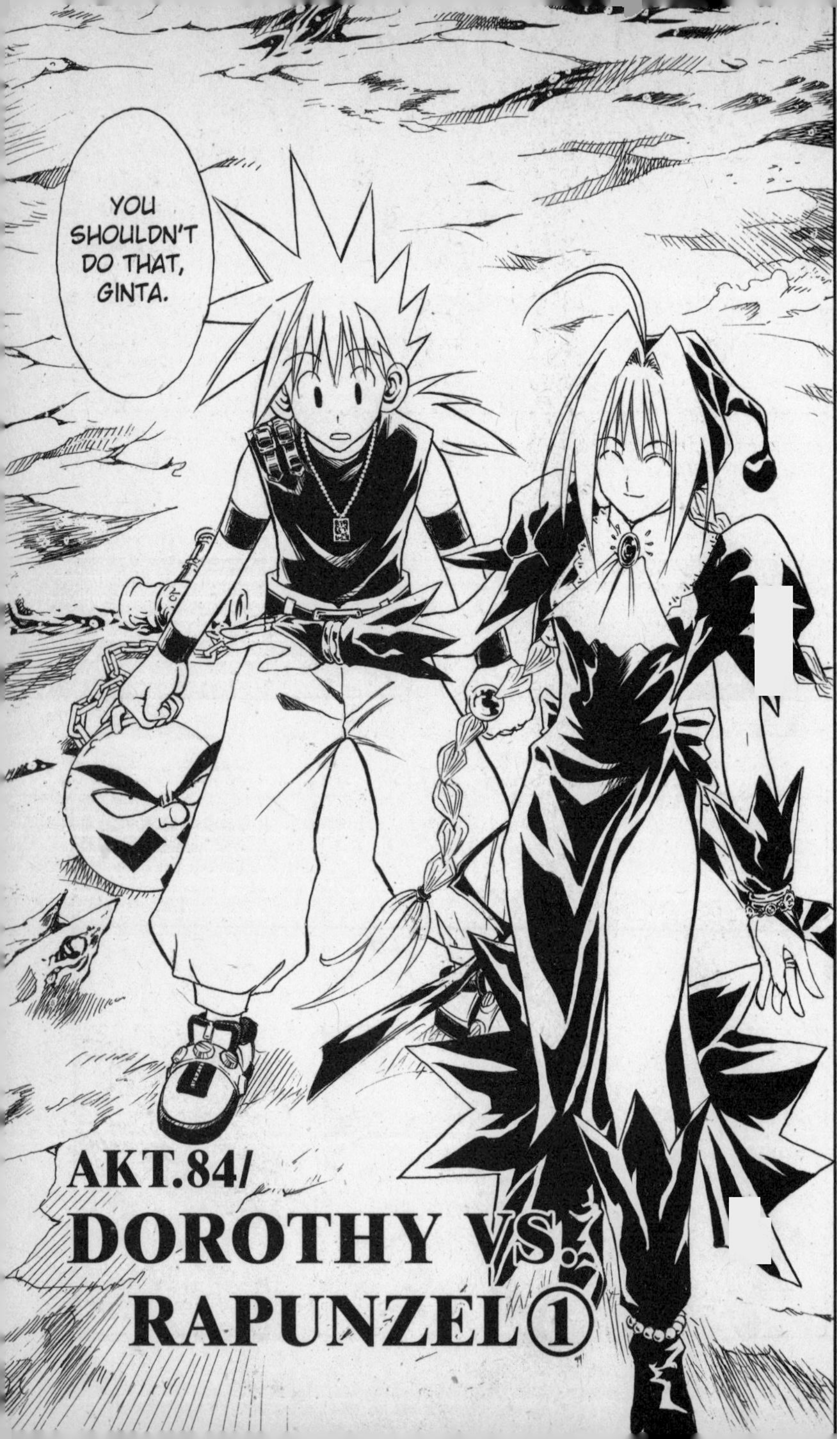
YOU SHOULDN'T DO THAT, GINTA.
AKT.84/
DOROTHY VS. RAPUNZEL①

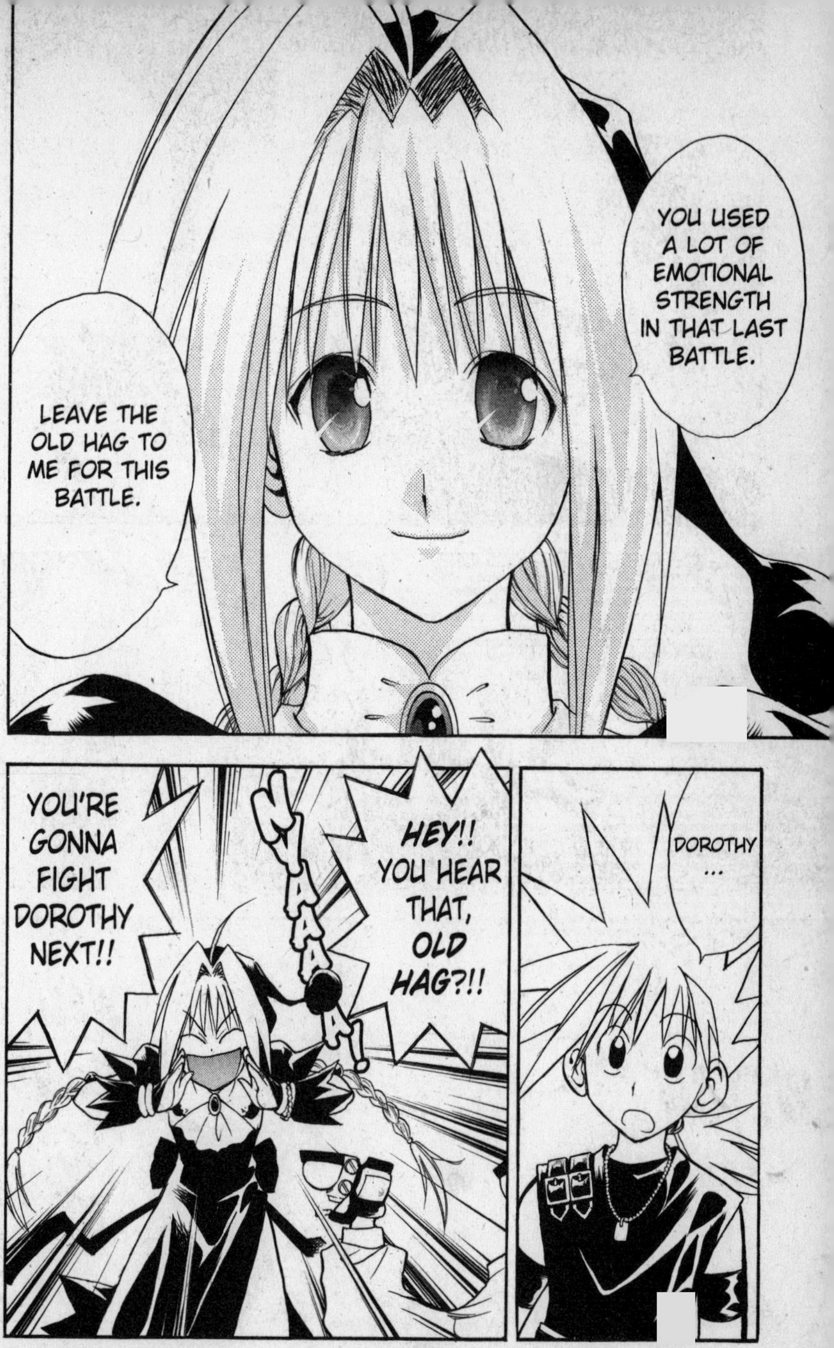
YOU USED A LOT OF EMOTIONAL STRENGTH IN THAT LAST BATTLE.
LEAVE THE OLD HAG TO ME FOR THIS BATTLE.
DOROTHY ...
HEY!! YOU HEAR THAT, OLD HAG?!!
YOU'RE GONNA FIGHT DOROTHY NEXT!!

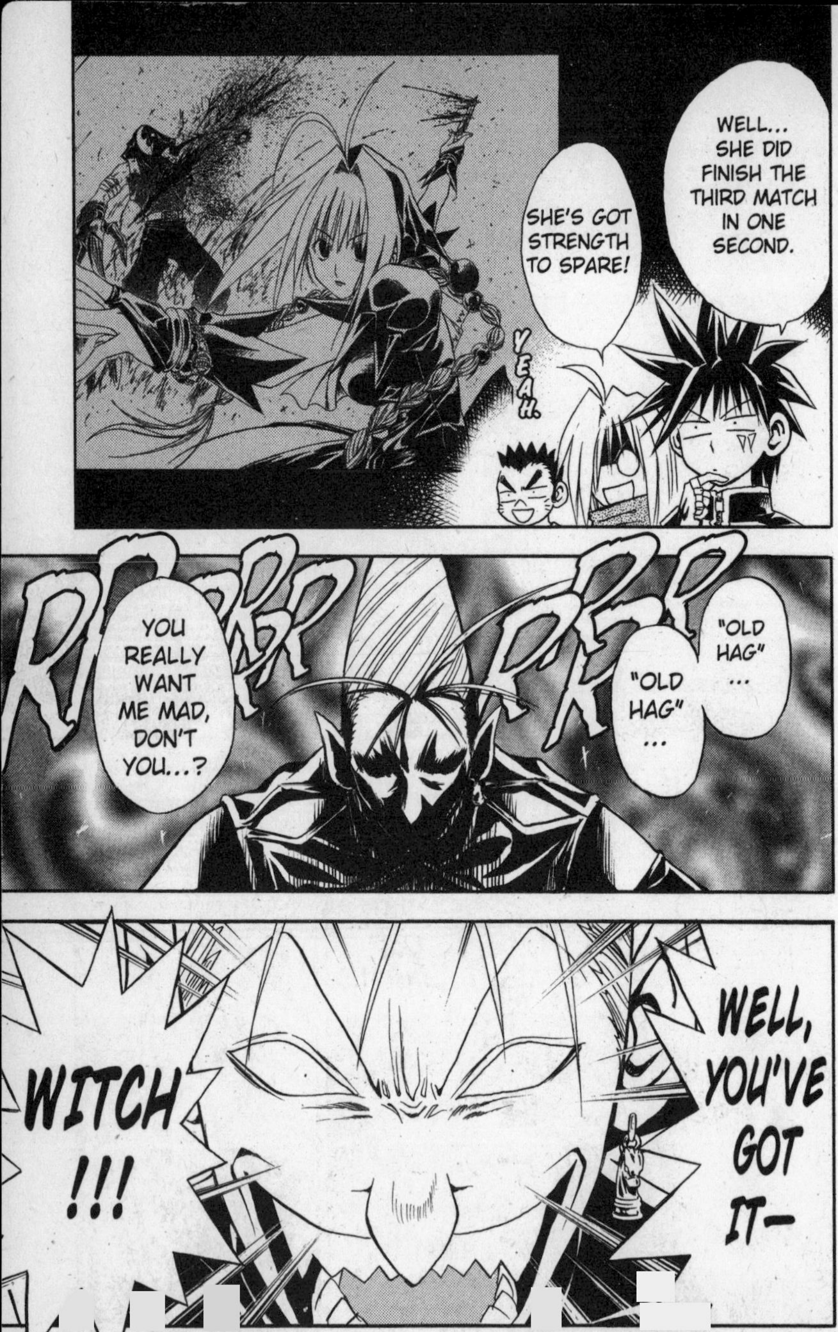
WELL... SHE DID FINISH THE THIRD MATCH IN ONE SECOND.
SHE'S GOT STRENGTH TO SPARE!
YEAH.
"OLD HAG" ...
"OLD HAG" ...
RRRR
RRRR
YOU REALLY WANT ME MAD, DON'T YOU...?
WELL, YOU'VE GOT IT—
WITCH !!!

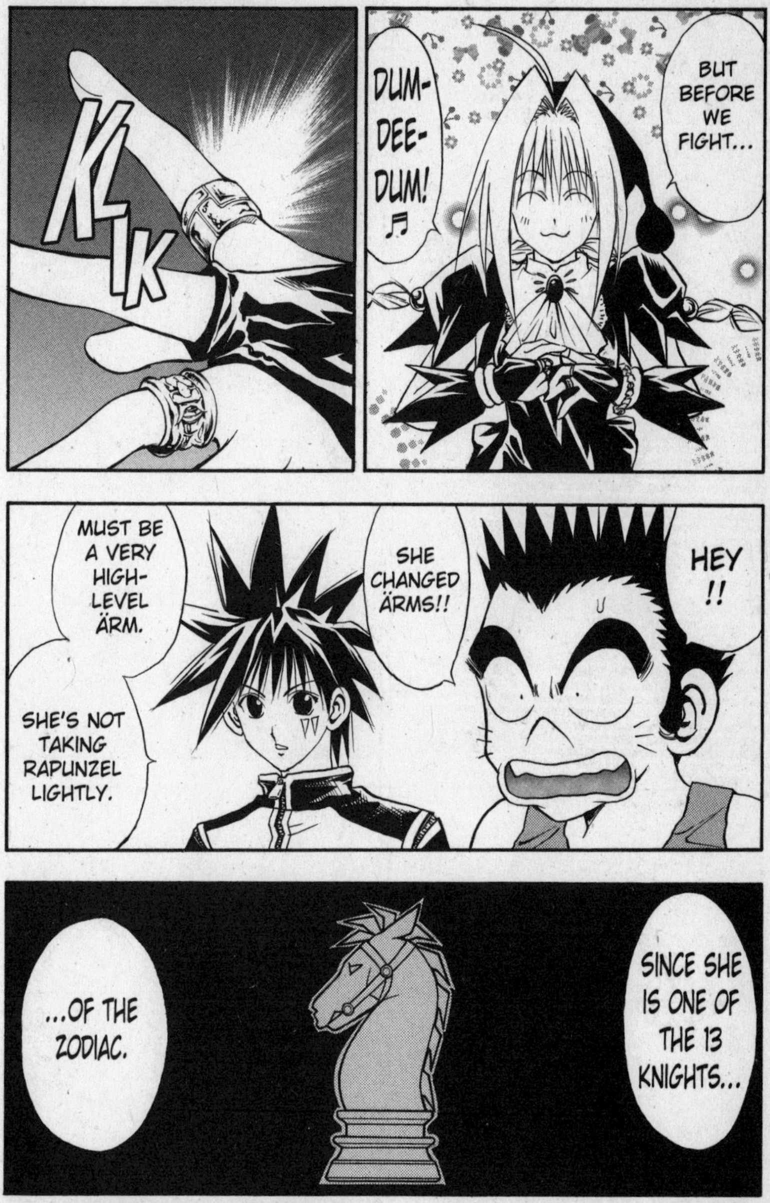
BUT BEFORE WE FIGHT...
DUM-DEE-DUM! ♬
KLIK
HEY!!
SHE CHANGED ÄRMS!!
MUST BE A VERY HIGH-LEVEL ÄRM.
SHE'S NOT TAKING RAPUNZEL LIGHTLY.
SINCE SHE IS ONE OF THE 13 KNIGHTS...
...OF THE ZODIAC.

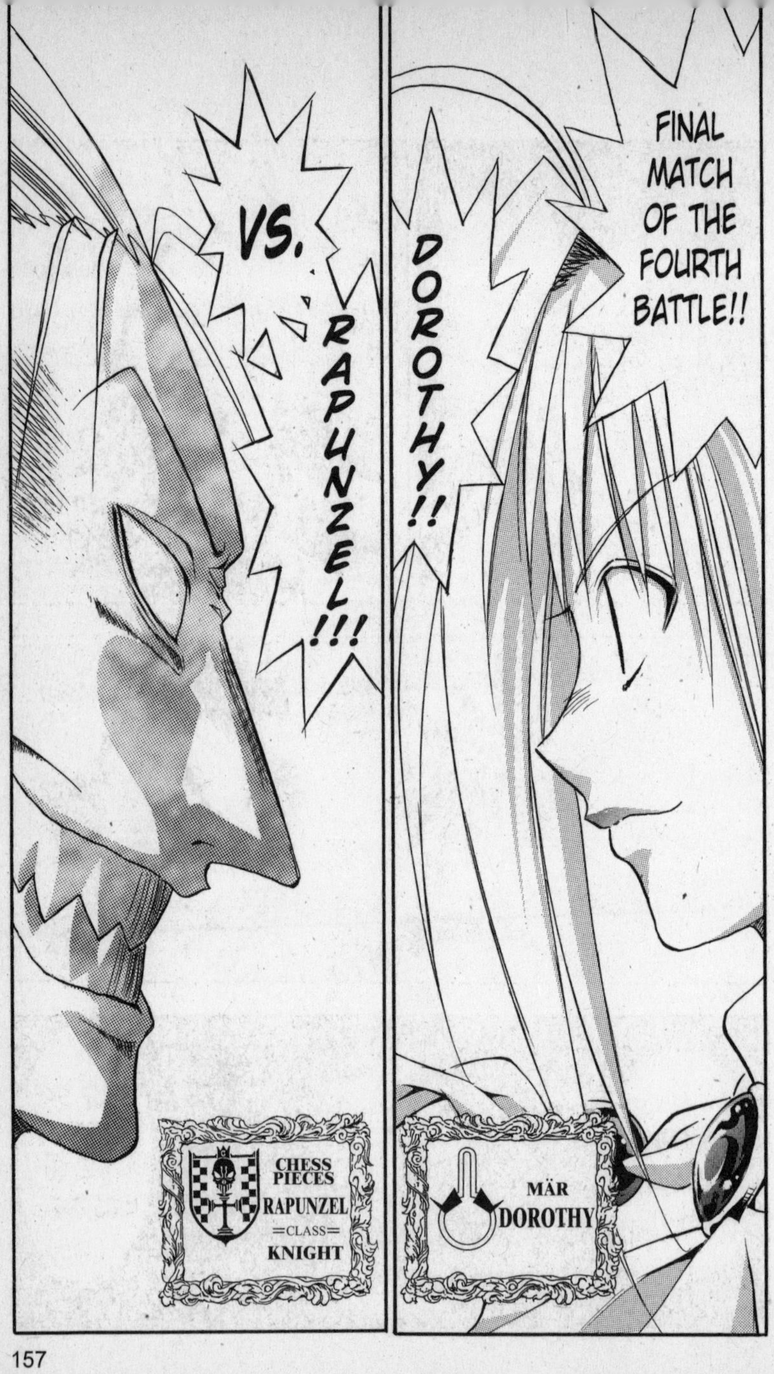
FINAL MATCH OF THE FOURTH BATTLE!!
DOROTHY!!
MÄR
DOROTHY
VS.
RAPUNZEL!!!
CHESS PIECES
RAPUNZEL
=CLASS=
KNIGHT

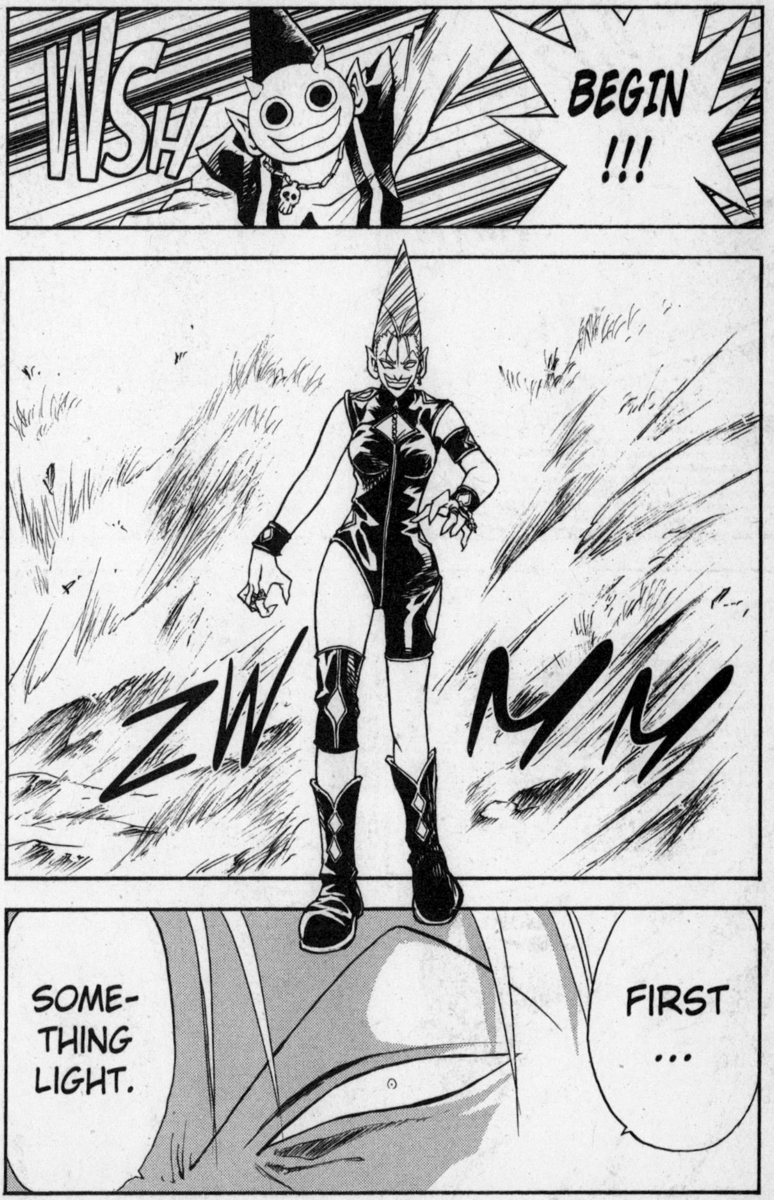
BEGIN !!!
WSH
ZWMM
FIRST ...
SOME-THING LIGHT.

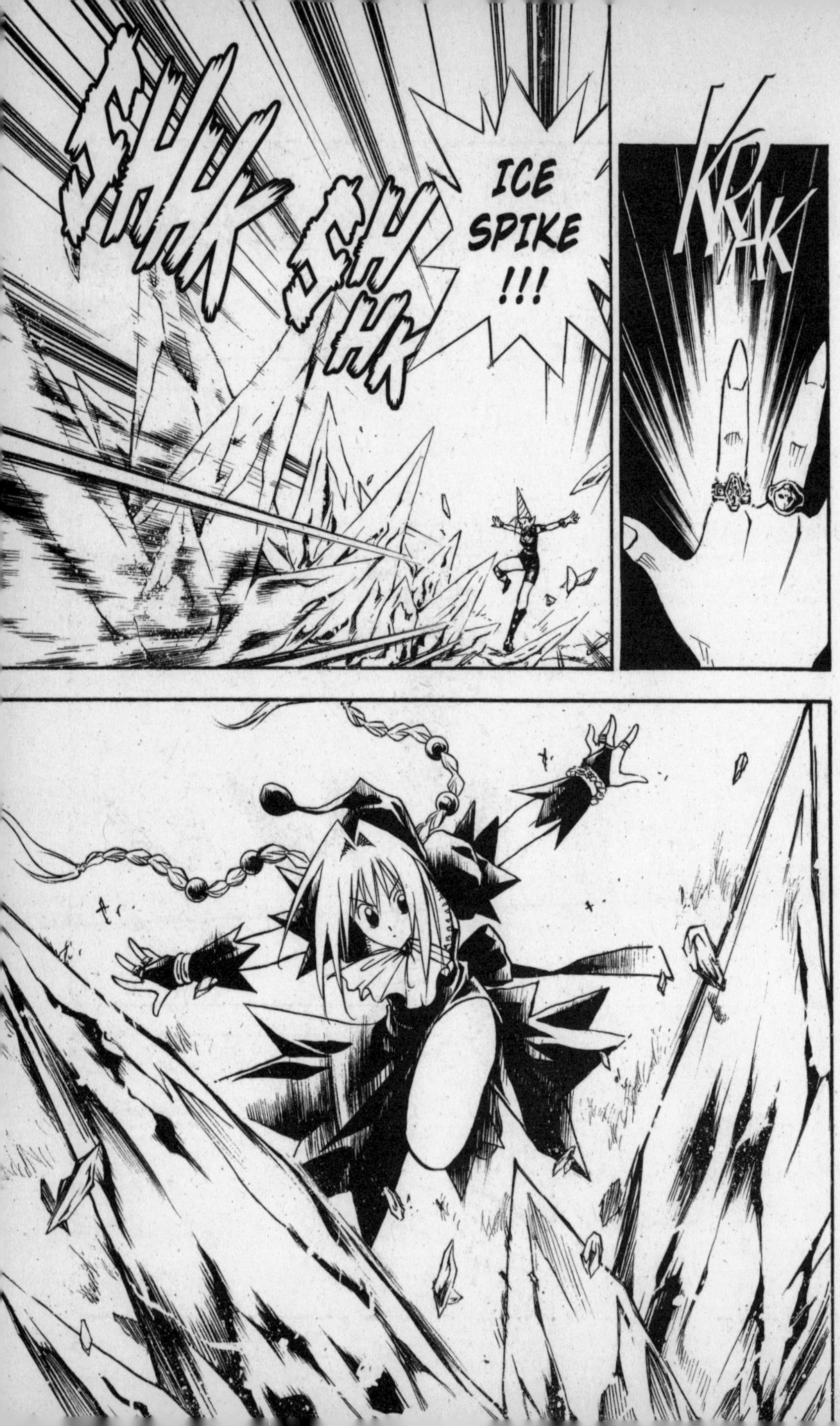
KRAK
ICE SPIKE!!!
SHHK
SHHK

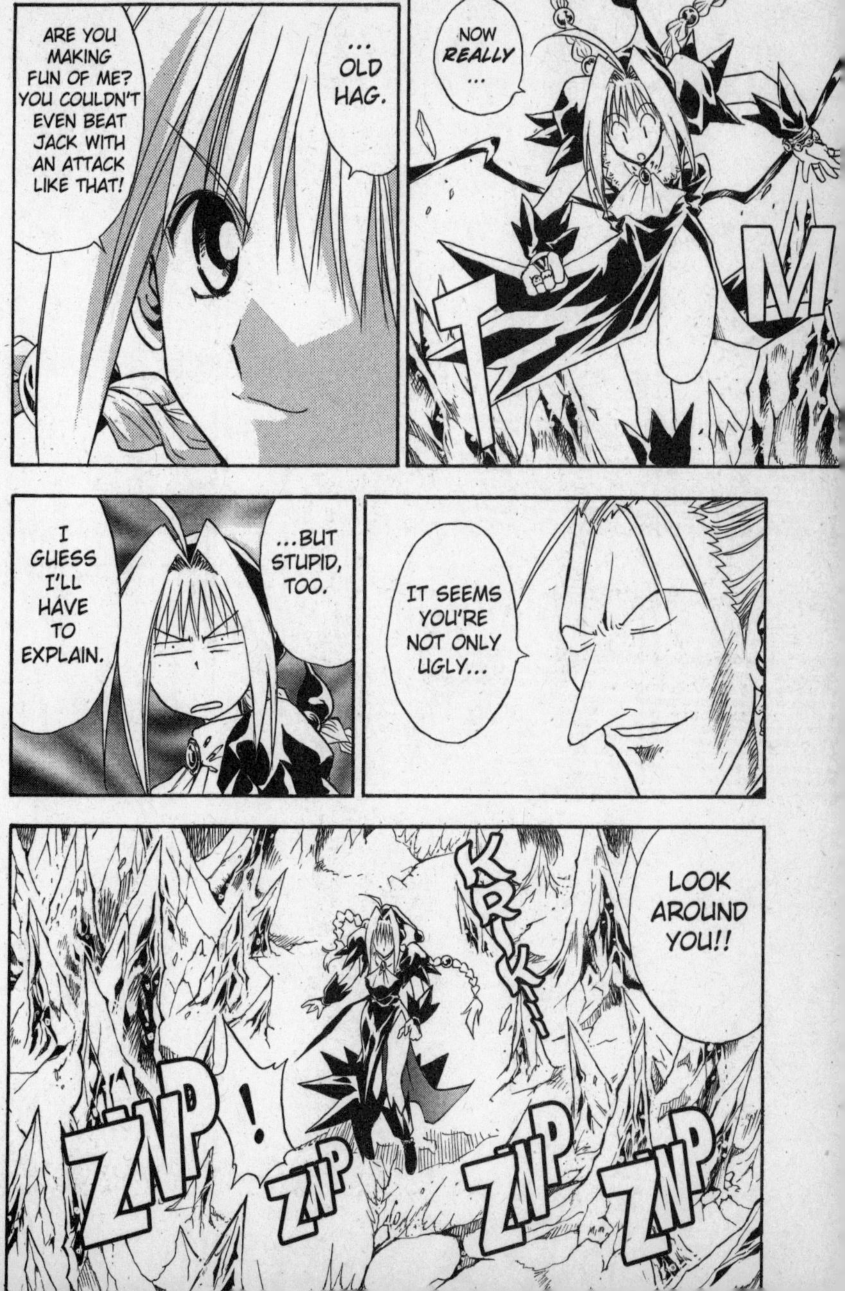
NOW *REALLY* ...
M
T
... OLD HAG.
ARE YOU MAKING FUN OF ME? YOU COULDN'T EVEN BEAT JACK WITH AN ATTACK LIKE THAT!
IT SEEMS YOU'RE NOT ONLY UGLY...
...BUT STUPID, TOO.
I GUESS I'LL HAVE TO EXPLAIN.
LOOK AROUND YOU!!
KRK
ZNP
ZNP
!
ZNP
ZNP

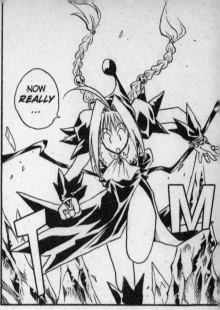

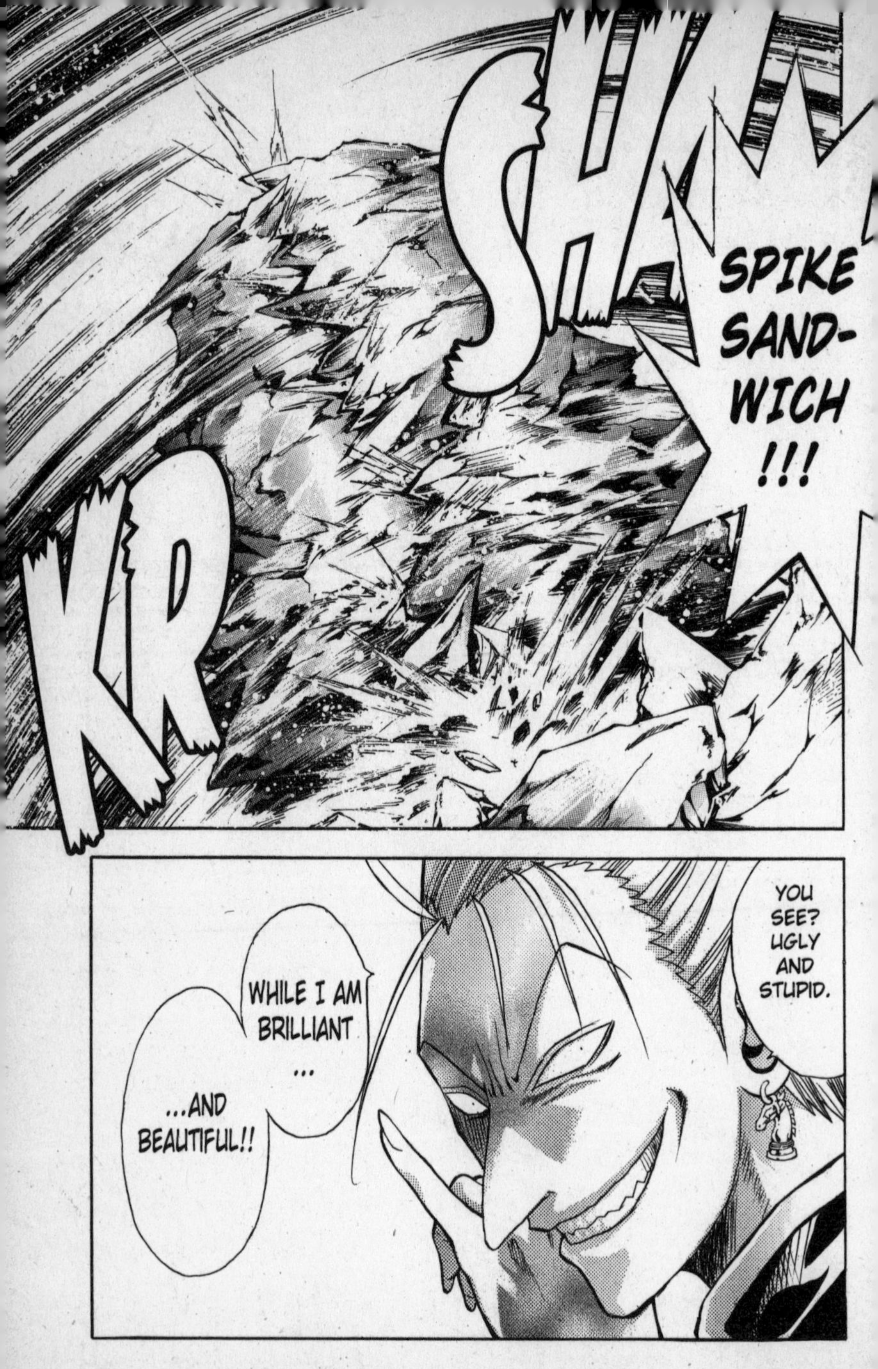
SHA
SPIKE SANDWICH!!!
KR
YOU SEE? UGLY AND STUPID.
WHILE I AM BRILLIANT...
...AND BEAUTIFUL!!

DORO-THY!!
OH ...
SHE'S ...!!
GRRRR

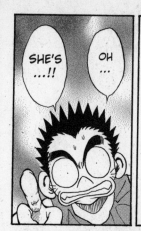

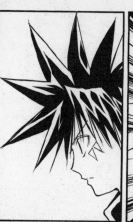

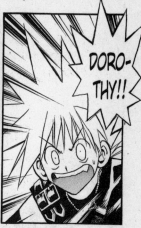

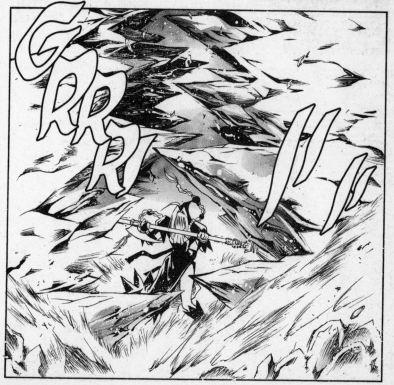

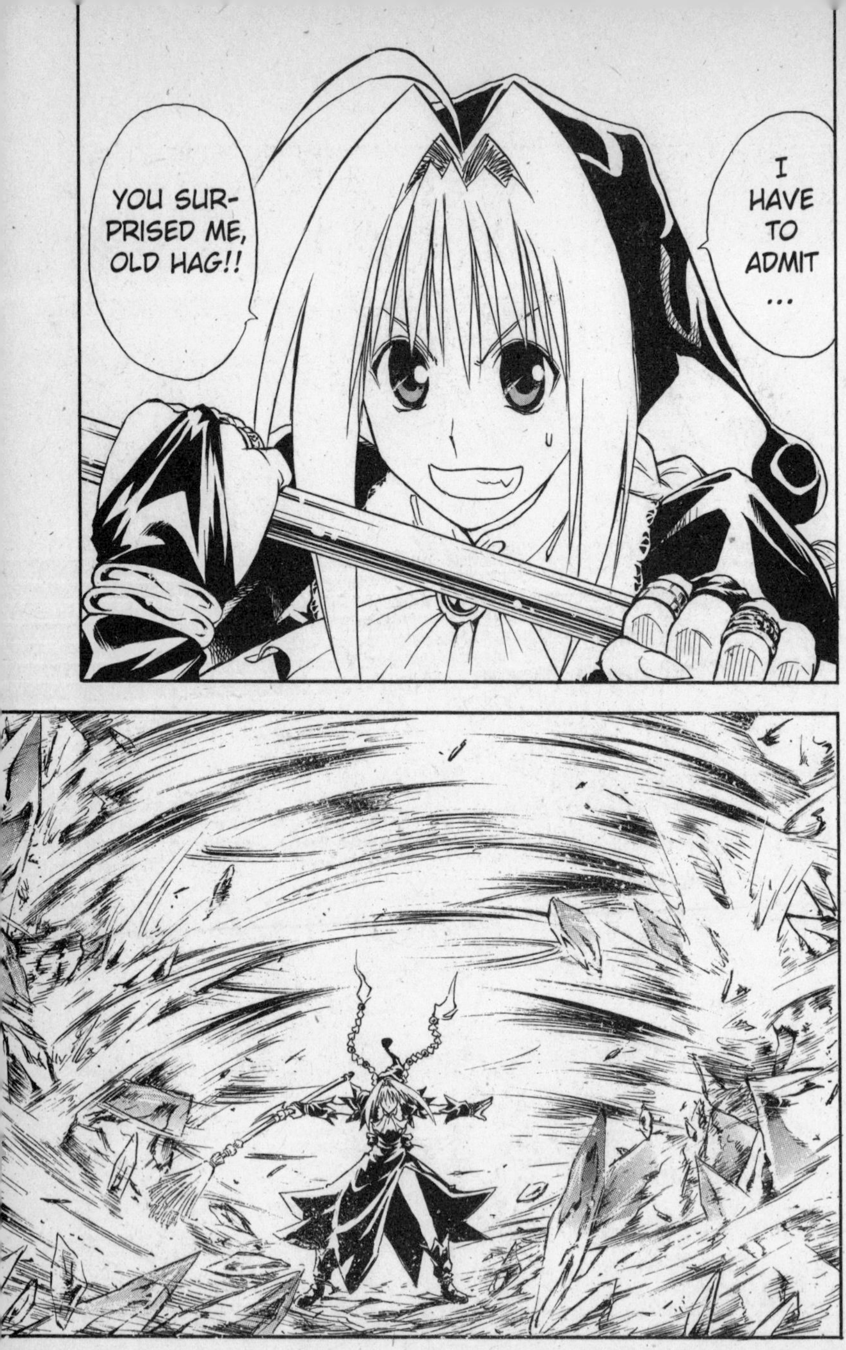
I HAVE TO ADMIT ...
YOU SURPRISED ME, OLD HAG!!

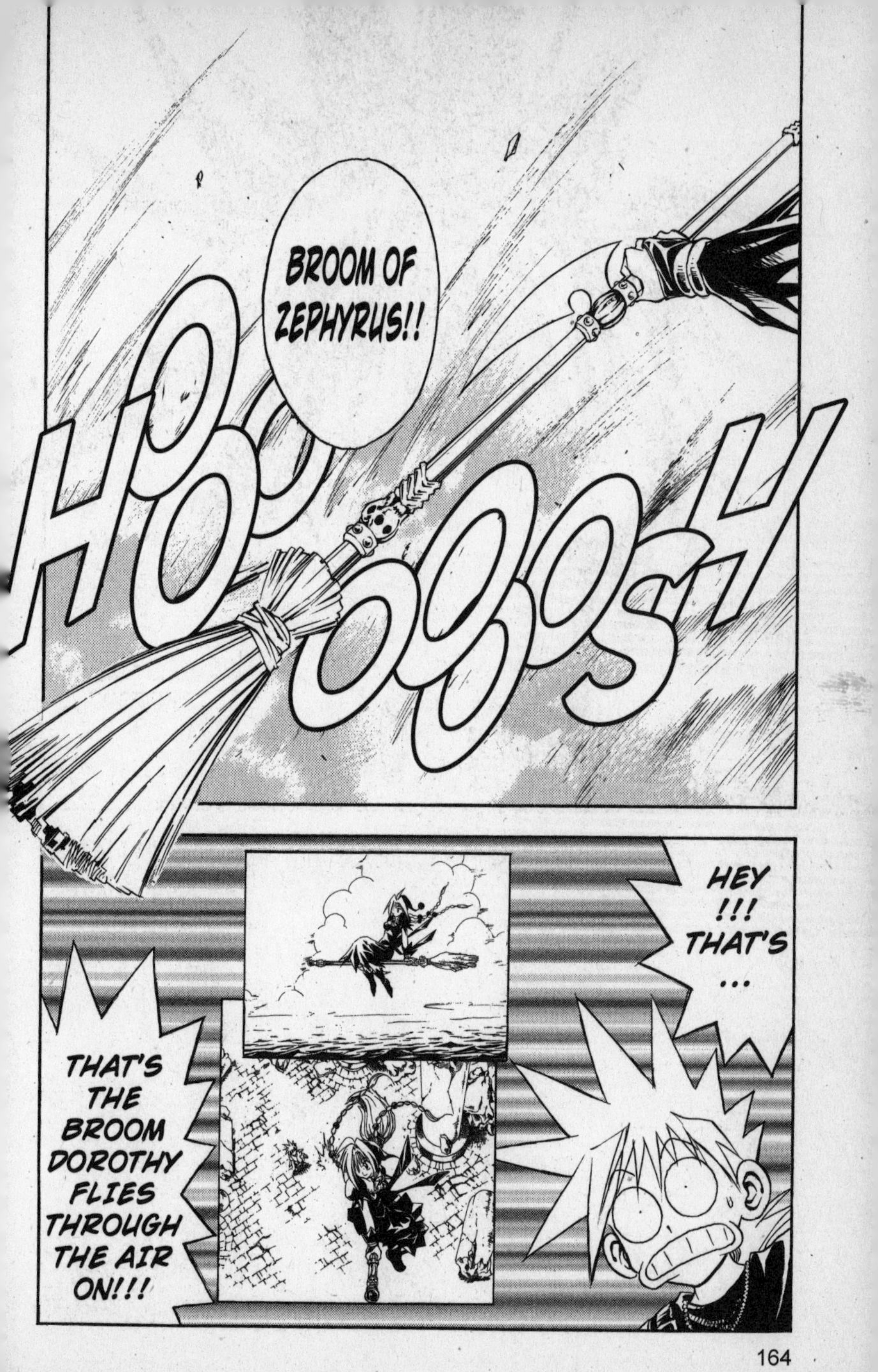
BROOM OF ZEPHYRUS!!
HOOOOOOOSH
HEY!!! THAT'S...
THAT'S THE BROOM DOROTHY FLIES THROUGH THE AIR ON!!!

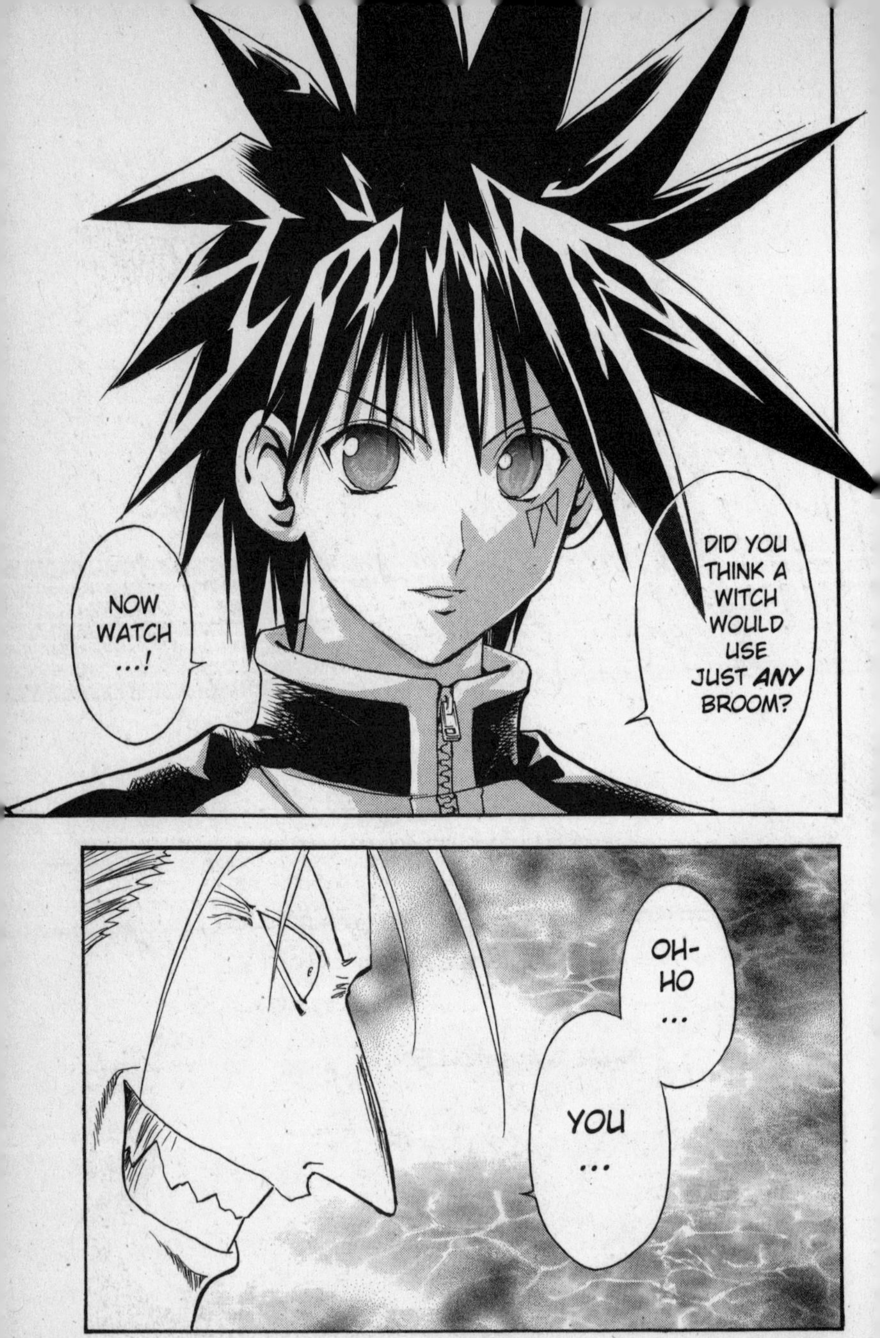
DID YOU THINK A WITCH WOULD USE JUST *ANY* BROOM?
NOW WATCH ...!
OH-HO ...
YOU ...

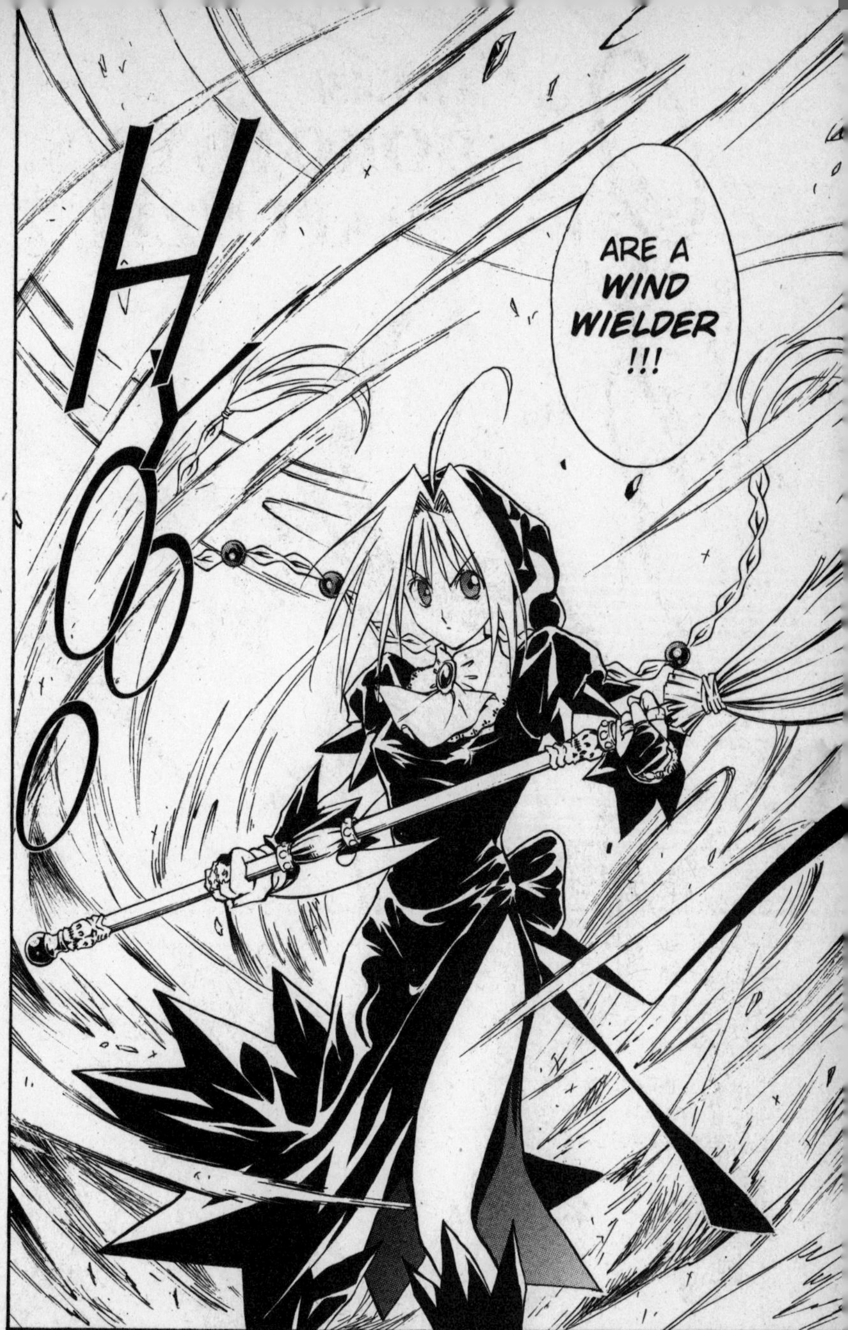
ARE A WIND WIELDER !!!
HYOOO

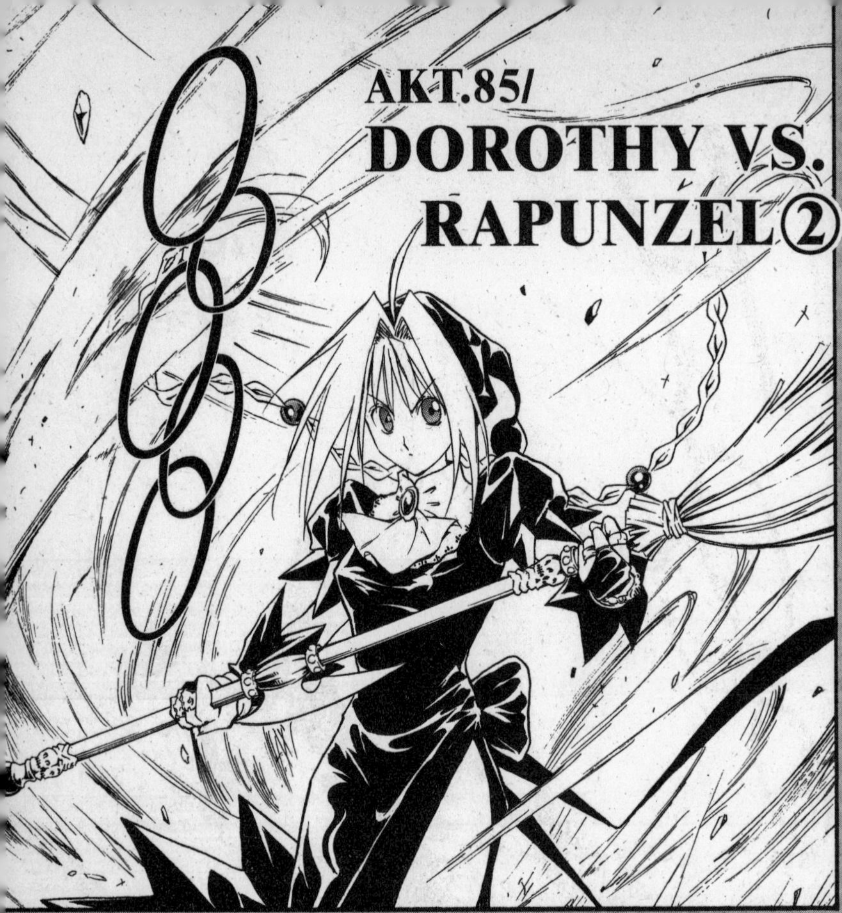
AKT.85/
DOROTHY VS. RAPUNZEL ②

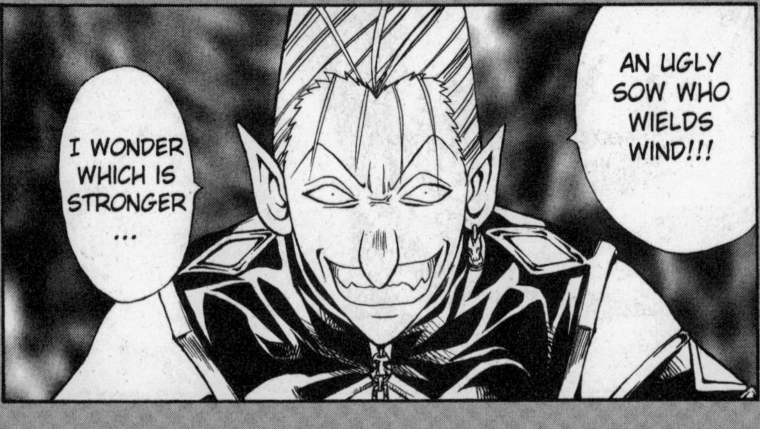
AN UGLY SOW WHO WIELDS WIND!!!
I WONDER WHICH IS STRONGER ...

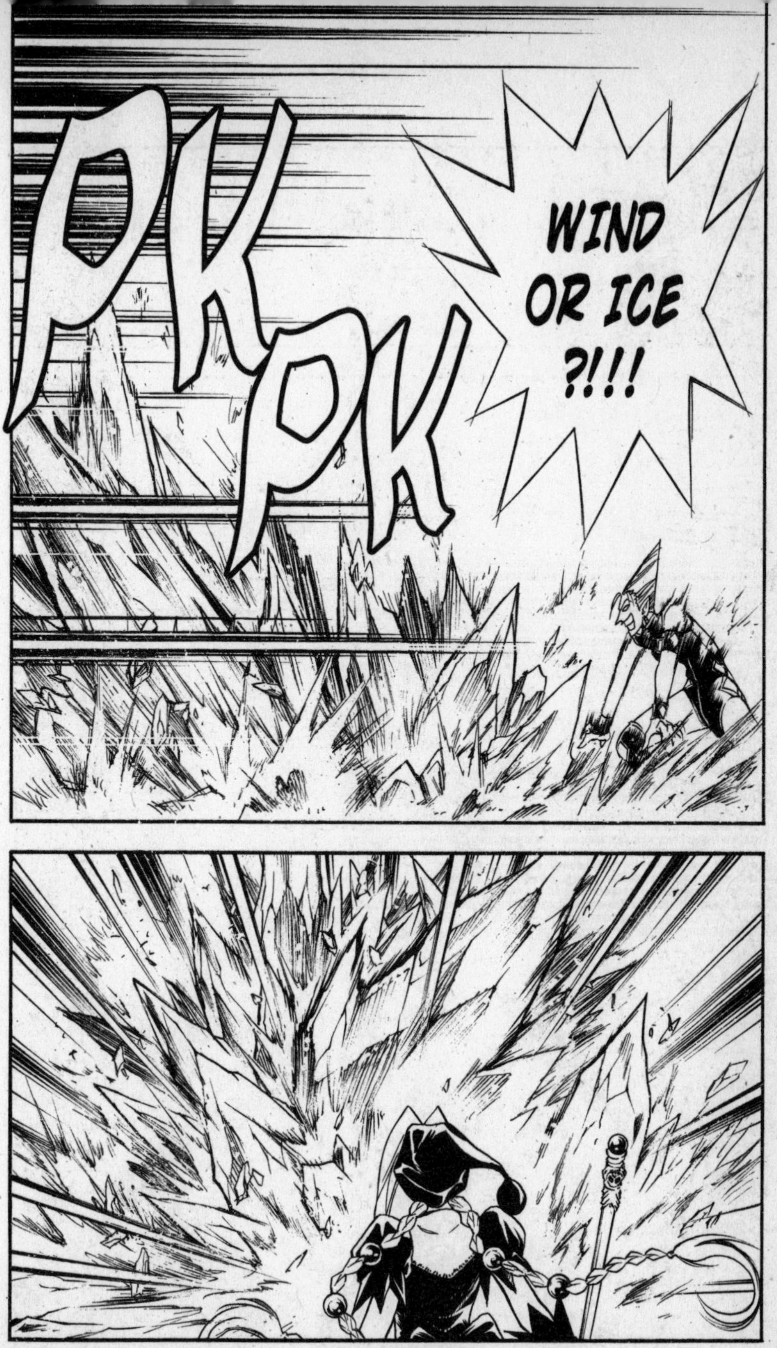
WIND OR ICE ?!!!
PK PK

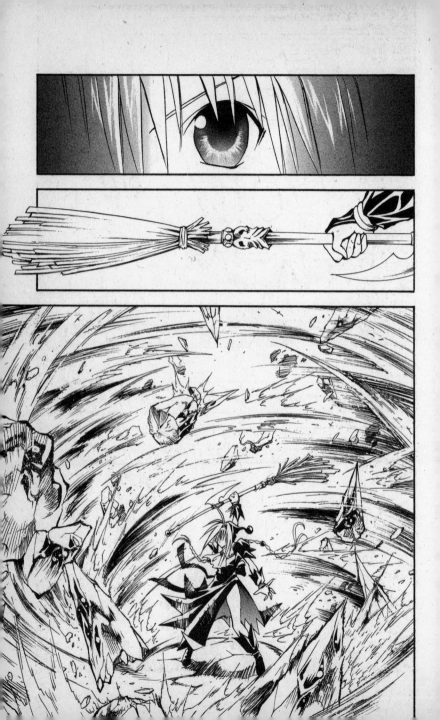

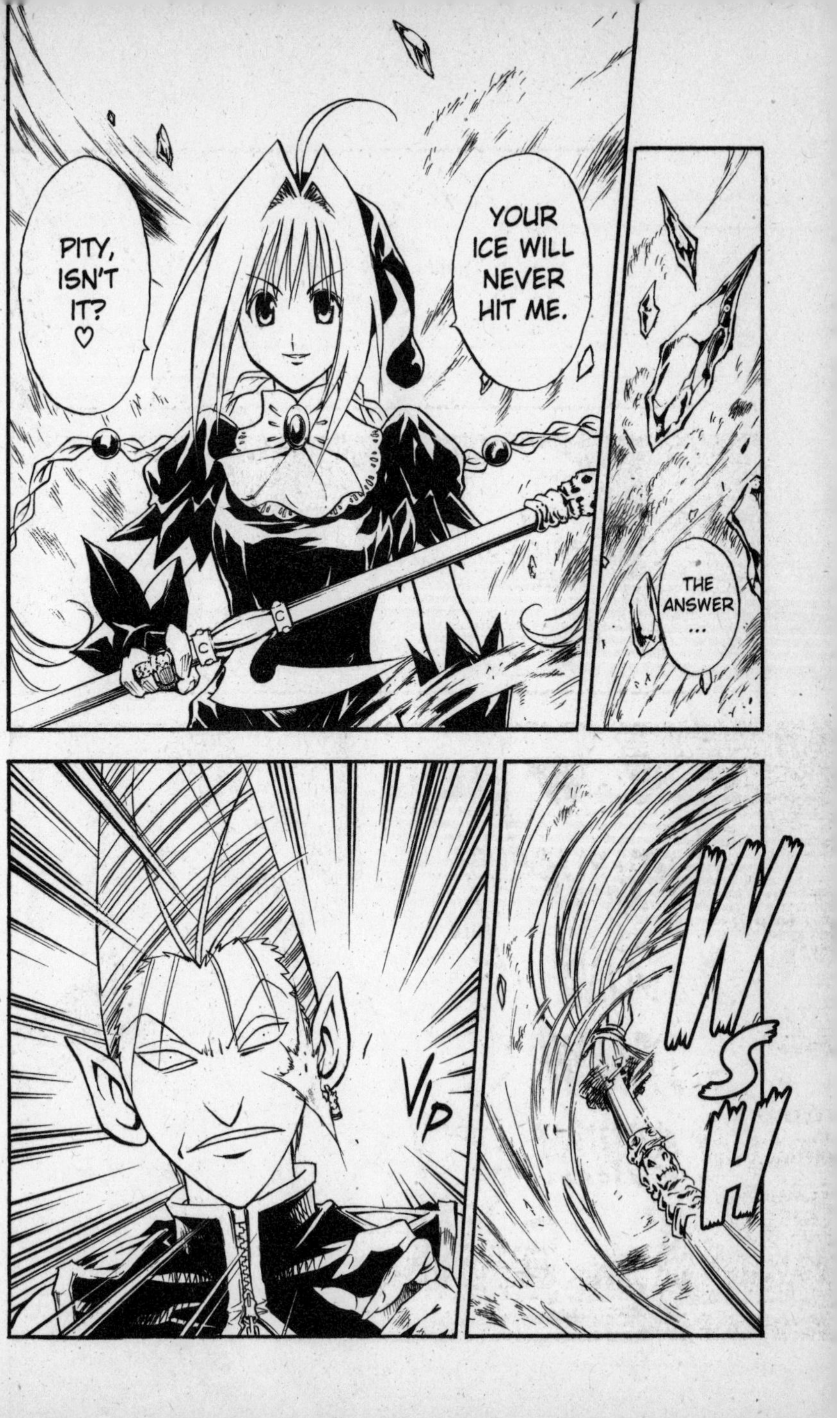
THE ANSWER ...
YOUR ICE WILL NEVER HIT ME.
PITY, ISN'T IT? ♡
WHSH
VIP

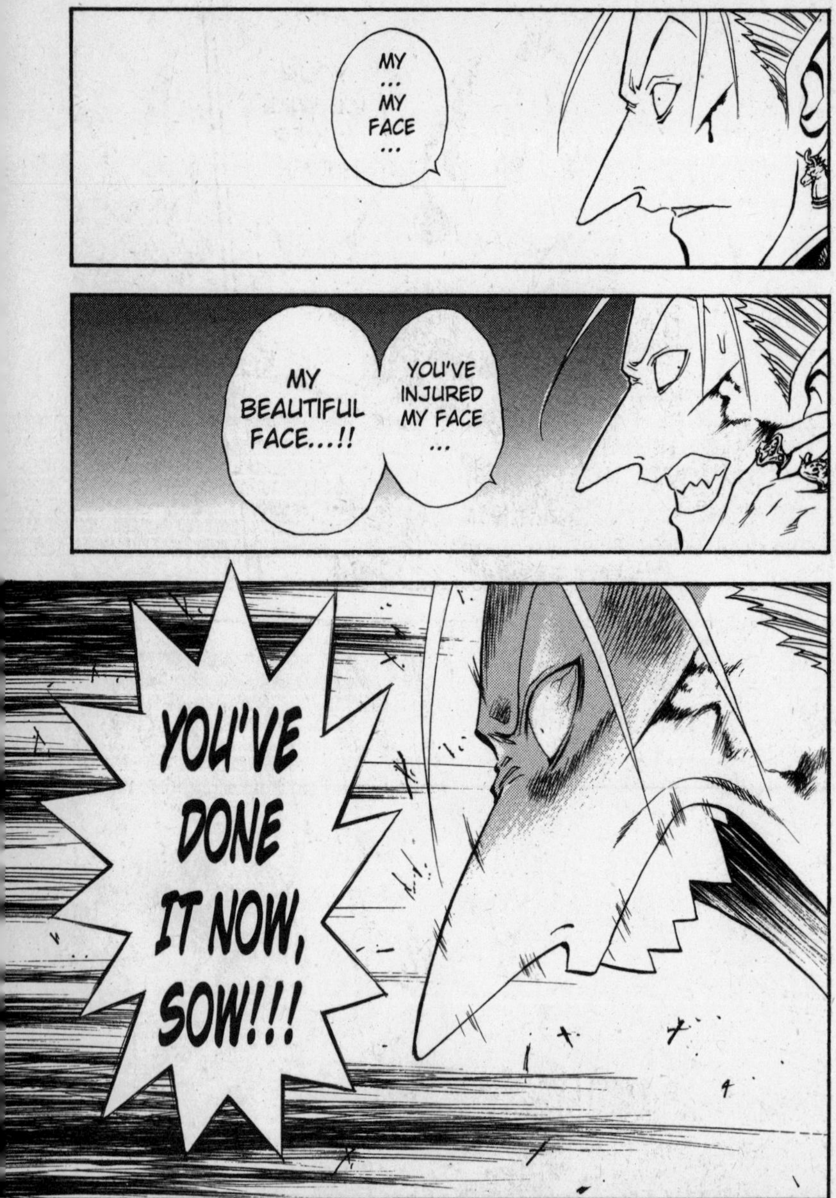
MY ... MY FACE ...
YOU'VE INJURED MY FACE ...
MY BEAUTIFUL FACE...!!
YOU'VE DONE IT NOW, SOW!!!

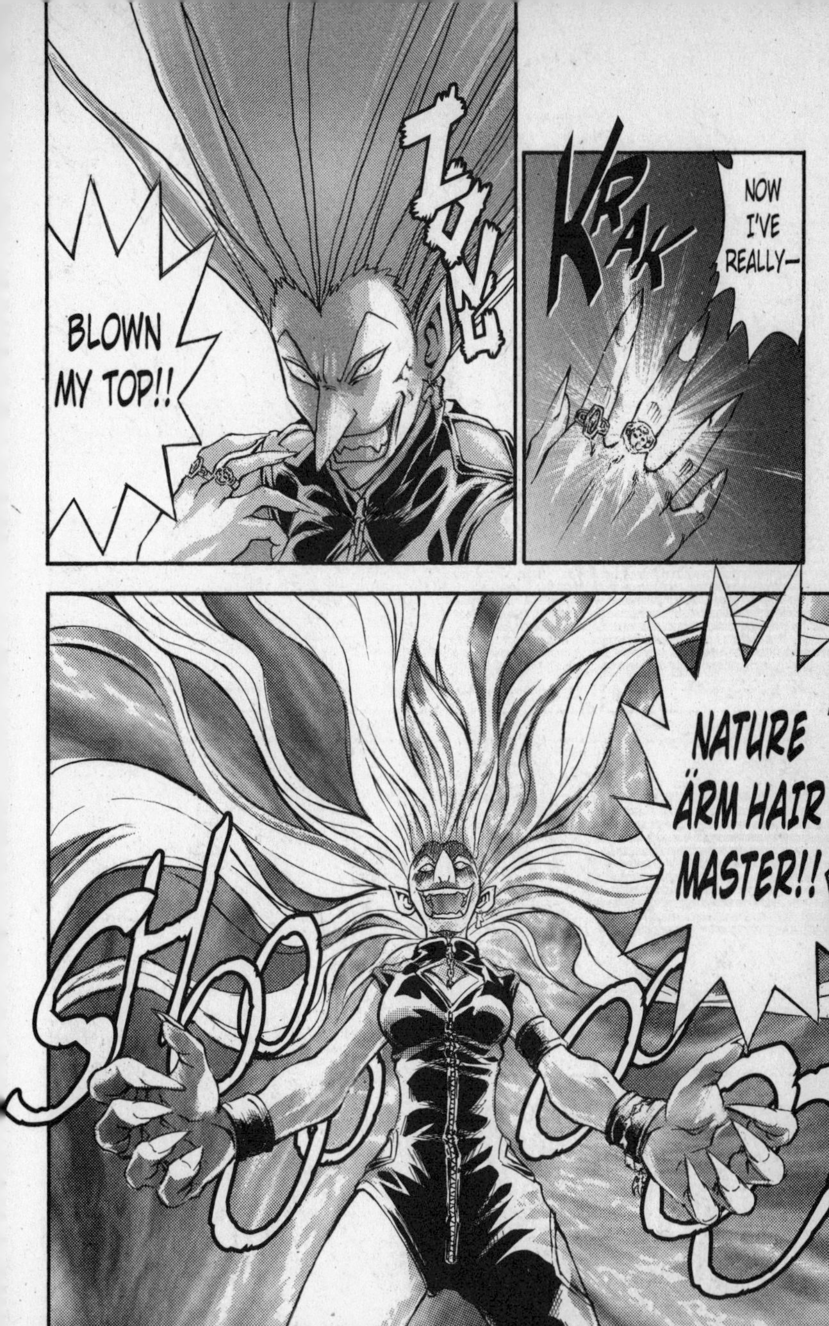
KRAK
NOW I'VE REALLY—
BLOWN MY TOP!!
NATURE ÄRM HAIR MASTER!!

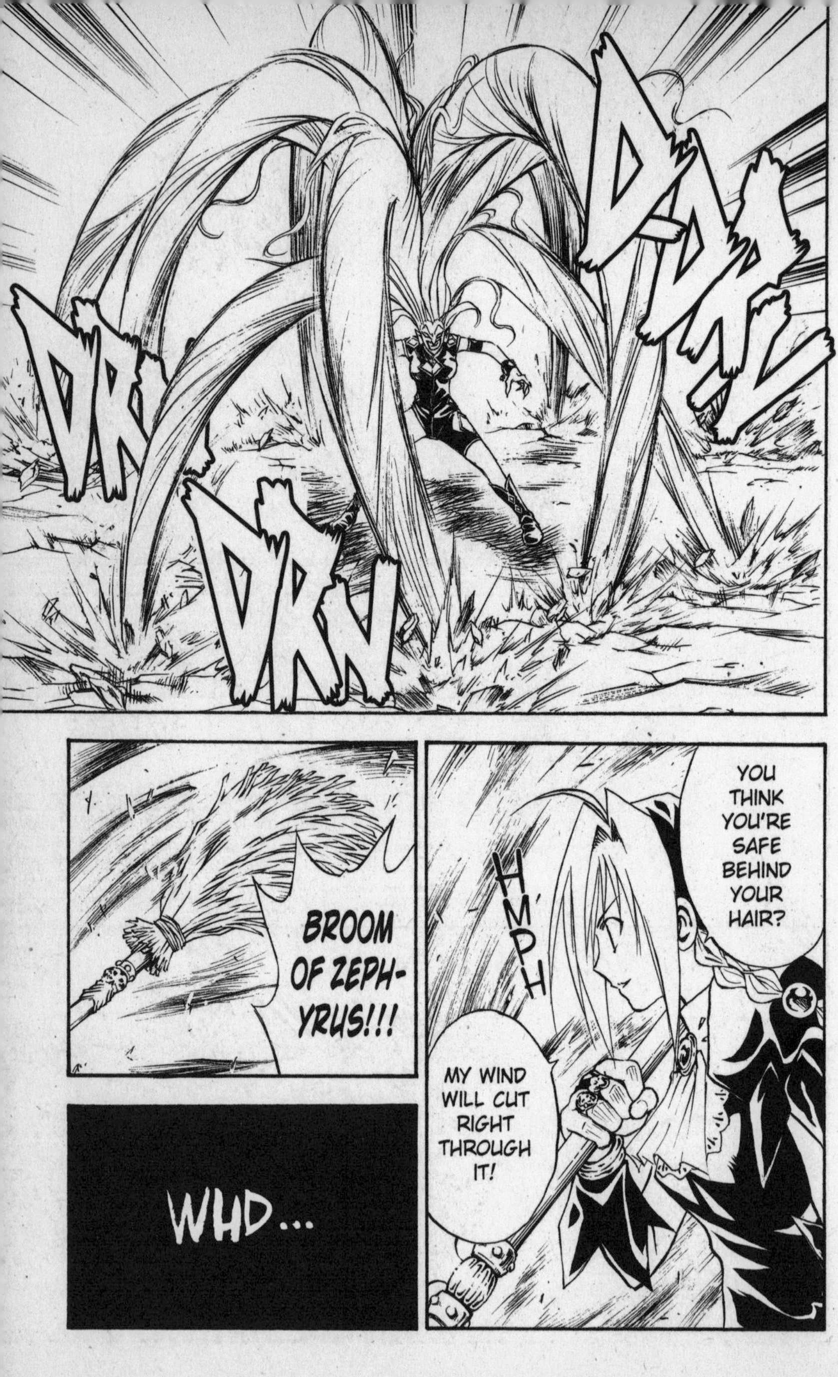
YOU THINK YOU'RE SAFE BEHIND YOUR HAIR?
HMPH
MY WIND WILL CUT RIGHT THROUGH IT!
BROOM OF ZEPH-YRUS!!!
WHD...

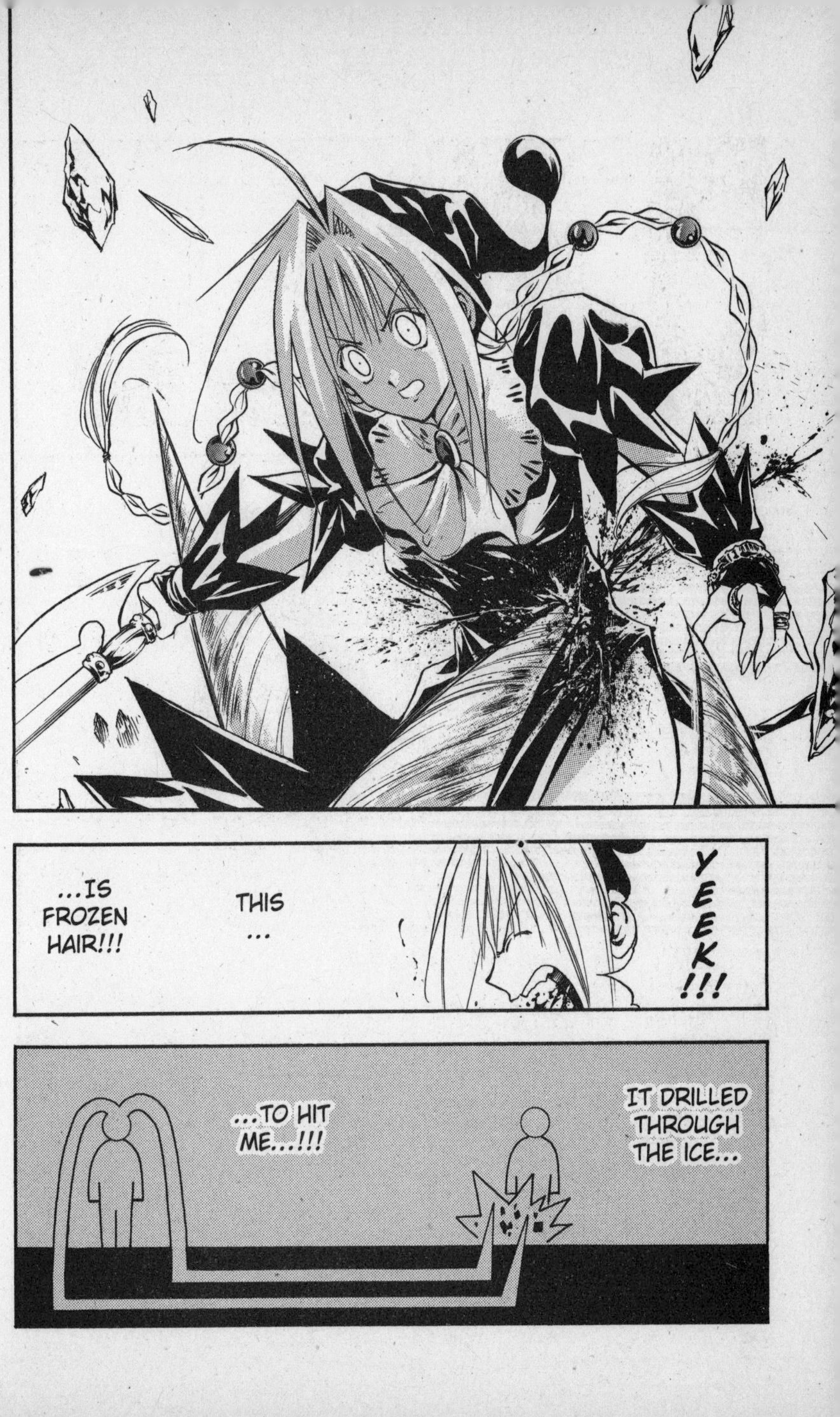
YEEK!!!
THIS...
...IS FROZEN HAIR!!!
IT DRILLED THROUGH THE ICE...
...TO HIT ME...!!!

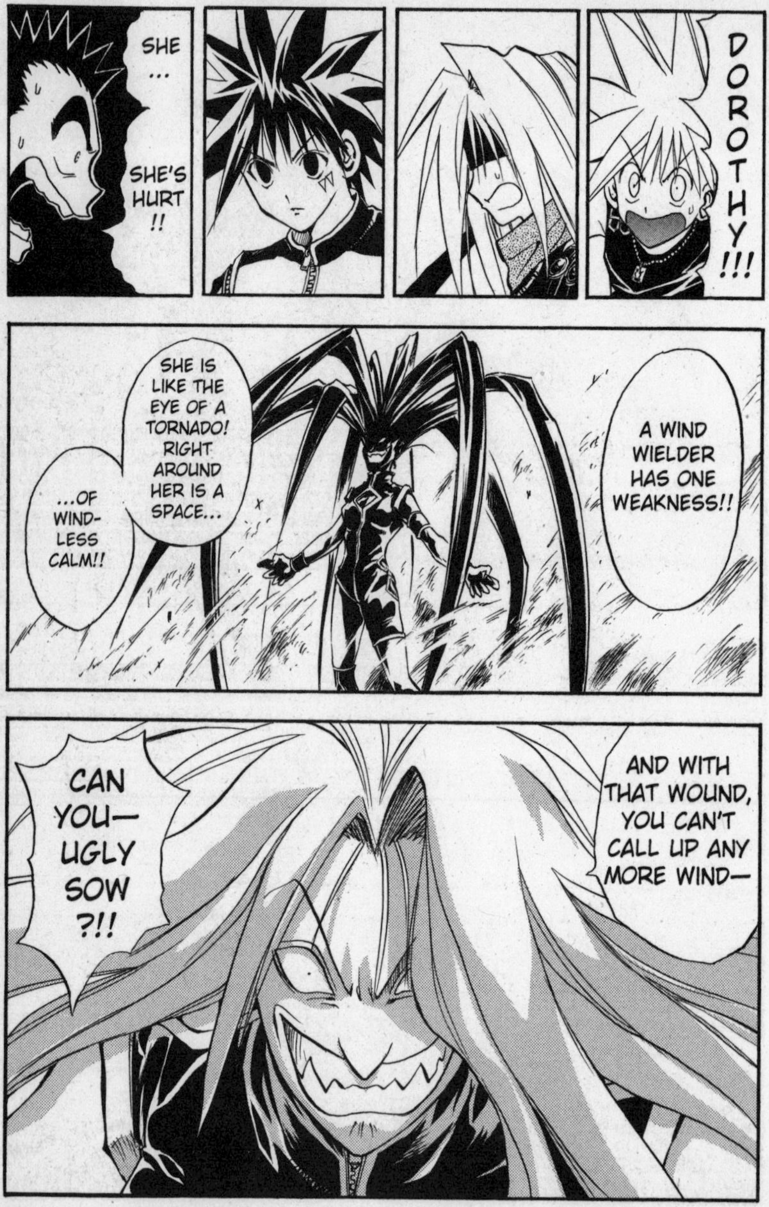
DOROTHY!!!
SHE ... SHE'S HURT!!
A WIND WIELDER HAS ONE WEAKNESS!!
SHE IS LIKE THE EYE OF A TORNADO! RIGHT AROUND HER IS A SPACE...
...OF WIND-LESS CALM!!
AND WITH THAT WOUND, YOU CAN'T CALL UP ANY MORE WIND—
CAN YOU— UGLY SOW?!!

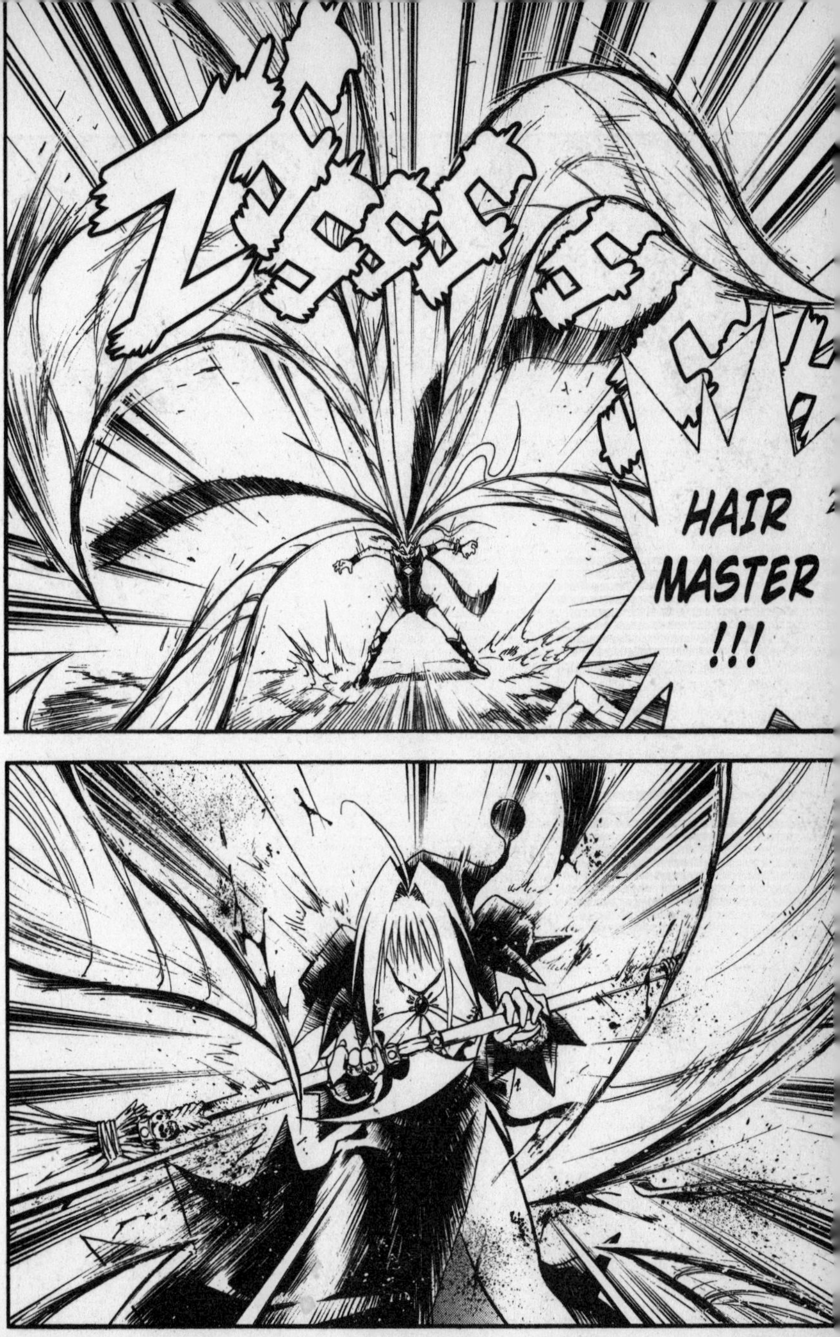
HAIR MASTER !!!

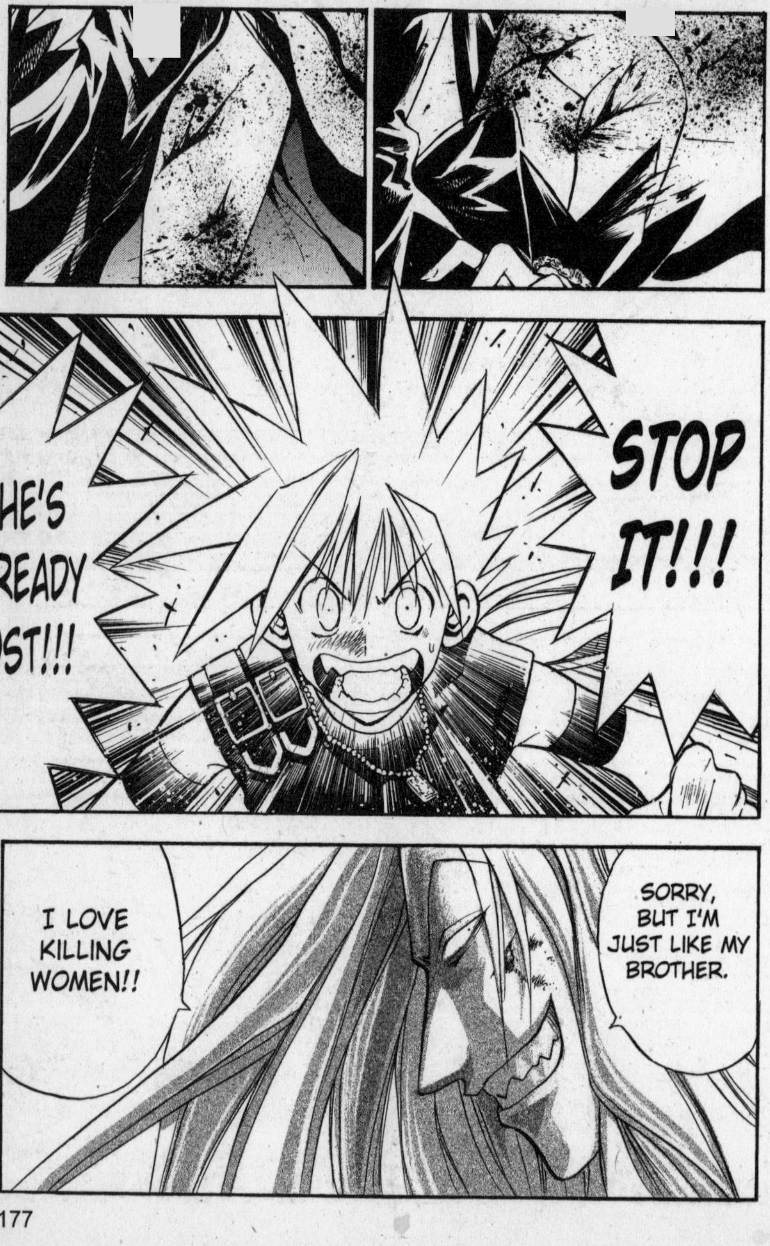
STOP IT!!!
SHE'S ALREADY LOST!!!
SORRY, BUT I'M JUST LIKE MY BROTHER.
I LOVE KILLING WOMEN!!

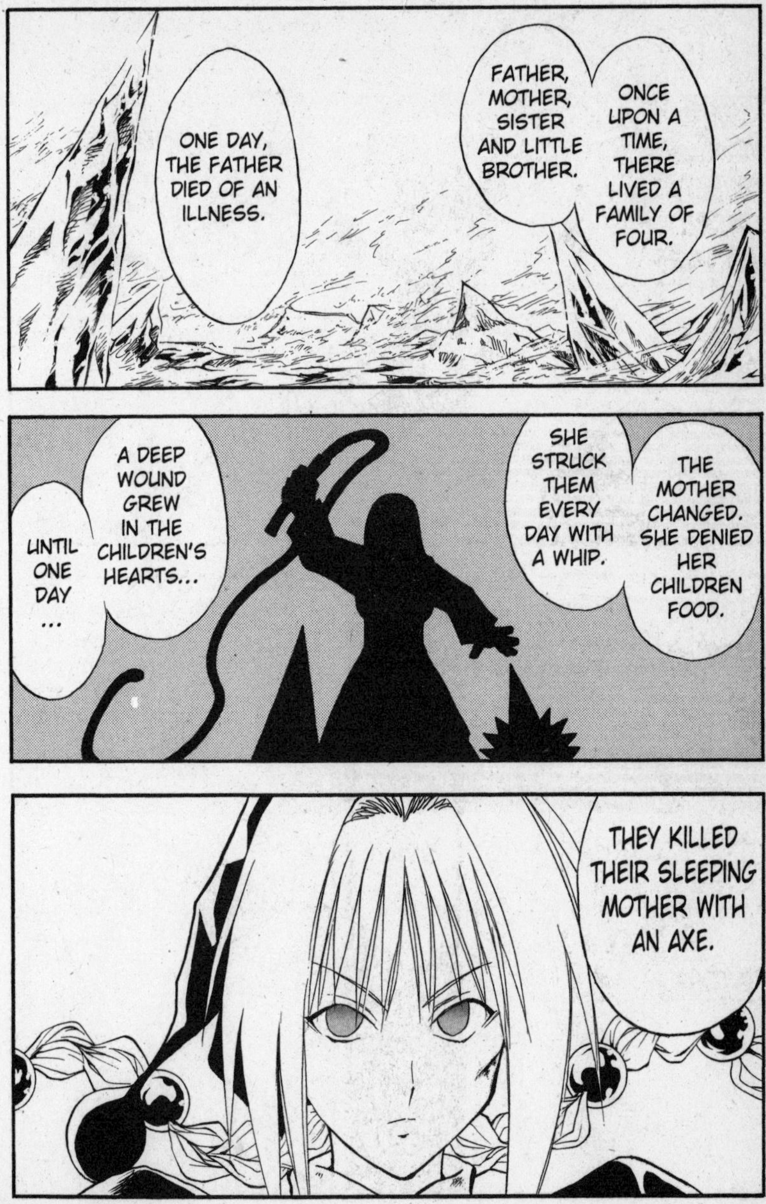
ONCE UPON A TIME, THERE LIVED A FAMILY OF FOUR.
FATHER, MOTHER, SISTER AND LITTLE BROTHER.
ONE DAY, THE FATHER DIED OF AN ILLNESS.
THE MOTHER CHANGED. SHE DENIED HER CHILDREN FOOD.
SHE STRUCK THEM EVERY DAY WITH A WHIP.
A DEEP WOUND GREW IN THE CHILDREN'S HEARTS...
UNTIL ONE DAY ...
THEY KILLED THEIR SLEEPING MOTHER WITH AN AXE.

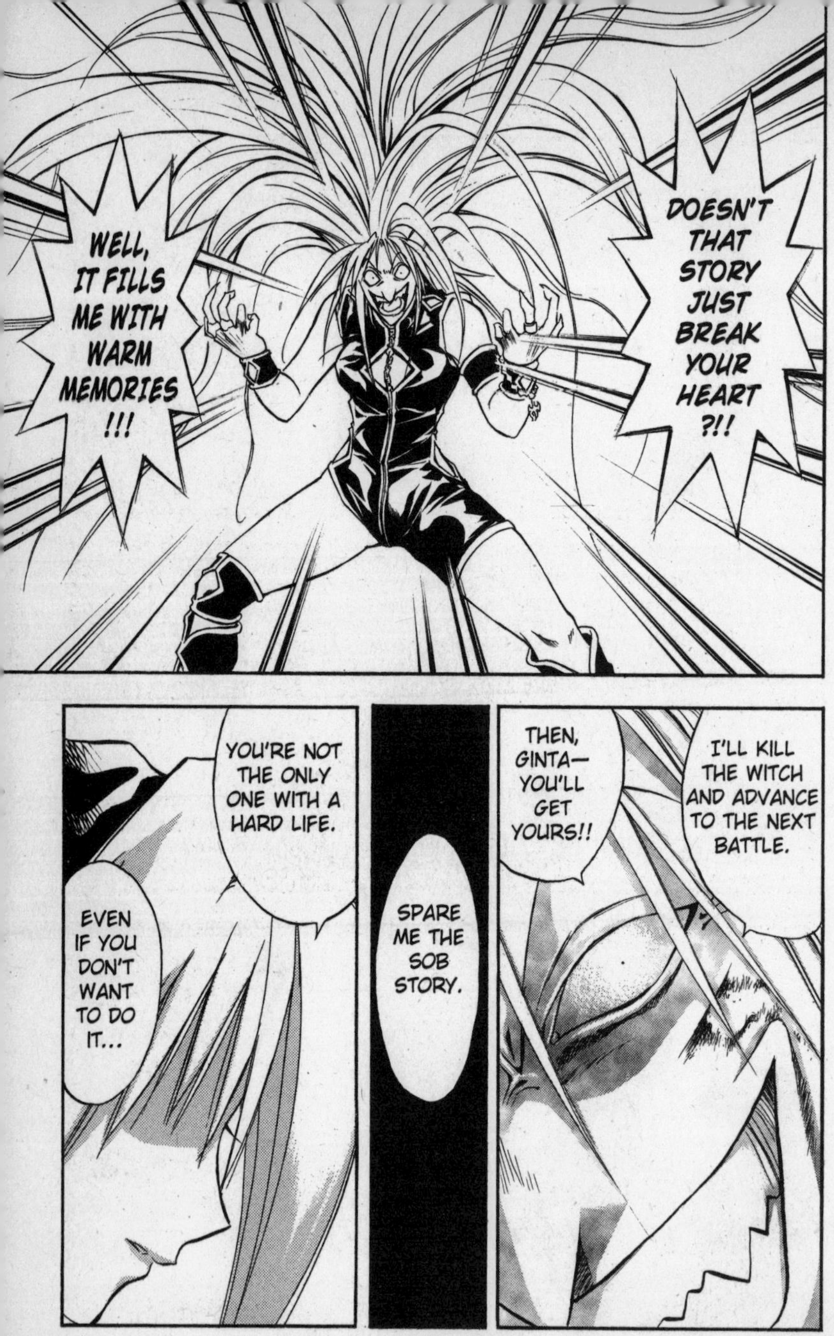
DOESN'T THAT STORY JUST BREAK YOUR HEART ?!!
WELL, IT FILLS ME WITH WARM MEMORIES !!!
I'LL KILL THE WITCH AND ADVANCE TO THE NEXT BATTLE.
THEN, GINTA— YOU'LL GET YOURS!!
SPARE ME THE SOB STORY.
YOU'RE NOT THE ONLY ONE WITH A HARD LIFE.
EVEN IF YOU DON'T WANT TO DO IT...

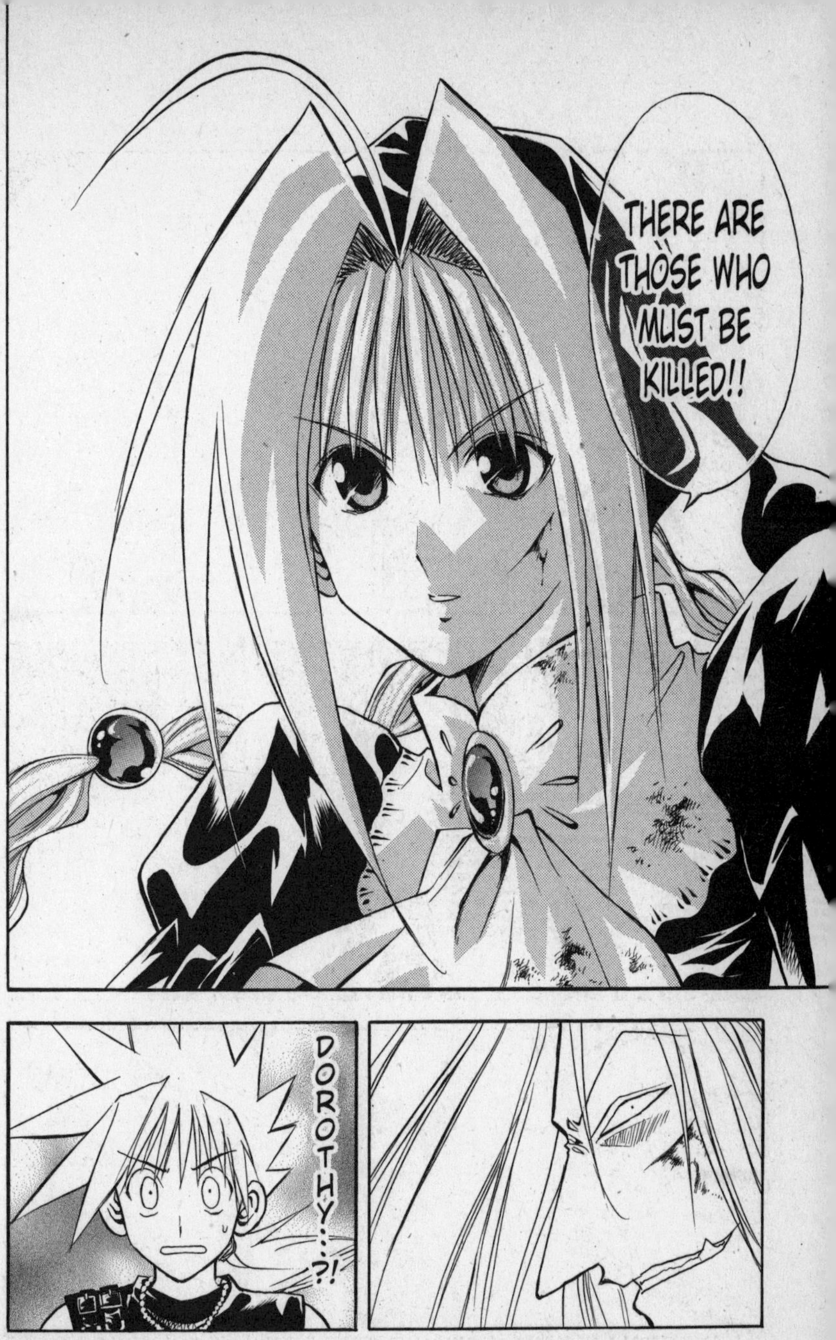
THERE ARE THOSE WHO MUST BE KILLED!!
DOROTHY...?!

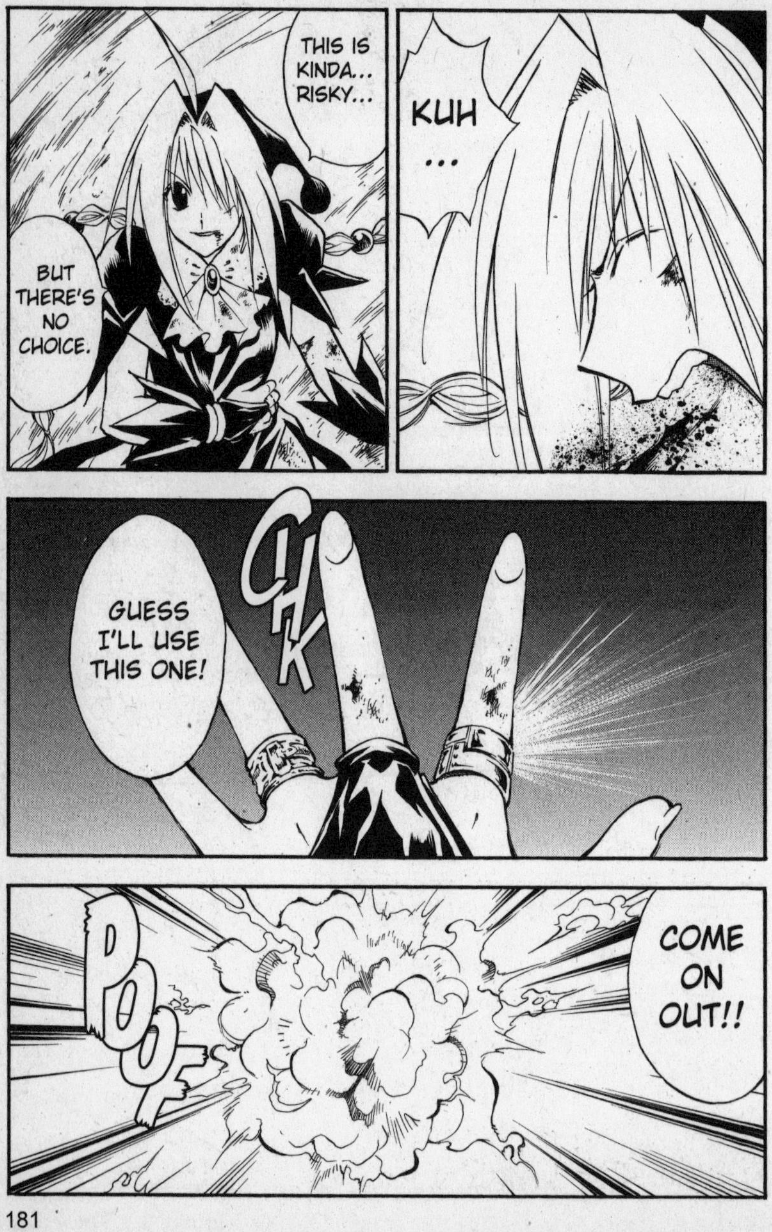
KUH ...
THIS IS KINDA... RISKY...
BUT THERE'S NO CHOICE.
CHK
GUESS I'LL USE THIS ONE!
COME ON OUT!!
POOF

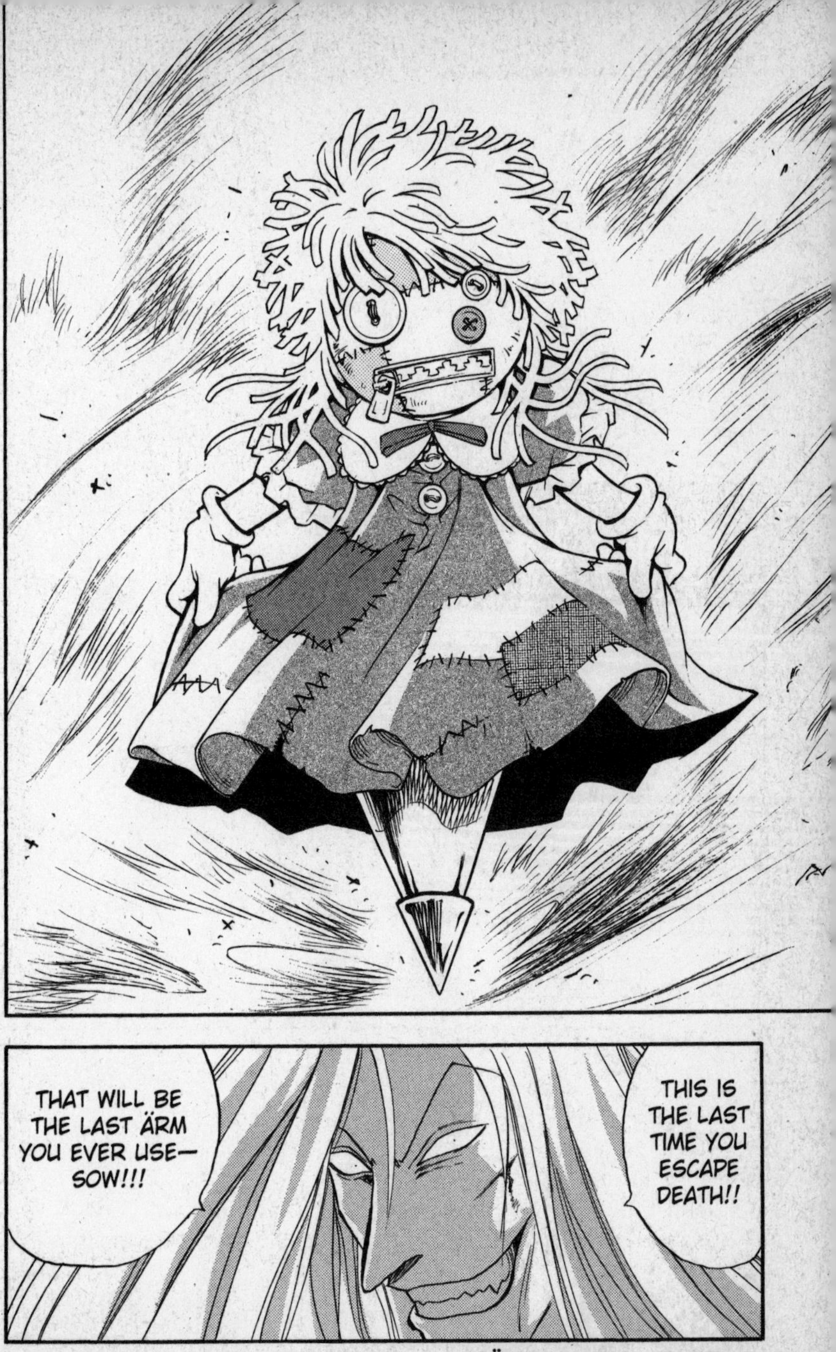
THIS IS THE LAST TIME YOU ESCAPE DEATH!!
THAT WILL BE THE LAST ÄRM YOU EVER USE— SOW!!!

MÄR Volume 8 – The End

THE EXCITEMENT BUILDS...

YOU CRAZY?!!
TOO BAD!!
CAUSE I'M CRAZIER THAN YOU!!

In the magic land of Caldia, a mystery is revealed.

COME WITH ME, TOMORROW... TO CALDIA.

Volume 9

COMING SOON!

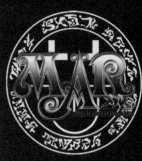

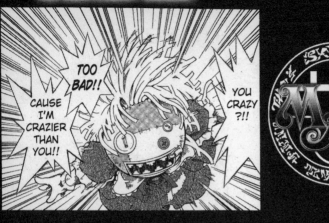

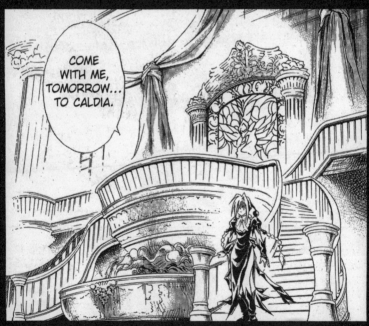

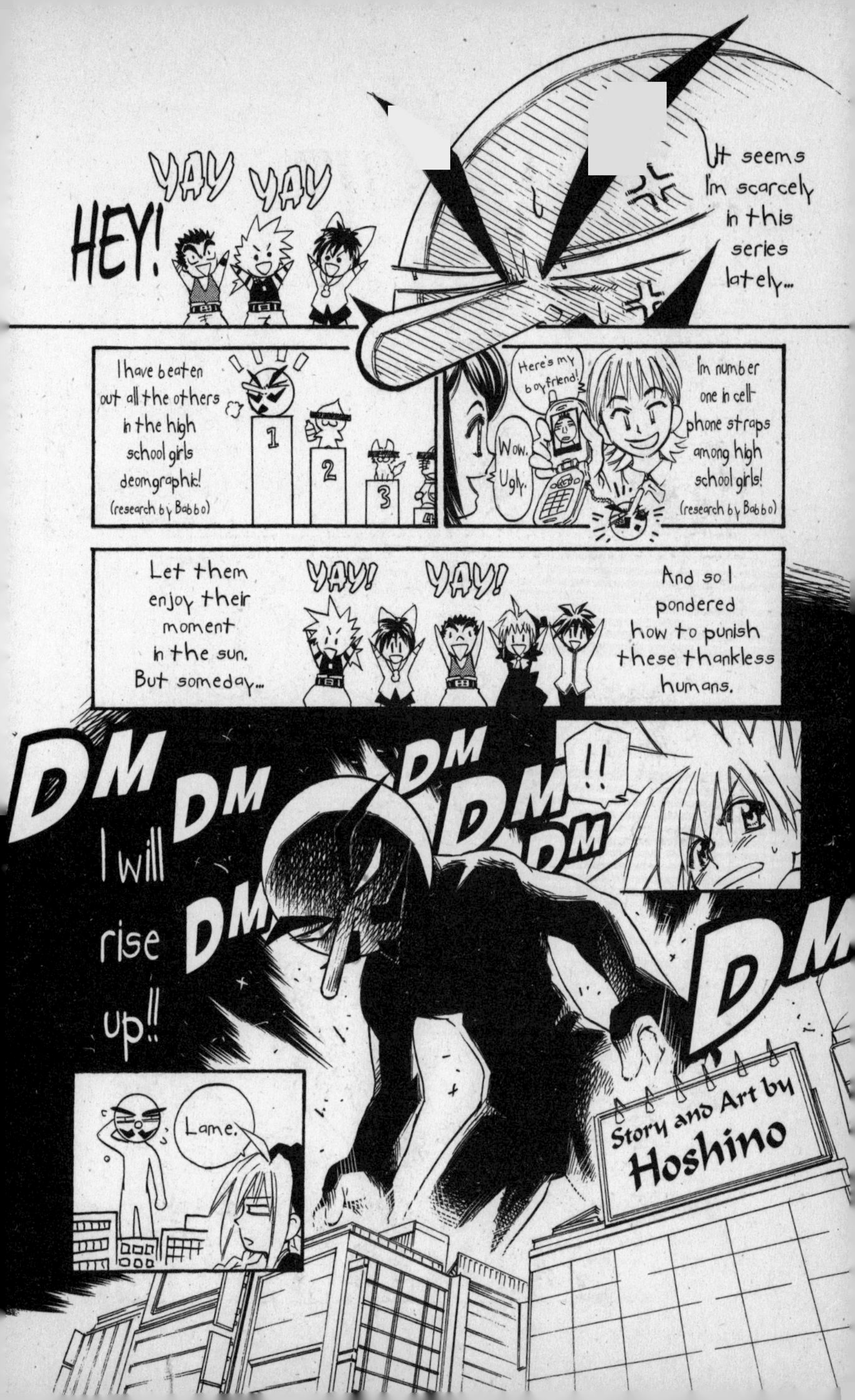
It seems I'm scarcely in this series lately...
YAY YAY
HEY!
I'm number one in cell phone straps among high school girls! (research by Babbo)
Here's my boyfriend!
Wow. Ugly.
I have beaten out all the others in the high school girls deomgraphic! (research by Babbo)
1
2
3
4
And so I pondered how to punish these thankless humans.
YAY! YAY!
Let them enjoy their moment in the sun. But someday...
!!
DM DM DM DM DM DM DM
I will rise up!!
Story and Art by Hoshino
Lame.

ACID VOMIT

By G.B.

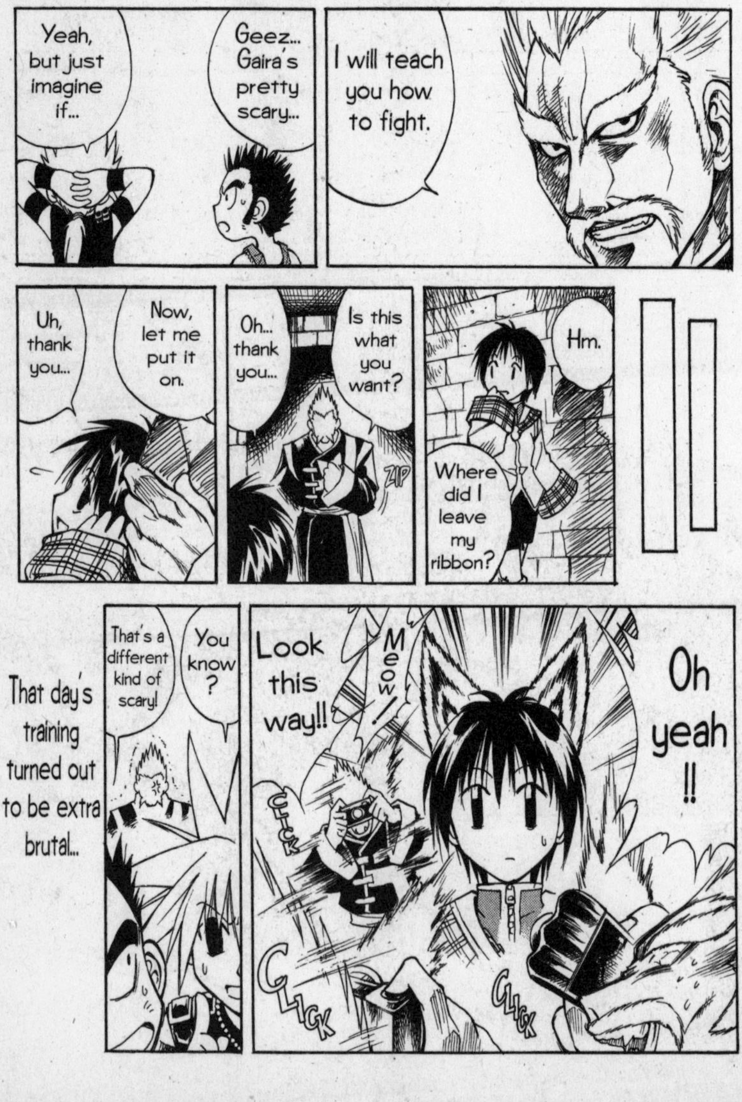
I will teach you how to fight.
Geez... Gaira's pretty scary...
Yeah, but just imagine if...
Hm.
Where did I leave my ribbon?
Is this what you want?
ZIP
Oh... thank you...
Now, let me put it on.
Uh, thank you...
Oh yeah!!
Meow!
Look this way!!
CLICK
CLICK
CLICK
You know?
That's a different kind of scary!
That day's training turned out to be extra brutal...

Title: **Actually...**

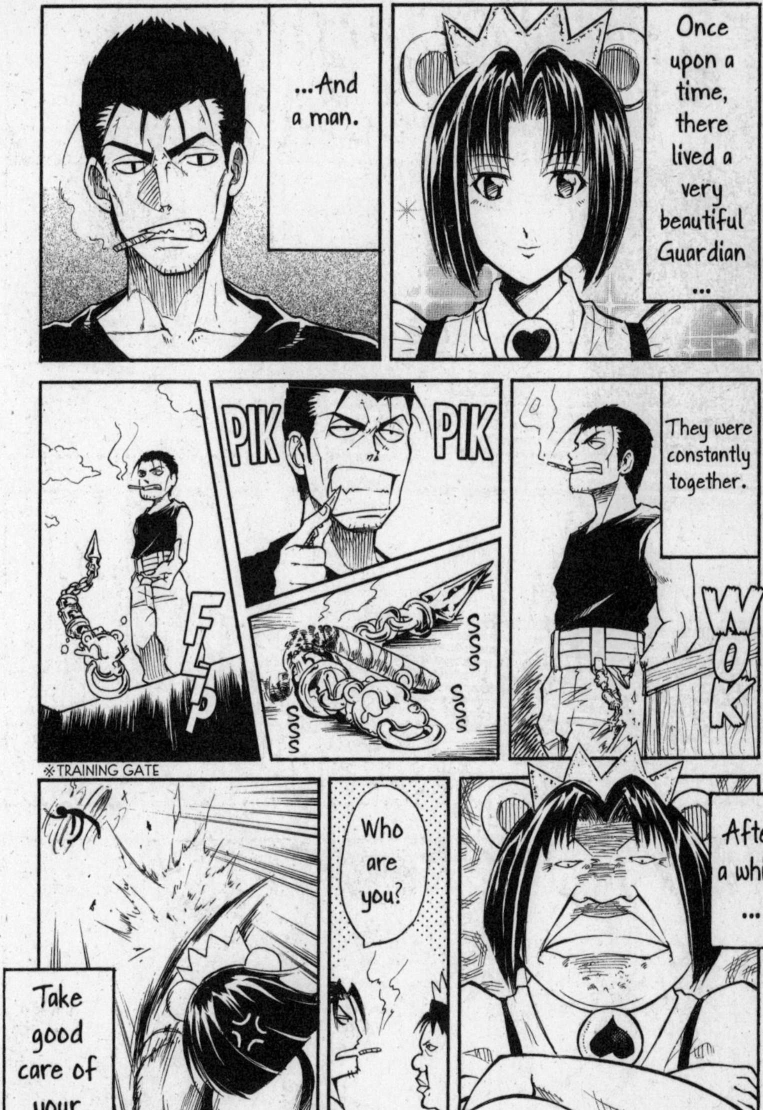

Once upon a time, there lived a very beautiful Guardian...
...And a man.
They were constantly together.
WOK
PIK PIK
SSS SSS SSS
FLIP
※TRAINING GATE
After a while...
Who are you?
Take good care of your things!

By Hechita.

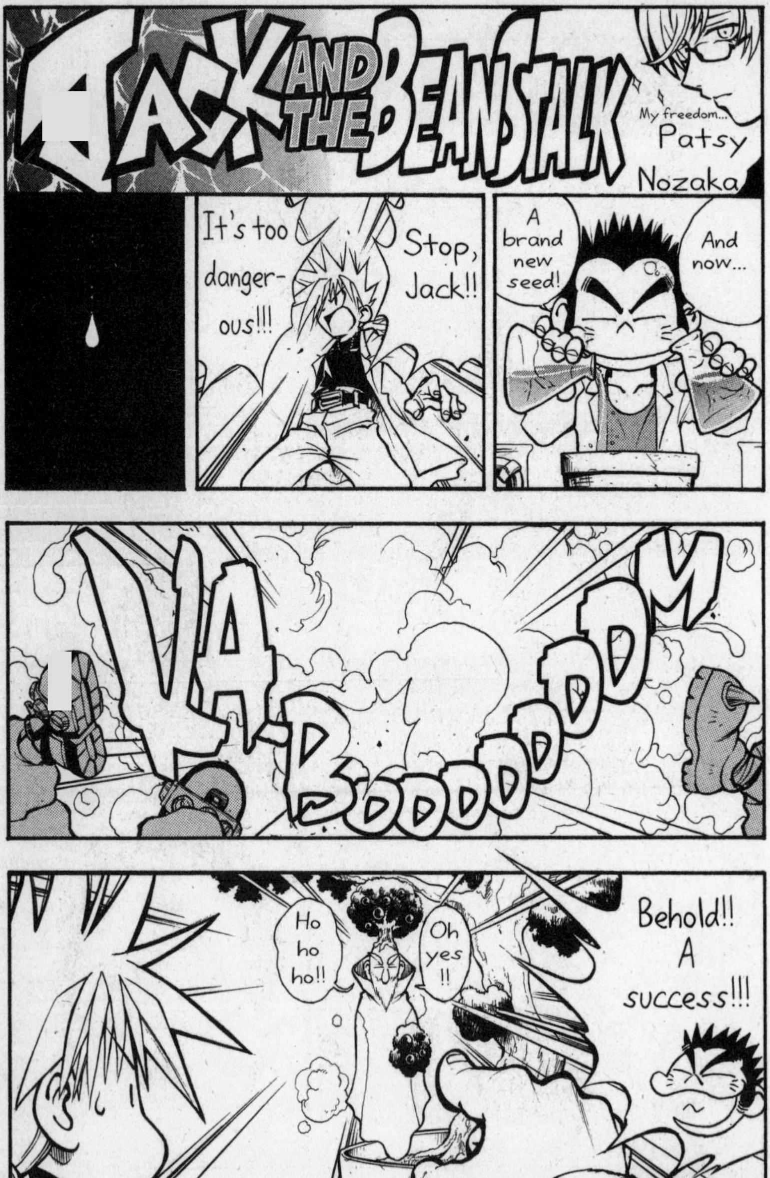
JACK AND THE BEANSTALK
My freedom...
Patsy Nozaka
And now...
A brand new seed!
Stop, Jack!!
It's too danger-ous!!!
YA-BOOOOOOOM
Behold!! A success!!!
Oh yes!!
Ho ho ho!!

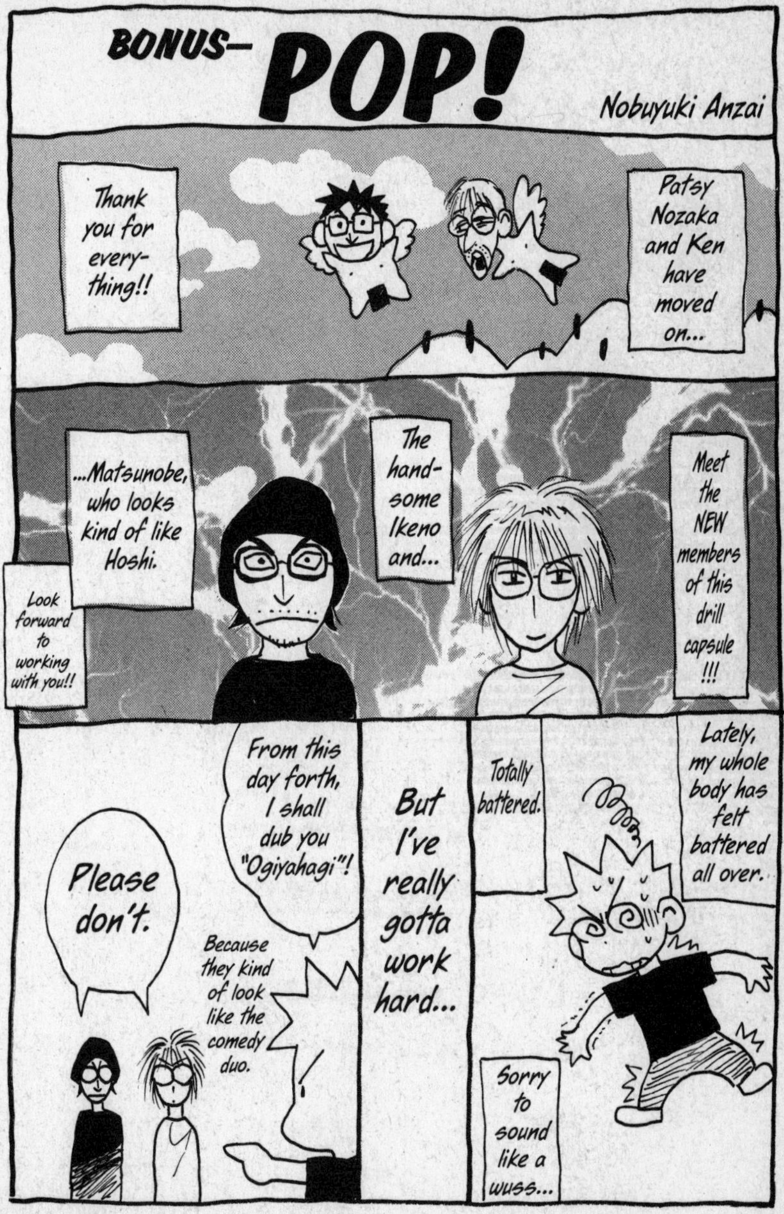
BONUS—POP!
Nobuyuki Anzai
Patsy Nozaka and Ken have moved on...
Thank you for everything!!
Meet the NEW members of this drill capsule!!!
The handsome Ikeno and...
...Matsunobe, who looks kind of like Hoshi.
Look forward to working with you!!
Lately, my whole body has felt battered all over.
Totally battered.
Sorry to sound like a wuss...
But I've really gotta work hard...
From this day forth, I shall dub you "Ogiyahagi"!
Because they kind of look like the comedy duo.
Please don't.

Author's Message:

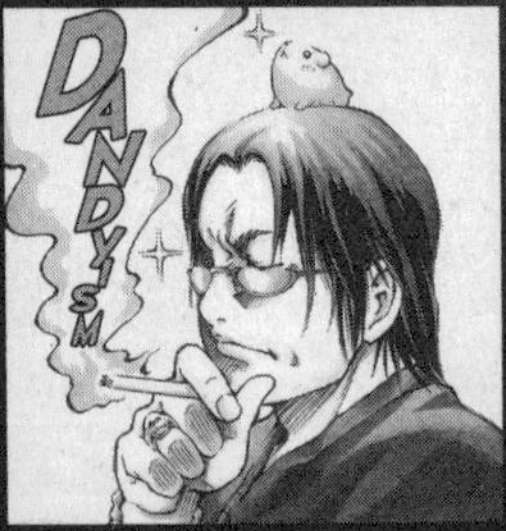
DANDYISM

Drawing by Masahiro Ikeno

NOBUYUKI ANZAI 安西信行 PRESENTS

Last week (today is Oct. 20th) I finally watched *Kill Bill*, volumes 1 and 2. It's now my favorite film. I especially love the battle scene with the main character and Gogo Yubari. Tarantino's movies are just great.

MÄR
Vol. 8
Story and Art by Nobuyuki Anzai

English Adaptation/Gerard Jones
Translation/Kaori Inoue
Touch-up Art & Lettering/James Gaubatz
Design/Izumi Evers
Editor/ Andy Nakatani

Managing Editor/Annette Roman
Director of Production/Noboru Watanabe
Vice President of Publishing/Alvin Lu
Sr. Director of Acquisitions/Rika Inouye
Vice President of Sales & Marketing/Liza Coppola
Publisher/Hyoe Narita

Printed in the U.S.A.

Published by VIZ Media, LLC
P.O. Box 77010
San Francisco, CA 94107

10 9 8 7 6 5 4 3 2 1
First printing, July 2006

www.viz.com
store.viz.com

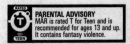

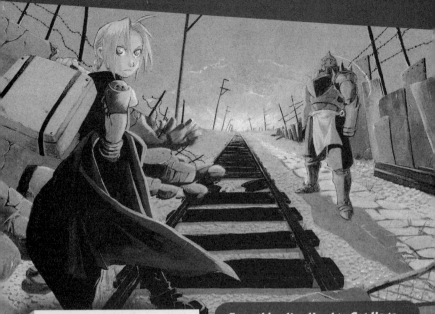
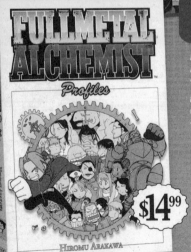
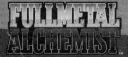

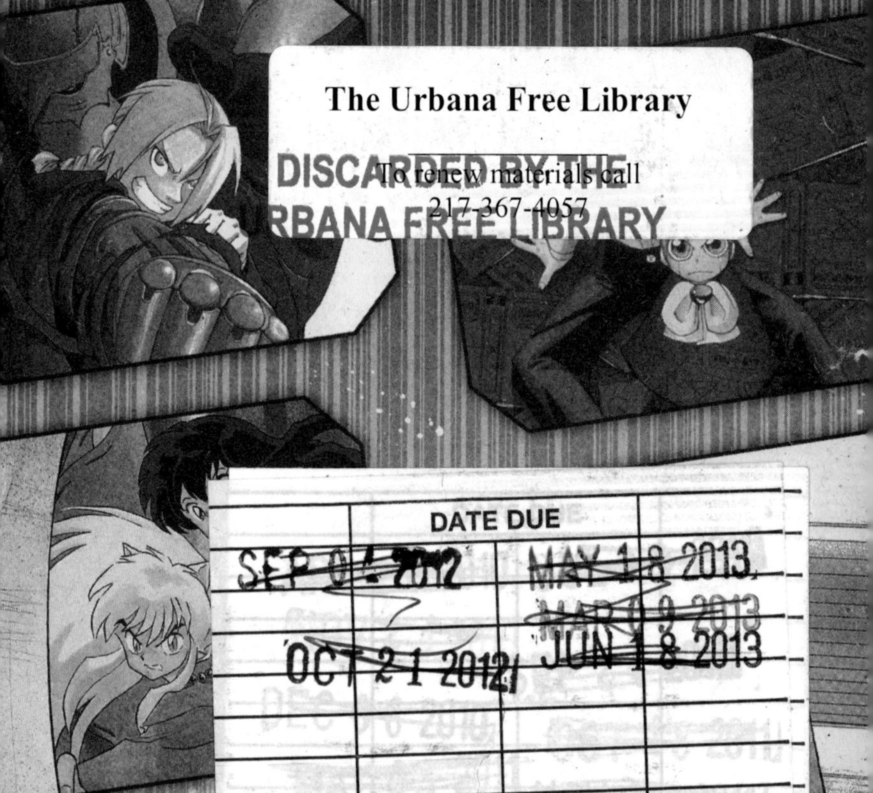